THE
SHAMAN
AND THE
JAGUAR

THE
SHAMAN
AND THE
JAGUAR

A Study of Narcotic Drugs Among the Indians of Colombia

G. Reichel-Dolmatoff

Temple University Press
Philadelphia

Temple University Press, Philadelphia 19122
© 1975 by G. Reichel-Dolmatoff. All rights reserved

Published 1975
Printed in the United States of America

International Standard Book Number: 0-87722-038-7
Library of Congress Catalog Card Number: 74-83672

Title page art adapted from a drawing by a Barasana
Indian of the hallucinatory image of mankind's first
dance (Figure 56)

CONTENTS

Illustrations vii
Foreword, by Richard Evans Schultes xi
Acknowledgments xv
Introduction xvii

1. Narcotic Snuff 3

2. In Search of a Jungle Vine 25

3. The Shaman and the Jaguar 43

4. The Forest and the River 61

5. Tukano Shamanism 76

6. Jaguar Transformation 108

7. Yajé: Myth and Ritual 133

8. A Yajé Session 157

9. Spirits of the Forest 182

10. Conclusions 198

Appendix: Desana Texts 205
Notes 227
Glossary 249
Bibliography 251
Index 273

ILLUSTRATIONS

Following page 24

1. Sketch map of Colombia
2. Guahibo Indians absorbing narcotic snuff
3. Guahibo shaman burning snail shells to obtain lime for snuff mixture
4. Snuffing tube of bird bone, Guahibo Indians
5. Snuffing tube of bird bone, Guahibo Indians
6. *Anadenanthera peregrina*
7. *Virola* sp.
8. Snuffing tube of bird bone, Barasana Indians
9. Bará Indian absorbing narcotic snuff
10. Snuff container of snail shell, Barasana Indians
11. Snuff container made of a dried fruit, Barasana Indians
12. Tatuyo Indian preparing powdered coca

Following page 42

13. *Banisteriopsis caapi*
14. Noanamá shaman holding a bundle of narcotic vines
15. Stems and leaves of *Banisteriopsis rusbyana*
16. Snuff container of jaguar bone, Guahibo Indians
17. Guahibo shaman consecrating a trough of freshly prepared *chicha* beer

Following page 96

18. Sketch map of the Vaupés Territory
19. The Vaupés River during the dry season

20. Cuyucuyú Falls
21. Painted shaman's stool, Desana Indians
22. Tatuyo Indians with ocelot skin
23. A Tatuyo youth dressed for a dance
24. A mask of painted barkcloth, Cubeo Indians
25. Taibano hunter with blowgun and quiver

Following page 156

26. Rock engraving at Nyí
27. Barasana Indians gathering yajé
28. Barasana Indians with bundles of *Banisteriopsis caapi* vines
29. Barasana Indian pounding the vines in a wooden trough
30. Barasana Indian preparing *Banisteriopsis caapi* vines
31. The narcotic potion being sifted into the vessel
32. A painted yajé vessel with a U-shaped design
33. A yajé session, Tatuyo Indians
34. Tatuyo Indians dancing
35. A Barasana dancer playing his instruments under the influence of yajé

Following page 174

36. A Barasan artist drawing hallucinatory patterns in the sand
37. A Barasana artist drawing hallucinatory patterns
38. A Barasana artist drawing a model in the sand before putting it on paper
39. Hallucinatory design motifs of the Tukano Indians
40. Phosphene patterns
41. House decoration representing hallucinatory patterns
42. Wall painting on a Taibano maloca showing the Master of Game Animals and hallucinatory patterns
43. Wall painting on a Taibano maloca showing hallucinatory patterns
44. Painted snake on housepost, Tukano Indians
45. Painted loincloth of tree bark, Tatuyo Indians
46. Painted loincloth of tree bark, Tatuyo Indians
47. Stamping tubes with painted designs
48. Gourd rattle with incised designs, Tatuyo Indians
49. Incised design motifs from a gourd rattle, Barasana Indians
50. Incised design motifs from a gourd rattle, Barasana Indians

51. Incised design motifs from a gourd rattle, Barasana Indians

52. Painted design from a drum

53. Painted yajé vessel

54. Drawing by a Barasana Indian representing the hallucinatory image of the first peopling of the world

55. Drawing by a Barasana Indian representing the hallucinatory image of origin of yajé

56. Drawing by a Barasana Indian representing the hallucinatory image of mankind's first dance

57. Drawing by a Barasana Indian representing the hallucinatory image of a jaguar, people on the Milky Way, and the U-shaped "entrance to the other world"

Following page 190

58. Wall painting in black and white from a Bará maloca representing hallucinatory patterns

59. Zoomorphic design from a Bará moloca

60. Fish design from a painted stamping tube, Tatuyo Indians

61. Anthropomorphic design from a Bará maloca

62. A painted stool carved from a single piece of wood, Tukano Indians

63. Design motif from a Bará maloca

64. Wall painting from a Bará maloca, representing hallucinatory patterns

65. Wall painting on a Taibano maloca, representing hallucinatory patterns

FOREWORD

Anthropologists have viewed with fascination the inordinate primacy that the mind of the Amerindian accords to certain animals. In some northern cultures, it is the buffalo. In Mexico, it is the deer. Birds and amphibians, both real and mythical, play similar roles throughout aboriginal concepts of Nature.

The peoples living in the humid tropics have tended to accord particular attention to the boa constrictor or anaconda and to various felines, and archaeological studies indicate that the special symbolic significance of these animals goes back at least four thousand years. But it is perhaps the jaguar that surpasses all other animals in aboriginal ideas of creation, of the supernatural regulation of earthly existence, of the otherworldly life—in short, in the very being of many of our American cultures.

Why?

All aspects of the jaguar's supremacy have long been noted and described in ethnological studies: the prevalence of the jaguar motif in primitive art forms; reproduction of jaguar sounds and habits in Indian dances and rituals; the role of the jaguar in aboriginal folk tales; the frequent propitiation of spirits associated with the jaguar; the constant use of words for the jaguar in denoting certain medicines and medical practices; references to the shaman as "the jaguar" and his dressing as a jaguar in magic rituals; the common connection of the jaguar with sacred hallucinogenic plants and their use. Recent attention has focused on the intimate ceremonial connection between man and jaguar, especially in relation to intoxicants. Much of the paraphernalia, both archaeological and modern, employed in preparing and using narcotic snuffs is richly ornamented with jaguars. Some tribes customarily keep the snuff in jaguar bones, undoubtedly because of the cat's magical significance. The frequency and importance of the jaguar motif in these snuffing objects are so striking as to indicate inexorably that more than pure chance underlies this culture trait.

Ethnologists have added to the store of our knowledge about the jaguar in primitive culture in many geographically and ethnographically unrelated localities. Among the Tukanoans of the northwestern Amazon, for example, older shamans assume the guise of jaguars and are feared above all others. A jaguar that attacks a human being is thought to be a shaman, and any shaman suspected of such an attack may himself be killed. The spirit of the murdered shaman, however, enters another jaguar, so the danger continues. In the Colombian Putumayo, Indians turn into jaguars after taking the hallucinogenic yajé and chase deer and tapirs in the forest with great ease. Beautiful ceramic vessels from the Chavin Culture of Peru, at least three thousand years old, clearly depict jaguars in association with the narcotic San Pedro cactus. Throughout South America, a number of indigenous names for "varieties" of hallucinogens refer to the jaguar, as among the Kamsá of Colombia, who call one of their strongest hallucinogenic plants *mits-kway borrachero* (intoxicant of the jaguar). The Kubeo of the Colombian Amazon relate that caapi-intoxication causes the men to see people in the bright colors of the jaguar.

The examples are countless. A long list of them would merely fortify what is already well known. The question is: What are we now going to do with this absorbingly interesting and significant mass of data?

Gerardo Reichel-Dolmatoff has come forward to grapple with this problem. His years of very original and searching field work have provided him with information on a scale not often available to many other ethnologists. I doubt that there is any researcher into this highly complex field who will not welcome and appreciate his contribution. Reichel-Dolmatoff's interpretations are definitely Freudian; few are ready to accept all of them, and I must confess that I am numbered among those who view with reservation some of the far-reaching conclusions which he offers. Yet this book will live. It is a masterly attempt to unravel, in one man's way of evaluating the most intricate of data, one of the greatest enigmas of modern ethnology. Its chief value may lie not in the success that the future will accord to all its interpretations and explanations, but in its originality, its boldness, its honesty and, not least of all, its effort to focus attention on the urgency of the task ahead and its encouragement of wider research and interpretative studies.

It has been said that the reason for the importance of huge snakes and large felines in native cultures is simply that the stealth and strength of these animals strike awe and fear into the Indian. But it is clear that such an explantation cannot withstand the scrutiny of any examination in depth. There have even been attempts to offer "biochemical" explanations: that the great frequency of jaguars and other felines and snakes in descriptions of caapi-intoxication might be due to an ability of the active chemical constituents of the hallucinogenic plant to induce visions of definite kinds of subjects. But there is not a shred of evidence that such specificity of action exists. One is left, then, with the near certainty that underlying the primacy of the jaguar in so many cultures are ancient, deeply ingrained and highly positive experiences that are now a part of the mind of aboriginal man. Reichel-Dolmatoff, with humility and sympathetic understanding, has tried in this volume to start us on the way toward clarifying some of the hidden reasons.

It might appear rather unusual that a plant scientist has been asked to write a foreword for such a book. The jaguar and shamanism both seem far removed from botany. At first, I felt somewhat apprehensive about accepting the invitation. But the day of the interdisciplinary approach is upon us. I consider it an honor to have been asked to offer my views on what the future may judge to be a major contribution to our understanding of thought in primitive Amerindian societies.

Man in primitive societies lives in a much closer and more personal association with his ambient vegetation than man in our modern technological cultures. Shamanism depends in great part on the supernatural powers resident in certain plants. These resident divinities are organic chemical constituents that allow mortal man to communicate through visual, auditory and other hallucinations with the spirit world that controls every aspect of man's earthly existence. Since natively used hallucinogens are, for the most part, of vegetal origin, the ethnobotanist comes face to face with those problems confronting the anthropologist, ethnologist, psychologist and other specialists. As plants are a basic element in man's very existence, the botanist claims his sphere of interest in how they may have helped shape society. It is in this spirit that I have written the foregoing words.

RICHARD EVANS SCHULTES

ACKNOWLEDGMENTS

During the years in which this book was written many individuals and institutions contributed in different ways to its development and completion. It is a pleasant duty to express my gratitude for the assistance received from them.

The initial field research was carried out under the sponsorship of the Universidad de los Andes, and I am grateful to this institution for the indispensable help given to me. Special thanks are due to the Committee on Urgent Anthropology of the Smithsonian Center for the Study of Man, which granted additional funds for research, and I wish to express my sincere gratitude to the program director, Dr. Samuel Stanley, for his help. The Instituto Colombiano de Antropología of the Colombian Ministry of National Education provided me with the necessary official authorizations and I am particularly indebted to this organization. In the field, the representatives of the Catholic Missions and the local civil authorities assisted me in many ways, and I owe my gratitude to Monseñor Belarmino Corréa, Apostolic Prefect of the Vaupés territory, and to the district commissioner, Dr. Narciso Matus Torres.

I am most grateful to the University of Cambridge, which honored me with a Visiting Scholarship in 1970 and where I was able to do part of my library research, and I wish to express my gratitude to the Centre of Latin-American Studies and to the Master and Fellows of Corpus Christi College for their gracious hospitality during my stay at Cambridge.

I am indebted to many friends in Bogotá from whose discussions I profited in many ways. Dr. Federico Medem, director of the Institute of Tropical Biology "Roberto Franco" (National University of

Colombia) at Villavicencio, shared with me his profound knowledge of the rain forest, and several distinguished psychiatrists, notably Dr. Francisco Cobos, and Drs. Jaime and Inga Villareal, gave most generously of their time in discussing with me many aspects concerning their particular fields of competence. Dr. Richard Evans Schultes, director of the Botanical Museum at Harvard University and a world authority on the narcotic plants of the Amazon area, constantly stimulated my interest in this field of research, and I am most grateful for his encouragement. My wife's contribution to this study has been substantial, both in the field and in the library, and her suggestions and criticism have been invaluable. My friend Alec Bright has patiently read most of my manuscript and has corrected my English.

All photographs are by the author, with six exceptions, for which grateful acknowledgment is made to Paul Beer (for Figs. 2, 3, and 17), to Alvaro Soto Holguín (for Fig. 25), and to A. Dussán (for Figs. 31 and 33). Line drawings are by the author. Figures 6, 7, and 13 were kindly provided by Dr. Richard Evans Schultes of Harvard University. The sketch maps (Figs. 1 and 18) were prepared by the Instituto Geográfico "Agustín Codazzi," Bogotá. It is unfortunate that the Gold Museum of the Banco de la República, Bogotá, did not collaborate by lending photographs of prehistoric objects from its collections, relating to the aboriginal use of narcotics.

I am deeply indebted to my Indian informants whose kindness and hospitality made this study possible. Antonio Guzmán, my Desana interpreter, aided substantially in the translation of many texts, and next to him many others deserve my lasting gratitude for the interest they took in transmitting to me their knowledge and experience.

INTRODUCTION

The main theme of this book is the use of certain narcotic drugs among Colombian Indians, and the jaguar transformation complex, which is closely related to it. The principal objective is to describe the traditions, rituals, and native interpretations connected with drug use and the hallucinatory sphere, and thus to call attention to a field of study which, it seems, has hitherto received too little notice.

The presentation is primarily descriptive; the contribution I hope to make consists in providing a body of references and textual documents on this aspect of aboriginal culture. It is urgent that this field of research be investigated by teams of specialists because, for this kind of study, it seems that time is running out very fast. If this book should stimulate others in formulating their research designs, it will have served its main purpose. The breakdown of native symbolic systems, the death of the older generation of Indians who still cherish the traditional way of life, and the rapid acculturation in all aspects of aboriginal culture are leading at present to the irretrievable loss of a vast accumulation of knowledge concerning the properties and uses of plants, acquired by the Amerinds over thousands of years. It is probable that much of this lore may be of great value to modern civilization, which already owes a considerable debt in this respect to the American Indians. Medicinal herbs, poisons, contraceptives, hallucinogens, and many other drugs form part of the Indians' culture, but this wealth of information will be lost if efforts to save it are not made quickly.

A few observations are in order, to explain the organization of this book and to describe the materials on which it is based. The first

chapters are an attempt to bring together some of the many isolated references to hallucinogenic drugs found in the literature. In
Chapter 1 I have tried to present a historical survey of the use of
narcotic snuff among Colombian Indians, basing my work mainly
on the early Spanish sources and, in a later period, on travel reports,
ethnological investigations, and other information. In this chapter
I have made liberal use of quotations because many of these sources
are not readily available to English readers, and in most cases I
give the original text in the Notes. I have found it necessary to re-
strict my survey to Colombian territory, but I am fully aware that
narcotic snuffs were, or still are, in use in many other areas. It was
not my intention to cover the entire field, however, since the
Colombian scene provides an abundance of data for the purpose of
an introductory study such as this.

In Chapter 2 I refer to *Banisteriopsis* potions, narcotic drinks
prepared from a jungle vine the existence of which was discovered
only in the last century by the English botanist Richard Spruce, and
whose use by the natives seems to be restricted to certain lowland
regions, mainly to the east of the Andes. My main sources, in this
case, have been the reports by botanists, travelers, and ethnog-
raphers who, in the last century and a half, have written on this
subject. Unfortunately, there is a lack of earlier references. In both
these chapters (1 and 2) I have added information on recent
botanical and pharmacological research, and I have quoted some
of the personal experiments made by individual investigators. In
Chapter 3, again on the basis of the early Spanish chronicles and
modern ethnographic reports, I have tried to relate the use of
narcotic substances to shamanistic practices and, through them, to
aboriginal jaguar imagery and symbolism. These three chapters,
then, form a unit which attempts to present a compilation of published data on native drug use and shamanism in certain Colombian
cultures.

Beginning with Chapter 4 I limit my field of inquiry to the rain
forest Indians of the Vaupés territory in the Colombian Northwest
Amazon. This chapter is meant to serve as a general introduction
to the local environment and its inhabitants. The material presented
in chapters 5–10 consist mainly of texts recorded in the field and
commented upon by the Indians themselves. These chapters, then,
are the result of field work and personal experiences.

After a brief visit to the Vaupés in 1951, my interest in this region was renewed in 1966 when I made the acquaintance of an acculturated Desana Indian, Antonio Guzmán. He provided me with a voluminous body of information on his view of his local culture, which led eventually to the publication of a book on some aspects of religious symbolism (Reichel-Dolmatoff 1971). This reconstruction of an elaborate belief system, seen through the eyes of one single informant, was, of course, likely to contain some misrepresentations, but the overall quality of Guzmán's information seemed to be such as to warrant the publication of this material. Although my informant had little firsthand experience with narcotic drugs as used within the context of his native culture, he implied that the psychotropic effects produced by these substances were at the core of many beliefs, and during our subsequent work I decided to concentrate on this aspect and to gather as much information as possible on it. This book, therefore, is in all essence a sequel to the volume mentioned above.

I hasten to explain that the data I was eventually able to obtain are incomplete and, in many ways, superficial. Although the Indians are generally not secretive about their use of narcotic drugs and about the manner in which they interpret their effects, any investigation into this aspect of their culture is difficult, not only because of its complex interrelationships with myth, ritual, and social organization, but also because altered states of consciousness are not easily defined, described, or explained in *any* cultural context. This is a borderline area of research in which, admittedly, one easily loses one's footing, and any attempt at interpretation is fraught with many dangers and pitfalls.

From 1966 to early in 1969 I worked with Antonio Guzmán—the native informant—and on several occasions I traveled with him to the Vaupés territory in order to record texts and elicit comments as detailed as possible on them with the assistance of this very competent interpreter. Although only a little more than five months were spent in actual field work, three of them in the general region of Mitú and two traveling on the Pira-paraná, the translations and comments on these texts occupied us for the better part of two years during which I acquired a sufficient knowledge of the Desana language to translate passages and discuss details of content and meaning. Most of this work concentrated on drug use and shamanism, but a number of interrelated topics were discussed and, on our occasional field trips, additional information was gathered from personal observation and from conversations with many other Indian informants.

In the description and interpretation of drug use among the Indians of the Vaupés I have used a number of texts which were tape-recorded in the field. These texts were translated and discussed with the help of many informants, and the results were checked repeatedly on subsequent field trips. The texts contain myths and tales, descriptions of ritual, songs and spells, and many spontaneous explanations of diverse topics. The principal informants were elderly men of the groups designated as Tukano proper, Desana, Pira-Tapuya, and Uanano, all of whom occasionally consumed narcotic drugs and many of whom had a detailed knowledge of shamanistic practices. One of the informants was a Tukano proper shaman of considerable renown, while among the Desana informants was an old man who was designated by his group as a *kumú*, a term used in referring to men with a special esoteric knowledge. He spoke no Spanish at all and was the least acculturated of the Desana group. The texts quoted in the present book were chosen from a voluminous body of transcriptions—more than one hundred hours of recordings—because they contained materials of special relevance to the theme of this inquiry. Additional information was gathered from a variety of informants and consisted of documents ranging from lengthy myths to simple conversations or brief comments on specific questions. Several extensive recordings were made during ceremonial occasions. I wish to point out, however, that, notwithstanding these personal observations and experiences, this book is not so much a field study as an inquiry based on textual materials and discussions with a selected group of informants.

A word must be said here about certain trends of thought and modes of expression which are common among the Indians of the Vaupés and might disturb some readers. Thus we shall note, again and again, references to sexual physiology, often enough expressed in images and situations which may appear somewhat gross. But, as we shall see in the chapters that follow, there is nothing lewd or erotic about these interpretations. The cosmological ideas of the Indians are, in essence, an outward projection of their image of the nature of man as a biological being, and preoccupations with sex and food are therefore constant. It is, then, "the cruel shamelessness of traditions"—in Cumont's words—which underlies these concepts, and to ignore it or underestimate it would be very misleading.

The results of this inquiry, even if we accept their incompleteness, have convinced me that the use of narcotic drugs by these Indians is an essential part of their culture and that, without a detailed knowledge of the role of these narcotics, any appreciation of social and religious customs would be very superficial indeed. But I am also aware of the fact that, in the chapters that follow, I have done hardly more than scratch the surface of much deeper problems in the exploration of which anthropology must combine its resources with those of many other disciplines, notably botany, pharmacology, and psychology. In fact, without the collaboration of these sciences any attempt at a valid cultural analysis would be doomed to failure.

It is with the hope that the cultural importance of narcotic drugs among Colombian natives will be the subject of further studies by others more competent than I that I have provided rather copious notes for the chapters; they will not only guide the reader to the original sources I have used, but also offer occasional comments or suggestions for further readings.

The following annotations are of importance and I must ask the reader to keep them in mind. All words in aboriginal languages are followed by bracketed capitals indicating the particular language: (T) for Tukano proper, (D) for Desana, and (LG) for *Lengua Geral*, a Tupi dialect. The term *Tukano* refers to the Eastern Tukano in general, while the term *Tukano proper* refers to the specific exogamic group known by that name. All words, sentences, or paragraphs set in quotation marks are literal expressions of native informants. I should add that whenever I write, "The Tukano say," or "According to the Tukano," the statement following the expression is based on a body of data that, in my view, seems to justify this generalization.

THE
SHAMAN
AND THE
JAGUAR

1

NARCOTIC
SNUFF

The priests who, in the late fifteenth and early sixteenth centuries, accompanied the Spanish troops on their conquest of the aborigines of the West Indies and the adjacent mainland, and those who in later years were put in charge of the conversion of the subdued tribes, were greatly disturbed by the many snares the devil had so industriously set to trap the souls of the natives. On the islands as well as almost everywhere on the newly discovered Spanish Main the Indians were found to practice superstitious rites which, to the friars' minds, were clearly instigated by him. In point of fact, the Indians themselves said so; they openly admitted that they believed in certain spirits who incited them to warfare and cannibalism, to drunkenness and all kinds of evil, and they described these spirits in terms which left little doubt as to their true identity. From the Caribbean coast to the highlands of the interior, from the Pacific to the Orinoco, the Indians told of strange beings who appeared to them in the shapes of monsters armed with pointed fangs, terrifying beings with glowing eyes and roaring voices who presented themselves in thunder and lightning and were recognized by the Indians as their overlords and masters. They were afraid of the monsters, it is true, but at the same time they respected and obeyed them. The priests were quick to recognize the New World image of the devil.

There were other supernatural beings, but these were of a tamer sort and were of less concern to the missionaries. There were the personifications of the sun and the moon, of rain and fertility; there were divinities that dwelt in mountain lakes or in caves, spirits of the forest or of the rivers, the supernatural masters of the game animals, and a host of others. And there were, of course, the culture

3

heroes of mythical times who had made order of the landscape and had taught their people to weave, to make pots, or to plant maize. Some of them had been lawgivers who had established a moral code, while others were half-forgotten chieftains who had been prominent in tribal wars of the past. But most of these personifications were only vaguely defined and were thought to exist in a remote sphere from which they exercised only occasional control over human affairs. They were venerated, and sometimes offerings were made to them, at certain spots and in certain seasons; they were remembered in myth and ritual, in songs and dances, but they remained distant powers, distant benevolent forces that watched over the course of worldly matters in a detached, impersonal way.

Yet there were these other, darker forces that were of much more immediate concern to people. In the humdrum give-and-take of everyday life—as humdrum as that anywhere—there existed conflicts that had to be resolved somehow, and all too often they were beyond the more lofty controls of the tribal deities. To begin with, there were envy and ambition; there were the meddling with women and the failure of crops; there were fights between neighbors, gossip, death and disease, fear and flight. And in all these situations, the tribal religion, as expressed in esoteric ritual and controlled by men with priestly or shamanistic functions, was of little avail because these were highly personal problems in the solution of which a benevolent sun-god or a culture hero could not be counted upon. These were problems of here and now, of food and sex, power or defeat, which had little or nothing to do with the order of the Universe, the change of seasons, or the cycle of decline and renewal.

And it is here where—as the missionaries saw it—the devil entered the picture. This was a force that could be called up at any time; it was an amoral force that could be bribed and used for personal ends: to harm, to kill, to gain prestige, or to forecast the future; to cure diseases, to gain possession of food, women or wealth, or whatever else was one's personal ambition.

And everywhere the Indians "talked to the devil," seeking his advice or asking him to do them this or that favor.

The early missionaries were, of course, well acquainted with demon worship and animal familiars. No matter how strange and fantastic the New World and its inhabitants might have appeared to them, these men coming from devil-ridden Europe immediately recognized the old pattern of the summoning of spirits by sorcerers, of diabolic possession and strange voices, of uncouth visions of ghostly beings. The suppression of these practices and their underlying beliefs became the missionaries' main task, and of this they wrote in their chronicles and in the reports they sent to their superiors, telling them over and over again how the Indians "talked with the devil."

This "talking with the devil," mentioned so frequently in the early sources, obviously refers to a widespread and very effective mechanism by which the natives entered a trancelike state during which they had visions or heard voices that seemed to pertain to a sphere lying wholly outside any rational experience. Today we know that this mechanism was provided by narcotic substances derived from plants, and that the images and voices perceived under their influence were creatures of imagination, but to the missionaries of those times the devil was much too real and omnipresent to be brushed off as a mere fantasy conceived by savage minds. And it was also obvious that these trances, during which the Indians claimed to establish contact with the forces of darkness, played an important part in their religious beliefs and were, therefore, an obstacle in their conversion to the Christian faith.

It was Christopher Columbus himself who, in his report on the second voyage in 1493–96, first wrote on these matters and who first mentions the use of a narcotic substance, a snuff, that was in common use by the Indians.[1] Speaking of the cult of the *cemis*, wooden images the natives of Haiti kept in special shrines or enclosures, Columbus writes: "In this house they have a finely wrought tablet, round like a thaler piece, in which is some powder which they place on the heads of these *cemis* while performing a certain ceremony; then with a cane that has two branches which they introduce in their nostrils they snuff up this powder. The words that they say none of our people understand. With these powders they go out of their minds and become as if intoxicated."[2]

Columbus took a personal interest in this ritual[3] and gave orders to Román Pane, a friar who had learned the native language, to make a study of their "rites and antiquities." The friar's report was published by Ferdinand Columbus, the admiral's son, and, among other things, again mentions the use of a narcotic snuff, called *cogioba* or *cohoba*. "The cogioba is a certain powder which they take sometimes to purge themselves and for other effects, as I shall mention later; they take it with a cane of about an arm's length and put one end in the nose and the other in the powder, and thus they absorb it through the nose, which purges them thoroughly."[4]

Speaking of a curing ritual performed by a local shaman, Friar Román continues: "It is necessary that he [the curer], too, purge himself like the patient, and to purge themselves they take *cogioba*[5] powder, absorbing it through the nose which intoxicates them so that they do not know what they are doing, and they say many things as if they were out of their minds, saying that they are talking with the *cemis* and that through them the disease has come."[6]

Another use of cogioba snuff described by Friar Román refers to a shamanistic practice during which contact with other supernatural forces was established. The natives, he reports, believe that, occasionally, a tree may make a sign to a passerby, perhaps by moving a root. When the shaman is told about the incident,

> the sorcerer runs immediately to where the tree stands, sits down next to it, and takes cogioba. . . . Having done so he rises and recites all his dignities[7] as if they were those of a great lord, and he asks the tree: "Tell me who you are? What are you doing here? What do you want from me? Why did you send for me? Say if you want me to cut you down or to come with me to make a house for you to own." Then the tree or the *cemis,* being an idol or a devil, answers him telling him the manner in which he wants this to be done and he cuts the tree and carves it in the manner indicated, makes a home for him to own and prepares *cogioba* for him many times a year whenever he prays to him to please him and to entreat him or to inquire from the *cemis* about evil things or good ones, and also to solicit from him great wealth.[8]

The narcotic powder was also used for other divinatory practices; Friar Román Pane writes:

> When they wish to know if they will be victorious over their enemies, they go into a house which no one enters except the men of importance, and their chief is the first who prepares *cogioba* and gives notice;[9] and while he is preparing *cogioba,* no one of his company speaks till he has finished; and when he has finished his supplication, he remains for a while with his head turned aside and his arms on his knees; then he lifts up his head and speaks while looking heavenward; then they all answer in unison in a loud voice, and when they have all spoken

giving thanks, he tells them the vision he has had while intoxicated with the *cogioba* he has absorbed through the nose, which goes to his head, and says that he has talked with the *cemis* and that they will be victorious; or that their enemies will flee; or that there will be a great massacre, or wars or famine, according to what occurs to him while intoxicated. Consider his state of mind and reason, for they say that the houses appear to be upside down and that the people are walking on their heads, with their feet in the air.[10]

There are other early chroniclers who mention the use of these snuffs in their descriptions of the newly discovered natives. Bartolomé de las Casas, who was to gain fame as the defender of the Indians, writes that the natives of Haiti "had certain powders of certain herbs well dried and ground, of the color of cinnamon or powdered henna,"[11] and he describes the instruments used for snuffing thus: "The snuffing-apparatus was made of the same kind of dark wood as the snuff-tray," the latter being "a round dish, not flat but slightly concavish or deep, made of wood; so handsome, smooth and pretty that it could not be very much more so even were it made of gold or silver; it was almost black and shone like jet."[12] Of the snuffing tube he says that it was "fashioned to the size of a small flute, all hollow as is a flute," and that "from two-thirds of its length onward it divided into two hollow canes."[13]

Gonzalo Fernández Oviedo y Valdés,[14] that extraordinary naturalist and historian of the Indies, gives a similar description of the object: "The caciques and chiefs had little hollow canes, about one xeme[15] long, or less, and of the thickness of the little finger, and these canes had two tubes joined into one, like the one illustrated here, and all in one piece." This description, however, is given by Oviedo when speaking of the use of tobacco, another devilish weed the Spaniards had discovered in Haiti, and from here on a certain confusion begins to appear in the early literature, tobacco smoking or snuffing not always being clearly distinguished from the use of other plants. In fact, before describing the instrument used to absorb the powder, the chronicler writes: "Among other vices, the Indians of this island have a very evil one which consists in taking a smoke that they call *tabaco,* in order to get out of their minds."[16] And, referring once more to the snuffing tubes, he goes on to say: "They put the two [branches] into the nostrils and the other one into the smoke and herbs that were burning and smouldering . . .

and they took the emanation and smoke—one, two, three or more times, as often as they could stand it, until they were out of their minds, lying on the ground drunk or overpowered by a deep and heavy sleep."[17]

From the various descriptions of the snuffing implements it appears that there were two different types of tubes with which to absorb the narcotic: a Y-shaped or bifurcated instrument and a straight tube, and it also seems that categories existed according to the rank of the consumer; the "caciques and chiefs" used the finely wrought artifacts mentioned by Columbus and Pane, while the common people used simple tubes or hollow canes.[18]

All authors agree that, under the influence of these snuffs, the Indians "went out of their minds," and that they talked wildly and incoherently, claiming to see visions and hear voices. Las Casas says that "they talk in a gabble, or like Germans, confusedly."[19] However, the religious character of the ritual is clearly stated, and Oviedo writes that "the taking of this herb and smoke was to them not only a healthy practice but a very sacred thing."[20]

The narcotic snuff could be taken collectively, but on occasions it was only the shaman or the chieftain who took it and then served as an oracle to the others. Oviedo's words deserve to be quoted in full:

> They worship the devil in diverse forms and images, as is the custom among these peoples in the Indies; because, as I have said, they paint, engrave or carve him in many objects and parts, in wood or clay, and also in other materials of which they make a demon they call *cemi*, as ugly and frightful as the Catholics represent him at the feet of Saint Michael or Saint Bartholomew; but not bound in chains, but revered: sometimes as if sitting in judgment, sometimes standing, in different ways. These infernal images they had in their houses in specially assigned and dark places and spots that were reserved for their worship; and there they entered to pray and to ask for whatever they desired, be it rain for their fields and farms, or bountiful harvests, or victory over their enemies; and there, finally, they prayed to him and had recourse to him in all their needs, to find a remedy for them. And inside there was an old Indian who answered them according to their expectations or in accordance with a consultation addressed to him whose evil image was standing there; and it is to be thought that the devil entered into him and spoke through him as through his minister; ... These

old men they greatly revered, and among the Indians they were held in high esteem as their priests and prelates; and it were they who most commonly consumed tobacco and the smoke mentioned above, and when they woke up they said if war should be declared or postponed; and without the devil's considered opinion . . . they did not undertake or carry out anything that might be of importance.[21]

The foregoing quotations suffice to show us quite clearly that narcotic vegetable substances played a most important, if not dominant, part in the religious practices of the ancient inhabitants of Haiti. They also show us that these narcotics were used in different forms—sometimes in mixtures—and that the specific manner in which the drug was consumed corresponded to certain occasions which, in each case, demanded specific results. The main objective was to establish direct communication with the supernatural sphere whose powers manifested themselves in the course of more or less prolonged states of hallucinatory trance. The problem arises now: What exactly were the plant sources of these hallucinogenic drugs?

William E. Safford,[22] one of the first botanists who paid close attention to this question, believed—probably quite correctly—that *cogioba* and *cohoba* were one and the same plant,[23] and that the narcotic powder was derived from the seeds of *Piptadenia peregrina,* a tree now reclassified as *Anadenanthera peregrina.*[24] In fact, Oviedo writes of the cohoba trees that "they bear peas or black beans that are round and very hard and are not eaten by man or beast. The cohoba bears certain beans and the pods are about a span in length."[25] This description points to *Anadenanthera peregrina,* a leguminous tree whose pods contain about a dozen black or brownish seeds. This tree is widely distributed in the tropical lowlands of South America and the Caribbean islands, and the seeds are now known to contain very potent hallucinogenic substances. But more about this later.

The other narcotic snuff was prepared from tobacco, the description given by Oviedo being quite unmistakable: "This herb is a stalk or shoot of about four or five spans in height or less, with wide and thick leaves that are soft and fuzzy."[26] It was from this that the "burning and smouldering" mass mentioned by Oviedo was prepared, and the chronicler writes: "This herb the Indians consider as very precious and cultivate it in their gardens and fields."[27]

We must turn now to the South American mainland and examine the early sources referring to the lands that became known as the Kingdom of New Granada, the modern Colombia.

The conquest of New Granada began on the Caribbean coast, a region that had already been partially explored during the last years of the fifteenth century and where, during the first decades of the sixteenth century, the first permanent Spanish settlements had been made. The foundation of Santa Marta in 1525, to the east of the mouth of the Magdalena River, was followed in 1533 by that of Cartagena of the Indies, lying to the west of it, near the fabulous country of Sinú where the Spaniards had discovered great golden hoards in the burial mounds of the local natives. The next step was to be the exploration of the valleys and mountains of the interior where the Land of El Dorado was supposed to lie.

The conquest of the coastal lowlands had been a continuous and violent struggle against a multitude of warlike tribes who harassed the small bands of soldiers by day and night with their poisoned arrows. This was no time for chroniclers and historians to write about strange customs and beliefs; the early reports speak of battles and ambushes, of looted villages and executed chieftains, but not of the way of life of the "Caribs" or other savage peoples. Once a semblance of peace had been established the conquistadors pressed on toward the south, toward the interior of the country. In 1537, a Spanish expedition under Gonzalo Jimenez de Quesada ascended the Magdalena River and, after great hardships, discovered the highlands of Cundinamarca, the homeland of the Muisca (or Chibcha) Indians. The Muisca had reached a fairly advanced level of cultural complexity, considerably above that of the tribal chiefdoms of the neighboring mountain valleys, but they offered little resistance to the foreign invaders and were soon subdued. The following year saw the foundation of Santa Fé de Bogotá, which from then on became the administrative center of the newly conquered lands, as well as the starting point for new expeditions into the unknown.

The Indians around Bogotá were a peaceful and cooperative people, and now that the Spaniards had settled down in their country to stay, the chroniclers and friars once more began to describe Indian customs. These highland Indians were quite different from those the Spaniards had encountered in the tropical environment of the West Indian islands and on the coast of the mainland. The

Muisca were an austere and withdrawn people, living scattered over the bleak highland basins and mountainfolds of the cordilleras where they tended their crops in the harsh Andean climate, so different from the sunlit beaches of the Caribbean. They had reached a remarkable degree of political cohesion; they had temples and priests who served the Sun and the Moon, and their chiefs were carried in litters, surrounded by attendant lords and slaves. But one thing they had in common with the natives of the coast—they used narcotic snuffs.

Again, it is Oviedo's history that contains the earliest information on this habit. Oviedo writes on the Muisca Indians:

> These Indians practice another idolatry and witchcraft, in that they will not take to the road, nor wage war, nor do any other thing of importance, without finding out beforehand what will be the outcome of their enterprise, or this, at least, they try to ascertain, and in order to do so they have two herbs which they consume, called *yop* and *osca* which, when taken separately and after a certain time span and interval, reveal to them, in answer to their inquiries, what it is the Sun wants them to do on these occasions. And having asked them how the Sun makes this known, once they have taken the herbs, they answer that there will be a twitching in a certain joint, after they have taken the herbs, which denotes that their wish and enterprise will be granted, while if other joints be twitching, it means that it will not be successful but to the contrary; and for the purpose of this extraordinary vagary they have classified, named, and observed all the joints of the body, some for good and some for evil.[28]

In another part of Oviedo's history the editor adds "*yop:* herb of divination, used by the *mojas* or sun-priests in the valleys of Tunja and Bogotá," that is, in the two main centers of Muisca culture; and "*osca:* herb of divination among the Indians of New Granada."[29]

This description given by Oviedo contains several interesting details. In the first place, the term *yop,* as the name of a narcotic herb or tree, appears here for the first time and, from here on, is mentioned frequently in the literature. In the second place, another "herb" is designated as *osca,* and Oviedo says that both plants are used for divinatory practices. We shall first try to identify the *yop* plant. This name appears in several early reports and is generally written *yopo* or *yopa,* sometimes *niopo* or *ñopo.*[30] Speaking of

Colombian Indians in general, the Spanish chronicler Bernardo de Vargas Machuca, writing in 1599, says: "They chew hayo or coca and jopa and tobacco, thereby going out of their minds, and then the Devil speaks to them."[31] The chewing of coca leaves is, of course, a well-known habit among many South American Indians, and *hayo* is the name of the coca plant (*Eritroxylon coca*) among the Indians of the Sierra Nevada of Santa Marta. But the use of *yop*—or *jopa*, as Vargas Machuca spells it—is of special interest here. Vargas Machuca continues and, speaking now of the Pijao Indians, a very warlike tribe of the upper Magdalena valley, refers to "their chief who was a sorcerer and mohan,[32] having taken jopa in order to speak with the devil."[33] And then he writes: "Jopa is a tree that produces certain small pods, similar to vetches, and the seeds inside are likewise, but smaller. These the Indians take ground, in the mouth, in order to speak with the devil."[34]

This description is of importance to our inquiry. It is sufficiently explicit to deduce from it that *yop*—at least the one used by the Pijao Indians—was *Anadenanthera peregrina,* the leguminous tree the seeds of which are known to contain a powerful hallucinogenic substance. We shall return later on to the discussion of the chemical aspects of this drug, and for the moment we shall continue to search for other early references to the use of *yopo,* as we shall from now on call this plant.

Some time before Vargas Machuca, approximately in 1560, the Spanish chronicler Friar Pedro de Aguado[35] mentions the use of yopo, this time among the Guayupe Indians of the Guaviare River, in the lowlands east of the Andes. The Guayupe were probably related to the Indians of the Vaupés territory, and Friar Pedro describes the customs of these Indians in some detail—of how they would kill their firstborn children by burying them alive or throwing them into the river; of their ritual flagellations and their curing rites, and of their habit of mixing the ashes of their dead chiefs with maize beer and drinking this brew during a most solemn gathering. And Friar Pedro goes on to say:

> They are accustomed to take *yopa* and tobacco, and the former
> is a seed or pip of a tree, and the latter is a certain leaf they
> keep, broad, long, and fuzzy, and these they smoke, sometimes
> by mouth or sometimes through the nose, until it intoxicates
> them and deprives them of their senses, and thus they become
> drowsy while the Devil, in their dreams, shows them all the

vanities and corruptions he wishes them to see, and which they take to be true revelations in which they believe even if told they will die. This habit of taking *yopa* and tobacco is general in the New Kingdom and, so I understand, in most of the Indies, and more so than any other occupation, for it being the instrument and means of which the Devil avails himself because, as I said, with the smoke the Indians take of these things they become intoxicated and deprived of their natural faculties, and in this manner the Fiend finds it easy to make them believe in idols and to follow other false tenets, such as he wishes.[36]

Another chronicler of the sixteenth century, Friar Juan de Castellanos,[37] who also had firsthand knowledge of Colombian Indians, mentions yopo among the Igneri Indians of Trinidad where he spent some time, and although this region falls outside our area of interest, the description is worth quoting here. Castellanos reports that "one takes tobacco while another takes yopa, in order to know the future; the squares, streets and roads were full of sorcerers and diviners."[38] It is perhaps significant that Castellanos should not hesitate to apply the term *yopo,* a name common on the mainland, to the drug used on that West Indian island. Knowing both regions and being a trustworthy source on Indian customs, he would probably have employed the name *cohoba* (or *cogioba*), had it been different from the yopo he knew from the mainland. But this is hardly more than a guess.

The following quotations will be useful to us in attempting to summarize the information contained in the chronicles. Friar Pedro Simón, a chronicler of the first decades of the seventeenth century, wrote extensively on the Muisca Indians; in his colloquial manner he tells the following story:

Not so long ago, finding myself in the Sogamoso Valley in one of our curacies called Tota, just after saying Mass, I met an old man by name of Paraico next the church door, a sort of buffoon and rascal, and knowing that he was a witch doctor, I had him undo the few rags he was wearing and found on him in a bag the tools of his trade, which were a small gourd vessel containing the powder of certain leaves they call *yopa,* together with some of same that were not yet pulverized, and a bit of mirror glass of ours, imbedded in a little stick, and a small broom, and a deer bone cut lengthwise in a slant and very well adorned, made like a spoon with which, when they practice this witchcraft, they take these powders and put them in their noses and which, because they are pungent, make the mucus flow until it hangs down to the mouth, which they observe in the mirror, and when it runs straight it is a good sign, and if crooked, the contrary, for whatever they try to divine."[39]

The following quotation is taken from the proceedings of an accusation of idolatry made, in 1634, against the Tunebo Indians, a tribe living to the north of the Muisca. The local priest, Father Pedro Guillén de Arce, writes:

That night, in spite of their being Christians and having received Holy Baptism, they summoned the Devil and called him up in their rites and ceremonies, complaining to him that the Spaniards had come to convert them and that the priests had deprived them of yopa . . . and in this manner, all night long the cacique and the Indians who were with him were taking yopa until they were seeing the Devil and were talking to him, taking the ground yopa out of a snail shell stopped up with a puma's tail, and an old man distributing it with a spoon made of puma bone . . . so they went on until dawn. The cacique had kept the women apart, with plenty of food and drink . . . and did not allow them to join their husbands that night, saying that the females could not enter the house . . . [because] the Devil was to foretell all the good and evil events, diseases, or deaths, that were to befall the Indians, their women and children, according to the filthy liquid that was running from their noses through which they take yopa, and which they watched in certain small mirrors.[40]

So far, we have observed the use of yopo among the Muisca and Tunebo Indians of the Andean highlands, among the Pijao of the tropical upper Magdalena valley, and among the Guayupe, a tribe of the border region between the grassy Orinoco Plains and the rain forests of the Northwest Amazon. Besides, Aguado had written that the use of yopo was "general in the New Kingdom."[41] But before we go further and investigate the precise use of the yopo plant, we must turn back once more and consider Oviedo's statement on the Muisca.

Oviedo had mentioned another plant—*osca*—that was taken for its narcotic effects; but what was *osca*?

A vocabulary of the Muisca language, dating from the early seventeenth century, translates this word (written *hosca*) as "tabaco, borrachero."[42] This last term seems to be significant. The name *borrachero,* from the Spanish *borracho*/drunk, was and still is the vernacular name applied to various species of the *Datura* plant, a solanaceous genus common in the highlands of the ancient Muisca territory as well as in the tropical and subtropical lowlands.[43] *Datura*[44] was widely used by the Indians for its highly narcotic effects[45] and was, as we shall see, well known among the Muisca. Castellanos describes the sacrifice of women and slaves among these Indians, who, at the death of their master, were buried with him: "and so that the women and the miserable slaves won't feel their death, before looking at the monstrous cavity, the xeques[46] give them certain draughts made of intoxicating tobacco, and other leaves of a tree we call borrachero."[47]

It is possible that the vocabulary mentioned above employs the term *tobacco* in a very vague and general sense, as if any narcotic plant might be designated as "the Indian's tobacco." We must examine the linguistic documents in more detail to explain this apparent confusion. Unfortunately, Muisca is a dead language; it already had disappeared in the eighteenth century, and all we have to go by at present are the few vocabularies collected during the colonial period by the Spanish friars.

The vocabulary from 1619 mentioned above is followed by a catechism and a treatise with rules for confessing the Muisca Indians that contain the following questions the priest asked of the confessant: "Have you been drinking tobacco or have you made others drink it in order to find [lost property]?"[48] In addition, the vocabulary contains definitions, among them: to drink tobacco/*hoscaz biohotysuca;* to drink tobacco on my behalf/*huas abiohotysuca;* to intoxicate oneself in this manner/*ityhyquynsuca;* to intoxicate someone else with borrachero/*btyhyquysuca.*[49] Turning to the questions put to the confessant we find that the first interrogation clearly refers to *hosca;* the text contains the expression *hosca miohotya,* from *biohotysuca*/to drink, and *biohoty*/beverage. But the other expressions quoted above—those that contain the verb "to intoxicate"—do not mention the word *hosca* but use the word *ityhyquysuca.* The corresponding noun is *tyhyquy* and as such it appears in the vocabulary as the name for "borrachero, a tree."[50] The word is probably related to *tyquy*/luck, fortune,[51] and might refer to the use of *Datura* in divinatory practices. Are we dealing, then, with two different plants, and could *osca* be tobacco, while *tyhyquy* is *Datura?* One would think that Oviedo, who had an excellent knowledge of the Indians of the West Indies and was interested in botany, would have said so if he had observed that the *osca* of the Muisca Indians was the same plant as tobacco. He knew tobacco from the islands, and he himself had described it in unmistakable terms as having "wide and thick leaves that are soft and fuzzy."[52] Why then does he mention *osca* only as an "herb for divination," without any further comparison?

We must leave this question open. Possibly the term *tobacco* was applied occasionally by the Spaniards to any narcotic plant, and when the vocabulary says "hosca; tabaco borrachero," it might refer simply to any beverage (*hizca*)[53] made of narcotic plants.

We can briefly summarize the evidence for the use of yopo among the Colombian Indians of the sixteenth and seventeenth centuries. Apart from the "general use" mentioned by Aguado, we have the following specific information: yopo was prepared as a powder (Muisca, Tunebo, Pijao, Guayupe); absorbed through the nose (Guayupe, Muisca, Tunebo); or eaten (Pijao), the latter form of use being somewhat doubtful and due, perhaps, to an error in the chronicler's observation. Yopo was used in combination with *osca* and tobacco (Muisca); with tobacco (Guayupe, Pijao). The paraphernalia described are: a gourd container (Muisca); a snail-shell container (Tunebo); a deer-bone spoon (Muisca); a puma-bone spoon (Tunebo); a stick with a piece of mirror glass (Muisca), and a "small mirror" (Tunebo). It was used for divinatory purposes, the principal objective in taking yopo being contact with the supernatural, the "Devil," and under the influence of the drug people "went out of their minds."

During the eighteenth century information on yopo becomes more common because by that time the Orinoco Plains, the principal center of snuff consumption, had been explored and settled. From our sources it seems that practically all tribes of this vast region used narcotic snuff and still do so to this day. This, however, does not mean that identical or similar snuffs were unknown among the natives of the rain forest areas—for example, the Vaupés, Apaporis, and Caquetá regions—but only that the Orinoco Plains was better known at that time than the humid tropical forest areas east of the Andean chain, which were still largely unexplored.

The Achagua Indians, an Arawakan tribe of peaceful, sedentary agriculturalists who inhabited the general region of the Meta River, were assiduous yopo snuffers. Father Juan Rivero, who in the early eighteenth century spent many years among these Indians, reports: "One of the deceits they practice consists in the use of certain powders which they obtain from the small seeds of certain trees which are tall and abundant in foliage; these powders they call *yopa*, and they use them for their prophecies . . . through the nose."[54]

After describing how the Achagua observe and interpret the flow of mucus, just as Simón said the Muisca did, Rivero goes on to relate the effects of the intoxication, and these observations begin to shed some light upon physiological and psychological aspects of the habit. Rivero writes: "They talk in loud and shrill shouts like madmen, making hideous grimaces and, even if many of them are gathered together, they do not converse one with another, but each one talks only to himself, with gestures and shakings, questions and cross-examinations, all of which demonstrates that they are talking with the Devil."[55]

Of another large tribe, the Sáliva, who were different from the Achagua in many cultural aspects, Rivero writes: "They are great herbalists and wizards, and renowned practitioners of *yopa* snuffing for their prophecies and superstitions."[56]

And of the neighboring Guahibo Indians, at that time a tribe of nomadic food gatherers, he writes: "The intoxication with *yopa* powder is never amiss amongst them, and they carry it in some large snail shells, the only equipment they take along on their wanderings; they use it with more excess and recklessness than the other nations, and employ it for their superstitions and prophecies."[57]

Father José Gumilla, a Jesuit priest, writes in 1745 about the Otomac Indians:

They have another abominable way of intoxicating themselves through the nose, with some malignant powders they call *yupa* and which deprive them completely of their senses, and furiously will they take up arms; and if the women were not clever in intercepting them and in tying them up, they would play cruel havoc every day; this is a tremendous vice indeed. They prepare these powders from *yupa* beans—whence their name—which smell of strong tobacco, but it is that which, by the Devil's diligence, they admix, that causes the intoxication and the fury: after having eaten some large snails which they

find in the marshes, they put the snails into the fire and reduce
them to quick lime, whiter than snow; they mix this lime with
yupa, in equal parts, and after reducing everything to a very
fine powder, the product is of a diabolical strength . . . before
going to war they make themselves brave with *yupa,* and
inflict wounds on themselves, and then—full of blood and
fury—they go to fight like enraged jaguars.[58]

Of the Tunebo, Father Rivero writes that "the use of *yopa,* which
is the principal instrument for their divinations and superstitions,
to which they are very much inclined, was well established among
them and is still practised among other savage nations."[59]

In 1802 Alexander von Humboldt ascended the Orinoco and
again observed the use of yopo among the Otomac Indians.[60] He
describes in some detail the preparation of the powder. The pods are
broken into pieces and, after water is added, are left to ferment.
The mass is then kneaded, with the admixture of manioc flour and
lime—the latter obtained from a snail shell—and is then baked over
a fire into little cakes. Parts of these cakes are then pulverized on a
small dish provided with a handle, and the powder is absorbed
into the nostrils through a forked instrument made of hollow bird
bones. The effect of this snuff is described by Humboldt as "a
state of drunkenness, one might say madness."[61]

Some fifty years later, Richard Spruce, the great English botanist,
traveled on the Orinoco, Rio Negro, and Vaupés. Spruce describes
the preparation of yopo from *Anadenanthera peregrina* seeds
among a group of wandering Guahibo Indians who had come from
the Meta River and were camping near the rapids of Maipures, on
the Orinoco. His detailed description is of interest and must be
quoted in full.

The seeds being first roasted, are powdered on a wooden platter,
nearly the shape of a watch-glass, but rather longer than
broad (9¼ inches by 8 inches). It is held on the knee by a
broad thin handle, which is grasped in the left hand, while
the fingers of the right hold a small spatula or pestle of hard
wood of the Palo de arco (Tecomae sp.) with which the seeds
are crushed. The snuff is kept in a mull made of a bit of the
leg-bone of the jaguar, closed at one end with pitch, and at the
other end stopped with a cork of marima bark. It hangs around
the neck. . . . For taking the snuff they use an apparatus made
of the leg-bones of herons or other long-shanked birds put

together in the shape of the letter Y, or something like a tuning
fork, and the two upper tubes are tipped with small black,
perforated knobs (the endocarps of a palm). The lower tube
being inserted in the snuff-box and the knobs in the nostrils, the
snuff is forcibly inhaled, with the effect of thoroughly narcotising
the novice, or indeed a practised hand, if taken in sufficient
quantity.[62]

He goes on to say:

Among the native tribes of the Uaupés and of the upper
tributaries of the Orinoco, niopo or paricá is the chief curative
agent. When the payé is called in to treat a patient, he first snuffs
up his nose such a quantity of paricá as suffices to throw him
into a sort of ecstasy, wherein he professes to divine the nature
of the evil wish which has caused the sickness.[63]

With Spruce's observation we are entering a new period, one of
research and of growing interest in the use of hallucinogenic drugs
among the forest Indians. By the end of the century and during
more recent times, a large number of European travelers and
ethnologists observed the use of yopo (*Anadenanthera peregrina*),
especially among the following tribes of Colombia: Guahibo and its
subgroups the Cuiva, Sicuani, and Amorúa;[64] Tunebo,[65] Piaroa,[66]
Piapoco,[67] Baniva,[68] Guayabero,[69] and Huitoto.[70] All these tribes
live east of the Andes and, with the exception of the forest-dwelling
Huitoto, inhabit the open savannah country of the Orinoco Plains,
an environment where this botanical species is most common.

We have spoken here only of the tribes of the Orinoco Plains,
mainly because this region was more thoroughly explored than the
rain forest area lying to the south. But turning now to the Northwest
Amazon and the forest Indians of the Vaupés-Caquetá regions, we
see the use of narcotic snuffs becoming much more complex.

In the historical and ethnological literature, a great deal of confusion has been caused by the many different names under which
South American narcotics are known, and it seems that quite often
too little attention has been paid to the correct botanical identification of the sources of these substances. From the Caribbean to
Argentina we find snuffs mentioned under the names *cohoba, yopo,
niop, paricá, curupa, sebil, vilca,* and others[71] and often it has been
taken almost for granted that all, or most of them, were derived
from *Anadenanthera peregrina* seeds. It is very probable that

Anadenanthera did play an important part in this complex, but there can be no doubt that there existed—or still exist—many other plant sources that provide narcotic substances for snuffing. The general distribution of *Anadenanthera peregrina* snuffing in South America seems to cover a large area that extends from the Caribbean coast southward to the Northwest Amazon, follows the Andean chain to northeast Argentina, and also includes a number of scattered localities over the Amazon drainage. However, present ethnological knowledge of this distribution is still incomplete, and a more detailed search in the literature and—as we shall see further on—in the prehistoric remains of many cultures would undoubtedly produce much more information. A most important point in trying to trace this wider distribution consists in the evaluation of the existing evidence and in the clear distinction between *Anadenanthera peregrina* snuffs and those derived from other sources. The description and analysis of the entire snuff complex in South America is, of course, far beyond the scope of this book; we must remain within the limits of Colombian aboriginal cultures and their immediate neighbors and cannot consider other regions where narcotic snuffs have been—or still are—in use. In any case, Colombia seems to be an important center of narcotic snuffs and other hallucinogenic drugs, thus providing an excellent field for our study.

We must turn then to the Colombian Northwest Amazon and explore these aspects of distribution and identity in more detail. Among the rain forest Indians of the Vaupés region, it appears that another, quite different snuff is prepared, from a different botanical source. This is a jungle tree of the genus *Virola*, a Myristicacea, several species of which (*V. calophylla, V. calophylloidea,* and *V. theidora*) contain in their bark a red resin that has strong hallucinogenic components. As the first step in preparing the snuff, the bark is stripped from the tree and is put into cold water for about an hour. After a while the reddish resin which exudes from the bark begins to congeal and can be scraped off. Water is then added to the resin, the mass is kneaded and then strained through a piece of barkcloth, and the liquid is kept in a small pottery vessel. Water is again added, and now the liquid is boiled for several hours until the bottom of the vessel is covered with a thick sticky mass. This mass is sun-dried and scraped off the inside of the vessel, after which it is finely ground with a smooth pebble. An equal amount of ashes is added, obtained from the burnt bark of the wild cacao tree (*Theo-*

broma subincanum Mart.), and then the powder is sifted through a very fine barkcloth. The dustlike snuff, now ready for use, is kept in a snail shell.[72]

Virola snuff is found today among the Puinave,[73] Kuripako,[74] Guayabero,[75] Cubeo,[76] and among many Tukano groups of the Vaupés.[77] The *Virola* is at home in a rain forest environment, while *Anadenanthera peregrina* grows in open savannah country; and so the Guaviare River seems to constitute a dividing line between the two areas of snuff use. Correct botanical identification in the field is therefore of the essence. The mere observation that this or that Indian tribe uses a more or less brownish powder does not warrant its identification with either plant source.

A clear distinction between different plant sources, and also between possible admixtures, is of importance because of the chemical reactions involved and, consequently, because of the variations in the psychotropic effects upon the user. The occasional admixture of alkaline substances such as ashes or calcined shells is probably of considerable importance in determining the intensity and general orientation of the hallucinatory experience. The possible consequences in the action of the drug of adding powdered tobacco are still insufficiently known, and, as we have seen, the early sources are often very confusing on this point.

This leads us to a brief consideration of the hallucinogenic substances contained in these snuffs. Recent chemical and pharmacological analyses have shown that the seeds or beans of *Anadenanthera peregrina* contain 5-Hydroxy-N,N-dimethyltriptamine (5-OH-DMT) or Bufotenine, all powerful psychotomimetic substances.[78] These act directly upon the brain, the tryptamines then producing their psychotropic effect. The physical symptoms of the intoxication are severe headaches, vomiting, and abundant perspiration and salivation, and occasionally the user may fall into a deep stupor. Agurell and his collaborators write that "considerable differences in the alkaloid composition of different parts of single plants were encountered, N, N-dimethyltryptamine being the major component in the leaves and 5-methoxy-N, N-dimethyltryptamine in the bark of *Virola theidora*."[79]

The ethnologist H. Becher, who took the narcotic snuff among the Waika Indians of southern Venezuela, describes his experience:

Immediately [after taking the snuff] I felt a splitting headache and became nauseated. . . . But shortly afterwards I had a strange sensation in that I felt to be a giant among giants. Everybody in my surroundings—people, dogs, and parrots— seemed suddenly to be of gigantic size.[80]

Another account is given by Horning, who injected himself with a dose of *N, N*-dimethyltryptamine (DMT) derived from *Anade-nanthera peregrina:*

> In the third or fourth minute after the injection vegetative symptoms appeared, such as a tingling sensation, trembling, slight nausea, mydriasis, elevation of blood pressure and increase of pulse rate. At the same time eidetic phenomena, optical illusions, pseudohallucinations and later real hallucinations appeared. The hallucinations consisted of moving, brilliantly coloured oriental motifs, and later I saw wonderful scenes, altering very rapidly. The faces of the people seemed to be masks. My emotional state was elevated sometimes up to euphoria. At the highest point, I had compulsive athetoid movements in my left hand. My consciousness was completely filled by hallucinations, and my attention was firmly bound by them; therefore I could not give an account of the events happening around me. After ¾–1 hour the symptoms disappeared, and I was able to describe what had happened.[81]

The snuff prepared from *Virola* also contains tryptamines, above all 5-Methoxy-*N, N*-dimethyltryptamine.[82] Richard Evans Schultes, to whom we owe many fundamental studies of Amazonian narcotics, took a dose of *Virola* snuff among the Indians of the Vaupés and describes his experience thus:

> I took about one-third of a level teaspoonful of the drug in two inhalations using the characteristic Y-shaped birdbone apparatus by means of which the natives blow the powder into the nostrils. This represents about one-quarter the dose usually absorbed by a diagnosing medicine-man, who takes about one slightly heaped teaspoonful in two or three inhalations at close intervals. . . . Within fifteen minutes a drawing sensation over the eyes was felt, followed very shortly by a strong tingling in the fingers and toes. The drawing sensation in the forehead rapidly gave way to a strong and constant headache. Within one half hour, there was a numbness of the feet and hands and an almost complete disappearance of sensitivity of the fingertips; walking was possible with difficulty, as in case of beri-beri.

Nausea was felt until about eight o'clock, accompanied by a general feeling of lassitude and uneasiness. Shortly after eight, I lay down in my hammock, overcome with a heavy drowsiness which, however, seemed to be accompanied by a muscular excitation, except in the extremities of the hands and feet. At about nine-thirty, probably, I fell into a fitful sleep which continued, with frequent awakenings, until morning. The strong headache óver the eyes lasted until noon. A profuse and uncomfortable sweating, especially of the armpits, and what might have been a slight fever lasted from about six o'clock all through the night. There was a strong dilation of the pupils during the first hour of the experiment.[83]

The same author describes the effects of *Virola* snuff on habitual consumers, that is, on Indian shamans:

The dose employed by the medicine-man is sufficient to put them into a deep but disturbed sleep, during which delirious mumblings or, sometimes, shouts are emitted; visual hallucinations or dreams are reported to accompany the narcotic sleep very often. These are "interpreted" by an assistant who awaits the prophetic or divinatory sounds. Some medicine-men, it is said, are affected more violently than others and uncontrolled twitchings of the fingers and facial muscles and a popping of eyes are not infrequent symptoms.[84]

A last quotation on the effects of dimethyltryptamine is of special interest within the context of aboriginal drug use:

The perceptual distortions are primarily visual in nature, and with closed eyes you can see illusions and color patterns, primarily geometrical patterns, moving very fast, having sometimes very deep emotional content and connotation. . . . There is an enhanced dependence on the environment for structure and for symbolic meaning, and increased association and search for synthesis.[85]

With these observations we have come to the end of our survey of the published sources, at least as far as Colombian territory is concerned. In any case, from what we know at present of the general distribution of narcotic snuffs, it seems that Colombia was—and still is—the main center of this habit, and that the taking of snuff has always been closely related to shamanistic practices.

The use of hallucinogenic snuffs is essentially a New World trait[86] that reached a wide distribution, especially in the tropical lowlands of South America and the Caribbean. Moreover, the ease with which the seeds of *Anadenanthera peregrina* could be traded undoubtedly contributed to the spread of the habit in areas beyond the geographical range of the tree itself. It is also probable that narcotic snuffs were already used in prehistoric times. Snuff tablets, tubes, and other objects pertaining to the snuffing apparatus have been found in many archaeological contexts[87] and suggest that snuff-induced trances played an important part in the ancient aboriginal cultures.[88]

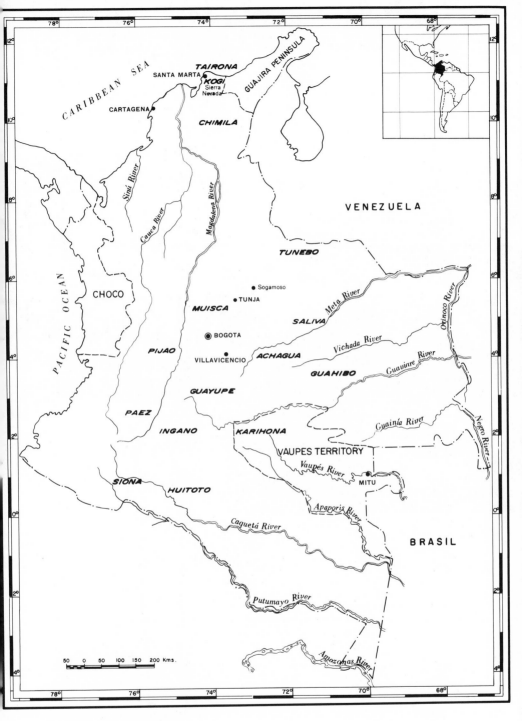

1. Sketch map of Colombia

2. Guahibo Indians
absorbing narcotic snuff
(*Anadenanthera per-*
egrina); Vichada River

3. Guahibo shaman
burning snail shells to
obtain lime for snuff
mixture; Vichada River

4. Snuffing tube of bird
bone (length, 20 cm.);
Guahibo Indians,
Vichada River

2

3

4

5. Snuffing tube of bird bone (length, 12 cm.); Guahibo Indians, Tuparro River

6. *Anadenanthera peregrina*

7. *Virola* sp.

8. Snuffing tube of bird bone with a small piece of mirror glass set in pitch into the base (length, 6 cm.); Barasana Indians, Pira-paraná

5

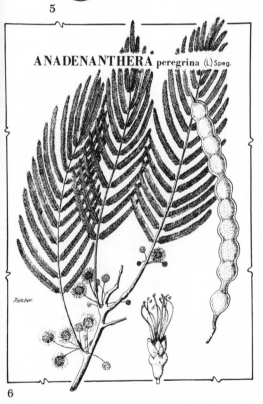

6

7

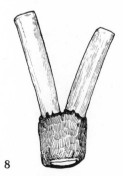

8

9. Bará Indian absorbing
narcotic snuff (*Virola*
sp.); Pira-paraná

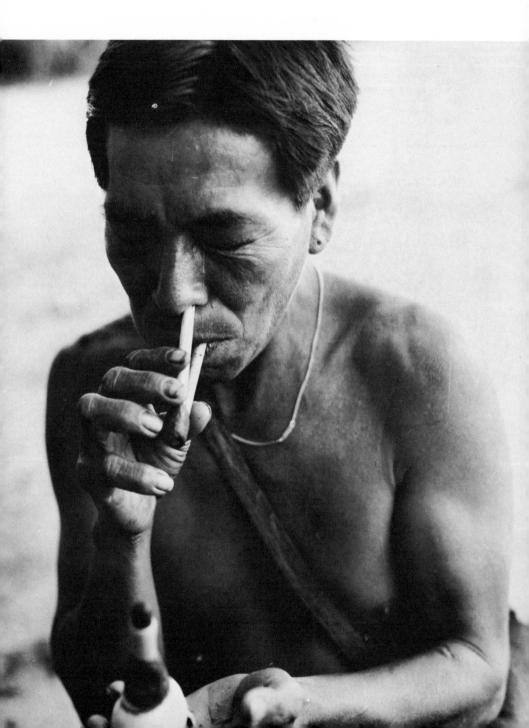

10. Snuff container of snail shell with a mirror glass set into the opening (length, 11 cm.); Barasana Indians, Pira-paraná

11. Snuff container made of a dried fruit (length, 9.5 cm.); Barasana Indians, Pira-paraná

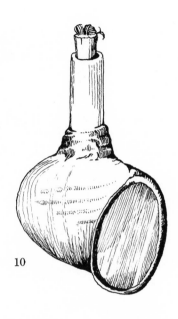

10

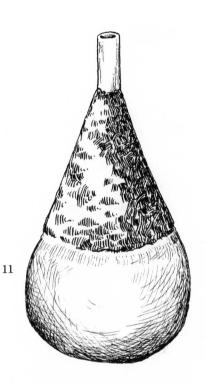

11

12. Tatuyo Indian pre-
paring powdered coca
(*Erythroxylon coca*);
Pira-paraná

2

IN
SEARCH
OF A
JUNGLE
VINE

For centuries the Vaupés territory was a terra incognita, a vast expanse of unexplored rain forest, as far removed from the administrative centers of Colombia as from those of neighboring Brazil. Only early in the nineteenth century, by traveling up the Rio Negro from Manaos, had a few missionaries ascended the Vaupés River and penetrated almost to its headwaters, even beyond the legendary Yuruparí Falls, but no permanent settlement was established then and they had had to return. In those years rubber had as yet no commercial uses, and any other natural resources, whatever they were, could not be exploited because of the innumerable difficulties in transportation, the great distances, and the almost complete absence of any outposts of civilization where trading posts might have been organized. The only occasional travel route—a long and difficult one—led up the Rio Negro from the Amazon and then crossed by way of the Casiquiare channel to the upper Orinoco drainage, passing on its way some small settlements of half-breeds who lived by fishing, hunting, and sporadic barter with visiting Indians. But the rivers that flowed out of the west—the Vaupés, Papurí, Tiquié, and others—remained almost unknown. Navigation on the Rio Negro, especially on its lower course, was hazardous because of the many rapids and falls, but the rivers coming out of the lands lying to the west were even more dangerous and more difficult to navigate. They were smaller and swifter; their foaming waters rushed over one fall after another, cascading over rapids of immense force which made boat travel a continuous risk. Besides, there were tales of "bad" Indians, of cannibalism, and of lonely adventurers' having disappeared forever. Only the mission-

25

aries had dared to penetrate this forbidding wilderness, and even they had come late; their initial efforts in establishing a foothold on the Vaupés had met with failure because of the formidable obstacles nature had set in their way.[1]

By the standards of those who lived or traveled before 1850 on the Rio Negro, the Vaupés Indians were mere savages who celebrated drunken feasts, believed in weird superstitions, and were dominated by rattle-swinging witch doctors; a miserable lot, of no interest whatsoever, except to be baptized and used as a cheap labor force. It was only around the middle of the last century that some travelers arrived who began to take an interest in the life of these forest peoples and were immediately impressed by them. These early travelers were the naturalists, and the palm of honor goes to two English botanists who were to achieve world fame— Alfred Russell Wallace and Richard Spruce.[2]

A third botanist, Henry Walter Bates,[3] had come to the tropics with Wallace, but after a while the three separated and Bates proceeded to the upper Amazon. Wallace and Spruce decided to ascend the Rio Negro and to visit the Vaupés. Writing of his expedition, Wallace says that this was a "country that no European traveller had ever before visited," and this may have been so; in any case, Wallace was the first one to take an immediate interest in the Indians: "The . . . most unexpected sensation of surprise and delight was my first meeting and living with a man in a state of nature—with absolute uncontaminated savages! This was on the Vaupés River."[4] Wallace traveled with Indian boatmen and lived in their huge *malocas* where he missed no chance to observe their colorful life. "The wild and strange appearance of these handsome, naked, painted Indians, with their curious ornaments and weapons, the stamp and song and rattle which accompanies the dance, the hum of conversation in a strange tongue, the music of fifes and flutes and other instruments of reed, bone, and turtle's shells, the large calabashes of caxiri constantly carried about, the great smoke-blackened gloomy house, produced an effect to which no description can do justice."[5]

Wallace traveled up the Vaupés River and for some time established his headquarters at Mitú, then a small Indian settlement, where he collected and described his plant and animal specimens. There were the umbrella bird, the cock of the rock, and a host of other strange and beautiful creatures; there were trees, and flowers, and butterflies; and the lonely naturalist worked to the limits of his physical endurance.

A year later, Richard Spruce, who had stayed behind and was collecting on the lower Vaupés River, had a strange experience. While he was staying at the Ipanoré Falls, a group of Tukano Indians who occupied a maloca farther upriver at Urubú-coára—the Place of the Buzzard—invited him to a *dabocurí* feast, one of the periodic ceremonial gatherings during which the Indians exchanged gifts between neighbors. In the course of that night Spruce was offered by his Indian hosts a cup containing a "nauseous beverage" the young men were drinking when they were not dancing up and down in the house. The name of the drink, made from a jungle vine, was *caapi*, and the natives attributed strong narcotic effects to it.

Spruce had heard of caapi before; the Brazilian *caboclos* had called it *yajé*, a word probably derived from the Tupi language they spoke, and they had told Spruce of the strange powers of this plant. Now he was able to observe its use by the Indians and to learn more about its peculiarities.

> In two minutes or less after drinking it, the effects begin to be apparent. The Indian turns deadly pale, trembles in every limb, and horror is in his aspect. Suddenly contrary symptoms succeed; he bursts into perspiration, and seems possessed with reckless fury, seizes whatever arms are at hand, his murucú, bow and arrows, or cutlass, and rushes to the doorway, while he inflicts violent blows on the ground and the doorposts, calling out all the while: "Thus would I do to mine enemy (naming him by name) were this he!" In about ten minutes the excitement has passed off, and the Indian grows calm, but appears exhausted.[6]

Spruce took one single cup of the beverage but did not care to take part in the entire ritual; he had a cup of coffee and retired to his hammock to watch the other participants.

The scene at which he was present that night was the beginning of an extraordinary discovery. Spruce inquired about the effects of caapi and then reported: "White men who have partaken of caapi in the proper way concur in the account of their sensations under its influence. They feel alternations of cold and heat, fear and boldness. The sight is disturbed, and visions pass rapidly before the eyes, wherein everything gorgeous and magnificent they have heard or read of seems combined; and presently the scene changes to things uncouth and horrible."[7]

These were acute observations, but Spruce's main interest was, of course, the correct botanic identification of the plant, and this he accomplished with great precision as soon as he had seen the jungle vine growing near the houses of the Indians. Spruce was thus the first botanist to identify caapi or yajé as *Banisteria caapi*, a member of the family of malpighiacea, and he sent voucher specimens to Kew Gardens. A few years later, in 1854, he met a band of wandering Guahibo Indians at the Maipures Falls on the Orinoco and observed that they "chew the dried stem (of caapi), as some people do tobacco." And again, in 1859, he found caapi in use among the Zaparo Indians of the Ecuadorean lowlands, there called *ayahuasca*, or "Dead Man's Vine," by the local natives. From the accounts Spruce was able to collect he concluded that the effects were the same as those he had observed among the Indians of the Vaupés.

Back in England, Spruce made a compilation of his notes on caapi and, in 1874, published a paper entitled "On Some Remarkable Narcotics of the Amazon Valley and Orinoco."[8] In this paper he presented a full description of the plant, and also of its use by the Indians. Spruce writes: "The lower part of the stem is the part used. A quantity of this is beaten in a mortar, with water. . . . When sufficiently triturated, it is passed through a sieve, which separates the woody fibre, and to the residue enough water is added to render it drinkable. Thus prepared, the colour is brownish-green, and its taste bitter and disagreeable."[9]

The description Spruce made of the serving of caapi deserves to be quoted in full: "In the course of the night, the young men partook of caapi five or six times, in the intervals between the dances; but only a few of them at a time, and very few drank of it twice. The cup-bearer—who must be a man, for no woman can touch or taste caapi—starts at a short run from the opposite end of the house, with a small calabash containing about a teacupful of caapi in each hand, muttering 'Mo-mo-mo-mo-mo' as he runs, and gradually sinking down until at last his chin nearly touches his knees, when he reaches out one of his cups to the man who stands ready to receive it."[10]

Caapi, as Spruce had observed during his travels in Ecuador, was the same as ayahuasca. This plant had been mentioned a few years earlier by an Ecuadorean civil servant, Manuel Villavicencio, who had been governor of the Río Napo district and had published an important volume on the geography of the country.[11] His de-

scription of the narcotic coincided with that of Spruce; there could
be no doubt then that, all over the Northwest Amazon, from Eastern
Ecuador to the Vaupés, and from there to the Orinoco Plains, the
Indians were using the same jungle vine to produce hallucinatory
trances.

From the descriptions given, however, the immediate objectives
of this intoxication could be manifold; on the Vaupés, Spruce had
observed that, when the Indians took the narcotic drink, they became aggressive and talked wildly about killing their enemies.
Now, among the Indians of the Ecuadorean lowlands Spruce found
that ayahuasca was also taken by the shaman "when called on to
adjudicate in a dispute or quarrel—to give the proper answer to an
embassy—to discover the plans of an enemy—to tell if strangers are
coming—to ascertain if wives are unfaithful—in the case of a sick
man to tell who has bewitched him, etc."[12]

It may be worthwhile to quote two descriptions of the effects of
the narcotic, one by Spruce on the Ecuadorean Indians, and another
by Wallace on those of the Vaupés. Spruce writes:

All who have partaken of it feel first vertigo; then as if they rose
up into the air and were floating about. The Indians say they
see beautiful lakes, woods laden with fruit, birds of brilliant
plumage, etc. Soon the scene changes; they see savage beasts
preparing to seize them. They can no longer hold themselves
up, but fall to the ground. At this crisis the Indian wakes up from
his trance, and if he were not held down in his hammock by
force, he would spring to his feet, seize his arms, and attack the
first person who stood in his way. Then he becomes drowsy
and finally sleeps. . . . Boys are not allowed to taste ayahuasca
before they reach puberty, nor women at any age: precisely
as on the Uaupés.[13]

Wallace gives the following description:

Presently the Capí was introduced, an account of which I had
from Senhor L. An old man comes forward with a large,
newly-painted earthen pot, which he sets down in the middle of
the house. He then squats behind it, stirs it about, and takes
out two small calabashes-full, which he holds up in each hand.
After a moment's pause, two Indians advance with bows and
arrows or lances in their hands. Each takes the proferred cup
and drinks, makes a wry face, for it is intensely bitter, and
stands motionless perhaps half a minute. They then with a start

twang their bows, shake their lances, stamp their feet, and
return to their seats. The little bowls are again filled, and two
others succeed them, with a similar result. Some, however,
become more excited, run furiously, lance in hand, as if they
would kill an enemy, shout and stamp savagely, and look very
warlike and terrible, and then, like the others, return quietly to
their places.[14]

Villavicencio speaks thus of his personal experiences with the
drug:

When I have partaken of aya-huasca, my head has immediately
begun to swim, then I have seemed to enter on an aerial
voyage, wherein I thought I saw the most charming landscapes,
great cities, lofty towers, beautiful parks, and other delightful
things. Then all at once I found myself deserted in a forest and
attacked by beasts of prey, against which I tried to defend
myself. Lastly, I began to come around, but with a feeling of
excessive drowsiness, headache, and sometimes general
malaise.[15]

Long before Spruce and Villavicencio's time, the existence of
ayahuasca among Amazonian Indians had been mentioned here and
there, in reports written by missionaries, travelers, or government
officials. Spruce alludes to this fact in the opening paragraph of his
paper on Amazonian narcotics. One of the earliest sources seems to
be Father José Chantre y Herrera's[16] history of the Jesuit missions
in the late seventeenth and early eighteenth centuries, in which he
speaks of a "diabolic brew" made of ayahuasca vines by the Indians
of the district of Mainas—upper Amazon—who used it for divinatory purposes. But as neither Martius,[17] Humboldt,[18] nor La Condamine[19] mention caapi or ayahuasca in their voluminous writings,
Spruce was the first naturalist to describe the plant and send samples of it to Europe.

Spruce's classical description of yajé (we shall use this term from
now on), its identity, use, and effects, was the starting point of a
search which continues at the present time. As a matter of fact, the
problems posed by yajé include not only that of precise botanical
identification, but also its phytochemical, pharmacological, psychi-
atric, and anthropological aspects, all of which appear to be of
great interest.

Most unfortunately, Spruce published his paper on Amazonian
narcotics in an obscure journal which probably did not come to the

attention of the travelers who, in later years, visited the Indians of the Vaupés territory. Coudreau[20] and Stradelli,[21] for example, who in the last decade of the nineteenth century explored parts of the Vaupés, mention yajé only in passing and add no significant details to Spruce's fundamental observations. So an important discovery remained almost unknown.

Spruce did not live to see his major works published. He died in 1893, after many years of ill health, and it fell to his friend and colleague Alfred Russell Wallace to edit and publish his journals. The two-volume work appeared in 1908 under the title "Notes of a Botanist on the Amazon and Andes" and contains, as we have shown, a wealth of ethnological information that makes it a most valuable source on aboriginal life in the Vaupés, as it was lived more than a century ago.

Until relatively recent times, then, no detailed study of the narcotic plants of the Northwest Amazon was undertaken, either by botanists or by travelers with anthropological interests. This was a most remarkable omission, especially in view of the fact that the use of hallucinogenic vines continued to be mentioned in occasional travel reports. Somehow, its true importance from a pharmacological and—above all—a cultural point of view was not clearly recognized; it was superficially observed and talked about, but neither was a systematic analysis of its chemical characteristics made nor was there any effort put forth to investigate the role this drug so obviously played in the religious and magical beliefs of the natives who used it.

Some confusion also arose as to the precise botanical species involved in its use, and this was due, in part, to the many different names under which this, or other similar vines, were known among the Indians. In the Northwest Amazon and the Orinoco the name caapi was in common use, while in the south, in the Ecuadorean and Peruvian *Montaña* region, the plant was known by the name of ayahuasca. In the territories of Vaupés, Guainía, and on the Rio Negro, the name yajé (or yagé) was widely employed, but individual Indian groups used local terms by which they distinguished certain kinds of yajé, according to their usage.

But we must return to the Vaupés. Between 1903 and 1905 the German ethnologist Theodor Koch-Grünberg traveled over much of the Vaupés territory and wrote a detailed account of his life with the Indians which is still a classic of ethnological travel literature.

While staying with the Tukano of the Tiquié River, to the south of the Papurí, Koch-Grünberg was able to observe, and take part in, a ceremonial dance during which yajé was consumed. Koch-Grünberg writes of this experience: "According to what the Indians told me, everything appears much larger and more beautiful than it is in reality. The house seems to be immense and radiant. One sees a large crowd of people, above all women. An erotic element seems to play a principal role in this intoxication. Large many-colored snakes entwine themselves around the houseposts. All colors are very luminous."[22]

On one occasion Koch-Grünberg took two small cups of the drink, and he describes his reaction thus: "As a matter of fact, after a while, and above all when stepping out from the house into the darkness outside, there appeared before my eyes a strange flickering and very intense light, and while writing, something like red flames shot over the paper."[23]

It is a pity inded that so acute an observer as Koch-Grünberg should not have gone into more detail but let it go at these few observations. He merely goes on to say that yajé was being consumed during the gathering of two neighboring groups, and also during initiation rituals, and expresses the opinion that the use of the drug might also be related to a ritual in which the men attempt to fortify their bravery. It is interesting to note that Koch-Grünberg[24] mentions two kinds of yajé, one called *kahpí*, identified by him as *Banisteria caapi*, while the other is named *kúlikahpiro*, pertaining to an unidentified plant species. We shall refer to this observation later on because it has some bearing upon the course of recent research.

At about the same time, the Colombian traveler Joaquín Rocha visited the Ingano Indians of the upper Caquetá River, an entirely different area of the Northwest Amazon. In his journal Rocha refers to the use of yajé and describes its preparation, which differs markedly from that observed in the Vaupés. "*Yagé* is a vine or shrub the Indians do not let white men see and which, therefore, I do not know. They prepare it as a drink by boiling it all night long, and once it has the appearance of thick honey, it is ready to be tasted. They diminish its effects when they administer it as a purge, by mixing it with other plants, mainly with an herb called *chiripanga*, which I don't know either. The use of *yagé* is not exempt of danger."[25]

Rocha goes on to describe the effects of yajé in very romantic terms. First, he says, the visions are interpreted as a means of identifying one's enemies and of locating propitious spots for hunting and fishing. Then there follow beautiful images of flowers and fruits, of half-naked dancing-girls, and erotic fantasies. In their hallucinations the men then turn into jaguars and pursue game. Suddenly the visions change into horrifying images which threaten and attack their victims. This report contains two points of interest: the pattern of several clearly defined successive stages, beginning with beautiful visions of blissful happiness but ending in the horrors of a nightmare; and the transformation into jaguars. We shall have more to say later on concerning these observations.

In 1914 the Montfortian Congregation, most of them Dutchmen, established a number of small mission outposts in the Vaupés, mainly among the Tukano, Desana, and Pira-Tapuya Indians of the Papurí River. According to many Indian informants who still remember those times, the missionaries immediately prohibited the use of yajé and destroyed most of the ritual paraphernalia connected with its use. Although the missionaries published several reports on ethnographical and linguistic matters,[26] the use of narcotic drugs was not mentioned by them, and it seems that during the first two decades of the present century no further observations on yajé were made in the Vaupés territory.

In 1937 the American ethnologist Irving Goldman[27] undertook a detailed study of the Cubeo Indians of the Cuduyarí River, a northern tributary of the Vaupés, and in his book, published only in 1963, he makes a number of interesting observations on the use of *mihí*, the name under which yajé is known among the Cubeo. Goldman writes:

This sequence of *mihí* transports a man from vague and mild visions of whiteness to intense hallucinatory experiences, bursts of violence, and finally loss of consciousness . . . At the beginning, the Indians say, the vision becomes blurred, things begin to look white, and one begins to lose the faculty of speech. The white vision turns to red. One Indian described it as a room spinning with feathers. This passes and one begins to see people in the bright coloring of the jaguar. When the final strong forms of *mihí* are taken the hallucinations begin to assume a disturbing and fearful form. One becomes aware of violent people milling about, shouting, weeping, threatening to kill. One

is seized wtih fear that he no longer has a home. The houseposts
and trees come alive and take the form of people. There is a
strong sensation that an animal is biting one's buttocks, a feeling
of the feet being tied. The earth spins and the ground rises
to the head. There are moments of euphoria as well, when one
hears music, the sound of people singing, and the sound of
flowing water. The Cubeo do not take *mihí* for the pleasure of
its hallucinations but for the intensity of the total experience,
for the wide range of sensation. I spoke to no one who pretended
to enjoy it.[28]

At Yavareté, at the mouth of the Papurí River, on the Brazilian
bank of the Vaupés, the Salesian Fathers had established a large
mission, which eventually came to include an anthropological research center. Father Alcionilio Brüzzi Alves da Silva published a
lengthy book in 1962 on the Indians of the Vaupés in which he refers to yajé.[29] According to his informants there were several different categories of yajé vines (which, he says, belong to the genus
Banisteriopsis) the stalks of which were pounded and then diluted
with water to prepare the drink. A Colombian settler who had taken
yajé told Father Alcionilio that he had very well-defined visions in
which he saw a series of geometrical designs. Another informant
said that he had seen women who twisted like snakes covered with
beautiful ornaments, and that the panpipes being played sounded
to him like a great orchestra. Father Alcionilio himself took a small
dose of yajé with the Tukano of Carurú Cachoeira, just above Yaua-
reté, but did not reach a hallucinatory trance although the other
participants claimed to see "globes and flames." He simply remarks
that "the effects mentioned by the Indians must be explained by
the easy excitability of their imagination."[30]

We may turn now to another area of the Colombian Northwest
Amazon, that of the Caquetá and Putumayo Rivers on the country's
southern frontier. Among the Siona Indians, a tribe belonging to
the so-called Western Tukano group that lives on the upper reaches
of the Caquetá, yajé is taken for magico-religious reasons. Father
Plácido de Calella, a local missionary, describes the preparation of
the drink and points out that, in this region, the liquid is boiled
before being consumed, a custom, as we have already observed, of
the neighboring Ingano Indians. After the first effects—nausea and
tremor—have passed, the participants fall into a trance during

which they have colorful visions. The shaman himself ascends to the sky, where he communicates with the tribal deities; he then descends into the netherworld, where *Supaí,* the Spirit of Evil, reveals his domain to him. The shaman describes these visions in a singsong voice to the audience, which occasionally formulates questions or comments. During these hallucinations the shaman and the other participants claim to see large crowds of people, Indians like themselves, all well adorned and painted, who are called "yajé people" (*yagé-paí*) and who sing and play musical instruments. When the trance is over the men copy the design motifs of the body paint of these spirit-beings and use them to adorn their own faces.[31]

Among the Huitoto the shaman takes a boiled concoction in order to make contact with the evil demon *Táife,* and his hallucinations enable him to diagnose sickness.[32] Whiffen reports of the same Indians that "the medicine-man also doses himself with a drink made from a certain liana. When thoroughly intoxicated with it he will run away, and shortly go into profound slumber. In this comatose state he is supposed to hold intercourse with the unseen world, to wander in spirit to other places, and, as a result of what he has hereby learnt, to be able to foretell the future when he awakes."[33]

But *Banisteriopsis* is also in use outside the Northwest Amazon. Among the Guahibo of the Orinoco Plains the stalks are chewed, and the shamans are known under the name of *huipa hai*/"the one who eats yajé."[34] The Piapoco Indians take *Banisteriopsis* in a concoction.[35] Moreover, *Banisteriopsis* is used by almost all Indians of the Pacific lowlands, an immense rain forest area stretching from Panama to Ecuador, beyond the Western Cordillera, where the Emberá tribe calls it *pildé,* and the Noanamá tribe, *dapa.*[36]

The many quotations given in the preceding pages reveal a fascinating picture which, although obviously lacking depth and detail, demonstrates the fact that yajé hallucinations play a most important part in the rituals and beliefs of many aboriginal cultures of the Colombian rain forests. The use to which these hallucinatory trances are put by the different Indian tribes varies from curing rituals to initiation ceremonies, and from the violent frenzy of warriors to ecstatic religious experiences. In all cases, it seems, yajé is thought to provide a means of being transported to another dimension of consciousness, which, in the daily life of the individual or of the group, acquires great importance. It would seem, then, that without exploring this dimension, a knowledge of aboriginal culture is impossible.

In Colombia, the center of the yajé complex is clearly the Northwest Amazon, including all tribes of the Putumayo-Caquetá area, the Vaupés-Guainía area, and the Orinoco Plains, no matter what linguistic family or cultural subdivision these groups may belong to. The use of the narcotic vine cuts across all dividing lines. It is found among the food-gathering Makú; the agricultural Tukano, Arawak, and Caribs of the rain forest; and the savannah-dwelling Indians of the regions to the north of the Guaviare River. This distribution, then, is known and documented in the literature. The question remains: What is yajé from a botanical and chemical standpoint?

Although Richard Spruce identified the vine of *Banisteriopsis caapi* more than a century ago, in the decades following this discovery no further studies of the genus were undertaken, and only in recent times were the botanical aspects of this plant systematically investigated. The research carried out by Richard Evans Schultes, director of the Botanical Museum at Harvard, is fundamental to our present understanding of the varieties and specific characteristics of yajé. Schultes, a world specialist in Amazonian plant life, particularly of narcotic plants, has spent many years in the Northwest Amazon, in part following the footsteps of his admired master, Richard Spruce, in part exploring regions where hitherto no botanist had ever collected.

The story of the botanical search for yajé and its variants is at first one of great confusion. When Spruce observed the use of ayahuasca among the Zaparo Indians of Ecuador in 1854, he wrote that "it was the identical species of the Vaupés, but under a different name." These words, written by the botanist who first identified *Banisteriopsis caapi*, are, of course, beyond questioning, and we might anticipate here that his identification of yajé and ayahuasca as the same plant has been borne out by all modern botanical studies. It is true that neither the Colombian Joaquín Rocha,[37] who in 1905 reported on the use of yajé among the Indians of the upper Putumayo-Caquetá region, nor the Ecuadorean M. Villavicencio,[38] whom we quoted earlier, collected specimens for botanical study; but the identity of yajé and ayahuasca was clearly established by Spruce. But then some highly contradictory theories appeared. In the first place Reinburg, a French anthropologist, published a lengthy study in 1921, in which he suggested that yajé and ayahuasca might be two quite different plants.[39] In the second place, Alexandre Rouhier, a French pharmacologist, expressed the opinion in 1926 that yajé was an *Aristolochia*,[40] a suggestion taken over by the Colombian chemist Fischer Cárdenas, who wrote a dissertation on this subject.[41] In addition, Reinburg thought that yajé might be *Prestonia amazonica*, and this suggestion, too, contributed to the confusion.

What was the basis of these assertions? It now appears that parts of Richard Spruce's work had been erroneously interpreted, and we owe thanks to Richard Evans Schultes for putting the record straight on this important point.[42]

As we have mentioned, Spruce's work on his South American travels was published by Alfred Russell Wallace, who in the course of editing the manuscript introduced a few slight changes into the text. In his book, Spruce, in describing the characteristics and use of *Banisteriopsis caapi* on the Rio Negro, mentions that there also existed another kind of caapi called *caapi pinima*, or "painted caapi," and that a small amount of the roots of this plant was occasionaly mixed with the macerated stems of *Banisteriopsis caapi*. According to Spruce, this "other" caapi was probably *Haemadictyon amazonicum* (at present called *Prestonia amazonica*). It seems that this observation was misread by some authors, who now began to claim that, in the area where the narcotic plant was known under the name of yajé, the drink was prepared exclusively from *Prestonia amazonica*. Schultes, who consulted Spruce's original field notes at Kew, found that Spruce had never made such a claim but had clearly stated that *caapi pinima* was nothing more than an occasional admixture. In addition, Schultes came to the conclusion that *Prestonia amazonica* is not used as an addition to narcotic drinks in the Amazon area, and that this very rare species is probably endemic solely to the Trombetas River on the lower Amazon where Spruce made his type collections in 1859. We now remember that Koch-Grünberg had reported that the Vaupés Indians used two kinds of caapi, one of which he identified as *Banisteria* (i.e., *Banisteriopsis*) *caapi*, while the other, called *kúlikahpiro* by the Indians, belonged to a species unknown to that author. In 1948, Richard Evans Schultes traveled in the same region and observed among the Indians of the Tiquié River the use of *Tetrapteris methystica*, another of the malpighiacea, with a strong narcotic effect. Having observed that the liquid prepared from *Banisteriop-sis caapi* had a dark-brownish color while the one prepared from *Tetrapteris methystica* was yellowish, Schultes suggested that the "painted caapi" Spruce had spoken of might well be the plant that produced the yellow-colored potion.

In 1912 an anonymous article appeared in the South American Supplement of the *Times* (London) mentioning yajé as a possible cure for beri-beri, and jointly there appeared a letter by the Colombian pharmacist Rafael Zerda Bayón extolling the "telepathic" powers of the plant. This article aroused the interest of Percy E. Wyndham, Esq., His Majesty's Minister in Bogotá, who in 1913 sent samples of what he believed to be yajé, gathered on the Caquetá River in southern Colombia, to the Museum of Economic Botany at the Royal Botanic Gardens at Kew. The plant was identified there by T. A. Sprague as a malpighiacea, possibly *Tetrapteris*. This identification proved to be correct and was confirmed by Schultes.[43]

In the twenties and thirties a number of botanists worked on the problem of identifying the different species of *Banisteriopsis* used by the rain forest Indians. An all-important point was to collect the plant in the field and to verify its identity by comparison with voucher specimens in herbarium collections and, at the same time, to observe exactly which plant—or combination of plants—was used by the Indians in the preparation of the drug. It had become clear by now that the utmost care was necessary to establish the precise composition of the drink because different species of the same genus proved to contain different chemical and psychotropic components; and, therefore, the problem of occasional admixtures —as observed by several authors—became of paramount importance to the understanding of the hallucinogenic effects of the drug.[44]

The occasional vagueness of some botanical identifications was, of course, a great obstacle to the chemical and pharmacological research now beginning to concentrate on Amazonian narcotics. In 1927 Perrot and Hamet summarized the current state of botanical knowledge of yajé in two important publications,[45] and in the following year a number of papers appeared—most of them by pharmacologists, chemists, and botanists trying to bring order into the mass of confusing, and sometimes contradictory, information. By the early thirties a number of different species of *Banisteriopsis* had come to be recognized by botanists, and now to *Banisteriopsis caapi* were added the species of *B. inebrians, B. quitensis, B. rusbyana, B. longlialata, B. metallicolor, B. lutea,* and others.

It is unfortunate that botanical and chemical research did not always go hand in hand at that time, and that many chemists and pharmacologists had to work with plant materials that were not sufficiently well identified. The Colombian chemist Fischer Cárdenas seems to have been the first to isolate, in 1923, a crystalline alkaloid from yajé which he called *telepathine,* but his specimens had not been identified as to species, and he suggested that the plant might be an *Aristolochia.*[46] In 1925, his colleague Barriga Villalba isolated two alkaloids from yajé, which he denominated *yajeína* and *yajenina,* and used the former in controlled laboratory experiments with guinea pigs and dogs.[47] Unfortunately, this scholar, too, used plant material that had not been properly identified botanically, and his suggestion that yajé was *Haemadictyon amazonicum,* that is, *Prestonia amazonica,* was erroneous. In 1929, Keller and Gottauf[48] isolated a harminelike alkaloid from ayahuasca, but the specimens lacked leaves and flowers, and botanical determination was therefore impossible. As long as there was no effective collaboration between field collectors and laboratory teams, the search for the true identity of the drug was hopeless.

It was not until 1939 that a definite breakthrough was made. In that year, Chen and Chen[49] identified three alkaloids in yajé vines (telepathine, yajeine, and banisterine) that proved to be the same harmine, the well-known alkaloid of *Peganum harmala,* a narcotic plant of the Old World. Now, for the first time, a chemical analysis was based upon properly identified plant materials; it was *Banisteriopsis caapi,* collected near Iquitos, a Peruvian town on the upper Amazon, by the botanist Llewellyn Williams.[50]

Although this was a most important advance, it did not mean that harmala alkaloids were the only psychoactive components of yajé, or that yajé—as represented by *Banisteriopsis caapi*—was the only source material used in the native preparation of the drug. The next step, then, was to analyze the other species known to be employed by the Indians. And then there was the problem of admixtures, of those minor ingredients added to the drink, the chemical action of which seemed to be crucial in determining the effects the drug had upon the human organism.

Klug and Cuatrecasas[51] collected another species, *Banisteriopsis rusbyana,* on the Putumayo River, where the Indians called it *chagropanga, yagé-úco* (or *oco-yagé*), while Schultes found the same species to be in use among the Indians of Mocoa, who, according to data given by local people, mixed the leaves of *Banisteriopsis rusbyana* with the pounded bark of *Banisteriopsis inebrians.* The latter species, which seems to be rather common on the Putumayo and Caquetá Rivers, is called *yajé de monte/*"jungle yajé," by the Ingano Indians and is the basis of their narcotic drink, but with an admixture of some leaves and young shoots of *Banisteriopsis rusbyana.*

From the numerous reports available it appears that the four species mentioned so far (*B. caapi, B. quitensis, B. rusbyana, B. inebrians*) are used, either individually or in mixtures of two, by most Indians of the Putumayo-Caquetá area and that, in many cases, the plants are cultivated near the houses for ready usage. It also appears that in this general region the drink is always prepared by boiling the stems and/or leaves for several hours, and that the potion is consumed in relatively small doses.

In the Vaupés area the picture is slightly different; the species in use are, above all, *Banisteriopsis caapi* and *Banisteriopsis rusbyana,* while the others seem to be lacking. As a general rule, it can be said that, on most occasions when yajé is being consumed by a group of people, only *Banisteriopsis caapi* is employed, but that in restricted shamanistic séances when what we might call "special effects" are desirable, *Banisteriopsis rusbyana* is added as an admixture. It is also possible that a number of hitherto quite unknown species are employed. Other additions observed are tobacco leaves or a few crushed leaves of *Malouetia Tamaquarina,* a poisonous Apocynacea, and the admixture of *Datura* has also been reported.

We must return briefly to the chemical and pharmacological properties of yajé. Harmala alkaloids are well known from the Old World, where the psychotropic properties of the seeds of *Peganum harmala* have been known since antiquity, and whose alkaloids were isolated more than a century ago. In the New World, the different species of *Banisteriopsis* found to contain these alkaloids grow mainly in the tropical rain forest of the upper Amazon and in the foothill regions of the eastern slopes of the Central and Northern Andes. The principal psychotropic substance contained in *Banisteriopsis* seems to be harmine (harmaline),[52] which, as we now know, is the same yajeine, banisterine, or telepathine of the early chemists. *Banisteriopsis caapi* was found to contain—besides harmine—two other beta-carboline derivatives: harmaline and d-tetrahydroharmine,[53] but harmaline proved to be missing in stems of *Banisteriopsis inebrians*,[54] although they do contain harmine. The analysis of *Banisteriopsis rusbyana*, a species that, next to *Banisteriopsis caapi*, seems to be the most common in the Vaupés, offered a surprise; it proved to contain N, N-dimethyltryptamine, a strong hallucinogenic and a base that occurs also in other psychotropic plants used by the Indians, such as *Anadenanthera peregrina* and *Virola* sp., the sources of narcotic snuff.

Research on the chemical constituents of the different species of *Banisteriopsis* is still under way or, rather, is still in an initial stage, together with the search for possible admixtures or, eventually, hallucinogenic plants that are as yet unknown to science. The Northwest Amazon seems to be a most promising area for this kind of research.

But ethnological investigations are still lagging behind. Ever since Spruce made his classic observations, it had been clear that the use of yajé played a role of great importance in these native cultures and that the hallucinatory experience itself offered a wide variety of cultural uses. Were the toxic effects of the drug the same in all cases? Was there a common basis to the visions they produced? And how were these visions interpreted by the Indians?

The symptoms accompanying a harmaline intoxication are described by Claudio Naranjo, whose laboratory experiments are of considerable interest.[55] Among the physiological aspects of the initial stages are the nausea, numbness, and general malaise we have mentioned already; but these tend to disappear in the following stages when visual and auditive phenomena begin to predominate. Distortions in the perception of the physical environment are rare, but frequently hallucinatory images are seen as superpositions on surfaces. The same author mentions rapid lateral vibrations in the field of vision; double and triple contours outlining objects; sudden flashes of light; colored visions with a predominance of red-green and blue-orange contrasts; and prolonged dreamlike sequences containing images of felines, reptiles, and staring eyes and the sensation of flying. Naranjo also points out that musical perception does not seem to be altered, but that buzzing or otherwise disagreeable sounds were reported by many individuals.

Of special interest is Naranjo's observation that "concern with religious or philosophical problems is frequent." In summarizing he says that "the typical reaction to harmaline is close-eyed contemplation of vivid imagery without much further effect than wonder and interest in its significance, which is in contrast to the ecstatic heavens and dreadful hells of other hallucinogens."

13. *Banisteriopsis caapi*

14. Noanamá shaman holding a bundle of narcotic vines (*Banisteriopsis caapi*); Calima River, Chocó Territory, Pacific Lowlands

13

14

15. Stems and leaves of
Banisteriopsis rusbyana;
Pira-paraná

16. Snuff container of
jaguar bone (length, 23
cm.); Guahibo Indians,
Vichada River

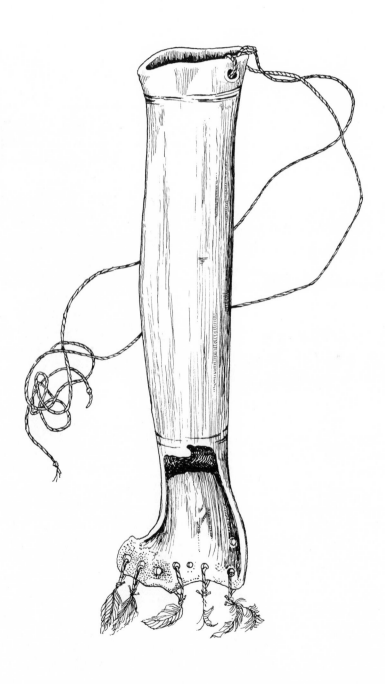

17. Guahibo shaman consecrating a trough of freshly prepared *chicha* beer; Vichada River

3

THE
SHAMAN
AND THE
JAGUAR

In the preceding chapters we have suggested that the use of hallucinogenic drugs—in this case, of *Anadenanthera* snuff and *Banisteriopsis* potions—has played, and continues to play, an important role in the shamanistic practices and religious beliefs of Colombian Indians. Collectively and individually, the mental dissociation produced by these narcotics is thought by these Indians to provide man with a ready means of establishing a direct contact with the supernatural sphere, which then reveals itself in images and voices—shadowy personifications that can be consulted on a wide range of human problems. It now remains to investigate some of the characteristics of these supernatural forces, of these shapes and images the native mind conjures and projects upon the screen of drug-induced hallucinations, and in order to do so we must turn to the shamanistic experience itself.

In tropical America, the close association between shamanism and jaguars or jaguar-spirits has long been a well-known phenomenon, and a great deal has been written on the subject.[1] The basic ideas underlying this complex of beliefs can be briefly summarized here.

To begin with, it is thought that a shaman can turn into a jaguar at will and that he can use the form of this animal as a disguise under which he can act as a helper, a protector, or an aggressor. After death, the shaman may turn permanently into a jaguar and can then manifest himself in that form to the living, both friend and foe, again in a benevolent or malefic way, as the case may be.

When speaking here of shamanism it is necessary also to include in this concept those higher levels of esoteric specialization that

43

must be designated as priesthoods, as would be the case in the more advanced native cultures. In the highly developed civilizations of Mesoamerica and the Central Andes, whose cultural influences upon neighboring areas were considerable in prehistoric times, these priesthoods were also closely associated with certain jaguar-spirits or, perhaps, deities. As priestly and political functions were sometimes combined in the same individual, a further association between kingship and jaguar imagery was present.[2]

Apart from this category of association between a feline concept and the magico-religious representative of society, the jaguar is frequently found associated with a number of natural phenomena such as thunder, the sun, the moon, caves, mountains, fire, and also certain animals. Sometimes the jaguar plays the role of Master of Animals, a protector of game, and thereby becomes associated with hunting rituals. In any case, in tropical and subtropical America, a connection with shamanistic beliefs and techniques is almost always present, and often enough this connection is so close that shamans and jaguars are thought to be almost identical, or at least equivalent, in their power, each in his own sphere of action, but occasionally able to exchange their roles.

We must leave the question why the jaguar should play this role for later discussion and turn once more to the early sources and ethnographic reports. Again, we must limit the field of inquiry to the Colombian scene and first search the Spanish chronicles for evidence.

We shall consider first of all the ancient Muisca Indians of the Andean highlands, a culture that, in the early sixteenth century, had advanced to the level of large village federations united into several incipient states. Among the Chibcha-speaking Muisca, chieftainship and priesthood were often fused so that certain major ceremonial centers such as Sogamoso, Tunja, or Chía were also centers of political consequence.

The names of several important chiefs or priests have been conserved in the chronicles. Some of them pertain to mythical personages, while others are those of historical figures, and it is notable that some of these names should contain the root of a feline concept. Puma or ocelot is *nymy* (*neme*) in Muisca[3] and we can trace this root in several names. One of the last chieftains, or *zipa*,[4] of Bogotá was *Nemequene*, whose name according to the chroniclers meant "puma's bone,"[5] while the chieftain of Sogamoso was called *Nom-*

pasum, meaning "puma's vessel";[6] *Nemocon,* another chieftain's name, meant "weeping puma."[7] Other names, not translated by the chroniclers but all of them containing the same root, are *Nompanem,*[8] *Nemqueteba,*[9] and *Cucinemegua.*[10] The principal culture hero of the Muisca was Bochica, known also under the name of *Nemterequeteba,*[11] and the deity *Nencatacoa* was the supernatural protector of "drunkenness, painters and weavers."[12]

This tendency toward feline names for important people can also be observed at present, especially in the Sierra Nevada of Santa Marta in northern Colombia, where several thousand Kogi Indians, another Chibcha-speaking tribe, still live.[13] The Kogi name for jaguar is *nebbi* (*nabi*) and the root *neb-, nem-,* or *nam-* occurs frequently in the names of mythical priests or chiefs, divine personifications, important mythical ancestors, and constellations of stars. Among the many names of mythical ancestors, most of whom are reported to have been chieftains or priests, we find *Namaku/* "jaguar-lord," *Namsiku/* "jaguar-man," *Namsaui/* "jaguar-devourer," all of them referring explicitly to "jaguar-people" (*nebbi-kve*), and occasionally female personifications will be known by such jaguar names; according to one myth the sun's wife was *Namshaya* (the moon)[14] while *Naboba* was the name of one of the divine daughters of the Mother Goddess.[15] We may add that jaguar names are still in use among some other tribes in Colombian territory; in 1958 the principal chief of the Chocó Indians[16] of the headwaters of the Sinú River, in northwestern Colombia, was known under the name of *imamá purrú/* "red jaguar,"[17] and in the early forties several Guahibo shamans of the Orinoco Plains had names derived from their word for jaguar: *negüiti.*[18]

Next to proper names, other jaguar attributes are frequently found among chiefs and shamans, from early Conquest times to the present. In the sixteenth century, the lord of Tunja, who was also a famous priest, was called by the Spaniards "the long-tailed chief" (*el cacique rabón*) because, according to a chronicler, "he had a long tail, like a jaguar's or a puma's, which he dragged on the ground."[19] On ceremonial occasions among the Muisca, groups of participants wore jaguar or puma dresses,[20] and in the same historical period the Tairona Indians of Santa Marta wore dresses of jaguar skins.[21]

Guahibo shamans still wear headdresses of jaguar claws turned upward, necklaces of jaguar teeth, and carrying-bags of jaguar fur that contain herbs, stones, and their snuffing apparatus. The narcotic powder is kept in a tubular jaguar bone closed on one end with pitch and on the other with a wooden stopper. An officiating Guahibo shaman paints his face with black spots in imitation of jaguar pelt marks, a form of facial paint that is used only by shamans.[22] Modern Kogi priests wear wooden jaguar masks during certain ceremonies, while the dancers will imitate the movements and growls of a jaguar and sing songs addressed to the jaguar-spirit.[23]

That a shaman can turn into a jaguar at will is one of the basic assumptions of the entire complex. Of the ancient Muisca a chronicler writes: "[They are] great sorcerers, some of whom can turn into pumas and jaguars at will, in order to behave then like those [jaguars] that make a practice of devouring human flesh."[24] Another chronicler adds to this: "It is very possible that, by means of communicating with the devil, there should result these illusions."[25] The sixteenth-century chronicler reporting on the Guayupe Indians writes that their shamans claim publicly to be able to turn into jaguars.[26] The modern Tunebo believe that their shamans are occasionally able to visit an otherworldly sphere where they turn into man-eating jaguars and that, at his death, the shaman turns into a jaguar and joins forces with the devil, who, in his turn, is also imagined as a jaguar.[27] Moreover, the idea that a man will turn into a jaguar after death does not seem to be limited to shamans only. The ancient Indians of Antioquia (Central Cordillera) believed that "the souls of those who die are transformed into jaguars."[28] An eighteenth-century text used by the Franciscan friars to confess the Siona Indians, a Tukano-speaking tribe of the Putumayo River in the extreme south of Colombia, contains the following interrogatory: "Have you believed in jaguars? Have you believed that, when dying, you will turn into a jaguar?"[29]

The Colombian traveler Joaquín Rocha, who in the early years of this century visited the Coreguaje, Tama, and Ingano Indians,[30] reports that "they imagine that the souls of certain individuals can pass into the body of a jaguar" and then goes on to tell of a jaguar that had attacked the inhabitants of a house, one of whom had taken a shot at the beast and had hit it in the leg. When it was simultaneously discovered that their local shaman had a wound in his leg he was accused of sorcery and was killed by the men.[31] The English traveler Thomas Whiffen writes of the Huitoto:

When a medicine-man dies he returns as a tiger, and even during his lifetime he can make excursions in tiger-form, and be so absolutely tiger that he can slay and eat the beasts of the wild. Every medicine-man possesses a jaguar skin that he is said to use when he turns tiger. By possession of a skin he has the power of resuscitating the tiger, he himself being the spirit of the tiger. He can thus work his will, afterwards returning to human form. An ordinary tiger might be killed, but a medicine-man in tiger form could not be. On one occasion a medicine-man I met had a bag made of tiger-skin hung round his neck, in which he carried all his paraphernalia. But the medicine-men never wear these skins as wraps or coverings. Each hides his tiger skin away, when not in actual use for magic purposes. The power to return after death in the shape of the dreaded jaguar is a further defensive measure, a precaution against hostile peoples, as in this shape both before and after death the medicine-man can attack the tribal enemies, and carry obnoxious individuals away into the bush whenever opportunity offers.[32]

Father Plácido de Calella, a missionary, writes on the same Indians:

The *éima* (shaman), when he is evil, turns into a jaguar and devours people. He can go from one place to another place far away, in an instant, like an airplane, but is invisible.[33]

Similarly, among the modern Páez Indians[34] it is said that evil shamans will turn into jaguars in order to steal cattle,[35] and that once upon a time a man turned into a jaguar to steal a "golden staff" from the neighboring Pijao tribe.[36] The Chimila of northern Colombia believe that their shamans turn into jaguars, and their Creation Myth says: "When Great Father saw that the earth was empty, he made a huge jaguar and set it free. Thus he created the jaguar, and there still exist jaguars of that breed."[37]

The Sikuani, a subgroup of the Guahibo, hold the jaguar in high esteem. After snuffing large quantities of *Anadenanthera peregrina* powder in the the preparation of which these Indians are said to be very competent, the men dance and sing: "We are jaguars, we are dancing like jaguars; our arrows are like the jaguar's fangs; we are fierce like jaguars." Among other Guahibo groups such as the Cuiva and those of the lower Vichada River, the jaguar is sometimes replaced by other felines such as the ocelot.[38]

The many early reports on Indian shamans "speaking with the

devil" obviously refer to auditory hallucinations which the shamans interpreted as supernatural voices.[39] Oviedo, the sixteenth-
century chronicler, writes of the Indians of the Caribbean lowlands
near Cartagena: "They say that the shaman speaks with the devil
and they affirm that they hear him converse with him, but that they
know neither with whom he speaks, nor do they see to whom he
speaks, nor do they understand what he says because they do not
understand the language in which they converse. And after they
have thus conversed, the shaman tells them what the devil has said
and that they do without fail everything he says the devil told him
to do."[40]

The Muisca priests (*jeque*) of the temple at Sogamoso "chewed
tobacco in his house so that the demon would manifest himself to
him."[41] He then made offerings and "transmitted to the people the
answer to what they had solicited from the devil."[42] The same
chronicler, writing of the ancient Tairona Indians, says that "the
demon . . . often talked to them, only to the shamans. . . .When they
were fasting, the demon talked to them, telling them a thousand
lies. . . . When the devil talked to them in his house, the fire that
burned there all night had to be extinguished by his orders."[43]

Sometimes the appearance of the devil was accompanied by a
violent storm: "When the devil came to talk to the shamans, he did
so with a great storm and hurricane that almost wanted to tear
off the house."[44] Of the Indians of Cumaná in Venezuela, an early
chronicler writes: "His guest, the demon, throws him to the ground,
and the shaman falls into convulsions and gives signs of horrible
suffering," and "through the mouth of the prostrate shaman answers
the spirit that has invaded him."[45] The Indians of Popayán, in the
upper Cauca valley of Colombia, were said to be "great drunkards
and sorcerers, who conjure the devil and speak to him,"[46] and
among the Muisca there existed wandering soothsayers, old people
who went from place to place "chewing tobacco and intoxicating
themselves with the smoke in order to divine."[47] When the ancient
Indians of Cartagena wanted to "speak with the devil," they prepared large quantities of tobacco because—so the devil himself
told them—all he wanted was "tobacco in leaves and powder, because this was a dish very much to his liking."[48] In summary, then,
these reports cover the entire Colombian territory, from the Caribbean Coast to the Andean highlands, and from the Orinoco Plains
to the Western Cordillera.

The ecstatic flight of a Muisca shaman of the sixteenth century is described by a Spanish writer, and the account is worth quoting in full since it contains several points of interest. The shaman of Ubaque, a village near Bogotá, was on what the chronicler calls very familiar terms with the devil and frequently talked to him. On one occasion "the devil took him through the air . . . and one night he took him to Santa Marta, a distance of almost two hundred leagues . . . returning him to his house in Ubaque that very same night." The shaman told of his extraordinary flight and said that "nothing frightened him more than to see the moon so big that it appeared to him five times larger than when seen from the earth."[49] Now, the phenomenon of macropsia, the illusion of perceiving objects much larger than they are, is frequent in hallucinations induced by narcotic snuff,[50] and the shaman's experience of seeing the moon greatly enlarged in size corresponds to well-known patterns of drug-induced hallucination. Of the same shaman another story is told that is significant in this context. The lord of Bogotá had a dream in which the waters of his ritual bath were turning into blood. Greatly worried by this vision, he consulted several shamans of renown who interpreted the dream as an augury of his victory in battle over his foe, the lord of Tunja. But the shaman of Ubaque did not agree with this interpretation and declared that the dream announced the imminent death of the lord of Bogotá. This proved to be true enough, but the point is that visions of blood—of pools of blood, or of the insides of houses covered with blood—are fairly common in drug-induced hallucinations among the modern Tukano Indians.

We may ask, perhaps, Who was this devil the Indians were talking to? How did they conceive him in their hallucinations, that is, what was the cultural image they projected upon their visions? An early chronicler, writing of the Indians of Guaca, in northwestern Colombia, says that "the devil appeared to them in the form of a very fierce jaguar."[51] Another early source, referring to the Anserma Indians of the Western Cordillera, says that "the devil appears to them . . . in the shape of a huge cat, of a jaguar,"[52] and another chronicler, writing of the same Indians, says that "[the devil] often appears to them on the trails and in their houses; and they depict him in the way they see him, and the loincloths *with their tails,* and the decorations they paint on their faces and bodies, are the designs of the devil they see."[53] The Indians of Caramanta, who in the sixteenth century lived to the north of the Anserma, partly in the Pacific lowlands, had in their temples "certain boards in which they carve the figure of the devil, very fierce, and in human form, with other idols and figures of cats which they worship. When they require water or sunshine for their crops, they seek aid from these idols."[54] We have mentioned that the modern Tunebo believe that the devil has a jaguar shape. The above quotations lead us to the relationship between the jaguar-demon and thunder and rain. Muisca priests prayed for rain,[55] and those of the temple at Tunja were said to be especially assiduous in this.[56] In the sixteenth century, the temple of the great thunder deity *Dabeiba,* in northwestern Colombia, had a jaguar for a guardian, and a loud thunderclap was taken to be a sign that the deity was angry.[57]

Finally, we should note that in some cases the jaguar embodies death. Among the Ingano, a Quechua-speaking tribe of southern Colombia, the appearance of a jaguar near a house heralds the death of the person who first sees the beast. In this case the jaguar appears neither as an aggressor nor as a helper but roams about the dwelling in a quite harmless way. According to these Indians this jaguar is the "spirit" of the doomed person.[58] A very similar belief is found among the mestizo peasants of the foothills of the Sierra Nevada of Santa Marta; should a person come upon a jaguar that is asleep or that otherwise presents himself in a harmless way—perhaps following the person on the trail, or just standing and watching him pass by—the beholder will die soon.[59]

It is clear that the foregoing notes refer to mere details; they are ethnographic minutiae this or that ancient or modern author observed or heard of and put on record—quite out of context—offering us tantalizing bits of information that lend themselves to easy oversimplification and speculation. To get a truer perspective of the complex ideas involved we must turn to the description of some specific aboriginal tribes of Colombia which, although widely separated, both geographically and in cultural level, nevertheless share in the basic ideology of the shaman-jaguar complex. We have sufficient information on some tribes to partially reconstruct this relationship and its underlying ideas, and once we have done so and shown the coherent system of these beliefs, we shall find it easier to evaluate and understand the isolated shreds of evidence from other tribes, both ancient and modern.

We shall refer first to a tribe of the southern highlands. The Páez Indians, a Chibcha-speaking tribe numbering several thousands at present, occupy a mountainous district called Tierradentro, between the headwaters of the Magdalena and that of the Cauca River. They are sedentary agriculturalists who live in small villages or scattered homesteads as farmers. During the Conquest, and still in the colonial period, the Páez were fierce warriors who fought for many years against the encroaching Spanish troops, but today they are peaceful peasants and, nominally at least, Catholics. However, this relatively isolated tribe has conserved many traits of the ancient belief system, and this living body of traditions is of considerable interest to our inquiry.

According to the Páez, their present tribal territory was formerly occupied by the warlike Pijao Indians, an enemy tribe that was expelled only after many legendary fights, when it was forced to retreat across the Cauca River toward the northeast.[60] There is historical evidence of the traditional enmity between these two native groups, and after the Spanish conquest the Pijao continued to raid Páez territory until they themselves were subdued by the Europeans. In Páez myths and traditions the Pijao are spoken of as cruel invaders, more beastlike than human, and endowed with extraordinary supernatural powers. It is said that they were the guardians of golden hoards, and that the power of their shamans was contained in "golden staffs" they carried. In many of these tales reference is made to the Pijao as abductors of Páez women whom they carried off or devoured on the spot, the Pijao being fierce cannibals.[61]

An important complex of myths is connected with this warfare, and among them are several that refer to the origins of the culture hero and, with him, of shamanism. It is said that in the beginning of time a young Páez woman was raped by a Pijao Indian who had turned into a jaguar, and that from this union the Thunder-Child was born.[62] In many Páez traditions the Pijao are identified with jaguars,[63] and this assault upon a Páez woman is a frequent motif of Páez myths. This child, who was the son of thunder—and is himself thunder—grew up into a man who became an important culture hero and shaman and eventually retired to a lake in the mountains where his spirit continues to dwell.[64] His name was *Tama*.[65] Thunder is a central theme of most Páez myths and is closely related with the jaguar-spirit, with the concept of fertility, and with shamanism. In fact, the prospective shaman receives his supernatural call to office from thunder, and it is near a mountain lake that apprenticeship takes place, accompanied by visionary experiences. A Páez shaman can turn into thunder, and an evil shaman can turn into a jaguar in order to do harm to other people.

We shall try to trace the individual components of this complex in greater detail. According to Páez mythology, the original Thunder-Jaguar has many children who combine in their features both feline and human traits. They are imagined as most voracious little creatures who, upon their appearance or birth, need several human wet nurses, young girls whom they kill, in the process of growing up, by drinking their milk and blood.[66] Once they are grown up they go to live at the bottom of a lake, and then they appear suddenly to people, sometimes ostentatiously displaying their male sexual organs and trying to abduct women, sometimes manifesting themselves to a shaman and offering to become his helpers.[67] A shaman's[68] apprenticeship takes place by a lake, at some lonely spot in the mountains, and a practicing shaman will periodically return to this place in order to consult the Thunder-Spirit.[69] A shaman should be very frugal in his food habits and should practice sexual abstinence; he should avoid salt and strong condiments such as peppers, in preparation for his activities[70] and in order to have supernatural visions. In these visions thunder will manifest himself and, eventually, will show him certain herbs;[71] above all, he will show him his staff, his magic wand called *tama.* This staff, from whose name is derived that of the Thunder-Spirit, is his "weapon," his emblem, and the wooden staffs all Páez shamans carry are said to be gifts of thunder.[72] Thunder will manifest himself in the lake by a roaring sound, similar to the growl of an enraged jaguar. The apprenticeship ends with a final visit to the lake during which offerings of raw meat are made, meant to be food for the Thunder-Spirit.[73]

Thunder, as a natural phenomenon, is called *capish,* but in his personification of shaman-hero or shaman-helper, he is *tama,* identified with his "golden staff." He may appear in the form of a child-like being or of a grown man, but most personifications and associations of thunder elaborate the feline character he has inherited from his jaguar progenitor. In one tradition he is said to have a tail, and his seat or stool to have a hole to accommodate it,[74] while his roar is compared to that of a jaguar. In his personification as a childlike spirit-being his voracity is emphasized, and it is pointed out that he assaults women sexually and carries them off to his abode. It may be added here that very similar beliefs are found today among the Indians of the southern Andes of Colombia, a region contiguous with the Páez territory. The local natives believe in the existence of childlike beings who live behind cascades and are associated with thunder, rain, and the rainbow. They, too, pursue women, sometimes appearing to them in erotic fantasies and causing them to waste away if not treated by a shaman. When annoyed, these little spirit-beings turn into jaguars and may attack a person or even a house, but then the men frighten them off by putting on masks.[75] In all essence, the transformations of the shaman into thunder and into a jaguar are one and the same thing; thunder and the jaguar-spirit form a single concept.

Thunder is associated with lightning, rain, and the rainbow and is also the guardian of gold.[76] In one tale the Thunder-Child turns into a snake and then into a rainbow,[77] and with this transformation a reptilian element is introduced which is a frequent component of the entire complex. Another tale reports that thunder, in the disguise of a prodigious hunter, covers his body with a snake skin,[78] and in some traditions the lakes where thunder lives are also the dwelling places of monstrous snakes.

Many shamanistic activities are concerned with the fertility of crops and the curing of disease. The Páez shaman chews tobacco[79] and uses a great many herbal medicines to effect his cures; occasionally he also uses jaguar and puma hair.[80]

Among the Páez there seems to exist no tradition of narcotic snuffs, but the use of other hallucinogenic substances is suggested by the following observations: Shamans are said to be able to turn into jaguars, and to accomplish this transformation they are said to consume a plant called *yutse*.[81] Now, an herb with a very similar name—*echyutse chime*—is masticated by shamans during curing rituals,[82] and a plant that, in all probability, is the same is mentioned in the following tale: A Pijao killed a Páez man, flayed him, and ate his flesh. He then filled the skin again with the bones, added *iutse* [sic] plants, and so restored the dead man to life, sending him back to his people. The revival, however, was effective only as long as no one spoke to the victim.[83] A plant that would produce this kind of transformation may well have been a hallucinogen. Besides, that narcotic plants are known to the Páez is demonstrated by the shamanistic use of the highly toxic *Datura*.[84]

An interesting event of recent times deserves to be quoted here. Near the village of Mosoco, a large puma had devastated the livestock of the Indians, and a group of men had killed the beast. The dead puma was carried to the village, where in one of the houses its body was laid out on a sort of altar crowned by an arch of branches beneath which the beast was put in a lifelike position. The room and the altar were adorned with red cloth, flowers, and candles, and the crowd danced around it to the sound of music. After the dance the carcass was butchered and small morsels of meat were given to all participants, but first a special warning was given to the effect that the meat should be prepared without salt.[85]

In summarizing the shaman-jaguar complex among the Páez Indians we can isolate the following components: the jaguar-spirit, or jaguar-monster, has shamanistic qualities and is the shaman's guide and helper. Moreover, he is associated with thunder, rain, and lakes. Many of his attributes are related to sexual aggression. In preparation for ritual actions the shaman must establish contact with the jaguar-spirit and transform himself into a jaguar. This contact and transformation are probably brought about through the use of narcotic drugs, and during his hallucinations the shaman can consult the jaguar-spirit or can do evil in the disguise of a jaguar.[86]

We turn now to another tribal culture, that of the Kogi Indians.[87] The Kogi live in the temperate and cool uplands of the Sierra Nevada of Santa Marta in northern Colombia, where they subsist on farming. The villages function mainly as places for social gatherings, most families living in isolated huts in the surroundings. All villages cluster around a ceremonial house or temple, attended by men with priestly functions, and several major ceremonial centers also exist where people gather during certain collective rituals. The Kogi are a deeply religious people who believe in a primordial mother-goddess who, together with her divine sons and daughters, established an elaborate religious and social code.

Among the Kogi many myths and traditions exist that speak of different jaguar personifications; of all these beings it is said that they were great shamans who were able to change freely from human to animal form and back again and who established rituals, fought wars, and exercised their dominion all over the mountains. The Kogi call themselves Jaguar People and claim to be the "Sons of the Jaguar," not so much in the sense of genealogical descent as in that of a spiritual participation in certain supernatural qualities they believe to be embodied in the beast. We shall return to this point later on, but first we must trace this jaguar image in Kogi traditions.

In Kogi cosmogony, the Universe consists of nine superposed layers or "worlds," the fifth and central layer of which is inhabited by mankind, the others populated by divine personifications or other spirit-beings. These layers were created by the Mother-Goddess and are her "daughters," each associated with a certain kind of agricultural soil. It is in the second layer that a mythical jaguar appears, the first of its kind in the whole creation.[88] In the fifth layer, that is, in our world, a number of jaguar-beings were created, the principal one being a divine son of the Mother, called *Kashindúkua*, followed by his son *Noánase* and his nephew *Námaku*. In one version of the Creation Myth, the deity *Eluitsáma* "first created a huge jaguar, and then a smaller one, and again a still smaller one."[89] Another myth refers to *Aldauhuiku*, a divine being who carried on his back a heavy bag full of noxious beasts—jaguars, pumas, snakes, and also *Kashindúkua* and his descendants. Another mythical being offered to help carry this load, but he soon became tired and put the bag on the ground, whereupon the beasts escaped.[90]

The myth of *Kashindúkua* is central to our understanding of the jaguar image, and we shall quote it briefly in a condensed form.

Kashindúkua, one of the divine sons of the Mother, was destined to be a great shaman who would cure all diseases by sucking the pathogenic essence from the patients' bodies. When his divine mother appointed him to be a healer of human ills, she gave him a "blue ball" and a jaguar mask, but warned him not to misuse the supernatural power of these objects. In fact, whenever *Kashindúkua* put the blue ball into his mouth and put on the mask, he was transformed into a jaguar and thus became able to perceive things in a different way, in the way a jaguar sees them. For example, when curing a patient, he would turn into a jaguar and then perceive the disease in the shape of a black beetle he then would devour in order to cure the patient. But this extraordinary faculty became his undoing. Once, when treating a female patient, he took the ball in his mouth and put on the mask. At this instant he saw a ripe pineapple lying before him and, suddenly becoming very hungry, ate it up. When he took off the mask and the ball, he realized that he had killed the woman and had devoured her.[91] From then on, every time he used the two tools of transformation, he became very hungry and continued to devour women, not only his patients, but also other women and girls, "eating" their sexual organs. In several cases he even committed incest with his own daughters and sisters. His elder brother, *Búnkuase*,[92] knew what was happening and reprimanded him severely, but *Kashindúkua* answered: "I don't need your advice; the Mother herself taught me to do this." Soon *Kashindúkua* had gathered a group of followers who also devoured women. *Búnkuase* now made a trap, a deadfall with a heavy log that, at night, looked like a woman. *Kashindúkua* fell into the trap; people arrived and killed him, wounding him in every part of his body. Before dying, *Kashindúkua* said: "From each pain you have caused me, I shall create a disease that will kill you. From now on, all of you shall be victims of disease."[93] When they cut off his head, they found that it was a jaguar's. They buried him in a cave. The myth ends with these words: "But *Kashindúkua* is not dead. One day, when the world is coming to an end, *Kashindúkua* will leave his cave and, in the shape of a jaguar, will go to all the villages and kill men and women . . . *Kashindúkua* is benevolent. He is our father because we, the Kogi, are Jaguar People and *Kashindúkua* is the Father of the Jaguar. This is his land. From him we ask permission to live here. To him we make offerings, and for him we dance."[94]

Another myth refers to *Noánase*,[95] *Kashindúkua's* son and also a shaman, who inherited from his father the blue ball and the mask. *Noánase*, too, devoured women and became "hungry" every time he transformed himself into a jaguar. One day, when he asked his uncle *Búnkuase* for food, the latter took him to a field planted with maize. On the trail, in order to test him *Búnkuase* transformed himself into different game animals "to see if *Noánase* really devoured people," but *Noánase* did not pay attention. The maize plants were, in reality, *Búnkuase's* men, ready to kill *Noánase*. When *Noánase* took the ball out of his mouth he saw himself surrounded by armed men and immediately put it back, the men turning again into maize plants. *Búnkuase* now led him to a ripe pineapple and asked him to allay his hunger. When *Noánase* inadvertently devoured the fruit, which in fact was a woman, *Búnkuase* killed him with his club. The myth ends with these words: "But only *Noánase's* human form died, because with the first stroke of the club the blue ball had fallen out of his mouth; *Noánase*, the jaguar, is still alive." He, too, will return when the world comes to an end.[96]

A third myth completes this cycle. In it, *Noánase* appears as the great shaman-chief of a village of Jaguar People on the western slopes of the mountains. The inhabitants of a village in the lowlands, who are not Jaguar People, occasionally visit *Noánase's* village, but whenever they go there they are in great fear of being devoured. The chief of the lowland village is *Ambu-ambu* and his wife is *Nabia*, a jaguar-woman from *Noánase's* village. *Nabia* often visits her relatives and, eventually, commits adultery with *Noánase*. She bears him a son, *Námaku*,[97] who grows up in the lowlands believing *Ambu-ambu* to be his father. *Nabia* falsely accuses *Ambu-ambu* of mistreatment and *Noánase* has him punished. *Námaku* knows that his mother hates *Ambu-ambu* and decides to tell *Noánase* that her accusations are untrue. When *Noánase* again sends his men to fetch *Ambu-ambu* for further punishment, *Námaku* follows them. To catch up with them he turns into a jaguar, but assumes human shape as he approaches the party. During the trial of *Ambu-ambu*, who by his silence tries to protect his wayward wife, *Námaku* suddenly realizes that *Noánase* is his father. When *Ambu-ambu* is condemned, he strikes *Noánase* down and usurps his power, becoming chieftain of the Jaguar People. When he learns of the adulterous behavior of his mother, he begins to exercise a reign of terror. He now feels that "part of him belongs to the jaguar," and he savagely punishes his subjects while he himself turns into a violator of women. At last, people rise against him and he has to leave the village. Turning to his step-father he says: "I must flee; I have become an evil person. In these days I have realized that I am evil." He finds refuge in a remote village but after some time is overcome by sadness and goes in search of his mother, *Nabia,* and his stepfather. When at last he arrives at their home, he finds that both have turned into stone.[98]

These three myths contain a fairly clear statement of the ambivalence that underlies Kogi philosophy. The "gift of the Mother" provides the key to another level of experience and consciousness which, when used for good intentions, can help to cure man's ills, but when misused for private ends, leads to the very depths of moral degradation. However, the Kogi consider their jaguar origin to be an inescapable inheritance, and the principle of Evil to be an essential condition of life.

We cannot go into the deeper problems of Kogi philosophy and religion here but must concentrate on the shaman-jaguar trans-formation complex. Some ethnographic details contained in the myths are highly significant to this inquiry. In the first place, the hallucinogenic substance consists of a "blue ball" called *nebbi kuái/* "jaguar's testicle" or "jaguar's sperm." The exact identity of this substance is uncertain, but it seems very probable that a poisonous puffball is meant. The Kogi are extremely secretive about what seem to be several drugs used by them.[99] In the second place, the use of this "blue ball" produces the illusion of the shaman's trans-formation into a jaguar. The jaguar mask is put on *after* the blue ball has been consumed; that is, its effects produce the jaguar vision. Another interesting point is the equation of eating and coition, the devouring jaguar being essentially a sexual aggressor. A point of major importance is that the tale of *Námaku* clearly describes an exogamic relationship between the inhabitants of a mountain village of Jaguar People and those of a lowland village. Residence rules are suggested to be virilocal and descent is de-scribed as patrilineal; in one of the most dramatic scenes—the trial of *Ambu-ambu* and the confrontation of father and son— *Námaku* recognizes his true father when he sees that both he and *Noánase* are wearing the same striped cloth that only Jaguar-men may use.[100]

Kogi society is divided into different patri- and matrilines, each associated with a certain animal.[101] Membership in one of these strictly exogamic groups descends from father to son and from mother to daughter, and there are sets of "male" and "female" ani-mals. Marriage rules imply that a man belonging to a certain group must marry a woman whose group is associated with an animal that is the natural prey of the man's animal. For example, men of the jaguar group marry women of the peccary group; men of the puma group, those of the deer group. There are, then, no jaguar-women or puma-women, nor are there peccary-men or deer-men; group membership is inherited by sex. Here again we can see the equivalence mentioned above, a man marrying, that is, "eating," a woman who represents the natural prey of his animal.[102]

As we have noticed, several groups are associated with felines— jaguar, puma—and we can add that others, too, recognize a certain relationship with felines such as ocelots and other cats. In any case, quite apart from these subdivisions, the entire tribe lays claim to jaguar descent, and *Kashindúkua,* in spite of his ambivalent role— or rather, precisely, because of it—occupies a most important place in myth and ritual.[103] *Kashindúkua* is the Master of the Temple, the protector of the uterine ceremonial house, and in former times it was the custom to suspend a jaguar skull near the main entrance of the ceremonial center.[104] The idea that the dead—not only shamans—are transformed into jaguars and return to earth to punish their relatives or, at least, those who have not made the prescribed offerings is common among the Kogi, and the return of the jaguars at the world's end is a common theme in myths and tales.

To complete this account of the Kogi, we shall quote a tale that, according to our informants, is based upon a historical event and shows how the jaguar imagery is being incorporated into recent local traditions. The tale tells of a girl who lived with her family in a region formerly inhabited by Jaguar People. One day the girl was attacked by a jaguar and bitten in the breast. The girl began to growl like a jaguar and died shortly afterward and was buried. During the night the jaguar returned and devoured the corpse. The men killed the jaguar and, upon examining the beast's body, discovered that one of its paws was shaped just like a human foot.[105]

Once more, we must briefly summarize our data. The tribe lays claim to mythical jaguar descent, and several of its exogamic units are particularly related to felines. Mythical chieftains and shamans are jaguar-beings; they turn into jaguars under the influence of a substance designated as "jaguar's sperm." Once they have assumed this shape they can do good or evil, according to the use they make of their new supernatural faculty of perceiving things in the way jaguars do. A shaman might use this faculty to destroy the essence of disease and to interpret natural phenomena, dreams, or signs in terms of a religious and moral code; but he can also do evil if, under the influence of the substance, he confounds—unintentionally or intentionally—the perceptive images of empirical reality with those of his visions and breaks the rules that regulate social relationships. The main point is the moral ambivalence of the jaguar image, a theme we shall find again and again, wherever we encounter the jaguar-shaman transformation.

The parallels with the beliefs of the Páez Indians are obvious. There may be variations in detail or emphasis, but the underlying ideas are very similar. And when we recall now the many isolated data from other tribes, ancient and modern, we now can see more clearly the wider context of jaguar-shaman relationships. A fundamental thought seems to be concerned with the problems of sex and incest, as defined by the local culture, and with the ordering of social relations, and these problems, as we shall see later on, are also basic in other native cultures of Colombia.

4

THE
FOREST
AND THE
RIVER

In the previous chapter we mentioned some aspects of shamanism and jaguar imagery in several Colombian tribes, as described in the historical and ethnological sources. We shall turn now to a region where, to this day, these cultural mechanisms are still operating: the tropical rain forest east of the Andes. It is from this region that by personal research we have been able to gather a certain amount of factual data which allows us to amplify the information presented so far, and to describe in more detail the shaman-jaguar complex and the drug-induced hallucinations. This chapter, then, is meant to provide an introduction to the wider scene of the rain forest environment, which is the stage on which the shaman, the jaguar, and the drug-possessed native act out their dramatic experience.

The Vaupés territory, a vast equatorial rain forest area of the Northwest Amazon, remains to this day one of the least-explored regions of the upper Amazon basin. Little is known of its geological structure, its soils and climatic conditions, its animal life, and less perhaps of its aboriginal inhabitants, the forest Indians.[1]

This lack of information is mainly due to the marked geographical isolation of this part of the country, in terms of connecting travel routes. Broadly speaking, the Vaupés territory is limited to the north by the Guaviare River—one of the major western affluents of the upper Orinoco—which marks the dividing line between the grassy plains, or *llanos,* and the Amazonian rain forest. To the west lies the heavily wooded chain of the Andes; to the south, the upper course of the Caquetá River; and to the east, the Río Negro and its tributaries. It is this somewhat marginal situation, on the northwestern rim of the Amazon basin, that makes travel conditions par-

ticularly difficult; the rivers of the Vaupés territory are not easily
navigable and do not offer the easy waterways one generally finds
in the South American lowlands. On the contrary, the streams
crossing this eastward-sloping land flow over beds of rocks and
boulders which form innumerable falls and rapids,[2] an ever present
obstacle to navigation. In the neighboring areas—the Orinoco
Plains, the Río Negro, or the Caquetá—the rivers are far less dangerous, there being few natural barriers to canoe travel, for those
approaching the periphery of the Vaupés—from any of these adjacent areas—the swift-moving rapid-blocked rivers of the Vaupés
forests make this a difficult country for river travel and, consequently, for settlement or trade.

The great, slow-moving Colombian rivers that flow from the
Andes toward the Orinoco—the Meta, Vichada, and Guaviare—
were already explored, in part at least, in the eighteenth and nineteenth centuries by travelers who descended their courses from
west to east. The early Jesuit missionaries played an important part
in the exploration and settlement of these vast plains, whose potential for cattle breeding was soon recognized by settlers from the
Colombian interior. These rivers flow mainly through open savannah country, and to cross from one to the other or to explore their
headwaters was not too difficult because one could travel on horse-
back and there was plenty of game and fish.[3] But south of the
Guaviare the rain forest began, and there travel conditions were
entirely different from those encountered on the wide, grass-cov-
ered plains. To the explorers proceeding from Andean Colombia,
the headwaters of the Vaupés River remained, therefore, almost unknown until fairly recent times;[4] to cross from the upper Guaviare
to the first small affluents of the upper Vaupés was an arduous and
time-consuming undertaking because there were no known trails
and the local Indians were said to be unfriendly or, at least, not at
all cooperative.

The quest for El Dorado, that powerful incentive to geographical
exploration, had lured some early European expeditions to the
western portions of the Orinoco Plains and to the rain forests to the
south, at the foot of the eastern slopes of the Andes. In the chronicles referring to these expeditions which, in the late thirties and
early forties of the sixteenth century, penetrated into these regions,
the Vaupés is mentioned for the first time.[5] After crossing the
Guaviare River the conquistadores entered the territory of the

Guapé Indians and soon afterward, pushing south, met a large tribe, the Omagua, who were said to be rich in gold and to live in spacious cities. However, these dreams of the "Dorado de los Omaguas" never came true, and the exhausted troops were forced to retreat and to abandon all further exploration. Unfortunately, the early records contain no reliable descriptions of the aboriginal peoples encountered during these expeditions, and once the quest for the Omagua treasures was abandoned, no further expeditions were undertaken.[6]

The Vaupés was explored, rather by missionaries and traders who ascended its course from the Río Negro, that is, from the Brazilian side. Most early reports speak of the long and dangerous ascent of the river, and it seems that only in the late nineteenth century did some Colombian traders and government agents penetrate from the northwest to the upper reaches of the Vaupés. Many of them were rubber collectors who, eventually, came into contact with Brazilians who had ascended the river from the east. Missionary activity also proceeded from the east, once a number of settlements had been established on the Río Negro. On the middle and upper Vaupés these efforts failed, and during the second half of the last century there seem to have been no mission stations on the Colombian part of the river. But the influence of the settlements on the Rio Negro and, with it, that of Manaos (the city lying at its mouth), which rose to prominence during the rubber boom, were strongly felt in the Vaupés territory. Rubber collectors in search of a cheap Indian labor force, and traders in search of such staple foods as cassava bread, contributed to the spread of the *Lengua Geral,* a Tupi dialect,[7] and also brought about changes by introducing many elements of material culture such as bushknives, cooking vessels, shotguns, and trade cloth. Early in the present century, in 1914, the first permanent Catholic missions were established in the eastern portion of the Colombian Vaupés, and in 1949 the Apostolic Prefecture of Mitú was established in the newly (1936) founded administrative capital of the entire district.[8]

A brief description of the main geographical features of the area is called for in order to acquaint the reader with the general lie of the land. The Vaupés is a major western tributary of the Rio Negro, the mighty Brazilian river that flows into the Amazon near Manaos. From its source in a small hill range in the west, the Vaupés flows in an eastern direction, approximately following the first parallel north until, in its lower course, it turns sharply to the south before it joins the Rio Negro. Next to the Vaupés, the Papurí is of importance, a stream flowing parallel to the former for its entire length, but joining the Vaupés at Yavareté, on its southward course. To the north of the Vaupés are several other large rivers—the Isana, Guainía, and Inírida—which, also flowing in a general west-to-east direction, belong to the Orinoco basin. South of the Vaupés and beyond the Papurí, the Tiquié River runs almost exactly along the equatorial line, and to the west of its headwaters the Pira-paraná describes a wide curve before flowing southward to join the Apaporis River. This last river is one of the major northern tributaries of the Caquetá River and may be said to form the western boundary of the Vaupés territory.

There are no mountains. The enormous floodplain is overwhelming in its monotonous flatness, its limitless expanse. Only here and there do a few level-topped or dome-shaped hills, small in extension, rise over the endless horizon, sometimes appearing like dark towers, at other times like islands floating in a sea of vegetation. They are the remnants of an earlier age, of the so-called Guiana-Shield, lonely remainders of the geological past that rise sporadically over the forest. In fact, the Vaupés territory is geologically the westernmost extension of the Guiana highlands. But otherwise the land is level, sloping almost imperceptibly toward the southeast and the great basin of the Amazon.

The overall monotony of the rain forest landscape gives the impression that this land forms a single homogeneous unit in terms of climate, soils, irrigation, and biota, but this would be far from the truth. In reality, within this vast expanse of forests and rivers many different zones exist, each characterized by a certain combination of soils, types of rivers, plant cover, and animal life, often showing marked climatic variations and thus forming a complex mosaic of larger or smaller micro-environments and ecological areas.[9] It is unfortunate that the Vaupés territory has not been studied from this point of view because it is clear that these different zones, so obvious to the traveler and to the local inhabitants, play an important part in the history and process of cultural adaptation to the rain forest environment.

At present the Indian population of the Vaupés territory can be estimated at some 7,000 individuals,[10] who live in scattered dwellings mainly along the rivers and smaller streams. In the past this was not an area of village life, but most Indians used to live—and some still do—in large communal houses, *malocas* as they are commonly called, and from one maloca to the next there was often a distance of a day's travel. The few villages that exist at present— Mitú, the capital of the district; Yavareté,[11] at the mouth of the Papurí River; Miraflores, on the upper Vaupés; Tipiaca,[12] downriver from Mitú; and a few others—are all recent foundations established during the last decades by missionaries and rubber collectors, but the traditional Indian way of life has always centered on the maloca, the large longhouse under whose roof a group of nuclear families is gathered.

The Indians who occupy the Vaupés territory at present belong to many different linguistic stocks. The majority come under the Tukanoan Family,[13] which is concentrated on the Vaupés, Papurí, Tiquié, and Pira-paraná Rivers, but some groups are found on the Rio Negro, to the east, and on the Apaporis, to the west. The Arawakan Family is represented mainly by groups living on the northeastern fringe, on the Guainía, Inírida, and Isana Rivers, a region that forms the so-called Comisaría del Guainía. These Arawakans are known generally by the name of Kuripako, but some others (Baniva, etc.), also of Arawakan stock, are found on the lower courses of these rivers.[14] The Tariana, also Arawakan, form a few small groups on the lower Papurí River and on the Brazilian side of the lower Vaupés. The Carib Family is represented by a small settlement of Karihona Indians who live at Puerto Nare on the upper Vaupés River.[15] Another native group, very different from those mentioned above, is constituted by the so-called Makú. These Indians live principally in a few interfluvial regions where they subsist as nomadic or seminomadic hunters and gatherers, leaving their forests only occasionally to join a sedentary Tukano group but returning after some time to their forest habitat. The Tukano consider the Makú little better than servants, as ignorant forest dwellers who occupy an inferior position, but a complex interrelationship exists between the two in which economic, social, and religious factors seem to play a role. Linguistically the Makú form a separate stock, with several dialects.[16]

A problem concerning these different linguistic groups and families is the demographic succession in the Vaupés. Unfortunately, hardly anything is known about the history of these various ethnic groups, and no archaeological studies have been undertaken. One might suggest that the Makú are remnants of an old sub-stratum of band-based hunters, and that the Arawakans, because of their widely scattered distribution, represent a later population eventually partly displaced and divided by Tukano invaders. Many Tukano traditions referring to the first settlement and the origins of social units speak of migrations that ascended the rivers, mainly the Rio Negro and Vaupés, starting from some remote region beyond Manaos. The detailed reference to place names and a step-by-step penetration into a new territory that figure prominently in many Tukano myths and tales may well contain a kernel of historical truth.

But these problems are beyond the scope of this book. We must return to the present-day Tukano and first give a brief description of some aspects of their culture.[17]

The Eastern Tukano are divided into more than twenty named exogamic groups. Descent is patrilineal and residence is patrilocal, with cross-cousin marriage said to be preferred.[18] Each group is subdivided into a number of ranked sibs and claims to be descended from a particular mythical ancestor whose first appearance is often associated with a certain topographical landmark, generally a rapid. Ideal marriage rules dictate unions between members of sibs of approximately equal rank, and between certain exogamic groups, but there are exceptions to these rules, and marriages be-tween low- and high-ranking sibs are fairly common. A rule strictly observed by all, however, is that of exogamy, and even among the most acculturated and missionized Indians marriage within the same group is unthought of.

A complete list of all exogamic units of the Eastern Tukano, in-cluding those who live in Brazilian territory, has not yet been established. We shall mention here only the principal ones, mainly those with whom personal contact was established. These groups are Tukano proper, Desana, Pira-Tapuya, Uanano, Carapana, Tatuyo, Barasana, Taibano, and Makuna.[19] A group that occupies a somewhat isolated position is the Cubeo.[20] The members of each of these exogamic groups speak their own language, but this does not constitute a barrier to intercommunication, since practically all people—men and women—speak several languages quite fluently and Tukano proper is understood by all and serves as a lingua franca throughout the Vaupés territory. This multilingualism is indeed a characteristic trait of the Vaupés Indians.[21]

Among the Eastern Tukano there is no tribal feeling, and, indeed, the concept of "tribe" cannot be applied to these scattered groups. On the Rio Negro and on the lower Vaupés River the concept of *tushaua*, a Tupi term meaning chief, still carries a certain prestige, but in the Colombian Vaupés it has little or no meaning. Occasionally one might speak of a headman, a "capitán," generally an elderly man who represents traditional values and has a large family, and whose authority is recognized beyond the limits of his household unit; but these cases seem to be rare, and more often each household or cluster of huts recognizes one of its members as its head and spokesman.

Exogamic marriage between these different linguistic units implies a complex and rigidly structured relationship between complementary groups, which is expressed in many patterns of reciprocity and exchange. The principal event consists in the gathering of two exogamic groups (a *dabocurí*, as these reunions are called), during which food is exchanged, a slightly fermented beer (*cashirí*) is served, and men and women dance, often for several days. Genealogies and origin myths emphasizing the tradition of reciprocity between the two groups are recited on many of these occasions, and in this manner their alliance is renewed and celebrated.

The economic basis of the Tukano is manioc agriculture, practiced in garden plots cleared in the adjacent forest. Hunting and fishing are mainly of a seasonal importance, as is the gathering of wild-growing fruits, honey, and edible insects. Most of these activities, both social and economic, are closely connected with ritual attitudes directed by the shaman—or *payé*, to use the common term in Lengua Geral. The payé officiates in the rituals of the life cycle (birth, initiation, and burial) and is also active as a curer of diseases. One of his main preoccupations, however, is directed toward the relationship between society and the supernatural, above all with the Master (or masters) of game animals, on whom depends success in hunting and fishing and who also commands many pathogenic agents the payé tries to neutralize. A few old men are known by the name of *kumú*, a title conferred upon them because of their exceptional esoteric knowledge, and they occupy a high status in their society.[22]

Nowadays most air travel to the Vaupés starts at Villavicencio, a rapidly growing town sprawling at the foot of the Eastern Cordillera, on the very edge of the Orinoco Plains. As the airplane turns and rises one can see the grassy savannahs stretching toward the east, the green cattle pastures, the tin roofs of the ranch houses glistening in the sun. This is still a cultural landscape, a plain crisscrossed by the straight lines of engineering, of roads and fences, irrigation ditches and cattle trails. But soon, as the plane turns southeast, the straight lines become bent and crooked; the roads disappear, and only the winding foottrails and some isolated homesteads bear witness to man's presence. And soon these, too, vanish. Now open savannah country, with dark strips of gallery forest, lies below, and as one approaches the Guaviare River the patches of forest grow larger and become more coherent. South of the Guaviare there are almost no grasslands. Now dense rain forest covers the ground, interrupted only by the gleaming bands of meandering rivers. There is no sign of human occupation; whatever houses or trails might exist in this green sea lie in the shadow of the forest, dwarfed by the enormous canopy of trees that covers every sign of life. One can fly for hours over these forests without seeing the least indication of settlements or fields.

But this breathtaking vista is gone as soon as the airplane slithers to a halt over the red clay of the airstrip, often not more than a small clearing hardly noticeable from the air. And now the forest and the rivers come to life.

The silver bands of water that appeared so calm, somnolent, and peaceful from the air look very different now. The rivers of the Vaupés territory are among the most treacherous of the Northwest Amazon. Their courses are interrupted by a large number of rapids and falls, sometimes formed by steep escarpments over which the water rushes in thundering currents and cascades. As there are hardly any overland trails and most travel is by dugout canoe, the hazards of these rapids are a constant peril to navigation. Often the canoe has to be unloaded completely and pushed and pulled over the danger spots, the boatmen wading up to their chests in the turbulent waters, stumbling over hidden rocks and crags while others carry the cargo over a forest trail on the riverbank until a spot is reached where the craft can be loaded again. Sometimes the force of the current is too strong and then the canoe itself has to be hauled overland, through swampy portages and over roots and ditches. Hours or even days may be spent in this way when traveling in the Vaupés.

The Indians are excellent boatmen, with an extraordinary knowledge of their rivers, and used to taking quick decisions. When paddling downstream and approaching a rapid, the roaring rush of which can often be heard at a considerable distance, the helmsman stands upright in the prow and scans the waters before him, looking for a passage through which the canoe may be steered without unloading. Obeying a few hand signals or head signs, the paddlers will advance carefully, and once the decision has been taken to shoot the rapids they will swiftly steer the canoe into the current, always watching the helmsman, who now crouches low and indicates with short rapid signs of his uplifted hand the direction to follow. There is a point of no return, and once the craft is riding the current it has to go forward regardless what might happen.

A change, however slight, in the water level of the river will affect the conditions under which a rapid can be passed or not. A sudden rainfall that fills the tributary streams above a fall, a few rolling boulders, or some floating tree trunks and branches that form a temporary obstacle may suddenly change the channels and passages, and so a rapid is never exactly the same as it was when last seen. At night the Indians will listen to the deep droning sound of a rapid and by its modulations will estimate its approximate water level and the channels that may provide a safe passage next day. When traveling upriver they will watch the leaves, flowers, or branches that float on the water and so will know if the level of the next rapid has risen or fallen; and when they approach the fall the foamy blotches floating on the surface will give them a measure of the current. These matters are common topics of conversation among men who travel, and the state of this or that rapid will be discussed in detail, in anticipation of the journey.

Between Mitú, the district capital, and Yavareté, the Brazilian border post at the confluence of the Vaupés and Papurí Rivers, there are more than sixty larger or smaller rapids, and above Mitú, toward the upper Vaupés, some ten others follow. The most famous of these is the Yuruparí Falls, which marks the dividing line between the upper and middle courses of the river. Located a few days' travel upstream from Mitú, it consists of a series of cascades and channels of a swiftness and violence not matched by the others. But farther up, beyond the Yuruparí, the river is calm; there are lagoons and swampy stretches of jungle, and innumerable small tributaries form the headwaters, a region in many aspects very different from the middle and lower courses. On the lower Vaupés the Yavareté Falls is of great size, and farther down, the falls at São Gabriel and Ipanoré are famous and feared. The other rivers, too, are dangerous, and one can hardly travel a day's distance without having to stop and unload, or take the risk of running the heaving waters of a rapid. On the Pira-paraná the Cuyucuyú and Meyú Falls divide the river into three main sections, each of which has its lesser rapids, according to the season, and on the Papurí and upper Tiquié Rivers small but violent rapids make navigation hazardous and slow. The Jirijirímo Falls on the upper Apaporis River is a most extraordinary sight: an enormous horseshoe-shaped cascade, deep in the forests of one of the least-known regions of the Vaupés territory.

All these falls and rapids figure prominently in Indian myths and traditions. Much more than any other landmarks, they are connected with aboriginal life and thought, with mythological scenes, with the origins of certain native groups, or with tales of strange monsters and uncanny happenings. They are the dwelling places of spirits, of dangerous forces that are supposed to inhabit the dark depths of the pools; as a matter of fact, they are imagined as "houses" where the water-beings have their abodes, much in the same way as people live on land. To the natives of the Vaupés, then, the rivers and their rapids are not only natural routes of communication but also spots where contact with another, supernatural, sphere is established.

The forest is a very different world. The forest is silent and unchanging. Because of its vast extent it is far less known to the Indian and, therefore, in his mind, harbors more dangers. On a stretch of river one can always see the sky and the wandering clouds casting their floating shadows over the water; one can watch the brilliant sunlight on the beaches and the vegetation on the riverbank. But the forest is dark. As soon as one enters its gloom one has to adapt one's vision to a closer range of things, to the roots and vines, the thorny branches and the slippery trunks that cross stagnant waters. And there is hardly a sign of life. Only from high up in the treetops can one hear the screeching of parrots or, sometimes, the chattering of a band of monkeys, but at ground level one can walk for hours without seeing an animal. When entering a clearing in the forest, perhaps an abandoned field or a spot where the wind has felled a

few trees, one might see a few huge blue Morpho butterflies fluttering in the hot air; there will be the hiss of cicadas and the hum of
bees and, perhaps, the sudden flash of a bright-colored bird; but
otherwise there will be silence.

But this silence is deceptive. Life is pulsating and alert everywhere. Without a sound the animals will hide behind a fallen
branch or between the roots of a tree; they will press their bodies to
the ground and lie flat on an overhanging branch, or move quietly
out of sight into the shadow of the underbrush. They will glide and
crouch, or freeze in their tracks, while watching out for approaching danger, and only after long experience will one be able to watch
this silent life of the forest. Wildlife is much more obvious near
the rivers, early in the morning or in the late afternoon, but in the
forest it is hardly noticeable to the unaccustomed intruder.

The rocky hills one encounters here and there in the depths of
the forest are feared by the Indians, who believe that it is there that
the supernatural masters of the game animals have their abodes.
These hills, much like the rapids and falls of the rivers, are thought
to be "malocas" wherein the animals live under the protection of
their master, and near these hills are clean and open spots where
they are said to gather to dance and play. At these spots, in the
presence of the Master of Animals, the deer, the peccary, or other
species will have their feasts, and then, the Indians say, the air will
be loaded with the musky smell of the aromatic herbs the dancers
use for anointing their bodies when they thus gather. These are
danger spots to the lonely hunter who may happen upon them; he
will fall ill with fever, pierced by the invisible tiny arrows shot at
him by the game animals in retaliation for the prey he has killed.
These dark and rocky spots are therefore avoided by all, and it is
precisely for this reason that they have become true sanctuaries
where wildlife is being preserved.

There are other dangerous spots in the forest. Sometimes one
finds a clearing, often quite large, where there is hardly any plant
growth or where the flat ground is covered by low herbs but lacks
trees or underbrush. These clearings are not man-made and are
not—as one might think—old, abandoned habitation sites; they
are spots where the chemistry of the local soils has special characteristics that inhibit the growth of larger forest trees or shrubs.
These spots, too, are feared by the Indians; it is said that they are
the gathering places of spirits, of the souls of the dead, or of ghostly

apparitions of unknown origin. Uncanny noises are heard there, and should someone come near such a clearing he will run the danger of falling ill.

And then there are the spots which, although well known by the hunter and traveler, are fraught with danger because of what has happened there in the past. There is the spot where a boy was bitten by a snake; the spot where a falling tree killed a man, or where a hunter buried the tongue of a deer he had killed so its spirit would not betray him; the spot where a forest spirit has been known to give his cry, or where a jaguar was said to have attacked a woman. There is the old habitation site where once a large maloca stood until it was abandoned when the shaman who inhabited it died and was buried in its center. Some of these abandoned house sites are also burial places because alongside the walls, all around the oval ground plan of the building, the inhabitants had buried their dead, one by one, until the last survivors left the place and the jungle closed in and covered it with undergrowth. There are the places in the forest where an evil shaman has cast a spell on all passersby or where the *boráro*, a monstrous forest spirit, was said to sun himself surrounded by blue butterflies. And there are spots or entire regions where the *uahtí*, small impish forest spirits, are likely to appear.

It is a fact that, for reasons largely unknown, there are tracts in the forest, large or small, where mammals or birds are scarce or practically absent. Although there seems to be no obvious reason— fruit trees or other food resources are present—it appears that certain regions are avoided by monkeys, peccaries, or rodents, and that even common birds are extremely rare. These are not circumscribed spots, but sometimes entire regions covering large areas that seem to be almost completely devoid of game animals, and it is not surprising that the Indians should consider these places uncanny, to be crossed in silence if they cannot be avoided entirely.

The forest, then, is a dimension full of unforeseeable dangers, many of which are quite real but most of which are of a supernatural and wholly unreal character. The forest is thought to be inhabited by many more different spirit-beings than the river because all mammals—or most of them—have spirit-natures that can be dangerous to people. Although the Indians move with the ease of long experience in the forest environment, they are never completely confident of their dominance.

The only places, then, that offer security are those that have been transformed by actual, present culture: the maloca and its immediate surroundings. The building itself, surrounded by the ring-shaped space of the yard, is the true center of life. Next to this there is another important space, the landing place, usually at a short distance from the dwelling. The narrow stretch of riverbank where the canoes are moored, where people bathe and talk, where the women wash and soak the fruits they have gathered, is of great importance in Indian life. It is there that contacts are established: contact between the forest and the river, between land and water, between the sexes, between culture and nature. It is the place for sexual intercourse and for ritual occasions, an emotion-charged place, and it figures prominently in myths and tales. Between the landing and the maloca, the trail that connects these two spatial units is another link of safety. Along this trail there lie discarded fishing rods or traps, pieces of old baskets or mats, small heaps of firewood, and perhaps an old canoe. This trail is an important tie between the household unit and the outer world, the river and all it stands for: travel, fishing, contact with neighbors.

Next there are the manioc fields and the trails leading to them from the maloca. They too offer safe ground for work and sex, not quite as safe as the landing and the yard, but safe enough. Most fields lie at a fairly short distance from the houses, and the trails are used every day by the women and children who go to work, or by the men who help them or go on from there into the forest for hunting. The animals one may encounter in the environment of the garden plots are harmless and friendly; they are the macaws and parrots, weaverbirds and hummingbirds, squirrels and mice. They do not "shoot arrows"; they are friends. But beyond the fields the forest commences, and with it a danger zone.

We must stop here and consider a few questions. How real are these dangers of river and forest? And how seriously do the Indians take the unreal perils they talk about so often?

As in any untamed natural environment, certain risks, do, of course, exist. The falls and whirlpools of the rivers are dangerous, no doubt, and many people have lost their lives in them. In the forest one may trip and break a leg; a dead tree can collapse, and a falling branch could hurt a passerby. One might be bitten by a poisonous snake. But, after all, these are most unlikely occurrences, and when asking someone for concrete cases one receives vague answers. Yes, someone was bitten by a snake some time ago and on another river; and years ago a relative drowned at this or that rapid. But such accidents are rare. The real dangers the natural environment presents are not the only cause of the anxiety so manifest in the tales told by so many people.

But then, what about beliefs in monsters and spirits, or in the necessity and efficacy of individual ritual action? Sometimes, after days and weeks of humdrum life, of eating and sleeping and small talk, of commonplace events and everyday matters, one can easily come to think that these Indians are quite realistic people who look at this world in a very matter-of-fact way. And they themselves will confirm this impression; no, there are no forest spirits anymore, someone would say; perhaps in olden times but not now, not since people got shotguns and electric torches. And the game animals? There are not many left anyhow, and they could do no harm; the old people—someone would say—had some ideas about them, but all this was being forgotten now, since the missionaries had come. Quite often one would find Indians who talked that way and openly questioned the old traditions. They had been under the influence of the missions, or the rubber collectors, and when they talked in the presence of unmissionized Indians, the latter would listen and nod; no, there were no spirits anymore. The old people had been wrong.

But then, maybe the next day, the scene would change. There would be men—mature and healthy men—who suddenly claimed to have encountered a bush spirit and now sat shivering in a corner repeating their story over and over again; men who calmly prepared a concoction with which to kill a distant enemy; men who, with almost fanatical voices, cast an evil spell over a burning cigar butt and threw it in the direction of an opponent. And then there are the burials, the initiation rites, and the gatherings, with dances and songs—all these tightly structured and highly formalized occasions when the members of neighboring malocas come together and reaffirm their alliance. No, that is not acculturation. Nor is the world interpreted then in realistic terms.

It is this dimension we shall try to explore in the following chapters, the dimension of what—in our culture—would be termed unreality, imagination, the fantastic. To the Indians this "other" dimension is just as real as that of ordinary everyday life, and for the individual to pass from one to the other is an experience shared by all. To accomplish this change, to see beyond the surface of things—through the hills and the waters and the sky—there exist means that can be handled and controlled; there is concentration, abstinence, and trance. Or sometimes this "other" dimensions will manifest itself quite suddenly and unexpectedly, allowing a brief and terrifying glimpse of dark powers. But more often the perception of this dimension will be produced quite consciously by chemical means, by powerful drugs under the influence of which the mind will wander into the hidden world of animals and forest spirits, of divine beings and mythical scenes. And in the preparation of these drugs the Indians of the Vaupés are specialists.

5

TUKANO
SHAMANISM

Shamanism is well developed among the Indians of the Vaupés, and the shaman (or payé,[1] as he is commonly called in that area), is probably the most important specialist within the native culture. It is he who, representing his local group, establishes contact with the supernatural powers and who, to the mind of his people, has the necessary esoteric knowledge to use this contact for the benefit of society.

The principal spheres of action of a payé are the curing of disease, the obtaining of game animals and fish from their supernatural masters, the presiding over the rituals in the individual life cycle, and defensive or aggressive action against personal enemies. In all these aspects the role of the payé is essentially that of a mediator and moderator between superterrestrial forces and society, and between the need for survival of the individual and the forces bent upon his destruction—sickness, hunger, and the ill will of others. In the course of his activities the shaman (we shall use this term interchangeably with payé) must therefore obtain the assistance of a number of spirit-helpers contact with whom is established through the use of narcotic drugs. Apart from this, the payé must obtain a series of concrete objects of wood, stone, or other substances that contain the essence of certain power concepts and form his instruments of practice.

The office of payé is not hereditary, but it seems to be fairly common for one of the sons of a well-known shaman to follow his father's calling. More important than family tradition, however, are certain psychological and intellectual qualities that mark a person as a potential payé, and that will be recognized in his youth

by those surrounding him. Among these qualities are a deep interest in myth and tribal tradition, a good memory for reciting long
sequences of names and events, a good singing voice, and the capacity for enduring hours of incantations during sleepless nights
preceded by fasting and sexual abstinence. But these are, perhaps,
minor qualities; there are others, more important, that develop
only in the course of long training and experience, if not in the
course of an entire life. Above all, a payé's soul should "illuminate";
it should shine with a strong inner light rendering visible all that is
in darkness, all that is hidden from ordinary knowledge and reason-
ing. This supernatural luminescence of the payé is said to manifest
itself when he speaks or sings, or when he explains his or others'
hallucinatory experiences. Of a payé whose explanations remain
obscure to the listener, it is said that "his soul is not seen, it does
not burn; it does not shine." This powerful emanation is thought to
be directly derived from the sun, and to have a marked seminal
character.[2] The sun's fertilizing energy is transmitted to the payé in
the sense that he himself becomes a carrier of a force that contains
procreative and fortifying components. Closely related to this concept is the ability of the payé to interpret mythical passages,
genealogical recitals, incantatory formulas, dreams, or any signs
and portents a person may have observed. The payé's interpretations thus "shed light" upon these matters, in the strict sense of the
expression. It is of importance, then, that the payé himself be able
to have clear and meaningful hallucinations (D: *yee inyári*/payé-
visions; *gahpí mahsá inyári*/yajé-people-visions). His vision must
not be blurred, his sense of hearing must be acute; that is, he must
be able to distinguish clearly the images that appear to his mind
while in a state of trance, and to understand the supernatural voices
speaking to him. Much of this capacity is, undoubtedly, acquired
over the years, the payé developing his own key of interpretation,
but some of it is said to be already discernible at an early age. The
older people will watch out for any signs a youth may give, and they
will discuss them with an experienced payé.

The formal training of a payé seems to begin rather late, perhaps
at the age of twenty-five. By that time the person is married, has
children, and occupies a well-defined position within the socioeco-
nomic structure of the larger unit. He may already have spent some
months living with a practicing payé, watching him during his
curing ceremonies and trances and learning from him and other

elders certain songs, spells, and incantations. But the real training takes place in isolation, in the company of one or two novices who go to live with a payé of renown for several months, or even a year or more, while receiving his instruction. Thanks to the multi-lingualism of the Vaupés area there are no language barriers, and prolonged sojourns in different regions are a fairly common feature of apprenticeship. The pupil, besides collaborating in his master's household, must pay a fee, perhaps several canoes or a shotgun or, more recently, a large framed mirror or a set of simple carpenter's tools.

First of all, a future payé must acquire a number of material objects he will use later on while officiating. The essence of these objects exists in the celestial sphere, in the House of Thunder (T: *bëhpó vii*), and in a drug-induced trance he must visit thunder (T: *bëhpó mahsë*) and ask for his help. It is thunder himself who gives him the essence—or even the material form—of these objects, designated as "weapons" (T: *uamó*), or who shows the apprentice where to obtain them.

To acquire these "weapons" the master and his pupils go to live for several weeks at an isolated spot in the forest where they build a temporary shelter that contains only the barest commodities such as hammocks, a few cooking utensils, and perhaps a few low wooden stools. No women are allowed to visit the spot. During the daytime the men go hunting, fishing, or gathering—activities, however, that are now strictly limited to certain plant and animal species and are controlled by many precise rules—but in the evenings they will dance and sing, smoke tobacco, and take narcotic drugs, mainly snuff and different yajé portions. It is during the narcotic trance that the power objects "appear"; they "fall out of the sky" and suddenly materialize before the apprentice.[3]

Thunder is closely related to the jaguar-spirit and may occasionally appear in the shape of a roaring jaguar. In the celestial sphere the harpy eagles are thunder's companions and messengers. Thunder wears earpendants (T: *bëhpó pini*) of shiny copper shaped like short tubes split in half. Thunder uses these ear pendants, which sparkle brightly, to produce lightning, and one of the attributes of a payé is the ability to control lightning and to cast a thunderbolt at his enemies. With a rapid circular motion of his arm he "throws" the pendant in the direction of the adversary and lightning will strike him or his property, no matter how far away they may be. These ear pendants, then, must be obtained from thunder. Another important tool of the payé is his gourd rattle, an instrument consisting of a large oval gourd decorated with incised designs, filled with seeds and small pebbles, and provided with a handle. The common gourd rattle used during dances or minor rituals has a straight rod for a handle which pierces the body of the hollow gourd, but a payé's rattle (T: *yaí toáte dëhéri*/payé-rattle-arm) has a handle of irregular shape branching out like a hand or, rather, like deer antlers, and it is made of a very hard reddish wood taken from the root of a water-worn tree submerged in a pool. Thunder will show where to obtain this wood. A small bow and some arrows (T: *behsú*) must be obtained in a similar way to serve as weapons against enemies, just as a diminutive paddle (T: *uahápi*) is used to stir the waters of the river to bring on the dry season. A certain porous stone (T: *ënoyá*) of a brick-red color, used on special occasions for facial paint, must also be obtained from thunder.

The quest for these power objects is difficult and slow. For nights on end the men will sit and chant, asking thunder to favor them with his power. Until, in their trance, they will see a tree, a piece of wood, or a stone and will suddenly know: this is mine, this is what thunder sent me! The drugged apprentice will mumble and groan in his trance. Close by, the payé is sitting. "What do you see? Tell me, what do you see?" he will ask insistently, and the apprentice will try to find words to describe his visions. "There is the bend of the river . . . a black rock . . . I can hear the water rushing. . . ." "Go on, go on!" the payé will insist, his ear close to the other's mouth. "There are birds, red birds, sitting on the lower branches of a tree. . . ." "Are they sitting on your left or on your right?" the payé will ask. And so they continue, haltingly, at times in deep silence, until the older man knows what kinds of images and voices his pupil is perceiving and can now begin to interpret them for him.

An essential part of a payé's equipment consists of a set of stones, so-called thunder-stones (T: *bëhpó ëhtá*). Some of them are used in the curing of different ailments, while others are lethal weapons to be employed against enemies. The principal stones are:[4] *ëhtá doátina ehkóyeka*/stone-patient-medicine, a small yellowish or light-brown chert with a very smooth, often shiny, surface;[5] *ëhtá doátina ëyaké*/stone–patient–look at, a small translucent quartzite of roughly rectangular shape; *ëhtá dëhpoányase miiká*/stone-head-ache-extract, a dark-grey, smooth pebble, about four centimeters in diameter; *ëhtá matína miiká*/stone–madness–draw out, a fairly large (12 cm.) brownish stone with a rough, scaly surface; *mari uahpëi ëyaké*/our enemies–look at–stone, a dark-grey pebble, about six centimeters in diameter; *uaheká ëhtá*/to kill–stone, a pebble similar to the former; *dohasé ëhtá*/to cure–stone, a piece of partly translucent whitish quartzite, about ten centimeters long. The different uses of these stones will be mentioned later.

Another magical tool of the payé consists of a set of sharp thorns or needlelike splinters (T: *uahkári*) of the wood of a palm tree. To "give these weapons" to an apprentice (T: *uamúkapohse*), the payé lays these splinters on the inside of the apprentice's left forearm, then takes the whitish quartz cylinder (T: *ëhtamboha*) that hangs from his neck and, placing it upon the splinters, makes the gesture of pressing them into the flesh. A similar gesture is made with the handle of the gourd rattle, and finally the payé puts his clenched fish upon the spot and blows sharply through it to make the splinters "enter" the arm, where they "disappear." From now on these splinters are thought to be like poisoned arrows which can be shot at an enemy with a violent movement of the arm.[6] The payé also places two small splinters upon the tongue of the apprentice and causes them to "enter" by repeatedly blowing through his fist, which is firmly placed upon the apprentice's mouth. These splinters are necessary to the payé, so that he can suck out the essence of disease from a patient's body, and they act as a counterpoison.

The fine white hairs (T: *yaí uihtó*) from the underbelly of a jaguar, and the fluffy white down (T: *a'apahke uihtó*) from the underside of a harpy eagle, animals that are both closely associated or even identified with Thunder, are put into the apprentice's ear so that he will be able to hear the voices that speak to him in his hallucinatory trance.

While the future payé is thus being initiated and invested with different powers, he and his master spend long hours singing and pronouncing incantations directed to *Vihó-mahsë*, the supernatural master of the narcotic snuff. During the entire period of the novitiate different kinds of yajé are consumed almost daily, and snuff is absorbed regularly because the specific details of a future shaman's knowledge are transmitted to him directly through *Vihó-mahsë*, who is always present and whose voice accompanies the imagery of the hallucinations. Thunder owns a special kind of narcotic snuff (T: *bëhpó vihó*) which is very potent. It comes in the shape of a hard resin, reddish in color, and bits of it are scraped off its surface with a piece of quartzite. This resin, too, must be obtained from thunder and suddenly appears before the men.

There are other elements and spirit-helpers a payé must acquire before he can practice his art.[7] He must obtain a stick rattle (T: *yaí-gë*), the phallic rod by which mankind descended from the sky; a hoe (T: *sió-yahpë*), formed like a wooden hook on the shorter arm of which a stone blade has been fastened with yellowish vegetable fibers; a forked cigarholder (T: *moënó seneno*) of finely carved hardwood in which to put the thick cigar rolled into a Heliconia leaf. He also needs a little wooden stool (T: *yaí-kumuno*/payé's stool, or *gahpí kumuno*/yajé stool). Then there are his snuffing apparatus of bird bone; his feathercrowns; and his seed rattles, which are tied to his ankles when he is dancing. During the entire apprenticeship his master will teach him how to manufacture these objects from raw materials gathered in the forest under his guidance, and while making these tools or adornments the apprentices will continue to sing their songs asking thunder and *Vihó-mahsë* to direct them and to endow the objects with their power. The novice will also learn to select and combine the different narcotic plants and to prepare snuff of different kinds; he will learn to pick the medical and magical herbs growing in the forest that will attract game to the hunter or will make a woman fall madly in love or will kill an enemy. There are herbs to cure diseases or to poison fish and aromatic herbs that can be rubbed on the body or worn in the belt while one is dancing at a gathering. All their different uses the future payé will have to learn.

In the course of his novitiate a payé will sometimes become utterly exhausted by dietary restrictions, lack of sleep, the toxic effects of the drugs he is taking, and by the sheer tension produced by the hallucinatory imagery in which shapes and voices mingle in a confusing and, sometimes, terrifying manner. But this state of extreme physical and psychological stress is said to be a necessary prerequisite and to constitute the true test of a payé's calling.

One last point: an individual cannot become a payé of his own will. He cannot say: "I shall become a payé and shall do this or that." All he can do is expose himself to a shamanistic experience and then observe his own reactions. The shamanistic power cannot be acquired; it bestows itself upon the person. The power selects its bearer, and not the reverse. Some people hear the call, while others do not, no matter how hard they listen in the solitude of their waiting and fasting.

When a newly initiated payé returns to his household, he finds himself in a very peculiar and dangerous state that demands many precautions, both in his own behavior and in that of other people. First of all, sexual abstinence continues to be essential, and all contacts with childbearing or menstruating women have to be avoided. Shortly before a woman has the menses a payé will know it is imminent because in his hallucinations he will see the houseposts dripping with blood and large blood stains covering the floor. He will then tell the woman to leave the house and to retire to a secluded hut in the forest where menstruating women and girls spend these days. Next in importance are further dietary restrictions; for several weeks or months the payé is not allowed to eat meat or any food prepared with peppers, but must consume only thin soups, bits of cassava bread, and some manioc starch. He may eat certain fishes[8] and ants,[9] but he must not eat fat larvae. No roasted food must be prepared in the house, nor should any game animal or fowl be singed nearby, the smoke and smell of both procedures being thought to be extremely harmful to the payé. Even some common food preparations should be avoided for the same reason.

Of special importance is the new payé's extreme sensitiveness to noise. Not only is the playing of panpipes or any other shrill musical instruments prohibited in his presence, but the womenfolk must be specially careful not to make any noise while preparing food. Cooking vessels should be handled carefully and with slow deliberate movements, being set on the fire or on the floor without the slightest sound. Pouring water from one vessel into another should be done with great caution so as to avoid the rush and splatter of the liquid. Basketry trays should be cleaned, not with sharp strokes with the flat of the hand, but with slow sweeping motions. Should there be any undue noise, the payé would become "confounded" (T: *yaí suriáse*); his ears would ring, and the buzzing sounds would drown the supernatural voices that speak to him. His vision would become blurred, the hallucinatory images fading away into meaningless shapes. To avoid all these harmful influences and contaminations the ritual objects of a payé are not kept in his house but are put into barkcloth bags or boxes of reeds which are hidden in a small hut in the forest. Although other people may know the hiding place they would never dare touch these objects. Only when officiating will a payé bring with him the necessary equipment, which, as we have noted, consists of objects so charged with different powers that it would be dangerous to keep them in one's living quarters where, at the same time, they might be exposed to damage and contamination.

Among the many activities of a Tukano shaman, one of the most important refers to his relationships with *Vaí-mahsë*, the supernatural Master of Animals. This spirit-being can manifest itself in many guises, but it is generally imagined, and seen in hallucinations, as a red dwarf, a small person in the attire of a hunter armed with bow and arrow. He is the owner and protector of all animals— fish, game, and all others that dwell in the forest and the rivers— and success in hunting and fishing depends largely upon his good will.[10] *Vaí-mahsë* is a payé in his own right; he owns all the "weapons" a payé obtains from thunder, except the copper ear pendants, and officiates in his realm just as a payé would among his own people. It is important to note here that some payés seem to derive their power mainly from *Vaí-mahsë* and not from *Vihó-mahsë*. They have to obtain *Vaí-mahsë*'s "arrows" (T: *Vaí-mahsë behsú*) and other objects hidden in the underwater houses of the Master of Animals, and the neophyte has to dive into the waters and search for these objects.[11]

The monotonous horizon of the rain forest is broken here and there by small hills, rocky formations with steep walls that rise over the forest like dark islands.[12] These hills, with their cliffs and dark recesses, are thought to be the dwelling places of *Vaí-mahsë*, in the interior of which he presides over the multitude of animals that are his charge, as if the hill were an enormous maloca. In his personification as Master of Fish, *Vaí-mahsë* also dwells at the bottom of the dark pools that form at the foot of the larger rapids. But not only animals inhabit these "houses" (T: *vaí-mahsë vii*); also living inside them are the forest spirit, *boráro* (or Curupíra,[13] as he is commonly called in the Amazon area); the *uahtí*, bush spirits that roam at night in the forest and frighten people with their uncanny noises and uncouth appearance;[14] and the *saaropë*, another category of beings that accompany the Master of Animals. The *saaropë* are creatures described as sometimes appearing in the forest in human shape, small naked people armed with blowguns who frighten the hunter with their sudden presence. Their characteristic means of communication consists in beating rhythmically with a stick against the flat, boardlike aerial roots that buttress the enormous trunks of certain trees, until the roots begin to vibrate with a booming sound. The *saaropë* are very shy and elusive, and quite harmless, but they frighten people in the depths of the forest, vanishing like shadows when approached.[15]

In the beginning of time, when *Pamurí-mahsë*, the "germinator," ascended the rivers of the Vaupés in his canoe in order to establish mankind on earth, he was accompanied not only by representatives of each exogamic group but also by a people called *vearí-mahsá*,[16] human beings who also were to live on this land. But soon the *vearí-mashá* were at odds with *Pamurí-mahsë* and began to quarrel with him about where and how to live on earth. The *vearí-mahsá* were exactly equal in number to the tribal representatives, but they proved to be so bothersome that *Pamurí-mahsë* decided to rid himself of their company. He wanted to kill them, but the Sun Father took pity and banished them to live forever in the hills and pools of *Vaí-mahsë*. There they continue to dwell, but they still represent a great danger to society because they are the exact doubles of all men and women that live on earth; they are the mirror images of mankind, the Doppelgänger, and emerging sometimes from their dark abodes, they sow confusion and terror among people.[17]

Inside the hills, but continually watching all approaches to them, are several animals that serve as sentinels. The bright orange-colored cock of the rock (T: *ënëténo*), the boraro's favored companion, will give warning with his hoarse croaking if any intruder should appear. A spiny-tailed lizard (T: *anyá dëhpoa*),[18] chief of all poisonous reptiles, watches from the crevices, together with his helper, a long-tailed lizard (T: *anyá dëhpoa kabi*),[19] and small green lizards (T: *anyá dëhpoa yasagë* and *anyá diákata*).

Vaí-mahsë, then, presides over a very mixed company composed of animals, spirits, and ghostly people, all of whom are masters of disguise and many of whom are bent upon doing harm to men. When *Vaí-mahsë* is angry he will use his charges to punish people, sending them diseases or poisonous snakes, or perhaps a jaguar or a devouring bush spirit. The game animals, at least certain species, will take men's weapons and will retaliate by shooting their arrows at the hunter, who will then become the victim of a disease.

It is the payé's task to maintain good relations with all these creatures, and to obtain from *Vaí-mahsë* the game and fish needed by
his people. Contact with the Master of Animals is established during hallucinatory trance and through the intermediation of *Vihó-
mahsë*, the Master of Snuff. The payé, lying in his hammock, will
absorb the narcotic powder and, in his trance, will ascend to the
Milky Way, the abode of *Vihó-mahsë*. With the latter's help he then
enters the hill where the Master of Animals dwells, and there they
begin to bargain for food or medicinal herbs, for vengeance upon
enemies or for a successful hunting season. The representatives of
the celestial, subterranean, and underwater dimensions thus meet
with the payé and, in a trance combined with songs and dances,
will now decide the destiny of men.

A hill inhabited by *Vaí-mahsë* is imagined as having four doors
located at the cardinal points. Near the northern entrance are the
jaguar-spirits and the poisonous *diaso* (T) snakes;[20] near the
eastern entrance, the *uahtí* spirits, the *vearí-mahsá*, and the *saaropë*
people; near the western door are the *boráro* and the *uahkéni-mana*
(T)—the latter noxious worms that destroy the fields and carry
diseases—together with the *piroa* (T) snakes. In his trance, the
payé arrives at the hill and approaches the northern entrance,
where he knocks three times with his stick rattle. From inside
Vaí-mahsë's voice asks: "What is it you want?" "I want food!" is the
payé's reply. Now the door opens before him and he enters the hill.
Inside, along the walls and on the rafters and beams, innumerable
animals are crouching as if asleep. In a corner several *boraro*-spirits
are sitting, somnolent and with hunched shoulders; jaguars and
snakes are lying on the floor, and brightly colored birds sit on the
rafters. "Take whatever you need!" says *Vaí-mahsë*. The payé fills
two large baskets with certain species of game animals and carries
them to the door. There the animals awaken as if from a stupor and
scurry away into the forest, always in pairs, a male and a female.
The payé returns for more and, with the help of *Vihó-mahsë*, carries two more baskets to the door. But, at the same time, when he is
taking the baskets out into the open, some noxious animals, too,
will escape from the hill and, always in pairs, will stray into the
forest—jaguars, snakes, and maybe a couple of bush spirits. The
game animals the payé sets free in the forest (T: *yaí ënë viori
uemi*/payé–forest–turn loose) are beings of flesh and blood, ready
prey for the hunter, but those that escape are spirit-animals. They
are clad in animal skins (T: *suti*), but inside they are hollow, filled

with air. These animals are very dangerous to the hunter because they cannot be killed but, in the form of snakes, jaguars, or other beasts, can do great harm to people. They are *Vaí-mahsë's* messengers and tools who punish people for their misbehavior, especially those hunters who fail to carry out all the necessary ritual preparations, such as observing dietary restrictions and sexual abstinence.

In exchange for the game animals, the payé must pay a fee, not so much to *Vaí-mahsë*[21] as to *Vihó-mahsë*, the intermediary. The payment consists of living people who now must die so that their spirits may enter *Vaí-mahsë's* domain. In his hallucinatory trance the payé kills these victims, whom he sees in the shapes of birds (which embody the life-essence of people) sitting on the rafters of the hill-house he visits. With the exception of personal enemies, a payé will rarely kill a relative, at least not in this manner and for these ends, but rather someone from a group living far away. And, when eventually news reaches him that, in a certain region, some people have died, he will know that his accounts with *Vihó-mahsë* are settled. The choice of a person who has to die is made by *Vihó-mahsë* himself, and he will tell the payé "who is paid for," that is, whose death corresponds to the kind and amount of game animals obtained.

Male initiation rites are of considerable importance among the Tukano, and occasionally several payés will be present to supervise their different phases and proceedings. It is usual for a fairly large group of boys to be initiated at the same time, their ages ranging from ten to fifteen years, and for this reason initiation rituals are not very frequent events. The term by which the group of initiates is designated is *amóa mahsá*/menstruation-people (T), and, as a matter of fact, the boys are compared to girls; it is pointed out to them that they will be in imminent danger of menstruating if they do not follow in detail the requisites demanded from them. The group of boys remains under the personal and continuous supervision of two or more men, at least one of whom should be a payé and the others well versed in the details of ritual procedure. Sometimes these men wear large dresses of painted barkcloth combined with masks that cover their faces and bodies. They represent spirit-beings (T: *amóyeri uahtí*/menstruation-spirit), and it is from them that the boys must learn their new duties as full-fledged members of society. During this period of initiation the boys must not see any women, and it therefore becomes necessary that the women of the household go to live somewhere else, or that the boys and their teachers establish themselves in isolation in an abandoned house or a temporary shelter.

The initiates must rise well before dawn and gather at the landing for their daily ritual of purification. The payé prepares large quantities of a strong emetic by scraping the bark from the *papuvárida* vine and mixing it with cold water. Each boy must drink from one to three bowls of the foamy blackish brew, until his stomach becomes visibly expanded, and then he must press his abdomen with both hands and vomit in the river. The extension of the foamy blotches that begin to float on the water is interpreted as a good omen. While bathing the boys "drum" on the water, making a hollow splashing sound by stirring the water with both arms. Occasionally they will cleanse themselves by absorbing drops of fresh chili peppers through the nose, using for this a small funnel made of a leaf. After these morning baths, sometimes also in the evening, the boys are whipped by their masked companions, with long thin rods similar to fishing rods, while the men shout *mamamamamá*/take![22] The swishing strokes with the thin elastic rods soon raise blistering welts on the backs, chests, and arms of the boys, who have to control all expression of pain and stand motionless before their teachers. The boys now return from the landing to the house but soon leave again, still before sunrise, and retire to a hut at a secluded spot in the forest where they will spend the day. On the way they play their small panpipes, of the kind called *mëhte-poro* (T), which are used only by boys. They are allowed to take with them small vessels of manioc starch, but otherwise they have to observe very strict dietary restrictions. During the daytime the boys go fishing and gathering, always accompanied by the men, but they may eat only certain small fishes, ants, wasps, and fruit. At nightfall they return once more to the house but are allowed hardly more than two or three hours of sleep, after which they must begin once more the daily round with their purification at the landing place.

This life continues for about one month, sometimes more, and during this period the boys are taught the songs, dances, and incantatory formulas all adult men must know. Special care is taken with the teaching of long and detailed spells in which exhaustive series of ants, wasps, larvae, peppers, tobacco, coca, and fish are enumerated and conjured so that they will not harm their future consumers.[23] After each category of these potential foods, condiments, and narcotics has been enumerated, with many details of size and color quoted, the category's constituents are magically deprived of their heads, teeth, stings, pincers, sharp fishbones and so forth, as the case may be, and these injurious parts are then exorcised with a special formula by which they are "mixed with yajé foam"/*gahpí soporo,* and thus neutralized.[24] The payé also prepares a special cigar (T: *mëëopëë*) the boys must smoke after he has said several spells over it. The main theme of these formulas is the preoccupation that the boys "might become like women, and begin to menstruate." The mythical origin and ritual use of the *yuruparí* flutes[25] is also taught, and the boys are instructed in the manufacture of these instruments. In the evening, when returning to the house, or sometimes in the early morning, they will play these instruments, walking up and down before the maloca or at the landing.

Once the seclusion in the forest is over, the boys return to the house, and with them the womenfolk. A new period begins, now within the household and in the company of several families. A girl who has not yet reached puberty prepares the boys' food, but they still can eat only cassava bread, starch, and a few cooked dishes prepared without peppers. No game may be eaten by them, and, in fact, only after marriage are they allowed to eat meat regularly. Every evening for about one month the boys consume narcotic potions prepared from a special vine called *kumuárida gahpí* (T) and administered only by a payé. This yajé is said to produce predominantly blue-colored hallucinations, and the payé now teaches his pupils how to interpret these visions, how to diagnose certain common diseases, and what spells to pronounce over food so that it may do no harm. Once this second period is over *cashirí* beer is prepared and now the boys can wear the feathercrowns of adult men for the first time and also play larger panpipes. From now on they can get married, eat food prepared with peppers, and take an active part in the periodic gatherings between neighbors. In any case, now they can have sexual relations, and the older ones will soon be looking for suitable marriage partners.[26]

The couvade is common practice among the Tukano. The father of a newly born child must interrupt his daily activities, observe a special diet, and remain inside or, at least, near the house for several days. He should not go hunting or fishing and should even avoid touching his weapons or fishing gear. The reason for this behavior is that *Vaí-mahsë* becomes extremely jealous at the birth of a child and might take revenge by harming his father. *Vaí-mahsë* is known to take a strong sexual interest in human affairs and to be attracted to women who go alone into the forest. At the birth of a child it falls to the payé to protect the family against any aggression from the Master of Animals. In a hallucinatory trance the payé constructs several fences (T: *misa*) of strong canes[27] around the house and the threatened family so that *Vaí-mahsë* cannot see them (T: *mahsá-pona vaí-mahsë yábuhkatina*/childbearing-people–*vaí-mahsë*–cannot see). The names of the fences the payé conjures (T: *ihkípini misa, buhpú misa, doropó misa,* and others) always indicate the cane or palm tree used in the construction. This imaginary fencing-in is then followed by long incantatory spells in which *Vaí-mahsë* is "turned around" so that he will face in another direction and go back to his abode. The formulas continue with the payé quoting at great length a number of delicious *cashirí* preparations *Vaí-mahsë* will find ready when he returns home.[28] The severity of the restrictions placed upon a father may vary according to his knowledge of magical spells. A man who knows a few incantatory songs against *Vaí-mahsë* will pronounce them, smoke his cigar, blow the smoke over his body and weapons, and thus will be able to continue his accustomed way of life without having to call a payé.

Many of a payé's activities are concerned with the curing of disease. Tobacco smoke, splashing with water, the sucking out of pathogenic substances, and lengthy incantations are all standard practice and are, in many cases, accompanied by the use of narcotic drugs. It is during his hallucinations that a payé can diagnose a disease, know its cause, discuss its treatment with *Vihó-mahsë*, and learn the correct formulas he has to pronounce over the patient. Sometimes the patient, too, must take a hallucinogenic drug, and he will then describe his visions to the payé, in search of clues to the causes and adequate treatment of the affliction. The curing ceremony usually takes place outside the house and in the daytime, the latter for the simple reason that evil spirits are less likely to wander about in daylight than after nightfall. The phases of the moon do not have any importance, but a sudden shower may be taken for an evil omen and the ceremony might be interrupted.

The different thunder-stones (T: *bëhpó ëhtá*) mentioned earlier are essential in the curing ritual. The yellow chert (T: *ëhtá doátina ahkóyeka*) is clasped together with the handle of the gourd rattle in the right hand, the power of the stone being thus transmitted to the rattle, which is agitated close to the patient's body. Yellow is a color with a seminal symbolism, and in many curing rituals white or yellowish objects such as stones, hairs, down, or cotton are used or conjured to lend their fertilizing and fortifying power to the sick person. The translucent stone (T: *ëhtá doátina ëyaka*) is held between thumb and forefinger as if it were a lens, and the payé will move it slowly close to the body of the patient and watch for sudden reflections or subtle changes in translucency. Once by means of his supposed extravisual ability the payé has located with precision the essence of the disease, the stone is laid upon the spot and the payé places his clenched fist on it, thumb upward, and he then sucks the air sharply through it in order to extract the disease, generally an intrusive object sent by an enemy. The essence thus extracted sometimes takes a visible form—that of a thorn, a hair, or a grain of sand—and the payé will show this object to his patient, displaying it on the palm of his hand before he throws it away with an exorcising formula. The sucking and spitting-out of pain and disease-causing matters or essences are processes that might take many hours or even days, the payé singing and smoking, taking *vihó* and yajé, and retiring once in a while to his hammock to consult in his hallucinations with *Vihó-mahsë*.

Many diseases are treated with ablutions of tepid water in which certain herbs have been prepared. Large vessels or earthenware dishes are placed on the floor, and the payé will splash the water over the patient's body will reciting his incantations and blowing tobacco smoke over the water and the afflicted body part. In the treatment of what are considered to be mental diseases[29] it is common practice for the patient, too, to take fairly large doses of narcotic drugs, generally *vihó* or *vaí-gahpí*, the strong "fish yajé." At the same time the payé mixes lukewarm water with the leaves of different plants[30] and pours it over the patient. During the treatment the payé often talks at length with his patient, mainly about the latter's enemies and sexual imbroglios, giving him to understand that the causes of his disease are to be sought more in the quality of his relations with other people than in organic disorders. The payé will explain that tensions in interpersonal relations are very "weakening" and make the person prone to attacks by *Vaímahsë* or other spirit-beings. These conversations are never public, however, and a payé will be very careful not to go into details and discuss names or specific animosities. In the treatment of some of these cases certain medical herbs are not taken by mouth or used in a bath but instead are kneaded into a damp mass from which drops are squeezed into the eye of the patient, two of each herb into each eye, once at midmorning and again in the early afternoon. These herbs should be collected before dawn and prepared while still fresh. It is essential that the payé collecting them should have abstained from food for several hours before, and that he recite the respective incantations while picking the herbs, walking from east to west and back to east. In many of these curing rituals it seems that the recital of incantations is the most important part of the act. The mere administration of herbal medicines, without lengthy spells and songs, is thought to be ineffective and even dangerous.

According to the season, that is, according to the availability or abundance of certain foods, the payé must recite spells that will protect the consumer of these provisions from any harm. The formulas employed refer in great detail to different kinds of food-stuffs—say, fishes, honey, or edible insects—and to the exorcising of all evil consequences their consumption might have. Similar spells must be pronounced over the food to be consumed by persons who are in a special and dangerous transition, such as during initiations and childbearing, or on the occasion of a young hunter's killing his first prey.

We have mentioned several times the importance of magical spells and incantations. These songs or formulas are not always the exclusive privilege of a payé; many of them can be learned and used by any man. In fact, the payés often complain that some people are negligent in this matter and will often pay too little attention to the learning of adequate spells, thus exposing themselves and their families to accidents or diseases which could have been avoided.

A Desana payé, when asked for an effective incantation against the wiles of the Master of Game Animals, provided the following text:

"When the masters of the game appear, they make us fall ill. Their *cashirí* beer is made of *umarí* fruit.[31] They also drink *cashirí* of groundnuts and of *nyahiamara*.[32] When they gather these fruits they appear near our malocas. When they thus appear, they make us fall ill. They give us to eat the transformed fish of *diroá-mahsë*.[33] This is why people have bad dreams. They make us eat these fish, and we eat them in our dreams. All sorts of fish appear in our dreams. All sorts of animals. Also all sorts of birds. Seeing this, the Masters of Game Animals appear near our malocas. For this reason we fall ill. They all drink *cashirí* made with swampy water and with clayey water. In our dreams they make us drink this. This is why we dream, confusedly, that we are drinking *cashirí*. In this way they diminish our life. This is how we fall ill. Their arrows are made of boa bones. They are adorned with the feathers of the oropendola bird, of the macaw, and of the parrot. The arrow is made of red and black boa bones. The arrows have black feathers of the oropendola bird. They arrive carrying small flutes and large flutes. They also carry red, white, and black blowguns. The masters of the game come playing their instruments. In our dreams, when we drink *cashirí*, they make us play music.

"Therefore, by anointing it with milk and with *tooka*,[34] they [the people] resist them. They resist the crowd of people, and touch them with milk and banish it. They anoint their *cashirí* vessels with milk and banish them. They anoint their *puuveherinyee*[35] ornaments with milk and banish them to where the sun is. They leave them up there. They anoint the arrow of boa bone with milk and throw it up there. This, too, they send to where the sun is. The blowgun, too, goes to where the sun is. All these things they anoint with milk and send them to where the sun is. They take away their hoes. They have splinters of the tree with green leaves and white leaves, of the *koragë*[36] river. With these the masters of the game want to hurt us. Therefore the splinters of the hoes are anointed with milk and with *tooka*, so they won't do harm, and they grasp them and resist the crowd. They leave them on the bench of the sun. When they [the masters] carry these, they are fierce, it is said. For canoes they have the bark of the tree of the opossum. With these canoes they arrive at our landing places. When they arrive, they tie their canoes to the houseposts. Then the food they eat arrives. They have vessels of green flowers and of red flowers. Their eating utensils, too, are the same. They invite us to eat from these vessels.

"By anointing the vessels with *tooka* and with milk, they get rid of them. They get rid of them leaving them in their canoes. They have the same kind of food vessels as we have. Soft vessels;[37] they, too, have them. They get rid of them by anointing them with *tooka* and with milk. By anointing them with milk and with *tooka* they resist them. Pushing them toward them, and grasping them, they push them into canoes. They tie up the canoes with the white rope and with the *piasaba*[38] rope. They get rid of them by anointing them with *tooka* and with milk, and by grasping them firmly. Grasping the canoe and anointing it with milk and with *tooka*, they push it away. There are splinters of white quartz, of red light, and of greenish light. They have splinters of transparent stone as well as of white and red stone. Pushing off the canoe they throw the splinters of stone into it and push again. With these splinters they destroy the canoe and make it sink. That is all" (Text No. 181).

In this recital, the supernatural Masters of the Game are described, quite realistically, as people, as a group of uninvited guests who arrive in their canoes carrying blowguns, darts, and hoes, playing their musical instruments, and bearing gifts of food. In other words, the spirit-beings are described in exactly the same terms as those one would use to describe a group of visitors from another maloca who came to celebrate an exogamic alliance. But these gift-bearing visitors are evil; they bring diseases to their hosts, who perceive them in their dreams. They are dream visitors, nightmares, and the dreamers fall ill as soon as they partake of the food offered to them.

The symbolic meaning of this visitation is not too difficult to understand. We must consider first of all the quality of the food the visitors are offering. *Cashirí* prepared from *umarí* fruit has a female connotation and figures prominently in several myths as a female element pertaining to "other" people. In some myths it is Tapir who is the Master of *Umarí*, and Tapir dwells above the Yurupari Falls, outside the Tukano territory. *Cashirí* beers prepared from groundnuts and *nyahiamara* (a kind of yam) is also associated with a female principle belonging to "other people," and they are not used by the the Tukano, as far as we know. These kinds of intoxicating "female" beverages, made with "dirty" water, are then pathogenic substances. Other foods the guests offer in that dreamlike state are fish, game, and fowl, many of them female elements in the sense in which the hunter's prey is always "female," the act of hunting being a kind of courtship during which the animals become enamored and finally submit to the hunter.[39] In summary, the visitors only pretend to be a group of people offering women in an alliance ritual; in reality they are deceivers trying to harm their hosts. The exorcism which follows includes all objects owned by the visitors: cooking vessels, weapons, ornaments, and the shamanistic paraphernalia of the deceivers. In fact, the cooking vessels represent women, the verb for cooking being a euphemism for sexual intercourse. All these objects are now banished by anointment with milk (*ahpikón*) and with the juice of the *tooka* plant, both seminal elements.

Another description of a spell, also referring to diseases sent by the Master of Game, describes the payé effecting his cure in a yajé trance. The spell is described thus:

"When seeing this [the diseases] the shaman takes 'fish-yajé.' When he is intoxicated he begins to sing. When he is singing thus he ascends to the rainbow. The shaman carriers a rattle adorned with the feathers of the oropendola bird. With this rattle he attracts all things. He attracts all the splinters and stones toward himself. With the rattle and with his shaman's stones he banishes the disease. Then he blows with his cigar that contains the spell. The splinters and stones become visible to him. In these cases he simply grasps them and throws them away. We, too, can see the splinters and stones. Over there in Carurú there were some. The splinters were of *patabá*[40] wood. These splinters have different colors: white, red, and whitish. It is the fever that causes the vomiting. A bit farther down [on the rattle] there are feathers of the toucan bird; not in a bundle, but like a sprout. This little thing causes us to have fits. The splinters make us feel sharp pains. There are other, similar splinters. On another splinter there is a bushel of hair, like a sprout. It is not tied into a bundle; it is like a sprout. On the other side it is yellow and yellowish. This splinter, too, causes fever and vomiting. One begins to vomit blood and then death comes. The one who leaves [sends] these things, talks like this, so whatever he wishes will happen. He buries these things at the landing. Under the effect of yajé the shaman sings and makes these things descend. He sees these things, high up, and with his rattle he orders them to depart. He blows tobacco smoke over the splinters and grasps them; these things are dangerous. If he did not extract them, they would grow. These splinters make the thread of feathers grow, a long thread. When they see this thread, those who command the thunder come with the thunder. When this happens, there will be fever, and vomiting and fits. When this happens there appear many fish and many Masters of Fish. Wherever a fish trap has been set, it will be full of fish. In this way, under the cover of this, they banish the disease to the Place of Lake Umarí. The fever vessel, too, they throw there. The vessel is similar to our yajé vessel. The lid, too, is similar. In there are the creatures of fever, the mosquitoes. When the lid is taken off, they emerge and sting people. White people do not know anything about all this" (Text No. 179).

Again, there is a female element involved: the vessel. A vessel full of disease is a well-known metaphor among the Desana and, generally, represents a forbidden marriage partner. Sometimes it is said of an evil payé that he will hide such a vessel near a maloca or the landing place of an enemy, who then will be "stung by mosquitoes."

Apart from the splinters of palm wood, hair is said to be an important pathogenic substance, especially monkey hair, a metaphor for pubic hair. The following Desana spell refers to this:

"There exists a confused mass of hair from the *guamo* monkey. This mass must be anointed with *tooka* and with milk in order to get rid of it. It is banished then to the River of Milk. There are white *guamo* monkeys. Their hair is also anointed with *tooka* and with milk, and thus anointed, it can be gotten rid of. It is banished to the River of Milk. It is done the same with all others [kinds of monkeys]. With the nocturnal monkey one does the same. Also with the bush dog. All this is sent to the River of Milk. Thus all the monkeys leave. This hairy mass entangles people. Then there are the birds. They, too, are sent to the River of Milk. Then there is the tangle of tapir hair. One makes incantations against the headache. One invokes the the sun and the rainbow. There are many rainbows, red like fire. This is why one becomes dizzy. Anointing the entangled mass with milk, it can be taken off and banished. If one knows how to do this, the headache is made to disappear."

Many diseases are attributed to these fuzzy masses of hair, or also to a kind of tissue or web which is thought to cover the patient and to separate him from his environment or from life itself. The cure consists in penetrating and taking off this tissue, often said to consist of hairs or feathers of certain animals which are the tools of the malevolent spirit-beings. This tissue is called *suriró*/garment, covering (D), and the verb *suriri* means to cover oneself with something or to wrap oneself into something. The same verb is used to express the idea of getting entangled, for example, in vines or branches. The noun *suriró* can be employed to designate any kind of dress: a shirt, a loincloth, a barkcloth, mask, or anything wrapped around the body. Moreover, the same noun is used to express the idea of being in a state of something, of being *invested* with something. To be in a state of disease is *doremoári suriró* (D), literally, to be "dressed in disease."

When speaking here of pathogenic monkey hair, several kinds of monkeys are referred to. The generic name for monkey is *gahkí* (D), a common synonym for penis. To "choke on monkey hair," a fairly common symptom of certain respiratory diseases, means, symbolically, a forbidden intercourse, the consequence of which is disease, not in a physical sense, but in a social and psychological one. Generally, two monkeys are mentioned. One is the *mere-siáme* (D), the *guamo* monkey—from *mere/guamo* (*Inga* sp.)—a small brownish monkey whose favorite food is the *guamo* fruit, which because of its white and gelatinous flesh has a seminal connotation. It is one of the complex of wild-growing fruits that symbolize fertility because of their textures, colors, and "sweet taste." The pods convey the idea of uterine covering, and the disposition of the fruits in rows is compared to a line of descent. The other monkey is *ukuámë* (D), a brown nocturnal monkey that feeds on insects, that is, an animal in many aspects opposed to the *guamo* monkey. The black bush dog is also said to be associated with a seminal concept because of a small yellow patch of hair on its neck. Red-headed birds (ducks, woodpeckers) are often associated with phallic concepts, while the tapir, the Master of Umarí, represents virility because of its large genitals.

The cure itself, then, consists in a repetition of the sex act, executed in symbolic form by the payé. The juice of *tooka* is semen, and while pronouncing the spell, the payé alludes to its "sweetness" and "honeylike" texture, both common epithets for sperm.

November is the last month of the rainy season, and it is at this time of year that the payés are said to prepare special gatherings. A group of men, perhaps three or four of them, will ask a payé to teach them how to cure certain diseases or how to harm their enemies, and then, in the company of their master, they will retire to a secluded spot in the forest where they will live in a temporary shelter and prepare themselves for the event.

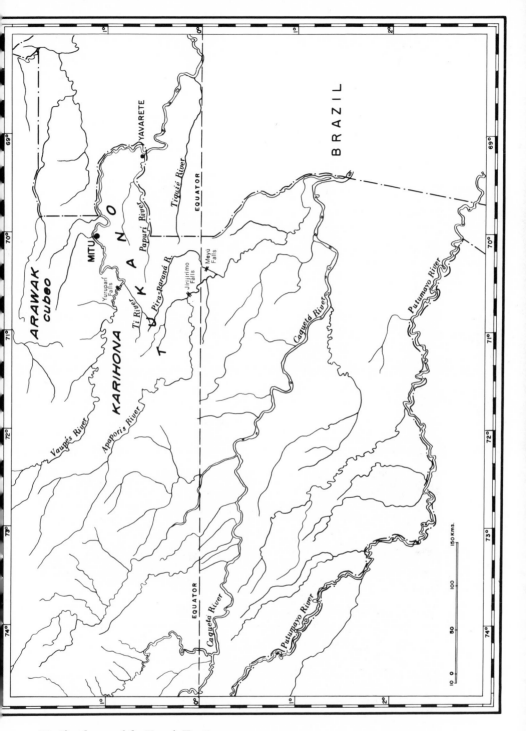

18. Sketch map of the Vaupés Territory

19. The Vaupés River
during the dry season

20. Cuyucuyú Falls;
Pira-paraná

19

20

21. Painted shaman's stool (length, 52 cm.); Desana Indians, Vaupés River

22. Tatuyo Indians with ocelot skin; Pira-paraná

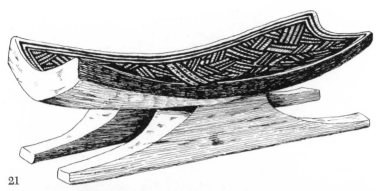

21

22

24. A mask of painted
barkcloth; Cubeo Indians,
Querarí River

25. Taibano hunter with
blowgun and quiver;
Pira-paraná

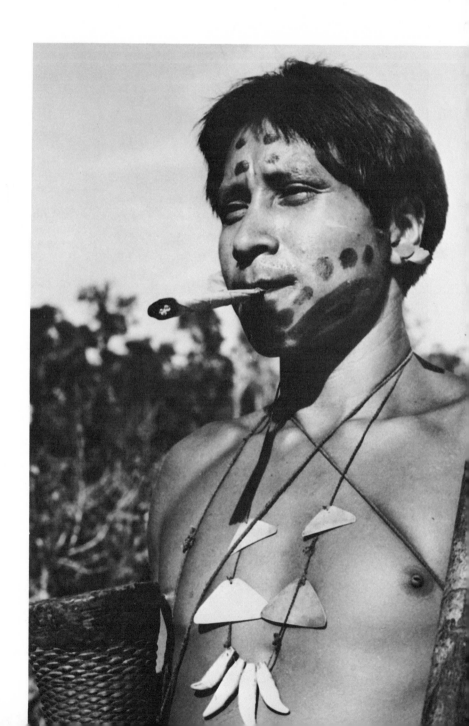

After the heavy rains that fall in October, the trees and shrubs are now in full bloom, and the damp forest is aglow with flowers and many-colored leaves, butterflies, and buzzing insects. This is said to be a propitious time to learn about medicinal and magical herbs, to watch the animals, and to collect remedies under the guidance of an expert. The men who accompany the payé will now tell him their personal worries, and once they have turned over to him their payment in shotguns, tools, or whatever has been arranged to that effect, the payé will ask them: "What is it you want to learn? To cure a patient or to kill an enemy?" One after another he will ask his companions, and each will explain his needs. This conversation is intended not so much to keep the payé informed of his pupils' desires as to convey the necessary information to *Vihó-mahsë*, who will be the intermediary and supernatural helper, and who is listening to what the men are saying.

In November, a strange-looking insect makes its appearance in the forests of the Vaupés. It is a large cicada[41] with grey-mottled wings and long snow-white streamers of a waxy substance on its body. The Indians say that this cicada sings *dari-dari-dari-yooo*. It is this buzzing, chirping sound that announces the coming of the dry season and the time for important shamanistic practices.

The wax-streamered cicada is called *iyá-mahsë*/worm-person (T), and November is *iyán dëhpóa* (T), the time of the worm. In fact, during this month there appear large numbers of blackish caterpillars, many of the edible, and it is *iyá-mahsë*, the white-tailed cicada, that is their master. There are many songs and tales referring to this event; of how the cicadas arrive in their celestial canoes, with the rainbow, and how they descend to earth and begin their song.

The payé and his companions now prepare themselves. First, they paint their faces with the powdered *ënoyá* (T) stone obtained from thunder—on the forehead a cross with a point in each angle, and on each cheek a triangle pointing downward and divided into two equal parts by a vertical line. Chanting and smoking tobacco, the payé now mixes a small quantity of the waxy streamers of a cicada with his *vihó*, adding a small amount of powder scraped off a whitish stone called *bëhpóta* (T), thunder-excrement.[42] But before absorbing the narcotic snuff, a special yajé potion has to be prepared from *vaí-gahpidá*/fish-yajé,[43] which is said to be extremely strong. At about midmorning each man drinks three small cups of this yajé, all the time singing and smoking, and after a while the payé will ask his companions: "What do you see?" The first visions are blurred; it is like smoke arising from nowhere, ascending slowly like a wall before their eyes. They now take their snuffing tubes and absorb the *vihó* mixture. Lying in their hammocks they now feel that they are ascending to the Milky Way. The payé chants: "Now we come to cure these people; now we come to kill these people; now we shall kill our enemies!" *Vihó-mahsë* replies with a loud thunderclap. But no rain is falling; it is noon and there are hardly any clouds in the sky, but rolling thunder announces *Vihó-mahsë's* presence and his willingness to guide the men on their quest for supernatural power. The ascent to the Milky Way is not easily accomplished. An apprentice will hardly ever be able to rise immediately to this sublunary region but, rather, will learn to do so only after many trials. At first he will barely rise over the horizon; the next time, perhaps, he will reach a point corresponding to the position of the sun at 9 A.M., then at 10 A.M., and so on, until at last, in a single soaring flight, he will rise to the zenith.

For weeks, perhaps a month or even more, the men continue to take the narcotic drugs, and the payé interprets to them their visions. To the left, the *uahtí* spirits will appear, threatening from the dark, but to the right there will be brilliant lights like huge torches, and in their radiance will appear the shapes of plants, of earthenware vessels filled with medicinal potions, gourd cups filled with draughts, and other objects, all demonstrating how this or that disease might be cured. And all the time the voice of *Vihó-mahsë* will speak to them, answering the payé's questions; explaining, exhorting, teaching, showing them herbs and poisons and telling them how to use them.

From the Milky Way the men now descend to *Vaí-mahsë's* abode in the hills, still in the company of *Vihó-mahsë*. There they learn how to command poisonous snakes to kill their adversaries. The hoe (T: *sióyahpë*) will turn into an *anyá* snake, while the seed rattles (T: *kihtió*) will become a rattlesnake; gesturing as if throwing the hoe or the rattles in the direction of the enemy, one frees the snake essence, and it will hurry forth to attack the victim. Such spirit-snakes cannot be killed, nor is there any antidote against their venom; they appear to be snakes, being clad in their skins, but beneath the skins they are hollow, devoid of flesh and bones. In the hill-house there are also many birds; those sitting on the rafters to the right contain the life-essences of one's kinsmen, while those on the left represent one's allies.[44] And while the men are looking at all these animals and objects the payé explains: "If you kill this bird, you kill a man," or "If you steal a man's snail-flute, you kill him." In one section of *Vaí-mahsë's* house are the skins and disguises (T: *suti*) of all kinds of animals—snakes, peccaries, jaguars, even of the *boráro* and the *veari-mahsá*, the doubles. The payé now shows his pupils how, with motions of their hoes, they can seize these skins and throw them over their bodies with rapid gestures, to roam in the forest under the disguise of these animals or spirits.

The shamanistic reunions celebrated in November play a major role in Tukano culture. They provide periodic occasions for relieving the pent-up tensions and anxieties of many people, who afterward feel secure and relaxed once more. The supernatural powers they have acquired and displayed during these sessions provide a sense of superiority and personal satisfaction which restores a lost or threatened equilibrium. When the participants return once more to their houses they have learnt to cure and to kill, and, should the occasion then arise, they will readily put this new knowledge to use.

The practice of aggressive sorcery aimed at harming·or killing personal adversaries occupies all payés. Not all of them, however, are really so inclined, but often they will yield to pressure, and many consider the practice of aggressive magic to be an unavoidable part of their office. Thunder and lightning play an important part in these matters. Thunder wears a yellow snake (T: *ëmoanopa*) for a belt, and sometimes he will tear it off furiously and cast it down through the clouds. The payé will have to show this snake and will have to learn to control it, to cast its essence upon an enemy. When a thunderstorm approaches, a payé will prepare himself by taking narcotic snuff in order to consult *Vihó-mahsë*. Who is it that sent this thunderstorm? When lightning strikes nearby, the payé hurries to the spot and examines the ground with the hope of finding some chips of translucent quartzite, the splinters of the thunderbolt of the enemy. Sometimes he will be able to recognize from them their owner, and then he will "return" them to him with *Vihó-mahsë's* help, throwing them with violent gestures in the direction of the enemy's house or landing place.

A particular fiendish way of taking one's revenge consists in causing the enemy to become the victim of a mental disease. It is said that during the dry season, at noon, a white foamy liquid exudes from small round holes in certain rock formations. This liquid (T: *ënëndi*/hill-blood) is said to cause madness. To gather this substance a payé must take precautions that consist in first collecting certain spiny leaves (T: *bara-nima piótase*) from three plants of different sizes, first on the eastern side of the hill, next on the western side, and once more on the eastern side.[45] The leaves and bits of bark of the same plants are kneaded together into a mass from which a drop is squeezed into each eye with the aid of a small funnel made of another leaf. This will protect the payé from going mad himself when he touches the liquid. The *ënëndi* foam is then collected in a small piece of barkcloth. The dried foam, or "blood," is mixed with tobacco, which might then be offered to an unwary enemy or sprinkled on his clothing or hammock. A more recently developed way is to smear the substance on the back end of an electric torch and, at night, suddenly flash the beam of light on the back of the unsuspecting victim.

A number of spells also exist that are aimed at "fencing in" an enemy's heart. Wooden fences of spiny branches or densely interwoven reeds are built around the victim, who suffocates under their increasing pressure.

There is no "natural" death in Tukano culture; death and disease are always regarded as the consequence of evil magic exercised by an enemy. And there is plenty of proof that one's enemies are busy: disease, accidents, crop failure, or a bad hunting or fishing season are constant reminders of their presence. In these circumstances it is perfectly reasonable to be constantly aware of one's foes and to try to get the better of them. It is a matter of gaining time, of killing or frightening one's enemies in the most effective way until, at last, one falls victim to the ruses of a stronger foe.

Enmities between payés lead to dramatic persecutions, duels, encounters and fights, all acted out in the hallucinatory sphere. The two contestants, both lying in deep trances in their respective houses, will meet in any dimension—the sky, the water, a hill, or under the earth. They will cast thunderbolts at each other, or disguise themselves as poisonous snakes or snarling jaguars. Using his spells a payé might build a "stone fence" (T: *ëhtambo imisa*) around his enemy's heart (T: *yaí heri-pona*) and close it in from all sides until the victim's world becomes smaller and smaller and no room is left in which to hide. The victim might turn into a tiny insect, but once the universe has reached the size of an orange, no

escape is possible any longer, and he is at the mercy of his perse-
cutor.[46] Other spells make the victim suffocate inside a steadily
diminishing world. Lying in his hammock, in a hallucinatory trance,
the payé will suddenly drop to the floor and die, his death attributed
to a heavy blow of his enemy's hoe, aimed at the neck. Occasionally
a fight between a payé and a *kumú* will take these dramatic forms;
the *kumú*, using a special formula (T: *uetíro*), turns into water and
disappears underground, while the payé seeks refuge in *Vaí-
mahsë's* houses, in the hills or in a rapid; or in the House of Thunder, in the sky.

The native term for payé, *ye'e* (D) or *yaí* (T), is derived from
the verb *ye'eri*/ to cohabit. It is the same name under which the
jaguar is known. The phallic attributes of the payé's office are obvious. In the first place, *Vaí-mahsë's* houses in the hills or under the
water are, in all essence, uterine deposits, an idea well recognized
by the Indians, and the payé's penetration into these womblike
abodes carries the connotation of a fertilizing act. Occasionally a
payé might even cohabit with the female game animals that inhabit
a hill and are "like people." *Vaí-mahsë* and *Vihó-mahsë* will sometimes celebrate a *dabucurí*, wherein the animals dance and sing in
human shape, drink yajé, and behave in every respect like human
beings. Quite often a payé, in his trance, will participate in these
feasts, to which a great fertilizing power is attributed. Sometimes
the supernatural inhabitants of a hill will have their dance outside
it, in a clearing in the nearby forest, and it is said that afterward
one might find on these spots a weapon or an ornament lost during
the tumultous dance. Soon afterward there will be a notable increase in the number of game animals in the forest, yet another
proof of the idea that *Vaí-mahsë's* dances are fertility rituals the
animals celebrate.

In the second place, the payé's stick rattle is a phallic rod from
which, according to the Creation Myth, the Sun Father's sperm
dropped down to earth. The cylinder of whitish quartzite the payé
wears suspended from his neck is called the "sun's penis" (D: *abé
yeeru*). The hoe is a phallic weapon, the yellow fibers fastening
the blade to the shaft being interpreted as sperm. *Vaí-mahsë*, the
"red dwarf," has the same characteristics in his realm, and his sexual activity is not limited to the propagation of animal species but
extends to the human sphere, just as a payé's may extend to *Vaí-*

mahsë's domain. The Master of Animals is said to pursue women in
the forest, to appear as an incubus in their dreams, and to take a
strong interest in human sex life, as in the case of the couvade. In
most of his activities the payé uses objects or concepts that are
imbued with a sexual—mainly seminal—meaning. The quartz crystals scattered by lightning which the payé collects are interpreted
as drops of semen; white down, yellow feathers, and cotton figure
prominently in a shaman's manipulations and have the same seminal character. Disease is often interpreted as a kind of magical
impregnation with an evil "seed" that has to be extracted and
exorcised so that the patient can be :"reborn" and cured. The seminal and, therefore, fortifying symbolism of white and yellowish
colors, whether shades of light, the coloring of animals, or the
mucilaginous flesh of certain fruits, is frequently mentioned in
incantations and spells, and the entire hallucinatory sphere is not
devoid of sexual connotations, the narcotic snuff itself being the
"Sun's sperm."

We have been speaking here of sex, phallic objects, uterine
abodes, and seminal substances. It would be very wrong and quite
unfortunate to see in these ideas and associations an obscene or
lewd element in Tukano culture. The truth is that the Indians are
deeply preoccupied with the concept of reproductive energy as
manifested in nature and society by fertility and growth. The existence of plants, animals, and people and of a viable balance
among them are thought to depend upon the continuity of this
energy, and the payé's or anybody else's tasks consist in maintain-
ing the cycle of reproduction and growth and in controlling it so
that there will be a balance between society and the natural environment. The underlying rules are reciprocity and complementarity, and the sexual symbolism, crude as it is, based on biological
facts which, in themselves, are morally neutral. It would also be an
oversimplification to believe that sexual reproduction is always the
basic model of the creative act; it is never more than a metaphor,
used to illustrate a point.

The preceding outline of Tukano shamanism shows several interesting patterns, and we must try to examine them within the
wider context of the native culture.

In the first place, it has become clear that practically all shamanistic attitudes and practices described so far are based upon

drug-induced states of mental dissociation and hallucinatory experiences. Moreover, it seems that these states and experiences do
not involve a mystical etiology; hallucinatory trances are used as
practical and efficient means of experiencing the presence of what,
in the native culture, is taken for the metaphysical. However, this
supernatural sphere is not the one of divine or godlike beings, but
one of morally ambivalent spirits who are sacralized versions of living beings and whose help has to be obtained for very practical
ends. As the Tukano see it, there exist supernatural beings—quite
apart from the Sun Father—who have absolute knowledge and
absolute power. Any illness has a cure, and any social ill can be
redressed if only one can find a channel of communication with the
forces that "know" the remedies and solutions. Narcotic drugs provide the key to this sphere of absolute knowledge, and the only
problem, then, is to understand the language of these spirit-beings.
Herein resides the ability of the payé, to interpret their utterings
and signs correctly.

Drug-induced ecstasy seems to have two main objectives in
Tukano shamanism: to find cures for diseases and ways to punish
one's enemies. As illness is not taken to be the natural lot of mankind but is always thought to be caused by the ill will of people or
their spirit-helpers, the problem of curing a disease is, in all essence,
a process of reestablishing workable relationships with others, even
in the event some of these "others" are spirit-beings, who, after all,
"are people." The ecstatic emphasis of Tukano shamanism can be
seen as a quest for clues and procedures that will allow the user to
restore a "dis-ease" produced by tension-fraught interpersonal relationships. Acting as a spokesman and intermediary, the payé is
not a mystic, but a practical specialist in communications.

The social functions of Tukano shamanism, therefore, are very
important ones, if we look at them in their wider relationship to
the particular conditions of the social environment. In its political
aspects Tukano society is very loosely organized, there being no
institutionalized authorities to settle legal conflicts and personal
feuds. There are no chieftains, no councils of elders, no organized
means whatsoever for solving conflicts or settling discords arising
from the social order, the rules of exogamy and reciprocity, or the
personal animosity between individuals. But shamanistic trance
provides a mechanism for conflict solution. As has been pointed out
already, the payé may discuss the causes of an illness in terms of a

social etiology, but he will refrain from making personal judgments or accusations. This pattern, of keeping the solution of social tensions within the bounds of private action, does not diminish the importance of the trance experiences as effective means of settling conflicts arising from social conditions. The aggressive aspects, then, take the character of cathartic rituals of great effectiveness.

In the second place, the concept of spirit-possession seems to be completely lacking in Tukano culture. A payé is always himself; never is he seized or invaded by a spirit; he simply interprets and transmits what this spirit shows him or tells him. He never becomes an instrument of other forces but always remains a translator and interpreter, a shrewd dealer trying to learn as much as possible from the beings that people the world of his visions; he never submits to them as a blind tool of uncontrollable forces. His soul may be wandering, but it is not being replaced by the intrusion of any external agency.

One might ask here: Who are the "enemies" the Tukano make so much of? Revenge is a recurrent theme in Tukano culture, and every man feels constantly threatened by people who wish him ill or by spirits that might be the supernatural helpers of these people. There is endless talk about fighting and killing; about taking violent vengeance on this or that person; about destroying the adversary with illness, lightning, or carefully prepared "accidents" while he is hunting or traveling. And in these matters people bide their time; there is already great satisfaction in long and careful preparations, the learning of spells, and the interpretation of dreams and visions. But, in reality, nothing much ever seems to happen. People hardly ever come to blows, and much less will they readily kill a man or destroy his property; the Tukano are a gentle, friendly people. All aggressiveness, then, is acted out in the hallucinatory dimension, or at least in a state of high excitement induced by the recital of spells and the violent gestures that accompany them. The idea that sorcery has a delayed action is, of course, important because of its essentially realistic aspect. Magical aggression has a good chance of bringing results if given time; thus, it is geared to probability. Given sufficient time, the individual can expect to see his enemy fall ill or die. Obviously, if more immediate effects were expected, the aggressor would often be disappointed.

To act "as if" is a common attitude underlying much of Tukano thought and behavioral patterns. Everyone knows that, in this world, a hill is a hill, and fish are just animals that can be caught and eaten; but everyone also knows that there is "another" world where the hills appear as if they were houses, and fish behave as if they were people. The conditional *as if* is explicit in spells and incantations in which nature is perceived as imbued with human motivations and possibilities of action. The hunter approaches his prey as if it were human; lightning strikes as if it had been cast by someone.

The transferral to the hallucinatory level of the acting out of aggressiveness caused by social pressures is, undoubtedly, a procedure of great importance. On the hallucinatory scene a great psychodrama is being performed, and tensions are relieved that would otherwise be intolerable.

When inquiring into the reasons for personal enmities between people, one soon sees clearly that malevolence and rancor are caused mainly by women. Adultery, or the suspicion thereof, between a woman and her husband's brothers is a frequent cause for bitter quarrels, and occasionally a widow or an unmarried girl will become the object of rivalry, jealousy, and accusations. In a society as controlled—one might almost say "possessed"—by the strictest exogamic rules, the slightest suspicion of illicit relationships will produce violent reactions, and sexual repression, homosexual attachments, and the laxity of women in obeying the restrictions imposed by the men also lead to open tensions. And then, of course, there is envy and there is prestige. The young and healthy, the successful hunter, and the graceful dancer are envied, especially if their prowess makes them appear desirable in the eyes of the opposite sex.

In Tukano symbolic thought food and sex are closely related, often identified. Many foods have a male connotation, of seminal, aphrodisiac, or fertilizing significance, while others are essentially female and related to fecundity and growth.[47] Chains of associations referring to details of shape, color, smell, or texture make the domain of foodstuffs one of great complexity, always closely related to sex in terms of fertility and fecundity. Some foods, or food preparations—ants, wasps, game, smoking, roasting—are thought to increase virility, and this is desirable in normal circumstances; but in others, when people approach the supernatural sphere on ritual occasions, they are to be avoided because then all energies have to be channeled into the visionary experience. Women are often equated with fish, and the consumption of fish, therefore, is occasionally subjected to the rules of exogamy by which a man might have to avoid eating fish caught on a certain stretch of the river, or fish of a certain species.[48] All this helps to explain the emphasis placed in many incantations and songs upon the danger of certain foods, and upon the need to exorcise them before they can be safely consumed. The emphasis on vomiting as a means of ritual purification is of interest in this context; vomiting is noneating, the opposite of food intake, and in this sense it is an asexual attitude.

One may wonder what outlet women have when beset by social pressures and personal conflicts. Homosexual attachments seem to be common among them, and they may provide a mechanism for relieving certain conflicts, but enmities and gossip are ever present. Women are not allowed to take narcotic drugs.[49] They dance and sing, and know about herbs and home remedies, but the hallucinatory sphere is closed to them. Tukano culture does not even provide them with that extraordinary means of expression—the solemn recitals and proclamations pronounced by the men at their periodic gatherings. This, then, is a field to be explored.

We have not mentioned in this chapter the meetings and dances during which yajé is consumed by a large audience, because we do not consider them to be part of shamanistic practice. They are social events with a religious overtone, visionary experiences in which a mystical ecstasy plays a certain role. They will be dealt with in another chapter. The shamanistic quest is of a very different nature; it is concerned with practical ends for individual purposes.

But however practical the quest may be, it is dangerous, both physically and psychologically. It entails hardships and acute discomfort, sometimes leading to utter exhaustion and even death. A payé does not simply "turn on"; he has a clear purpose; a passionate interest in learning more and more about the powers he perceives in his visions, and if he sometimes uses them to harm others he does so with the conviction that he is restoring a balance that cannot be achieved by ordinary social controls.

A final word must be said here about the practitioner himself. As far as we were able to judge, there is nothing psychologically abnormal about a payé. Hysteroid or epileptoid symptoms seem to be wholly absent, and anything resembling fits or seizures is simply the consequence of intoxication, not a trait of a psychotic personality. On the contrary, the payés we have known always gave us the impression of being sober, level-headed people, quite normal members of their society.

What distinguishes a payé from others is that he is an intellectual. As such, he is not much given to small talk and the simple pleasures of the home. He often has a tendency to keep apart from others, to be silent, and to abstain from noisy conversation and ribald joking. He may take lonely walks, mumble spells, or sit staring into the dark. But he is immensely curious; he is always interested in animals and plants, the weather, the stars, diseases—anything that, to others, is unpredictable. He is a humanist, in the sense that he is interested in the "pagan" antiquities of his own cultural tradition: in myths of origin, in archaeological sites, in long-forgotten place names, and in stories of legendary migrations. And he will enjoy the company of other, like-minded men. When a few friends gather he will talk and sing all night long. He will recall past events, speak of some special "cases" in his practice, and will be a great raconteur.

A Tukano payé does not receive a sudden call to office, in an overwhelming traumatic experience, but develops his personality slowly and steadily, the driving force being a truly intellectual interest in the unknown; and that not so much for the purpose of acquiring power over his fellowmen as for the personal satisfaction of "knowing" things which others are unable to grasp.

6

JAGUAR
TRANS-
FORMATION

We must turn now to present-day use of narcotic snuff among the Tukano Indians and examine the ideological context in which this toxic is employed. Here is a brief summary of the most general aspects.

All Tukano payés take *vihó* snuff prepared from *Virola* sap, and any man may occasionally take the snuff, usually under the guidance of an experienced payé. The trance produced by the narcotic is said to be the most important means by which one can establish contact with the supernatural sphere in order to consult the spirit-beings, above all *Vihó-mahsë*/"snuff-person" (the owner and master of snuff), who dwells on the Milky Way whence he watches continuously the doings of mankind. *Vihó-mahsë* has to be called upon for help, often as an intermediary with other powers, and therefore the payé has to ascend to the Milky Way and visit him. A payé cannot communicate directly with *Vaí-mahsë*, the Master of Game Animals, nor with any other spirit-being; he always has to act through *Vihó-mahsë*, for example, if he wishes to know where game is to be found or when a fishing expedition is to be organized. In the curing of disease the assistance of *Vihó-mahsë* is essential, and the payé has to take snuff because, in his trance, *Vihó-mahsë* will give him instructions concerning the cause and treatment of the illness. Furthermore, in order to take vengeance upon one's enemies, one also needs *Vihó-mahsë*'s help.

All this is common knowledge. But the striking point—mentioned in passing by the Indians, but obviously of prime importance—is that occasionally a payé or other men will take large doses of narcotic snuff and then will turn into jaguars.

We have already mentioned that not everyone can become a payé, that there are many psychological and intellectual requirements the novice has to meet before an older and experienced master will accept him as an apprentice. A future payé has to have shown a true interest in esoteric matters since his youth; he has to have a good memory for reciting genealogies, myths, and spells; and, above all, he has to be able to interpret the hallucinations of others. He has to know of diseases, of the habits of game animals, of weather conditions, and of astronomy. And, most important, he has to have that interior luminescence, the illumination that—through him—makes things hidden in nature and in men's minds visible, so that they can be understood and controlled.

The test comes when the novice has to take *vihó*, in the company of his master or of several other apprentices. After months of fasting, of sleepless nights spent in chanting spells, the group of novices will be called together by their master and they will snuff *vihó*. And then, the Indians say, they will turn into jaguars.

When speaking of these matters, a Desana payé said, "He does not choose his *vihó;* the *vihó* chooses him," and this statement was confirmed by others. In explanation, it was said that not all people were equally affected by the snuff; some only became nauseated and felt ill for days, while others, after an initial spell of headache and dizziness, ascended to the Milky Way and turned into jaguars. Their bodies were lying in their hammocks, but their souls soared up high, or took on animal shape, and so they could roam in the forest, unrecognized.

This idea, then, that the snuff "takes its choice," is based upon observation; it is obvious that in the reaction to the drug many personal factors are at play, and that the nature and intensity of the hallucinatory trance depend upon a combination of specific psychological, physiological, and social circumstances.

We have no detailed myth on the origin of *vihó*, but only some fragmentary tales referring to this event. According to these stories it was the daughter of the sun who obtained the first *vihó* "by scratching her father's penis." In fact, *vihó* is said to be derived from the sun's sperm and to owe its existence to the Sun Father's incest with his daughter.[1] The container in which the powder is kept on ritual occasions is called *abé yeeru* (D) or *muhipu nuri* (T), that is, penis of the sun.

The following Desana text (Text No. 30) refers to the ritual use of *vihó* and describes a group of men who have gathered for the purpose of transforming themselves into jaguars.

"It was *Pamurí-mahsë* who brought us the penis of the sun. That was in the beginning of time. Our ancestors were already payés. They owned the *vihó* of the devouring jaguar. They had *vihó* to turn into jaguars and into people. They had *vihó* to turn into doubles.[2] All this can be done with *vihó*.

"The *vihó* is inside a tube. It has a cover. And this is how it was since the beginning of time. To snuff *vihó* one must first open the tube. They put it in the center. The *vihó* affects those who are susceptible. They sneeze. It affects the kidneys. Once they react this way they take more snuff. When they take this snuff they lie down. When they are lying there only their hearts are beating. Now they are devouring jaguars. To become a jaguar they turn their bellies up. They do this to hide their hearts. Part of the face is like a gourd bowl. In this way, if someone should shoot at them, they won't die. Together with the other jaguars they roam in the forest. They have their dwellings on the headwaters of the West. That is what our traditions say. These jaguars wander about and devour people. Distance does not count for them.

"An old woman takes care of them. On one occasion this old woman scolded the jaguars and said: 'Bring some food for me too!' They agreed to bring her a share of the prey. They brought the leg of a woman; it still had some body paint on it. When they returned they put the leg into the cooking vessel and when the old woman came they said to her: 'Grandmother, we brought you some food. Eat it with your pepper-pot!' When she saw it was a human leg she became afraid and scolded the jaguars.

"The men have a macaw that is also fasting and taking *vihó* snuff so that it can turn into a jaguar. When a jaguar-man fails, the macaw replaces him in jaguar form. The macaw will turn into a jaguar. When the macaw returns to the maloca its beak is stained with blood. When this happens, they take his bone away. There are other, real jaguars, too. They live in other places."

A few explanatory notes are in order here. According to this text *vihó* snuff can be used for two ends: to turn into a jaguar, or to turn into a "double," a *vearí-mahsë*—that is, one of the anthropomorphic spirits who are the mirror images of mankind. Both forms are used to attack enemies, but jaguar transformation is said to be more common and to be the principal means of taking personal vengeance.

The "tube" in which the narcotic powder is kept, designated as "penis of the sun," is a short piece of white stalactite, hollowed out longitudinally. According to other reports, the snuff container is made of a jaguar bone, while the stalactite is an element apart; a small quantity of lime is scraped off its end and is mixed with the *vihó* powder. All informants agree that the distribution of the snuff takes part in the center of the house where the men are gathered. The concept of the magical importance of the "center" is often found in Tukano rituals, which mention a "central spot," or the act of "centering" an object so that it will occupy a determined spot. In the Creation Myth the Sun Father "centered" his stick rattle until it stood upright, and from other descriptions it can be inferred that this act of "putting something in the center" has a certain sexual connotation related to the idea of establishing a contact with the precise, the only adequate, opposite element, in terms of exogamy.

Under the influence of the drug the men now "turn into" jaguars in a quite literal, physical sense, the convulsive behavior being described as "turning their bellies up." We shall return to this point later on and meanwhile keep in mind this important aspect of the transformation.

Some people say that no woman should be present and that the men should do their own cooking or other household chores while they are engaged upon their power quest, but it is also said that sometimes an old woman or a woman at least past menopause can accompany the men. The role of the macaw is not wholly clear; because of its yellow and red plumage this bird is often associated with shamanistic practices, both as a helper and bearer of fertilizing colors, and also as a spy, a messenger who may overhear an enemy's conversation or warn a payé of approaching danger. The red stains on a macaw's beak can, of course, be explained as the red juice of certain fruits the bird has been feeding on.

Another Desana text (Text No. 99) adds further details and must be quoted in full.

"They usually take the sun's penis snuff in the Summer of the Caterpillar. Then they turn into jaguars and devour people. Forming a circle they open the sun's penis, standing in the middle. It [the snuff] is contained in a tube and they open it, standing in the middle. They do this in the middle of the circle. Then they leave it in the middle, so the snuff can take its choice. When the snuff penetrates the person, he sneezes. Having sneezed, they continue to take snuff. When doing this—and having fasted beforehand—they devour people. They use the jaguar's costume. They do not move and they lie there covered with ashes; only their hearts continue to beat while they are roaming at large in the shape of jaguars, to devour people. Thus they are roaming. Clad in their jaguar garments they turn up their faces. Their backs turn downward to where the stomach is. This is how they can penetrate into the other world. Once they have turned into jaguars they go and kill their enemies. When they devour people, all other jaguars become fierce, too. The jaguars of the forest become fierce; very fierce they become. This is what they say when talking. His head is a gourd bowl; the forehead has the shape of a gourd bowl."

This text is followed by one of the many anecdotes people will tell about jaguar-men, and we shall quote it here as an illustration of the imagery involved in this complex.

"Once upon a time the jaguars devoured a man. Seeing the dead man, people said: 'His son-in-law killed him.'"

At this point the informant interrupted his story and, by way of explanation, said: "Only *one* jaguar lets himself be seen. A jaguar always kills from behind. While one [man] is watching one jaguar, the other one attacks from behind. They seize and devour one, and leave the head impaled on a tree trunk. This is what they did here. The jaguar-men themselves do not devour, but the other (natural) jaguars take advantage and devour; this is what they say."

After this, the story continued: "They [the jaguars] were lying in wait for those who went to fish with traps. They appear quite visibly. A man was taking fish out of his trap when a jaguar killed him. He defended himself as well as he could, but he was killed. At that time his son-in-law had been visiting him. He had gone to visit his father-in-law. The son-in-law said: 'I shall kill this jaguar!' Thus he said and went to get a fish trap. The others said: 'There are many jaguars around—man-eating jaguars,' but he did not listen to them. There was the fish trap; it had been set in the *umarí* season.[3] Fearing the jaguars he did not look for fish. When he climbed up the riverbank the jaguar seized him. The others saw that he was late and that he had not returned. They said: 'Something has happened to him,' and the next day they went to see. They went to see and they found only his head. There were also his bones. They gathered up the remains and went home weeping. Thus they returned home. One of them went ahead and when he climbed the hill the jaguar was lying in wait for him. But he, too, was a payé. He was one of us, a Desana. He turned back; the others arrived and were weeping. They went by and wept, but the jaguar was already approaching. There were three jaguar-apprentices. One of them was a jaguar-man who had taught the others; he was the one who attacked. His whiskers were blood-stained. He was the one who attacked. His apprentices went ahead of the Desana. Three of them went ahead of him. When they were ahead of him, he noticed them. When he saw him, the jaguar said, 'Don't shoot!' but the man shot him and hit him near the shoulder blade. The jaguar fell down and died. He cut off the dead jaguar's tongue.[4] In this way he killed the jaguar. But the next day the man died, quite suddenly. The jaguar-man, being a Desana himself, had killed him. He killed him with a spell. They had been enemies. He said, 'I, too, have taken snuff,' and he killed him in revenge. He killed another man while he was eating ants. Having seized him, he devoured him. The natural jaguars devoured him. The others were lying in wait, watching the jaguars gathering the corpses. They killed one of the apprentice-jaguars, and they also killed his master. They killed both."

When the informant had arrived at this point, he added emphatically: "The real master is invisible; the others are visible! Take note of this!"

Again, the tale continued: "This done, they buried the two dead jaguars. They had killed the jaguar-apprentices. When they were about to burn them in a huge fire, their carcasses burst with a noise: po-tooo! Their souls had escaped.[5] Their souls were returning to life. They had killed the garment only. When the jaguars kill people they also turn into 'doubles.' Sometimes they will devour people in the guise of an anaconda. Out of revenge they do this. In the river, the anaconda, and on land, the jaguars and the doubles. They all appear in this manner, people say. This happens when they snuff the penis of the Sun. When they do this, they take their revenge. It is dangerous then. That is all."

Another text (Text No. 140), referring to the same theme, was given by a high-ranking Desana payé:

"When they are taking vihó snuff, they sit in a circle. The snuff takes hold of them of its own accord. The snuff is kept in a tube, in the penis of the Sun, and they open it, in the center of the circle. When they take this snuff their only nourishment consists of cassava soup; they mix it with manioc starch. After two or three

months they begin to feel its effects. When they are thus intoxicated they begin to feel as if they were possessed by wild beasts.
They begin to utter cries. They make *hihihihihihi*. And then they
cohabit with their women, saying: "It is not prohibited!" But this
does upset them. Then they roar again, *hihihihihihi*, being now still
more deranged. So they say.

"And then all things open up before them; the horizon opens
like a door. They now put on their jaguar garments. At the river
mouth they gather *vëhë* reeds to make baskets. With these reeds
they make manioc squeezers which turn into anacondas, to devour
people. They conceive many other things, rapidly. They also conceive the disguise of the doubles. The abodes of the jaguars, too.
And this is how they disguise themselves: they turn their under-
sides up to where the back is. Their faces they cover with a gourd
bowl. 'Otherwise they might kill me . . . ,' they say, and so they protect themselves. This is what they do. And in this way they roam
about as jaguars. They go wherever they have enemies. Those of
them who venture into the forest, they kill with their hoes. This is
what they say, elder brother. That's how it is, yes."

The text now continues by quoting mythical and anecdotal materials: "In the beginning of time, the Sons of Aracú [i.e., the
Desana] were like this. They had what is called 'day-snuff.' This is
how the meddling with the women started. Not all people are
suitable. Over here, the Sons of Bëgëyéri devoured many people in
the disguise of jaguars. It is also said that they killed many Tari
people.

"Women are sometimes wicked. There was one who did not prepare cassava soup in time. Her husband wanted to go fishing early
in the morning. 'She always does this to me,' he said and took
his fishing gear and left. At that time of the year people were taking
vihó snuff. Just as I mentioned before. He came to where we were
living then, at the Cumare Creek. He went down to the creek and
crossed it on a fallen tree trunk and went to fish. He was fishing
for catfish. After a while he went to another pool. Looking at the
water he saw the reflection of a huge shadow behind him. 'What
animal is this?' he said to himself; 'It is coming to devour me,' he
said and gathered up his fishing gear. At that time certain Brazilian
bushknives were in use, called *pacao*. He had one of these bushknives. He was fleeing from the jaguar when he became caught
in a mudbank. He was trying to struggle free when the jaguar over-

took him. But the jaguar, too, got stuck in the mud. He jumped at the man. But he got entangled in some vines. Being caught in the vines the man hit the jaguar over the head with his bushknife. The jaguar was bleeding. He was losing strength. The man shouted: 'The jaguar is devouring me!' People were coming; 'The jaguar is devouring him,' they said. They came shouting to help the man. When they arrived, the jaguar fled. Next day the man, who was a Son of Bëgëyéri, went to hunt early in the morning. While he was hunting the jaguar seized him. The jaguar attacked him from behind just when he was lifting his gun. Seeing that he did not return home his wife went to look for him. 'There are many jaguars around,' she said. She found his gun lying on the ground and next to it was the man's head. The body was lying farther off. They went to catch the jaguar in a trap. And so they killed it. They shot it through the lattice of the trap. Then they gathered plenty of firewood and burned the jaguar, and then its carcass burst. When this happened, the body died. They devour people only as long as the effects of the snuff last. When the effects wear off they become human again. It is as if they were returning from somewhere. That is what they do. That's all."

The foregoing two texts (Text Nos. 99 and 140) contain a number of interesting details but, above all, they allow us to isolate certain phases, certain individual scenes which have to be considered separately: the general setting of the *vihó* experience, the process of transformation, and the exploits of the transformed participants. We shall refer to these three units in the same order and turn first of all to the particular environment in which the gathering takes place.

During the last few months of the year, sometimes as early as August, large quantities of caterpillars appear in the Vaupés territory, several species of which are edible and are assiduously collected by the Indians.[6] Tradition says that these caterpillars navigate through the night sky in large canoes, the outlines of which can be recognized in certain dark areas in the Milky Way, and that they descend to earth on the eastern horizon, whence they are carried along by the winds, by long silvery threads of saliva. The yearly arrival of these caterpillars is much talked about, and the payés use many incantatory formulas in which reference is made to this event. Each species has its "master," who is addressed in spells and songs[7] describing the characteristics of the animals and their yearly return. In November, shortly before the dry season sets in, the large cicadas[8] mentioned in the last chapter make their appearance, and their coming marks the high point of the season because they are said to be the true "masters" of the caterpillars and also of certain kinds of narcotic snuffs. The cicadas, then, announce the propitious time for shamanistic practices[9] which, in a very specific way, are connected with jaguar transformation and imagery.

The following text (Text No. 96) represents the words of a Desana payé while looking at the night sky.

"Well, there it is, isn't it? There, at the river mouth, yes. There are the heads of the *ii* caterpillars; aren't there? Yes, *ii* caterpillars with red heads, yes. When these heads appear we say they are coming in their canoes, and when the *ii* heads come, the winds come with them. The canoes come with a rushing sound, we say. The wind is like a torrent. Then those here [the payés] take *vihó* snuff; they snuff it and absorb it, yes. And once more they take snuff. They mix it with the starch of *carayurú*.[10] They also have 'water-snuff.' In this manner they go over there to look for snuff in the canoes. In our visions we then see a crowd of people who try to kill us. That's the way it is, elder brother. That's it. They say they have red heads. Then there are some with spiny heads, too. Those with spiny heads are evil. Then the *vihó* snuffers gather there. This is why it thunders.[11] That is what they say; isn't it? But they come later, the spiny heads; the red heads come first. These *ii* heads are dangerous in their time; but not now. Now they do not make any noise. [But] then the windy currents come, the wind of these canoes; don't they? This is why we say they are coming with the wind, and then there is danger. That's the way it is; so they say. It is like thundering canoes. It is such that it produces nightmares in us. In our visions we can see them singing. They are adorned with macaw feathers. The 'water-snuff people' are dancing in a crowd, with their masks. Those with the feather ornaments are the ones that use *carayurú* snuff. Those with the *yuí* ornaments[12] are the ones who use 'water-snuff.' When they behave like this, in a crowd, they throw us into confusion; yes, elder brother. It makes us nauseated, the women and the canoes of the *ii* caterpillars. This is why we become nauseated. This is what they say when talking. That's all."

The Tukano divide the seasons of the year into a sequence of more than twenty alternating "summers" and "winters," or rather, short periods of more or less rainfall, heralded by the appearance of

certain constellations in the night sky. The "Summer of the Caterpillar" falls in the month of November, the most propitious time
for taking *vihó* snuff. Those who take the snuff are one or two payés
or, sometimes, just one payé with his apprentice. For this purpose
they go to an isolated hut belonging to the payé where the novice
or novices have spent some time during their previous apprenticeship. Only an old woman is allowed to be present, and she has to
prepare a special diet for the men, who spend most of the time in
their hammocks. Cassava bread, tapioca, and ants constitute the
main part of the food they are allowed to consume.[13] When speaking of this preparatory stage, some Indians pointed out that not
always does one have to go to a secluded spot in the forest but that
occasionally the group of men might stay in a maloca. In the payé's
text (No. 140) it had been mentioned that the men would impreg-
nate their women under the influence of the drug, an act that was
considered very dangerous for both sexes. After all, a woman might
bear a jaguar cub if she became pregnant and, besides, prolonged
sexual abstinence was an important prerequisite during apprenticeship as well as during the initial *vihó* experience. The main purpose
of social isolation was to avoid this possibility, but according to
specific circumstances this isolation could be maintained in the
maloca, wthout having the men live apart in the forest.

The payé had said (Text No. 140) that the effects of *vihó* began
to be felt "after two months," and from further commentaries, cor-
roborated by others, it appears that the taking of snuff is not always
an act limited to a certain moment; it may consist of a slow process
of intoxication produced by steadily increasing doses of the narcotic
substance. It would be difficult indeed to imagine that the men
would spend two or three months in their hammocks without dedi-
cating some of their time to household tasks, conversation, or occasional work in the fields, but the possibility that this actually is
the procedure cannot be excluded; the informant insisted on this
point.

The idea that "the snuff takes its choice" and that it "takes hold
of them of its own accord" was further elaborated by the informant's saying that different people reacted very differently to
the narcotic and that a potential payé did not develop the more
unpleasant symptoms of intoxication such as severe headaches and
nausea. Several informants pointed out that one had to have courage and determination when one took the snuff because one could

never be sure of its immediate effects; if one faltered and became afraid, the substance could do great harm to one's health.

According to all our data, the Indians' manifest purpose in taking *vihó* snuff on these occasions was to become transformed into jaguars. In this process two aspects have to be distinguished; in the first place it is a trial, a test devised to ascertain who of the novices has the true disposition to achieve this dangerous transformation. In other words, it is a test of vocation in terms of the snuff's "taking its choice." It is, in all essence, an initiation. In the second place, the objective of turning into a jaguar is to take revenge. This point proved to be difficult to discuss and to interpret, in conversation with the Indians. Although there was much elaboration on the themes of killing, devouring, decapitation, blood-stained whiskers, and so on, there was also a tacit agreement that jaguars did not behave this way. Jaguars, all Indians are ready to admit, are not particularly dangerous beasts, and when one tries to verify the tales of hunters who speak of jaguars attacking them, or the stories of women who are said to have been pursued or devoured by jaguars, one soon discovers that they are based on hearsay. The fierceness of the beast toward people is largely a matter of imagination, and the hair-raising stories one hears so often about jaguars are hardly ever based on real experience but seem to express a fantastic confabulation of violent and ambivalent emotions. But it is also obvious that, to the Indians, this dark world of monstrous feline creatures is all too real and that this imagery plays an important role in their thoughts.

Revenge is a theme that is often mentioned in conversation, and the idea of taking revenge against one's enemies occupies an important place in Tukano thought. But in the daily round there is little evidence for such deep-set enmities. There are always some sinister tales circulating about this or that person's having been slighted during a dance, or about someone who suspects his wife of adultery and is going to kill the offender, but very rarely is there any physical aggression, and it seems rather that this wild talk forms part of an institutionalized bragging and threatening behavior which, although certainly expressing very real tensions, hardly ever leads to bloodshed. But more of this later.

To describe the onset of the hallucinatory trance with the words "The horizon opens like a door" is fairly common. The expression tries to convey the idea of a sudden luminous phenomenon which lights up a previous state of darkness. Once this has happened, the men have different ways of going about their business. Of some payés it is said that they can turn into anacondas which then take on the appearance of large manioc squeezers, the elongated sleeve-like instruments the Indians use to press out the poisonous juice of the grated manioc. The parallel is obvious: the elastic basketry press is compared to the strangling coils of the huge snake. These supernatural manioc squeezers are said sometimes to float in the river, turn into anacondas, and devour their victims. A payé could also turn into a poisonous snake and thus kill his enemy.

The transformation into *vëarí-mahsá* is an entirely different matter. In many myths and tales reference is made to this most dangerous category of spirit-beings, whose name is sometimes translated as "deceivers." In reality, the name means "big people,"[14] and they are imagined as spirits which take on the physical likenesses of relatives and friends, even imitating their voices and gestures, in order to seduce women or kill men. They are said to appear on lonely trails, at the landing, or at dusk near the maloca, and to invite an unsuspecting girl or a lone hunter to accompany them. They then rape or kill their victims who realize their mistake only when it is too late. We shall refer later on to some aspects of this transformation complex which are of special importance.

It is interesting to note the payé's statement (Text No. 140) that, in the beginning of time, the Sons of Aracú, that is, the Desana themselves, turned into jaguars and devoured many people. The Sons of Bëgëyéri, a Desana sib, derive their name from *bëgë*/old man, and *yé'eri*/to cohabit. The *Tari* people, a name unknown at present, seem to have been inhabitants of the north and, according to the payé, lived in the region of the Guainía and Isana Rivers, being related to the Kuripako, an Arawakan tribe of that area.[15] Now in commenting on this story, the payé added that when he said the Desana devoured other people he had meant to say that they abducted women from other groups. In saying, "This is how the meddling with women started; not all people are suitable," he was referring to exogamic rules broken by the Desana "jaguars," who had devoured, that is, had cohabited with, women who were not eligible as marriage partners.

Another point developed in detail was that in a group of men-turned-jaguars the leading payé was said to be invisible, at least when the pack was about to attack the victim. The others were merely his dupes, his helpers who did the actual killing and devouring. In the case of a lone payé-turned-jaguar, however, he would be invisible and would look just like a common jaguar. The rapid *hihihihihi* the men uttered at the onset of the trance represents the sound with which the Indians commonly imitate the panting of the beast. It was then that they put on their jaguar garments.

Here a question comes to mind: If one should be walking in the forest and come upon a jaguar—how does one know it is not a payé? How can one distinguish between a common jaguar, *yebá yee*/an "earth-jaguar," and *yee mahsá*/jaguar-people?

We have discussed this matter with a number of Indians, among them several payés, and we shall quote their words here.

"A common jaguar is like a dog. But a payé-turned-jaguar is upside down. Everything is reversed. What is below, is up, and what is up, is below. The heart is on the back, and the backbone is where the belly was. They do this to hide their hearts. So, if one has to shoot a payé-jaguar, one has to hit him high on the back, where the heart is, and not on the shoulder blade, where one would shoot a common jaguar."

The same had been said in Text No. 30: "To become a jaguar they turn their bellies upward. . . . Their backs turn to where the stomach is." Upon further questioning, our informants demonstrated this position by lifting up their clenched fists to eye level while, at the same time, bending back the body in an intensely strained posture. In other words, the position of the jaguar-man was depicted as the same as the convulsive posture adopted by a person under the influence of narcotic snuff. This parallel is difficult to explain. If the convulsions of an intoxicated man meant that he was ready to turn into a jaguar, the image of an "upside down" jaguar was, in all probability, also based upon an observed fact. Inquiries about the comportment of jaguars in their natural habitat produced correct observations on hunting and mating behavior. It was also said that, when the female was in heat (T: *mehé kanisé*/with heated blood), an invisible red thread extended between it and the males, attracting them and leading them for miles to where the female was. The spectacular mating behavior of jaguars and other cats was well known to the Indians, but their descriptions did not fit into the image of the "upside down" jaguar.

The answer, or at least a suggestion of it, was obtained on a different occasion. The conversation was concerned with animals which, according to the Indians, had a knowledge of medicinal herbs. It was pointed out that certain birds of prey would devour poisonous snakes and then eat a few leaves that were an antivenom, that dogs would eat grass, and that monkeys when wounded would use green leaves as poultices. Someone mentioned that animals would purge themselves by eating certain herbs. "A jaguar will chew and eat yajé vines to purge himself," it was stated. The Indians went on to explain that they had seen jaguar tracks near trees the trunks of which were covered with yajé vines, and that they had seen the torn and chewed stems, at ground level. Now yajé has strong purgative effects, but the point is that all felines are extremely sensitive to drugs and are likely to display the strangest behavior under their influence, such as writhing on the ground in convulsions. Besides, large felines such as jaguars are known to have the habit of chewing and eating leafy jungle vines.[16] The combination of these two facts may possibly provide the clue to the problem. The Indians may have observed jaguars that had chewed yajé vines and were writhing in convulsions. To the observer the conclusion must have been obvious: these jaguars were payés.

But we must return to the interpretation of our texts. Although the main objective of a jaguar-man consisted in killing his enemies, the informants add that he would also attack women. Some of them he would kill and devour on the spot, while others he would abduct and they would disappear forever. This suggests that there exists a sexual incentive in the transformation complex, and there is some evidence for this in many myths and tales. In these traditions jaguar-men are said to have raped or abducted women, and occasionally to have procreated hybrid offspring which, eventually, displayed jaguar traits. The assailants were generally described as being jaguar-men from other tribal groups with which there were no institutionalized marriage relationships; in cases where they were of the same group (e.g., Tukano), their sexual assaults were of an incestuous nature, the jaguar-men attacking female relatives of their own exogamic unit.

The general pattern of jaguar transformation described above is based upon information and texts obtained from Desana and Tukano proper Indians. A Pira-Tapuya Indian gave a modified version of some aspects of the procedure which is of interest because it demonstrates that, although the underlying concepts are largely the same, a certain amount of local variation exists in shamanistic techniques, owing to personal elaborations of individual payés. According to our Pira-Tapuya source the diet of the apprentice should consist exclusively of manioc starch, all other foods being considered extremely harmful. Once they had been transformed into jaguars (P: *yaí-base*), the men would not kill their enemies on the spot but would carry them to the house where they were taking *vihó* and devour them there, even eating their bones. Then they would resume human shape again and proceed to "dry" their jaguar garments by putting them tail end upward, on a sunny spot, flat and not stretched out on stakes. This had to be done in a special kind of small clearing in the forest, called *s'túutu* (P) or *suhtutu* (T), where there was no plant growth at all. Besides, the Pira-Tapuya are said to have a preference for turning into the yellowish, even-colored kind of jaguar and not into the spotted kind, which has clearly defined pelt markings and is said to be less fierce than the others. It was added that a Pira-Tapuya payé would not turn his entire body into a jaguar, but only his heart. "The payé's heart is in the jaguar; nothing else," explained our informant. From this and other information obtained from members of different exogamic groups one can see that the details of ritual practice and the personal expectations involved allow for a wide range of local variation.

Another Desana tale (Text No. 31), although not directly concerned with drug-induced jaguar transformation, contains important additional material and is worth quoting in full here.

"When a jaguar is roaming and it thunders, there is no danger; that jaguar is different. The jaguar of the East is black, and the jaguar of the West is spotted. There is also a *Heliconia* jaguar and a deer jaguar.

"Once upon a time a woman rejected her husband and he wandered off alone into the forest. He came upon a jaguar in human shape. The jaguar-man was carrying a basket that contained his jaguar garment. The jaguar-man asked the man where he was going and he said: 'My wife does not love me and so I'm going to lose myself in the forest.' The jaguar-man asked where the woman was living. 'Over there,' said the man, and the jaguar-man said: 'I shall help you to bring her back to you.' The jaguar-man was carrying a hoe over his shoulder. The devouring jaguars always carry that hoe. Only jaguar-men use it. They use the hoe to seize people with. The jaguar-man went to lie in wait for the woman;

he went in human shape but in truth he was a huge black jaguar. The woman went to the landing carrying a vessel. When she was close enough, he seized her with his hoe. She only saw a huge jaguar. The other people saw only bloodstains and jaguar tracks. The jaguar-man went and took the woman back to the man. 'This is the one who does not love you,' he said; 'Come with me to the maloca of the western headwaters; we are going to drink *cashirí*,' he said to the couple.

"When night fell the couple made a fire. 'What is it you people eat?' asked the jaguar-man. 'We eat game,' they answered. 'You go ahead and eat; I won't,' he said. When the two were asleep he changed into his jaguar garment and lay down. When they woke up they saw a huge jaguar lying there and they talked about it. But the jaguar was listening. He moved his ears as if to say: I am listening. Then he took off his jaguar garment. 'What are you talking about?' he asked; 'Don't be afraid of me,' he said; 'This is how I change my dress.'

"They visited many malocas. Each time the same thing happened. The jaguar-man showed them everything. They had become tired. 'We are almost there,' he said; 'Now I shall change my garment.' He told them what he was going to do. He also showed them his garment and his whiskers; he was a huge jaguar. He had his jaguar blowgun. When they arrived at the end of their journey they saw a large painted maloca. 'Take hold of my tail!' he said; 'Grasping my tail you can follow me.' He was the chief of all the others there. He had come to dance with them. He arrived on the exact day. The others, too, were just arriving and they were many. They all greeted the black jaguar. He received them with greetings. The two were still clinging to his tail. When he entered the maloca he took off his jaguar garment. There they danced and when they had danced they returned. When jaguars travel thus one can hear their panting. The jaguar-man took the couple back to their maloca and warned them not to speak of what they had seen. 'If you tell of it, you shall die,' he said; 'If you tell, at once you will have to come to my maloca. Next year, if you are still alive, I shall come back for you and take you with me again,' he said. A long time had passed since the couple had been gone from their home, a year or so. The jaguar-man returned to his maloca of the East. The other people asked them what had happened, but they refused to tell. First they listened to all the questions, but in the end they got tired and told what had happened. They both died that very same night."

From several myths and tales it can be deduced that the East and the West are associated with certain jaguar personifications of different colors. Black jaguars are fairly numerous in the Northwest Amazon and are said to be particularly fierce, while, as we were told by the Pira-Tapuya, the common spotted kind is thought to be less dangerous. A payé-turned-jaguar will occasionally "travel with the sun," from East to West, it is said, and there is a special spell by which an enemy payé can make the sun become invisible so that the sky traveler will lose his way. But above all, the jaguars of the East and the West live in a relationship of reciprocity expressed in periodic visits during which each group participates in the dances prepared by the other. We may add here that, in many texts, the expression "to dance with others" symbolizes an exogamic relationship and is equivalent to sexual intercourse.

But there are other categories of jaguars we must mention first: the Heliconia jaguar (D: *ohopú yee*) and the deer jaguar (D: *nyamá yee*). Near the rivers and creeks often grow dense stands of *Heliconia bihai* L., a broad-leaved plant not dissimilar to a small banana tree, but wild-growing and bearing inedible fruits. The withered leaves and stalks of Heliconia turn a soft yellowish brown, which according to the Indians is the color of a certain kind of jaguar. Jaguars often hunt on Heliconia-covered riverbanks, obviously a propitious place for rodents and other small game that prefer a riverine environment, and it is true that jaguars tend to specialize and to develop, individually, a preference for a certain local environment and a certain kind of prey. The Desana name for Heliconia is *ohopú*/bat-leaf, and it is a fact that Heliconia thickets are often inhabited by large colonies of bats. The deer jaguars, of course, are said to have a predilection for deer, and the color of their coats to be very similar to that of a deer.

The frequent "change of dress" is another point of interest. From the story (Text No. 31) it becomes clear that when traveling the jaguar-man always appears in human shape, but that when sleeping, attacking, or visiting he adopts feline attire. When we elicited comments on the jaguar garment, our informants offered different interpretations. Some said that the jaguar-man was obviously a payé and that, as such, he had been taking *vihó* snuff and had turned into a jaguar. Others were inclined to take the story at face value; the man had a jaguar skin in his basket and simply threw it over his back or took it off, as the case might be. A third group, composed mostly of elderly men, explained things in a different way. According to them, the jaguar skin was no skin at all, but an essence, a state of mind which made a person act like a jaguar.

When speaking of the jaguar skin or garment our informants employed the term *suriró* (D). Although this is the common word used to designate any garment or attire, be it of cloth or bark, it is also used to describe a particular state, in the sense of a person's being invested with, that is, clad in, certain qualities. The elder informants—and we have no reason to doubt their words—insisted that it was in this sense that the transformation had to be understood. In fact, it became clear that many emotional attitudes could be described by this term, it being understood that on these occasions the person was imagined as being covered by a kind of invisible envelope expressing his mood or state. For example, the Desana term *gametarári suriró* meant "to be in love"; *doremoári suriró*, "to be ill"; *bayiri suriró*, "to be under a spell"; *gamekëári suriró*, "to be enraged"; *muhkú miríri suriró*, "to be happy"; and *áriri suriró*, "to be" or "to exist." It seems that the noun *suriró*/garment is derived from the verb *suri*/to paint, to anoint, and that it is related to the verb *suirí*, which means "to become entangled" or "to be covered by something."

The initial attitude of the man who, so the story went, had gone into the forest "to lose himself" because his wife did not love him is rather striking because romantic love does not seem to be a common sentiment among the Tukano, much less so in marriage. The term used to describe his act of entering the forest was *suári* (D), a verb that means "to enter," "to penetrate into," and it is used in this precise sense when one describes the act of going from an open space into the forest or a thicket. The verb is pronounced with a long *a* sound, but if one should pronounce it with a short *a* its meaning changes somewhat and comes to stand for "to squeeze into a cleft," a euphemism for cohabitation. The informants pointed out this double entendre and added jokingly that the man, having been rejected by his wife, was looking somewhere else for sexual adventures.

The next scene shows the jaguar-man engaged in bringing back the reluctant woman to her husband. In commenting on this, our informants explained that what was meant was a sexual assault.

The jaguar-man attacked and "killed" her, the bloodstains bearing witness to the aggression.

The theme of the equivalence of food and sex was further elaborated in comments on the travelers who sit at their campfire and on the jaguar-man's question, "What is it you people eat?" When told that the couple's food is game, the jaguar-man refuses this kind of food. The point is that the jaguar eats his food raw, while the couple, having built a fire, prepared theirs in cooked form.

In Tukano thought, the difference between the raw and the cooked is the difference between prohibition and permission in sexual contacts. Within the Tukano territory all people are considered to be "cooked" (T: *doase*), a term one can also translate as "added," "joined," "forming a unit." The "raw" territory is that surrounding the Vaupés and lying beyond the limits of the Tukano habitat. According to myth this zonification was established by the Sun Father, who put the dividing line between the raw and the cooked at certain large rapids: the Yuruparí Falls on the upper Vaupés, the Jirijirimo Falls on the Apaporis River, the Meyú Falls on the lower Pira-paraná, and the falls at São Gabriel on the lower Vaupés. The jaguar-man who traveled toward the West was taking his companions into the "raw" territory.[17] Although, in order to protect them, he introduced them there as "his people"—the act of grasping his tail was explained by our informants as touching his penis—they were strangers there.

The story comes to a sudden end when, tired of all the questioning, the couple tell of their adventure. They die, and now their souls must go to the maloca of the black jaguar. A Desana payé, when asked about the meaning of this punishment, said: "They danced in the malcoa of the West, there were other men and women there, and they danced together. They were not of their kind." The story, then, was essentially a cautionary tale pointing out the dangers of sexual relationships outside the prescribed norms—dangers brought about by a woman, in the first place, and aggravated later by the man's adventurous trip. It describes two sets of exogamic relationships: that of the man and his wife; and that of the two jaguar-peoples, those of the East and of the West. When their trails crossed, when they treated women of the other set, they violated their own exogamic rules and the punishment of the couple was death, social death, as soon as their behavior became public knowledge.

From the foregoing discussion it has become clear that jaguar imagery is related to sexual aggression. Be it in the drug-induced hallucinatory sphere, or in the mythical sphere of jaguar-people and jaguar-spirits, this sexual component frequently appears, and, often enough, a clear suggestion of incest. We must, then, make a brief inquiry into the relationship that seems to exist between the jaguar image and the idea of incest.

In many myths the jaguar is closely associated with the moon. Sometimes the moon is directly identified with a jaguar; at other times the jaguar is a descendant or otherwise a relative of the moon. In one Tukano myth, sun, moon, and jaguar live together in the sky until jaguar decides to descend to the earth, transforming himself into *omé-mahsë*/"smoke-person" (T). The moon, according to the Tukano in general, is the expression of incestuous love. In some myths the moon commits incest with his daughter, or with the daughter of the sun, his brother. The following is a condensed version of one of these tales.

Sun and moon were brothers, and the daughter of the moon was living on this earth. At night the moon descended and committed incest with her. The girl had prepared black body paint in a bowl, and one night, when her lover came, she put her hand covered with wet paint on his face,[18] in order to identify him later. Shortly afterward she left the maloca and saw the moon, his face covered with the imprint of her stained hand. Ever since, the moon has hidden his face out of shame, for three nights each month.

The connection with the jaguar becomes clear as soon as we recognize that what the two have in common is the spots. The story of how the jaguar got its spots is related to the previous one.

When the jaguar noticed the spots on the moon's face he went up to the sky and asked: "How did you soil your face?" The moon answered: "I slept with my daughter." The jaguar told the other felines and they all went to see the daughter of the moon. At that time they all were of one color and did not have spots. The girl had prepared body paint for a dance: a black paint (T: *uée*) and a red one (T: *kahtákasone uée*). The jaguar puts his paw into the liquid and daubed it on his body; the black jaguar put his whole hand into it and smeared it all over his fur. The puma painted himself red, and all the others, ocelots and their kind, began to splash paint on their bodies.[19]

The Tukano recognize a category of spotted things, and spotted

things are said to be evil. Cutaneous and other diseases break out
in spots; there are spots on rotten fruit and on the leaves of diseased
plants. Certain spotted fish should not be eaten. Yellow, black-
spotted animals are said to be especially dangerous because of the
similarity of their markings to the pelt markings of a jaguar, and
sometimes their very names refer to the jaguar: the spotted sting-
ray (T: *yaí anyá*), a very poisonous spotted wasp (T: *yaí uhtia*), a
certain spider, and some poisonous plants. The prototype of all
these spotted things is the spots on the moon's face, and the
spotted category is a constant reminder of the prohibition of incest.
They are, in other words, *maculae*.

The jaguar, then, is feared by all. To dream of a jaguar is an evil
omen, and to come upon a jaguar in the forest implies the danger of
the beast's being a spirit-jaguar or an enemy-turned-jaguar. Should
a spirit-jaguar have harmless intentions he may wear behind an ear
a yellow and black spotted orchid (T: *yaí oro*/jaguar-flower), but
few people would take a close look. What is feared, however, is not
the "earth-jaguar," not the spotted cat one can hear cough in the
forest or whose tracks one can see in the sand of the riverbank; what
is feared is the enemy that may hide behind its disguise. The evil
payé, the unknown foe, the anonymous malevolence incorporated
in the feline cause terror; not the zoological species.

There are many spells to ward off the dangers personified in the
jaguar. The following (Text No. 102) is a Desana spell.

"His ears are his ornaments,
His ears are his ornaments;
They are the white feathers of the harpy eagle.
When he is thus adorned, he is fierce;
Then he is armed with his bow;
Thus he is adorned.
    Now they take his bow away from him;
    They take it away.
    Also the hoe;
    They take it away.
    With this he cuts.
    We grasp it and he grasps it;
    They cut it off and take it away;
Thus they take away his ornaments;
They take away his hoe;
Taking it away, they put it on the platform of the sun."

The following (Text No. 100) is a commentary on the spell.

"The jaguar spell, that is what you want to know. There were some jaguar apprentices, they say; large ones. When the spell is said one lights a fire at the spot where they used to spend the night. One makes a fire on that spot. When this fire burns, the reflections of the mat and of the charcoal are spreading. Also the *mirití*[20] mat, the *anato*,[21] the *nyumú*[22] mat, and the glowing charcoal mat spread their reflections. When doing this, a trail is being formed to the maloca of the headwaters. One puts paca, deer, and agouti on that trail; they are his prey, and meanwhile one finds protection under the mat. Then once more one gathers firewood; wood from *nyumú* and *mirití* palms; this firewood will sputter sparks. One looks for firewood that sputters sparks, so there will be plenty of sparks when the jaguar sees it. One puts the spirit of puberty behind the mats. Then come the fishing rods, the black one and the thin one and the one of *moaburebo*[23] wood; one gives him these for weapons. Also the rod of starch. With these rods one strikes the mat from behind: papapapapa. This is what they do. This is the spell against the jaguar. One prepares a trail to where the sun rises. And also to where it sets. Thus he can eat behind the mat. Then the jaguar will not come near us, but will stay far away. This is what they say. That's all."

The informant added: "They do the same with the ornaments of the ears. Thus they say. In this way they appease him because he is fierce when he is adorned. This is how they cast the spell. They make him go to his maloca. Casting off his ornaments they make him enter it. That's all."

Like many similar incantations, this spell mentions the manufacture of certain "mats," or, perhaps rather, "fences," that protect and cover the supplicant. In Desana, *imikéya* is a palm wood that is used in the construction of fish traps, and *imikéyáru* is a finely woven mat or grid, a kind of lattice work. The two terms are often employed in shamanistic formulas as protective measures, and the different palm-wood maps mentioned here belong to the same category. The "spirit of puberty" is a rather cryptic expression, but a Spanish-speaking Desana insisted upon this translation. The term was *uáhti gamuyéri*, literally "bush-spirit-together-to cohabit."[24] The significance of the fishing rods also remained unexplained. But otherwise the spell is similar to those used against the Master of Animals, the *boráro*, or any of the malevolent supernatural personifications. The pattern is the same; the person hides behind a fence or mat while the spirit-being is disarmed and offered food, slowly being enticed to take a specially prepared trail that leads it away. There is no fight, no threatening confrontation, but gentle manipulation, a sort of enchantment during which the dangerous spirit loses its fierceness and becomes docile and harmless.

We must turn now to a brief discussion of this transformation complex and inquire into its deeper motivations and functions. It is obvious, perhaps, that for the Indian the jaguar embodies raw nature in her most uncontrolled and aggressive sense. The feline is the dominant power in the forest, a bloodthirsty beast which, by its cunning and sheer physical force, subjects all other mammals or reptiles, even those larger than himself. The jaguar is also assertively familiar with all dimensions of its natural environment; it roams in the densest forest, climbs trees, and swims in the water, and its prey ranges therefore from ground-dwelling animals to monkeys and birds, fish and turtles, or even caymans. It is the most conspicuous single carnivore of the tropical lowlands, and as a most resourceful hunter it is a fierce competitor of man. The jaguar's versatility makes of him a great transformer; the fact that black jaguars are fairly numerous in the Vaupés expresses, in the eyes of the Indians, an ambivalence, a dichotomy, that no other beast personifies more clearly, and the different local races of jaguars, with their varieties of protective coloring, have not escaped the attention of the natives. There is only one jaguar, true, but it can appear in many different forms. To this image we may add the "spotted" aspect of the jaguar, interpreted as the stigma of incest, which associates it with the moon and with the wider category of evil spotted things. Its spectacular mating behavior, its suggested habit of chewing jungle vines—perhaps yajé—its fierce fangs and claws all combine into an image unmatched by other beasts.

Upon most, if not all, animals of the forest and the river, the Indians have projected a social order. A colony of weaverbirds, a school of fish, or an anthill are obvious examples, but even on an individual level animals are often seen as members of categories which, in many ways, display a patterned behavior similar to that of people. A deer with its young, a lone tapir, a chattering monkey behave in humanly understandable and predictable terms. Not so a jaguar; the jaguar is the antithesis of the organized, patterned way of life the others lead; it is everybody's foe; it is the powerful carnivore amongst the meek and timid herbivores, and thus the jaguar is an outsider.

It would, perhaps, be tempting to see in the jaguar transformation primarily a mechanism for changing from Culture to Nature. The opposition to all cultural manifestations is stated in many cases; amongst others, in its attitude toward fire, its eating of raw food, and its implied incestuous tendency. In one of the texts (Text No. 31), when the couple prepare cooked food, the jaguar says: "You eat, but I won't." In another text (Text No. 30), the jaguar-men devour a woman in the forest, but the leg they bring for the old woman they put into a cooking vessel so it can be boiled. We could quote many other instances where this idea is stated in myths and tales. For the jaguar, then, fire is culture, and man-made fire is the great transformer of raw food into cooked food and, by extension, of forbidden sex into culturally approved sex.[25] What man consumes must be processed first, be it food or women. The jaguar-men's shying away from fire seems to express their rejection of exogamic rules, of all rules regulating sex in society.

In the spell against the jaguar the opposition is shown in other ways. To appease the beast, it is offered wild game, which is its natural food, while people seek protection under different-colored mats. And again, the jaguar is held at bay by the building of a fire that sputters sparks. It appears, then, that the jaguar cannot be subdued by force, by "natural" means, but only by the most subtle of cultural manipulations: fire, traps, mats, open trails, baits, fishing rods. And in the end the jaguar is killed by fire.

But the man who pretends to change himself into a jaguar conceives this transformation, in all essence, as operating on a sexual level, and as a change from strict exogamic rules to complete sexual license. The jaguar-man "devours" and rapes without distinction; he kills men or women who may be his close relatives. In contrast to this, the man in one of the tales (Text No. 31) is almost led to suicide because his wife has rejected him; he is the victim of his cultural conventions. Of course, his penetrating into the forest "to lose himself" seems to repeat the Culture-to-Nature reversal, especially if we remember the ambivalence of the verb suári/to enter a thicket or a cleft. The restrictions to which men are subject in Tukano society appears so suffocatingly contre nature that, it seems, men must escape sometimes, and it is the payé who takes it upon himself to effect this transition or to lead others on the way to it.

The question is: How like a jaguar does a man become? A payé-turned-jaguar is, for all exterior purposes, a true jaguar: he has the voice of a jaguar, he devours a raw meat, he sleeps on the ground, and he has the highly developed vision and olfactory sense of the feline. The reversal is expressed even in the translocation of his internal anatomy, his "hiding of the heart." But in one aspect he is not a jaguar at all: in his attitude toward human beings. In this, he does not behave like a jaguar, but like a man—a man devoid of all cultural restrictions, but still a man. The motivation of revenge and the acts of sexual assault, of attacking from behind and in a pack, and of severing the victim's head are not jaguar but human traits. What turns into a jaguar, then, is that other part of man's personality that resists and rejects cultural conventions. The jaguar of the hallucinatory sphere, the jaguar-monster of Tukano tales, is a man's alter ego, now roaming free and untrammeled, and acting out his deepest desires and fears.

7

YAJÉ:
MYTH
AND
RITUAL

Yajé is widely used among the Tukano, and drug-induced trances of varying intensity form part of many ritual activities. The principal occasions on which the potion is consumed are the gatherings of people from two or more exogamic units and consist of solemn events accompanied by dances, songs, and recitations. These collective trances, during which the participants are gathered together for one or several days, are religious ceremonies. The interpretation of the hallucinations emphasizes the law of exogamy, and the principal objective of the total experience is to demonstrate the divine origin of the rules regulating social relationships. But on other occasions, it may be only a small group of men that consumes yajé, in search of supernatural experience. And then sometimes, a lone person may take the drug, for his own particular ends. The potion is also consumed during most rituals connected with the individual life cycle, such as initiations or burials and, above all, during the *yuruparí* ceremony. Often, yajé is taken in preparation for fish-poisoning expeditions, or when a party of people has gathered some specific wild-growing fruit in the forest. During curing rituals, not only the payé will take yajé; sometimes the patient, too, will have to imbibe the drug, in order to search in his visions for causes and remedies.

In trying to describe the function of yajé trance in Tukano society, we must inquire first into the mythical origins of the drug. These myths and tales provide the justification of the institution of narcotic trance and give it its sacred character in that they explain the divine origin of the plant, together with the ritual norms that must be observed during its use.

The following text is a translation of a Desana myth:

"It was a woman. Her name was *gahpí mahsó*/yajé-woman. It happened in the beginning of time. In the beginning of time, when the Anaconda-Canoe[1] was ascending the rivers to settle mankind all over the land, there appeared the Yajé Woman. The canoe had arrived at a place called *dia vii*, the House of the Waters, and the men were sitting in the first maloca[2] when the Yajé Woman arrived. She stood in front of the maloca, and there she gave birth to her child; yes, that was where she gave birth.

"The Yajé Woman took a *tooka*[3] plant and cleaned herself and the child. This is a plant the leaves of which are red as blood on the underside, and she took these leaves and with them she cleaned the child. The leaves were shiny red, brilliant red, and so was the umbilical cord. It was red and yellow and white, shining brightly. It was a long umbilical cord, a large piece of it. She is the mother of the yajé vine.

"Inside the maloca the men were sitting, the ancestors of mankind, the ancestors of all Tukano groups. The Desana were there, and the Tukano proper, the Pira-Tapuya, and the Uanano; they were all there. They had come to receive the yajé vine. To each one the yajé vine was to be given, and they had gathered to receive it.

"Then the woman walked toward the maloca where the men were sitting and entered through the door, with the child in her arms. When the men saw the woman with her child they became benumbed and bewildered. It was as if they were drowning as they watched the woman and her child.

"She walked to the center of the maloca and, standing there, she asked: 'Who is the father of this child?'

"The men were sitting, and they felt nauseated and benumbed; they could not think anymore. The monkeys too, yes, the monkeys were sitting and were chewing herbs; they were *bayapia* leaves.[4] The monkeys could not stand the sight either. They began to eat their tails. The tapirs, too, were eating their tails which, at that time, were quite long. The squirrels, too, were eating their tails and were chewing herbs. The squirrel made a little noise—kiu-kiu-kiu—as it was chewing. 'I am in a bad way,' the squirrel said; 'I am eating my tail.' 'What is going on?' the monkeys said and touched their tails, but the tails were gone. 'We are in a bad way,' the monkeys said; 'Poor me!' said one of the monkeys; 'I shall go mad eating my tail! Poor me!'

"The Yajé Woman stood in the center of the maloca and asked: 'Who is the father of this child?'

"There was a man sitting in a corner and saliva was dripping from his mouth. He rose and, seizing the child's right leg, he said: 'I am his father!' 'No!' said another man; 'I am his father!' 'No!' said the others; 'We are the child's fathers!' And then all the men turned upon the child and tore it to pieces. They tore off the umbilical cord and the fingers, the arms, and the legs. They tore the child to bits. Each one took a part, the part that corresponds to him, to his people.[5] And ever since each group of men has had its own kind of yajé."

At this point the tale was interrupted and the question was asked how the woman had become pregnant.

"It was the old man, the Sun Father; he was the phallus. She looked at him and from his appearance, from the way he looked,[6] the seed was made because he was the Yajé Person. The Sun Father was the Master of Yajé, the master of the sex act. In the House of the Waters she was impregnated through the eye. By looking at the Sun Father she became pregnant. Everything happened through the eye.

"The Yajé Woman had come with the men. While the men were preparing *cashirí* the woman left the maloca and gave birth to the yajé vine in the form of a child. It was night. The men were trying to find a way to get drunk. The Yajé Child was born while the men were trying to find a way to become intoxicated. They were just beginning to sing; their song rejected the child. They rejected it with a stick rattle of *sëmé* wood.[7] The animals that were eating their tails were cohabiting because they had become intoxicated. The yajé should have produced only pleasant visions, but some became nauseated and so they rejected it.

"The woman had walked to the center of the maloca. There was a box of feather headdresses; and there was a hearth. When she walked in, only one of the men had kept a clear head and had not become dizzy. The men were drinking when she had her child, and at once they became dizzy. First they became dizzy; then came the red light and they saw red colors, the blood of childbirth. Then she entered with her child, and when she stepped through the door they all lost their senses. Only one of them resisted and took hold of the first branch of yajé. It was then that our ancestor acted like a thief; he took off one of his copper earrings and broke it in half, and with the sharp edge he cut the umbilical cord. He cut off a large piece. This is why yajé comes in the shape of a vine. They all tore off bits and pieces of the child. The other men had already taken their parts of the child's body when at last our ancestor, *boréka*,[8] took the part corresponding to him. Our ancestor did not know how to take advantage of yajé; he became too much intoxicated."

We must pause here and consider this text in some of its details. The essential framework within which the yajé theme has been developed is the Creation Myth. This myth is recited on many ritual occasions, but many minor variants exist because each group has its own emphasis and its particular manner of focusing on certain places or events related to its lineage. We must begin, then, by recapitulating the broad outlines of the myth.

The divine creator was the Sun Father, in all essence a phallic concept,[9] but still a deified abstraction, who originated life by fertilizing the earth, which is imagined as a female principle. The fertilizing power of the Sun, conceived as procreative energy, manifests itself in different forms, but, above all, in that of an intense yellow light. The yellow color has for the Tukano the connotation of seminal impregnation, and according to the intensity of the color the fertilizing power is graded into several categories. The Indians distinguish at least seven shades of yellow ranging from a dull, opaque, or "dirty" yellow to a bright orange tint. The importance of distinguishing these different shades is shown in many ritual actions, especially in songs and spells, in which fertility—in terms of the increase of animal and plant life, or of society and specific segments thereof—constitutes the central theme. The colors are named in a sequence of increasing intensity, and the particular names pronounced with great care, after which a short exclamation condenses the formulation of a desired end, such as an exhortation to plentiful reproduction or to a banishment of evil influences. Animals of a yellowish color—birds, mammals, insects—play an important part in these songs and spells, since they are thought to be imbued with the sun's powerful life force and, in some ways, to be the sun's direct representatives on earth.[10] Fire, the yellow flames of the hearth, also expresses this power. The complementary color is red, because of its association with the fecundity of the female principle. Yellow and red, male and female, phallic fertilization and uterine productiveness, thus form a pattern of recurrent motifs in most cosmogonic and cosmological ideas and pervade, through ritual, practically all aspects of existence. The basic model is always the sun.

In the beginning of time, long before mankind had been created, the Sun Father, his brother the moon, and the sun's daughter, a bright star, lived together, alone, in the sky. Both fell in love with the girl, and while the Sun Father lived openly with her in an incestuous union, the moon only visited her furtively as a celestial incubus whom she mistook for her father and lover. Once, when the moon asked for her favors while she was menstruating, she pushed him away with her bloodstained hand, and ever since the moon's pale face has been marred with dark spots.[11]

The original act of incest between the Sun Father and his daughter had taken place at the Wainambí Falls[12] on the Macú-paraná, an affluent of the Papurí River, and the ancient petroglyphs that cover some of the large boulders near the falls are said to represent the traces of this scene: two hollow depressions made by the girl's buttocks, a chain of small holes or "drops" where she urinated, and several other marks bearing witness to the event. But soon afterward the sun became aware of the gravity of his crime. Although some versions of the myth suggest that, at first, the girl was not overly displeased with her new relationship to her father, she soon fell ill and began to waste away. She bore her divine father a son, but the infant died and in this manner death came into this world. Incest had led to death, and this fatal consequence now become the Sun Father's first principle when he created mankind. Thus the law of exogamy was established.

From some myths it appears that the "bright star," the daughter of the sun, was Venus, and that the incest theme expresses a "confusion," a mistaken identity, patterned on the appearance of Venus Matutina and Venus Vespertina. The double image of this planet and the manner in which it seems to follow the sun or to approach the moon are aspects often mentioned by the Indians and seem to be the model for this tale.[13]

Our Desana text began with the words "In the beginning of time," and the meaning of this expression—*neo gorare*—is of interest. The root *go* expresses a uterine concept, the idea of origin and birth; *goró* is vagina, *gobé* is a cavity or hole, and *gorá* expresses the idea of a vital force emerging from somewhere. *Gorosiri* means "place of origin," but also place of death and of return, and the same term *goró* is also used to designate a burial place.[14] It is from the uterus, the maternal womb from which life is born and to which —in the form of tomb and paradise—it returns. It is not surprising then to find that this concept of birth should be related to that of legitimacy; both *gorare* and *gora* mean true, authentic, legitimate, pure, and *gorata* means truly, in reality; *gorege* is true, real. The initial expression *neo gorare*—in the beginning of time—contains therefore the idea of truthfulness, of the true and legitimate origins.

This physiological aspect of origins is complemented by the Sun Father's attitude, described as "the yellow intention." When the sun had the yellow intention he decided to create mankind in an act, or a series of acts, the sexual character of which is but very thinly disguised.

In the first place, the Sun Father began to travel upriver in his canoe, in search of a propitious spot for the creative act. Now the symbolism of rivers and of river travel is rather complex in Tukano thought. In English we speak of the *headwaters* of a river, and of the *mouth* of a river. We are always interested in locating the sources of rivers, in finding the exact spots where the waters spring from the *bosom* of the earth, and we associate with these spots the idea of purity, of a mysterious immaculateness watched over by benevolent forces and containing a life-giving and -preserving quality. To our minds, the sources of a river are a beginning, while the river mouth is an end.

The Tukano do not think this way. To them, the origin and the true force of a river are at its mouth, and from there these qualities ascend, ever diminishing, until they reach the headwaters, the end. All rivers are imagined as snakes, their undulating glistening bodies stretching over the land, their tail ends lying in remote and isolated regions while their powerful bodies develop into fierce heads at the river mouths. The ripples on the skins of these winding snakes are the falls and rapids; it is there that the river flexes its muscles and where dark powers are thought to reside, unfathomable dangers contained in the thundering waters and the silent pools that follow them. Again, in our culture we speak of snakes as one single category of animals, and at times we are puzzled by the occasional ambivalence of snake symbolism. For the Tukano there are two entirely different categories of snakes, which can never be confused: the anacondas and other water-dwelling snakes represent a female principle, devouring and entwining, a powerful force which attracts and seduces; while the land-dwelling snakes—above all, the diverse boa constrictors and the many colorful and often poisonous species—symbolize a male principle, an outward-acting and aggressive force. Rivers, then, are essentially water snakes, and, therefore, female elements.

The mouth of a large water snake is sometimes compared to a female sexual organ, and the ascent of a river is symbolically related to a sexual act. The verb *pahári*/to glide or float on the surface of the water, is used in referring to a canoe, but it is also a synonym for cohabitation. The verb *mëriri*/to ascend, be it a tree or a river, expresses the act of "climbing up" with an effort and is another synonym. In a Desana metaphor "the river opens like a flower" (*paríri*) before the traveler, who, if he is of a supernatural character, now takes the "yellow path" (*bahsíri maa*) that leads along the bottom of the river and is the route of communication of all spirit-beings associated with water. A synonym is *dia koré maa*/"river-vagina-path," an expression underscoring the fertilizing aspect of the voyage, and in several myths it is stated that it was this path the Sun Father took when he was about to create mankind.

The rapids and falls also have a sexual character; they are female elements, uterine whirlpools to be overcome by great effort, not devoid of dangers. The deep pools at the foot of these falls are thought to be the dwelling places, not only of the supernatural Master of Fish, but also of monstrous man-devouring snakes in whose abodes the drowned victims lead a shadowy existence. These falls and pools are designated as "traps," as female organs into which the male is being sucked and drowned. A number of myths speak of the exploits of those who have had to brave these danger spots on their travels. But the rapids and their pools are also important way stations on the road to mankind's dispersal. They are "houses," malocas, designated by specific names that refer to creative acts that took place there, or to certain plants or animals with sexual connotations. The designation "House of the Waters" thus includes a number of specific spots mentioned one by one in relating a particular myth.

Already at several hundred meters below a rapid the traveler will be able to observe scattered blotches of whitish foam floating on the surface of the water, and these increase steadily as one approaches the spot where the river rushes over the boulders. This bubbling froth, gushing out from the turbulent waves and currents, provides an emotion-charged spectacle to the Indians, who see in it

an image that combines the elements of procreation and birth. To
the mind of the Tukano, anything that bubbles and foams contains
the essence of creation, be it the contents of a cooking pot on the
hearth or a yajé potion being stirred in a vessel before the drink is
distributed. The fermentation of a trough of *cashiri* beer is interpreted in the same manner. The key concept is "yajé foam" (*gahpí
soporo*), a vision-producing, creative liquid imagined as having
seminal and hallucinogenic properties. The rapids and pools, then,
are places of creation where man and his institutions originated,
sprouted forth, welling up from the deep thronging regions of the
waters. The verb *pamurí*/to bubble, to germinate, to froth, is associated with this image and is found in certain place names and in
the names of mythical beings who were instrumental in the Creation. To pass over a rapid is *yërësé* (T), a verb denoting a passage
in the sense of a transformation; the rapid is the climax of the
ascent and is the spot where the river "flowers" (T: *yurári*), a verb
that, having the meaning of "to rise," "to overflow," "to sprout," "to
flower," is also used to describe sexual sensations. After this comes
the descent, which is letting oneself float with the current, expressed by the verb *yuríri*.

It was at these roaring and foaming falls that the Sun Father
was searching for the precise spot to create mankind. The tool he
carried with him for accomplishing this act was the stick rattle, a
long, thin, lance-shaped staff the upper end of which had a small
oblong chamber containing a few dry seeds which produced a
vibrating, rattling sound when the stick was shaken. Part of this
polished staff was adorned with the brightly colored feathers of
certain hummingbirds.[15] The stick rattle, called *yeegë* (from *yee*/
jaguar, *yeeri*/to cohabit), is the phallic staff still in use on many
ritual occasions, and in the hand of the Sun Father it was the tool of
fertility.

The myth continues, recounting that the Sun Father occasionally
stopped and thrust the pointed end of his stick rattle into the riverbank as if to test the soil, but proceeded on his way as soon as he had
observed that the staff stood obliquely. He knew that on the spot
he was searching for the stick would eventually stand vertically, but
this spot was difficult to find and the myth describes the many trials
and vain attempts of the divinity to locate this place.

We have already mentioned that the concept of finding the

"center," or of centering an object—generally related to creative acts—plays an important role in Tukano myth and ritual. The center, or precise spot, is associated with a female principle and is also the spot where an *axis mundi* can be placed, a connecting link between this earth and other cosmic levels that may lie above or below it. The object itself—a staff, a house beam, a tree, a vine serving as a ladder—then becomes a means of communication and, in another sense, one of fertilization. The phallic axis which penetrates the earth and the precise point at which this happens are complementary elements, and the heavenly penetration must find its true counterpart. The staff stands erect only when it joins the female complement, its partner in terms of exogamic law.

Several landmarks in the Northwest Amazon are pointed out by the Indians as the places where mankind had its origin, owing to the fact that each major tribe or group has its own creation story, based on dim memories of migrations or on vague traditions of its members' having come from a certain direction. But all of them have this in common: they are huge rocks and boulders lying at large waterfalls, and most of them are covered with ancient petroglyphs. Two of these spots are of special importance to the Vaupés Indians: the rocks of Ipanoré on the lower Vaupés River, in the Brazilian territory, and the Rock of Nyí, near the Meyú Falls on the Pira-paraná, in Colombia. It so happens that both spots lie almost exactly on the equatorial line, and it is this fact that contains the key to the Sun Father's search. It is on the equator that the sun's rays fall vertically upon the earth, that is, that the phallic stick rattle stands upright. The Sun Father was "measuring the center of the day" (D: *ëmë dehko*). In fact, to one standing on the equatorial line and looking eastward or westward, all constellations appear to rise or set vertically, while, to one observing them from a spot lying a few degrees to the north or south, they appear to rise and set obliquely. The equator, then, is a zone of verticality, and this is why the Creator chose this place.[16]

The momentous act of the Sun Father's visit was commemorated on these spots by bygone generations of natives who carved a number of petroglyphs on the rocks that lie at the falls. These of Ipanoré[17] are at present badly eroded and are hardly recognizable at all, most of them lying somewhat below water level and visible only during the height of the dry season. But the Rock of Nyí is adorned with some of the best-preserved petroglyphs in the entire

Vaupés area, and it rises above the waters at all times of the year. The huge boulder, roughly rhomboid in shape, presents a flat, perfectly vertical surface, on which a large symmetrical design has been deeply cut into the rock. The design shows a triangular face, interpreted by the Indians as a vagina, and immediately below it a stylized human figure, somewhat similar to a winged phallus.[18] At the foot of the rock, cut into the flat surfaces of smaller boulders, are several other designs, concentric circles, some of them with short spikes radiating from the periphery. These designs are variously said to be the imprints of the Sun Father's blowgun or of the flutes he carried with him. Two other groups of petroglyphs, both located at important rapids, are found on the headwaters of the Tiquié River, in Brazilian territory. Located just east of the Rock of Nyí, they also lie on the equator, at Pari Cachoeira and Carurú Cachoeira, respectively. The motifs engraved on these rocks show stylized anthropomorphic figures and several spiral designs, all said to be connected with the Creation Myth of the local Tukano groups.

But we must return once more to our origin myth. When the Sun Father's staff at last stood upright, without casting a shadow, drops of sperm flowed down from it upon the earth, which received them and brought forth the first men.[19]

Just below the Rock of Nyí lies the Meyú Falls, and on some of the large flat boulders lying on the western shore these first beginnings of mankind are said to have left their traces. *Meyú* is a Tupi word meaning cassava (*beijú*), and it is said that at the Meyú Falls people prepared food for the first time. Several large circular depressions in the rock represent the cooking vessels, and some thin whitish veins crossing the dark surface of the stone begin at these depressions and are said to be the traces of the thick soup of manioc flour which poured over the boulder when the vessel overflowed because of "too much heat." But this is one level of interpretation. When standing at these boulders and discussing the matter, some Indians said that the circular depressions were the marks of female buttocks and that the light-colored veins were the traces of the Sun Father's sperm. The act of cooking was interpreted as coitus, and the "vessel that overflowed" was the first woman.

Nearby there are a few natural depressions in the flat rock, quite similar to human footprints, some of adult size and, following them, a few smaller ones, apparently of children. The Indians interpret these as traces of the first women and children, but here, it seems, they were mixing two different mythical traditions, that of the Sun Father's lonely trip upriver to create the first men and that of *Pamurí-mahsë's* (the "germinator's") Anaconda-Canoe, which held the first men. As there were no women at that time, the petroglyphs of the Meyú Falls seem to be associated with another, later aspect of the Creation Myth.

When traveling in an open canoe under the low-hanging vegetation of the jungle-covered riverbanks, one must constantly duck and crouch to avoid branches, tree trunks, or sharp, backlashing sticks and canes. No warning is given and each passenger must fend for himself, ducking rapidly under a rotten trunk or twisting his body sideways to dodge a looping vine or a sharply splintered branch. Sometimes one passes under a wasp nest, or a snake stretched out on an overhanging branch, and then silent gestures are all that is necessary to call attention to these potential trouble spots. One day, not far from the Meyú Falls, our canoe was gliding through a small affluent when a vine brushed my shoulder and a sharp thorn tore my shirt and skin. The vine was long and thin, but extremely resilient, and the hooked thorns were fine and strong.[20] "That's how our ancestors caught the first woman!" one of my Desana boatmen shouted. Calling back and forth from prow to stern my companions now told me that, in the beginning of time, the first men had gathered on the shore and, with the help of this particular vine, had hooked and caught the beautiful Daughter of *Aracú*, the fish called *boréka*, who was to become the first Desana woman. The fish-girl—others elaborated on the story—had watched from under the water the fire the men had built on the shore, and around which they were dancing while playing their flutes. Enticed by the "yellow light of the flames" she had swum closer and closer and, catching sight of the first Desana, had become enamored of him. It was he who caught her with the hooked vine, and when she thus fell into his hands, he offered her honey, an irresistible gift to any woman.[21]

"Woman are fish," say the Indians, and there is ample proof for this interpretation in many aspects of Tukano culture. The courtship of women is often ritually represented as "fishing," and the yearly run of fish is a model for many dances and songs in which women and fish are described and compared in terms of fertility and their character as "food for men."[22]

There are many songs among the Tukano of a solemn and monotonous kind, accompanied by dances, which are known by the general term *vaí bayári*/fish songs. *Bayári* means to dance and sing, and *bayíri*—a related word—means to implore, to enchant. The word *vaí* is mainly applied to fish in everyday usage, but when combined with certain other particles it may mean any animal or living being in general (D: *vaí méra*) or may refer to a category of game animals (D: *vaí bëgë*). Sometimes the word can stand for all animated life, depending upon the context. When used in the fish songs, *vaí* refers both to women and to their offspring, and the words of the songs speak with monotonous intensity of the fruitful river, the "deep furrow," the vagina belonging to them, to the men only, and in whose depths stretches the "line of succession" of the continuity of life.

The following is a fish song of the Desana:

What line is this?
It is the line of the river;
There are fish in the river;
Maní fish, lover of the river;
The line of the river continues;
Maní fish, lover of the river;
There are fish in the river;
Maní fish, lover of the river;
Erect yourself inside her!
There are fish in the river;
Maní fish, lover of the river;
The line is continuing.
 Join her, I say;
 Lying with her, I say: Bite her!
 Erect yourself inside her!
 Within her, erect yourself!
 There are fish in the river;
 The breeding places of *maní* fish;
 River of yajé.
She goes on forming them;
There are fish in the river;
The fish are within her;
The line of fish is calling;
She is opening up, opening up;
There are fish in the river;
Maní fish, lover of the river."[23]

The song tells of the "river of yajé," and after this long digression we must pick up the thread once more and return to the Creation Myth.

When the Sun Father had thrust his stick rattle into the ground, its pointed end penetrated far beyond the earth, down into the land of *ahpikondiá*. With this term (derived from *ahpikon*/milk, and *diá*/river), the Indians designate paradise, the underworld abode of the Sun Father and the source from which all life springs and to which the souls of the virtuous return after the body's death. This paradise, presided over by the sun, has a uterine character; it is a land where there is neither hunger nor fear, bathed eternally in the yellow-greenish light the color of tender *coca*[24] leaves. *Ahpikondiá*, the River of Milk, is entirely surrounded by a shell, a protective cover called *ahpikon-víi*, House of Milk. It was into this House of Milk that the stick rattle penetrated.

Tukano ideas connected with the generative powers of this cosmic womb are highly involved. The Sun Father's sperm, which fertilized the womb, was of a supernatural character and therefore had to undergo a transformation in order to be able to bring forth ordinary human beings. This biospermatic energy remained constant and unchanged, but its product was to be a new life such as had not existed before and which had to be "filtered" and "combined" in a special way in order to accomplish the transformation from a spiritual, supernatural seminal essence into a human being. The key word around which these ideas revolve is *taër'ro*/"that which is constant, that which is a beginning." According to our Desana informants, the related verb *tariri*/"to happen," "to come to pass," and, in a wider sense, "to manifest itself," is connected with this concept. The womb of *ahpikondiá* is designated as *taëró-víi*/"manifestation-house," in the sense of its being a place wherein the supernatural essence manifested itself in a visible, human form. Many myths and songs refer to this process of transformation and to the "sifting filter" through which the original sperm passed before it became "diluted" in the cosmic womb. Once this had happened, newly created mankind issued forth, climbing up the stick rattle until it reached the level of our earth and there emerged as full-grown men.

Thus ends the first part of the Creation Myth, the first major chapter in which the Sun Father himself visited the earth. The next part describes a different theme, that of the peopling of the land, of the slow, progressive dispersal of ancestral groups, and at

the same time we are told how women came into this world, how
animals and plants began to breed and spread, and how certain
artifacts and social institutions came into being.

Pamurí-mahsë, the germinator, had been put in charge by the
Sun Father of the establishment of mankind on earth, and we next
find him laboriously ascending the rivers in a large canoe shaped
like an anaconda. There were only men inside this craft, one of each
tribe and each exogamic group; what we learn about the manner
in which they were ranked and the personal attributes they carried
with them depends on who is telling the tale. Each Tukano group
has its own variant of this myth, and the different episodes described in them vary according to local tradition.

The slow ascent of the rivers is described in all these myth variants. Step by step the riverbanks are settled, the men disembark
and build their homes, clear their fields, and take possession of the
land. Place names are mentioned, many of them still in common
use, where this or that incident occurred, but the sequence and
colorful elaboration of detail depend completely on the person telling the story. Some versions are laconic, while others monotonously
repeat some episodes over and over, with only slight variations in
names and dramatic detail. Often enough several versions are
garbled, and also parts of entirely different myth-complexes are introduced while important scenes of the Creation story are left out
or are transformed almost beyond recognition.

In most versions, however, the building of the first maloca is
given a prominent place. In the myth we quoted at the beginning
of this chapter it was at a place called *dia vii*/House of the Waters,
where the first maloca stood and where the Yajé Woman made her
appearance. From what had happened before it seems that women
did not exist until then; at least none is mentioned as being present
during the dramatic scene of the birth and dismemberment of the
Yajé Child. The Yajé Woman, it seems, was the first woman of
Creation.

Contradictions occur, of course, owing to the interpenetration of
different traditions. Not only will certain groups claim that their
particular female ancestor was truly the first woman, but other
groups will claim that some women had already been created when
the Yajé Woman arrived. But no matter; what seems certain is that,
judging from the behavior of the men and animals present, the

appearance of the Yajé Woman introduces a crucial sexual element into the sequence of events that had been taking place during the original peopling of the land. As a matter of fact, this is a turning point in the entire Creation Myth.

In our attempts to unravel the tangled web of events in the phantasmagoric scene in the House of the Waters, we elicited comments and explanations and soon noted that the informants pointed out with great insistence that the men, on seeing the Yajé Woman, "felt like drowning," and that therein the true key was to be found to the impact the woman had made upon the concourse of men and beasts. We must examine this expression in more detail because, from the study of a large number of original texts, it appears that its meaning is of special significance to the question of how yajé is related to sexual experiences.

The term in use is *miriri* (D), and its nearest translation is "to drown." However, the word has several meanings which are important if we want to learn about the interpretation of the myth at various levels of abstraction. In the sense of "drowning," the word *miriri* can be used of persons, animals, or an inanimate object which falls, plunges, or sinks into the water. It can also be used in the sense of a patient's sinking into unconsciousness or coma, or of a person's having hallucinations. In a somewhat different sense, *miriri* means "to dilute, to mix, to confound oneself," and in this sense the word can be used, for example, in describing what happens when a drop of water falls into a pool or when—as in the Creation Myth—the Sun Father's sperm is diluted in the cosmic womb. A third meaning is that of overpowering, overwhelming, and dominating. This does not imply physical force, but rather the influence of a state of mind; of alcohol, poison, or a drug. Another meaning of *miriri* is "to throw into disorder, to perplex"; and a last group of possible meanings is contained in the terms "to saturate, to overflow." All of these are used in describing the physiology of sex.

In the face of this wide range of meanings, the interpretation of the mythical scene in the House of the Waters becomes, perhaps, more comprehensible. The myth says that, when the Yajé Woman entered the maloca, *gahpí noméri miria vaya*/"yajé-images–she drowned them with." The term *noméri* is of interest here. The hallucinatory images produced by the ingestion of yajé are usually called *gahpí gohóri*/"yajé-figures," an expression derived from *gohsisé*/reflection, aureola. The term *noméri*, in this context, has a similar meaning, although it stands here for "to paint with red dots," an expression that may be used when referring to facial paint but that also describes luminous phenomena such as reflections upon water or clouds, or even the flash of a gun. One of the informants said: "When one drinks yajé one sees images that move and dance. Yajé is female and produces these images."

When speaking of hallucinations and the terms employed in describing them, the Indians repeatedly pointed out that the same words would be used to describe a sexual experience. During coitus the person "drowns" and "sees visions"; the act is described as a state of intoxication (*niaróre*), of drunkenness, a state of rapture in which anxiety and bliss combine and transport the male into another dimension of physical and spiritual consciousness. In the myth, the anguish of the men's state is increased when the Yajé Woman reaches the center of the maloca; the text says: *beetëonyati paro*/"it was unbearable." To the Tukano, this close association between sex and hallucinatory trance is quite natural; these two experiences, because of their intensity and rapture, have much in common, and the myth simply explains how they came into being. In fact, according to the Indians, in explaining the origin of yajé, the myth explains the origin of sex, and in linking the two it links the law of exogamy to the religious sphere. But more of this later.

We must briefly refer to the symbolism connected with the maloca—any maloca. A maloca is said to be a womb, the "uterus of the sib," and the entrance door is imagined as a vagina. This, then, is a danger spot, a zone of transition between two different spheres where things are being transformed while passing from one to another. The maloca is fertilized through the door, that is, the sib's continuity is guaranteed, but gestation takes place in the center of the dwelling. Hearth and womb, according to the Tukano, are the two great transformers, the crucibles wherein nature becomes culturally sanctioned, wherein the raw turns into the cooked, the sperm gives birth to a new member of the household. These ideas are closely related to certain ritual attitudes a hunter must observe when bringing his prey from the forest, and with food preparation in general, and we have referred to this aspect in another context.[25]

The oblong boxes of plaited leaves and canes in which the dance ornaments are kept when they are not in use are also uterine symbols and are often mentioned in this sense in mythological and ritual contexts. Their contents are the headdresses covered with white down, the ropes of monkey hair, and many other ornaments used during different rituals, and many of these objects have a seminal significance which is kept and guarded within the box.

From what our informants explained, it seems that, when the Yajé Woman enters the maloca with her child and walks toward the center where the hearth and the box are located, her behavior symbolizes a sexual attitude. This scene—not the dismemberment of the child—is pointed out as the climax of the tale, and that this act caused an extremely anguished reaction is clearly indicated in the myth. There is an element of confusion, of indecision, accompanied by deviant behavior. Some of the beasts, many of them considered to be phallic animals, begin to eat their tails, an action interpreted by our informants as a sex act.

Whenever we referred to this state of confusion and asked about its nature and significance, we received the answer "There were no rules yet; people behaved like animals." From these comments it becomes clear that this statement refers to the absence of precise marriage rules, and that the Sun Father's preoccupation with the "right spot" was concerned with the establishment of the law of exogamy and the definition of social segments between which the future exchange of women was to take place. In addition, from several texts and further comments it appears that sex itself did not yet exist, that it was introduced, together with yajé, in a kind of initiation rite. In one of our texts there is a significant allusion to this; when describing the ascent of the river, *after* the Yajé Woman had made her appearance, the text says: "Now they were floating on the surface of the water" (*iro pamutúa arinyora doha oó vehká arinyora pare. Vehká ira vagá pányoma*), an expression which, as we have mentioned earlier, is a description of the sex act. Moreover, all our informants insisted that the law of exogamy was introduced simultaneously with yajé. Now men and animals were separated, and each group of men was assigned certain groups of women. These, in turn, were now associated with certain animals—mainly fish—and plants, and in this manner the origin of yajé became closely linked to the mythical origins of social organization.

From the symbolic representation of the yajé complex, as de-

scribed in myth and tradition, we must turn now to its social aspects
and ritualization. The preparation of the narcotic potion is formalized in detail and several texts explain the various stages in the
collective consumption of the drug. The following text (Text No.
173) reproduces the words of a Desana payé:

"The yajé vessel is painted with yellow and white designs. The
yellow color we call *boré* and the white color we call *ebobohó*. It
is with these colors that the vessel is adorned.

"There must be two men who blow tobacco smoke over the vessel. And while they are blowing they chant: 'This is what we are
going to see when we are drinking yajé!' They begin with the
snake, a snake like a bead necklace. Singing of this snake they
speak of its colors which are like those of a necklace with bright
designs, blurred designs, and white designs. Then they sing of the
white and the black boa constrictor. They imagine the two boa
snakes as the central beams of the roof of the maloca, the white boa
lying on the left and the black one to the right. The houseposts,
too, they imagine as shining brightly, and they imagine the houseposts as entwined by snakes that are curled around them. And they
sing: 'We shall have bright visions, we shall have blurred visions.'
The *yonero*[26] snakes come, too, and, grasping their shapes and colors,
they push them into the maloca. Then come the *boréka*[27] snakes
and, grasping them—their shapes and their colors—they push them
into the maloca. Then comes the *mahká*[28] snake, and they push it
into the maloca. There is a light-colored boa constrictor, with bright
and blurred markings, and the image of this snake they push up
onto the houseposts. 'All this we are going to see,' they sing. And
again they blow smoke over the vessel. They smoke the same tobacco that is used during the gatherings. Then they sing of *buia*[29]
and they imagine the maloca to be painted the color of *carayurú*.[30]
They also push the yellow and the yellowish colors into the maloca.
Then they sing of the ornaments and feather headdresses, and they
imagine them as fruits, and push them into the maloca. They put
the red and the yellow colors in the center. 'This we shall see,' they
sing, 'When we are drinking yajé.' They are not sitting quietly; they
are preparing the images. 'The conical design[31] must be in the
center,' they sing. 'The shrimp-shaped designs, the female design,
must be heard; the *vahsú*[32] design must be heard. When we are
under the influence of yajé, we shall hear these sounds; we shall feel
as if we are drowning,' they sing. They take the black deer-bone

flute and the white deer-bone flute, and put their sounds into the maloca. The sound is: oré-oré-oré-rooo-rooo-rooo-erúuuu-erúuuu-erúuuu. All this they will hear later under the influence of yajé. Whatever music they play now, they will hear later. The red deer-bone flute sounds: pi-pari-pá-pira-pu. 'This we shall hear,' they say; 'And the sound of the music shall overpower us and we shall fall silent.' Then they shall hear the sound of the clay trumpet: mooo-mooo-virá-virá-virá-mooooo. All these sounds they are shaping while blowing tobacco smoke over the yajé vessel. And again the sound of the flutes: te-to-te-to-teto-te-rooo-te-rooo. 'This we shall hear,' they say. With their words, and blowing smoke over the yajé vessel, they create these sounds. And they take the vessel and lift it up high, and when they do this they know that their visions will be bright. When they do this, the people will not become nauseated. To sing well, they support it with macaw feathers. If we do not do this, one cannot sing well."

So far our information has described the preparation of the vessel. Apart from this, the different yajé vines[33] must be prepared by saying a spell over them. The following Desana text (Text No. 141) refers to this procedure:

> The vine of fish-yajé makes us dizzy;
> Vine of red fire, vine of white fire.
> Anoint the vine with *tooka* sap, with *tooka* peppers, to grasp it.
> By grasping the nausea its power is destroyed and banished to
>   the river mouth.
> Take the nausea away and take it to its spot at the river mouth.
>   The vine of fever-yajé is at the headwaters of the rivers;
>   Fish-yajé of green vines, red vines, white vines.
>   May our visions not produce nausea.
>   These are the potions of the Master of Game Animals.
> The *bayapia* plant makes us dizzy;
> The *bayapia* plant with red vines, white vines, green vines.
> Ours is the same, the same in kind;
> Green vines, white vines, red vines;
> They all make us nauseated.
>   Banish the nausea by anointing them with *tooka* sap;
>   Banish it by grasping it, and by doing so, take it away;
>   Destroy the evil power of the potion!
> The narcotic snuff is the penis of the Sun Father;
> When they prepare it, they have their containers;
> For firewood they only use *puikarogë* and *oyodiigë* wood.[34]

Taking these firewoods, they separate them;
By grasping them, they banish the nausea.
    Then comes the red starch;
    The macaw feathers are maddening to us;
    The *bayapia* people make us dizzy;
    Grasping it, our people banish the nausea;
    Grasping it, they throw it into the river mouth;
    Thus they destroy the nausea.
The *bayapia* people return once more;
Red vines, white vines, green vines;
Destroy the nausea by grasping it;
    Our yajé comes next;
    korépida vine, *merepida* vine, *duhtu-puusere* vine;[35]
    Then comes the yajé vessel;
    The vessel with yellow designs, with white designs.
    These designs anoint with *tooka* sap!
    The stirring rod is next;
    As it stirs the potion, so it is stirring us.
    Anoint it with *tooka* sap and destroy the nausea!
    In this way the evil visions will disappear.

Our next text (Text No. 174) refers to the pounding of the yajé vines and the preliminary preparations for the event.

"The yajé vines are pounded outside the door. The leaves are torn off and [the stems] are put in a heap. Then they mash them, by pounding them in a special way[36] while they whistle. The leaves that will be added are mashed apart.[37] Then the yajé vessel is put under a sieve. Then they light the cigar for their incantations, and blow smoke into the vessel. The vessel in which they prepare the admixture[38] is different. They leave the vessel inside the maloca, near the door. 'Will it do?' [they ask], and two men taste the drink. They take little draughts of the liquid, in a small gourd cup. They drink two cups and say: 'It is all right.'

"Then they take up their stick rattles. Armed with the stick rattles they go and announce the drink. When they thus begin to sing, the others begin to converse.[39] 'We have a beverage,' they say; 'Let us go and drink it.' This said, the two return. Those who are going to sing are talking now. They all are going to drink. Now they converse: iiii aaa ëë–iii aaa ëë. Then one of them stands up in the center. He fills two gourd cups with the potion. They begin to drink. They drink twice and then they sit down on their stools. Those who follow them come again to drink. The old men gesture in defiance and sit down again. All the men drink. All those who drink gesture in defiance. So do all of them, and now the old men who will sing step forward. They hold their stick rattles and their shields.[40] After having taken two drinks they shake their stick rattles. They defy their enemies. Then they begin to take out the ornaments, and the one who directs [the event] takes the ankle rattles. Now all the men adorn themselves and step forward in pairs."

This description refers only to the preparatory stage of the ceremony; the potion has been tasted and now several men are sitting, facing each other and beginning a ritual conversation.[41] But it is understood that they do not yet wear their feather ornaments. These are distributed only shortly before the dance.

Another description (Text No. 78) takes us a step further:

"Carrying up[42] the yajé vessel to our elders, they say: 'I shall offer you this drink; Drink it!' They say: 'I shall prepare yajé for you!' The young people do this; one of them stirs the potion; the one that carries the cups has the stirring rod. Another one distributes the drink. The one who distributes it, what does he do? He says: 'We shall return the favors of those who give us women; sitting here we shall saturate ourselves.'[43] This said, they return and fill the cups again. Now when they approach once more the others begin to whistle. They say: 'We shall reject you immediately so that fishes will emerge from the mouth of the vessel instead from our mouths.'[44] They tell the yajé vessel to go and lie crying on the floor.[45] Addressing the vessel they shout: 'I shall drink your contents and then I shall fill you with dirt. And then I shall kick you with my foot!' And the others shout at the vessel: 'I shall drink what you contain, but then I shall defecate into you!' Then they go to the center of the maloca and there they dance and sing. They all wear earrings. Thus they offer the gourd cups. Thus they come, saying: 'Take!' They come with two cups and offer them. They approach again and make a clapping noise.[46] They exclaim; others come, again and again; they approach and exclaim, once more offering two cups. Then they go back and when they return again they make a clapping noise. [This scene is repeated several times in the text.] The dancers wear their shields and hoes; it is imposing, isn't it?[47] 'Drink this!' they exclaim; 'This is our life! It is as vital to us as the bones of fish are.' Then they give the cups to the others to carry, and take the stick rattles. They crouch and posture,[48] and then they hit the sticks against their shoulders to make them vibrate loudly. 'This to you, enemy of our ancestors!' they shout;[49] 'This is the way I shall thrust you with my stick rattle!' And then they return to their posts, and when they arrive they stamp firmly and call out: 'I shall kill the enemy of my ancestors!' Then they sit down and rest. And then they take the yajé vessel and they lift it up high, and then they crouch and stamp loudly and return to the back of the maloca.[50] Then two others step forward and do the same; they advance and then they turn back. And then they leave the vessel and go back to their seats.

"At this instant it happens! A shiver runs through our bones. No, they have not yet consumed all the yajé, but the shiver comes and grasps you. You almost die. Yes, almost. And then the sounds come and the music says: 'Bear it!' All the songs come, all the spells; now you can hear them and they all say: 'Bear it! Bear it!'

"First is the bitterness of the potion;[51] everybody mentions it; the Cubeo, all of them talk about it. They all speak of the bitter part and of the red part.[52] The red hallucinations are blinding, they say. They rise before us, they rise. They pervade everything. Those who first were boisterous now become somnolent; they cannot speak, they cannot find words. Seeing these visions they almost go mad. Our bodies feel light. Some babble nonsense; they are worthless. But some are silent and understand. And while this happens, the old men sing and dance. This is why one should not sit down to rest; one should dance. The bone flutes sound: rerererere. When one hears this, one also hears the deer-bone flute: piraripa-pero-puuu-paririri-pirararara. One can hear this music even if no one is playing the instruments. It is the effect of the incantations. Also the snail flute can be heard: mooo vira-vira-vira. This is the music one hears when drinking yajé.

"But our whole bodies are trembling then. When this happens, our women exclaim: 'O the poor miserable ones!' All this happens when we drink yajé. These are the sounds. It is better to sit down, then. When this happens and when the incantations were well done, one can hear the flutes. The incantations influence the flutes. But it can be very harmful, too, they say.

"The old men continue to talk. The one who carries the shield sits down. Taking the shield, the one with large edges and the one with small edges,[53] he protects himself and sits down. He sits on his stool which is adorned with painted zigzag designs.[54] Taking the stick rattle, the smooth one and the knotty one, he sits down.

"And then the Star-People descend, with their shining eyes, with their brilliant eyes, and surround those sitting on their benches. The scintillating lights come and try to carry them back to the Milky Way. This is what they say."

The foregoing descriptions show how highly formalized a yajé ceremony is said to be. Each phase, practically each individual movement, is prescribed in detail, and if we add to this the specific forms and meanings of feather headdresses, musical instruments, dances, songs, and gestures, the overall picture is one of great complexity. As we shall note further on, however, ritual details among the Tukano are easily modified or condensed to their essentials. No two yajé ceremonies are alike; there is always variation, and the texts we have quoted represent rather a standard model which serves as a mere outline.

The question was put to our informants whether the mythical scene in which the Yajé Woman first entered the maloca was similar to the textual descriptions given above. A Desana payé answered in the following words:

"Yes, this was what they felt. Only one of them kept a clear head. The mere presence of yajé and the sight of childbirth made them feel nauseated. They were drinking *cashiri* beer while the Yajé Woman was in labor, and at once they became nauseated. First they became nauseated; then the red visions came and they saw red colors, the blood of childbirth. Then the woman entered with her child, and when she stepped through the door they all lost their senses. Only one of them remained conscious, and he took hold of the yajé vine; he cut the umbilical cord."

Now the problem remained of why the Sun Father should have created yajé, and of his intentions when he gave this drug to mankind. Here follow the words of a Desana payé, in answer to this inquiry:

"It was the yellow light. People were like animals; they did not know how to use the yellow light. The Sun Father had to teach them how to use it. He acted in the form of an oropendola[55] bird when he created yajé. He took the great heat of the Universe and put it into the Yajé Woman. The oropendola bird traveled upriver and during four days he created yajé. The Sun Father was traveling in his canoe, alone, at the beginning of time, ascending the river. Sometimes he stopped and took his stick rattle and pointed it here and there, trying to find the exact spot where the power of yajé might be located. Mankind needed a means of communication; it was for this reason that the Sun Father was searching for yajé. He thrust his stick in the ground, in the riverbank, wherever he stopped at a rapid. But the stick did not stand erect; it stood inclined. So he went on and tried again. But once more it stood inclined. He went on and on, and at last it stood straight, it stood upright; this was the spot. This happened at the Ipanoré Falls, and at the Rock of Nyí. It happened there where the Sun Father, in his form of an oropendola bird, was trying to find the spot for yajé. When he had found the spot, the Sun Father returned to the House of the Waters. He returned out of shame, because of the purity of the color, the yellow color of the sun, the power of the sun. The color was ashamed. Now he sat for three days thinking and thinking of how to use the color in the right way, without doing harm. First he thought that the color of the heat of the Universe was similar to the color of the *caimo* fruit;[56] but this was not true. No, it was a different color. He thought and thought until he found the right color which the people should use when they chose their women. He gave the color to the people; he gave them the yellow light. He gave them yajé. And by giving them yajé, he gave them their life; he gave them the rules by which they should live. Once they had yajé, they had found their fields, their conversations.[57] Now they had yajé, and so many other things besides with which to reciprocate: conversations, songs, food, and also evil things. Now they had found their place, even if it was in the midst of troubles and errors. Sitting there, in the House of the Waters, they had found their way of life."

We may recall here that at some other point in the Desana Creation Myth it was said that the Sun Father had created mankind when he had the "yellow intention," and that this expression was explained as referring to a sex act. The Desana payé now added that the preoccupation with the "right color," the right shade of yellow, referred to the definition of specific groups of people between which women were to be exchanged. According to our informants, the search for the right shades of yellow was the search for marriage rules.

26. Rock engraving at
Nyí, near Meyú Falls,
Pira-paraná (total height
of engraving, 1.40 m.)

27. Barasana Indians
gathering yajé
(*Banisteriopsis caapi*);
Pira-paraná

28. Barasana Indians
with bundles of
Banisteriopsis caapi vines;
Pira-paraná

28

27

29. Barasana Indian
pounding the vines in a
wooden trough; Pira-
paraná

30. Barasana Indian pre-
paring *Banisteriopsis
caapi* vines; Pira-paraná

29

30

31. The narcotic potion
being sifted into the
vessel; Pira-paraná

32. A painted yajé vessel
with a U-shaped design;
Pira-paraná

33. A yajé session;
Tatuyo Indians, Pira-
paraná

34. Tatuyo Indians danc-
ing; Pira-paraná

32

33

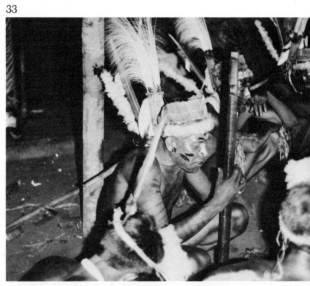

34

35. A Barasana dancer playing his instruments under the influence of yajé; Pira-paraná

8

A
YAJÉ
SESSION

In this chapter I shall give an account of a yajé ceremony I was able to witness among the Barasana Indians of the Pira-paraná. In the description of this ceremony we shall be able to observe the variability of certain details of procedure, together with the basic pattern underlying these ritual gatherings.

I had been asked by the Indians if I wanted to take part in a yajé session and I had expressed my intention of doing so. In the days that followed this conversation the matter was not mentioned again, but about a week afterward I noticed that some of the men were leaving the maloca, taking with them their hammocks and fishing gear. I gathered that they had been sent to visit several malocas in the neighborhood, perhaps a day's travel away, in order to invite guests. In fact, as the days went by several canoes arrived with men from another exogamic unit, some of them accompanied by their women and children. After lengthy ceremonial greetings the men put up their hammocks in our maloca, while their women-folk gathered in the back, chatting with the other women, grating manioc, and taking part, after a while, in the daily tasks of food preparation.

The next day, shortly after noon, I found myself almost alone in the house. The men had gone fishing or were gathering wood, and all the women and children were down at the creek soaking the red *mirití* fruits in the water. Only three men—one whom I shall call Biá, and his two younger brothers—were sitting at the door, one of them polishing a blowgun and the others idling or drawing with their fingers in the sand. After a while Biá rose and came over to where I was sitting. "Let's go and gather yajé," he said. He took up his bushknife and left the maloca.

I walked behind him and the two young men followed us, jostling and running. We went down the trail to the creek where the women were busying themselves with their baskets full of fruit. Paying no attention to them the men went by, jumping from stone to stone, crossing the water and wading through the mudbank on the opposite side of the creek. We entered the forest, and the trail was ascending now, but soon we arrived at the top of a small hill. Biá had stopped and pulled at some leafy vines that were hanging down in profusion from the trees surrounding us. He broke off a piece and chewed it for a moment; then he spit out the splinters and pulled at another vine. A shower of dry leaves and ants fell over us and the men laughed, slapping their shoulders and thighs. Now they all began to pull down the vines Biá had pointed out to them, and they cleaned off the leaves and small branches, cutting off a bundle of finger-thick stems of about arm length. We then went to another tree nearby and then to a third. Each time Biá first chewed a piece of the stem of the vines before he and the others pulled down the required quantity. "This is *guamo*[1] yajé," he said, showing me the stems he had taken from a height of about three meters; they were of a light-brown color and the surface of the bark had some slightly raised ridges. Other vines, taken from a height of about two meters, he called "mammal yajé"; their color was brownish with light spots, and the surface was smooth. A third category was "head yajé," taken at ground level, and the dark-colored stems were knotty and twisted. As far as I was able to ascertain, all three bundles of vines belonged to the same botanical species— *Banisteriopsis caapi*—but Biá insisted that they were three different kinds of yajé. We now had some twenty-five stems, each about sixty centimeters in length.

It was almost four o'clock in the afternoon when we returned to the maloca. Biá cleaned the wooden trough that was lying outside near the entrance and began to break the leafless stems into smaller pieces he now threw into the trough. Then he took his club of heavy redwood and with the blunt end began to macerate the stems with heavy rhythmical blows. While continuously stamping the mass he murmured and, once in a while, broke into a chant.

Muhipu, the headman of the maloca, had taken down the painted yajé vessel that had been hanging outside from a rafter, and he was cleaning it carefully, but without washing it. He also murmured and chanted, and then he went into the maloca and walked along the walls chanting and gesturing with a small torch he held in his hand. The other men had removed the hammocks, tools, and baskets that had been lying about, and the women had swept the floor and were now stirring the *cashirí* beer in the large trough standing in the center, slightly to the right.

Outside, a group of men was sitting. After dipping small cylindrical roller stamps of carved wood into *genipa*[2] juice, they painted their legs and arms. The stamps had longitudinal perforations, and with thin straws introduced as axes they could be rolled over the skin, leaving behind bands of geometrical designs. Some of the older women were there, and they painted their husbands' backs and shoulders, all serious-faced and working with great care. Near the back entrance other women and some nubile girls were carefully painting their arms and breasts and dipping little sticks into the liquid paint to trace lines and dots on their faces.

Biá had been pounding the yajé vines for more than one hour. He now poured cold water, about eight litres, over the shredded mass and then began to pick out some bits of woody splinters that were floating on top of the liquid. Muhipu brought a small gourd-cup with some water in it and put a few small splinters of shredded yajé vine into it. He watched it closely as the water turned a cloudy white. "It is starchy! It is good!" he exclaimed; "We shall see many images!" He now put the yajé vessel on the floor and brought a large circular basketry sieve. A group of men crouched in a circle and lifted up the sieve horizontally, holding it over the vessel while Muhipu filled a large gourd-cup from the trough and poured it slowly over the sieve so that the sifted liquid dripped into the vessel.

It was becoming dark now and we entered the maloca. Just inside the door the men had arranged two rows of little wooden stools, and now they began to open the large boxes containing the feather-crowns, the rattles, and the painted loincloths. Bëhpó, the oldest of the men present and the headman of the visiting party, opened a box lying before him on the floor, lifted up a large feather headdress with both hands, and put it slowly on his head. It was 6:20 P.M. He now took another feathercrown and handed it to his neighbor; then another and another. More boxes were brought, and all the men adorned themselves. They tied the large seed rattles to their

right ankles and fixed others on their left elbows; they stood and
walked about, fitting on belts and crowns, sometimes stamping
sharply to make the rattles sound. Others were blowing shrill tunes
on their flutes. It was about an hour before all the men were properly dressed.

Now they sat down in a semicircle facing the interior of the
maloca, with their backs to the main door. There were twelve men,
who were now talking and laughing. It was dark now and one of
them lit the *turí*, the large resin-covered torch standing near the
center of the room, and it began to shed an intense red light over
the scene.

There was a sudden hush. Bëhpó rose and walked to the center
of the semicircle. He was holding a stick rattle horizontally in both
hands, the rattle pointing to the right. He shook it sharply and exclaimed: "hö-hö!" Again he shook the thin stick, holding it before
him, almost touching his thighs. Now he took the stick into his left
hand, the rattle pointing downward before him and the hand high
above his head. A sharp stroke with the right palm against the stick
made the rattle vibrate loudly, and now he swung it in a wide circle,
clockwise, the sound of the rattle filling the room. Again and again
he hit the stick, letting the lower end circle, hanging from his uplifted hand. After a few minutes he changed his stance; grasping
the stick in the middle with his right hand and holding it with
bent elbow horizontally and pointing forward, he knocked it
against his right shoulder with sharp, rapid movements. "Hö-hö!"
he called again.

Now he sat down in the middle, among the other men. There
was a shrill noise of flutes and whistles. A man began to play an instrument of turtle shell, rubbing the wax-covered projection of the
plastron with a sawlike motion of his right palm while pressing the
shell against his body with his left upper arm. The chirping, rasp-
ing noise rose rhythmically, increasing rapidly. There was no music
yet, just noise, each man using some instrument as if tuning it.

There was another silence. A boy approached with a large bowl
of fresh *cashirí* beer and we all drank a sip of the brew. Bëhpó now
lifted up a large horn of black pottery decorated with yellow and
white designs and, without rising from his stool, blew on it. The
blaring sound, long-drawn like a foghorn, filled the air. As if in
answer to it the other men, also without rising, stamped their feet
and sounded their rattles. Now they rose and took up their posi-

tions for the first dance. They were standing in line, each man with a painted stamping tube in his left hand, the right hand resting lightly upon the shoulder of his neighbor. Again they stamped fiercely, and then they began to sing, moving forward with rapid steps and dancing toward the interior of the maloca. Encircling the first four houseposts they danced for a long while.

It was shortly after eight o'clock when Muhipu put the yajé vessel in front of him and began to stir the liquid with a little rod. The rattling sound it made was a signal; the men returned to their seats, perspiring and breathing deeply. Muhipu filled two small, black gourd-cups with yajé potion and, holding a cup in the hollow of each hand, began to chant rapidly: "mamamamamamamá!" He offered a cup to the man sitting next to him. He took it and, throwing back his head, drank the potion. Then he coughed and spit noisily. A young boy handed him a cup with *cashirí* and the man took a sip. After having given the second cup to the next man, Muhipu walked back and refilled the empty cups. Going back and forth, always chanting "mamamamamá!" he offered a cup to each man. While drinking the potion the men grimaced and screwed up their eyes as if the draught were very bitter and nauseating. They coughed and spit; some of them shook their heads as if in disgust.

When Muhipu offered me a cup I drank it, swallowing rapidly like the others. It tasted not at all as bitter or unpleasant as people had warned me it would. My pulse was 100; I felt a slight euphoria, and after a while a fleeting drowsiness set in.

The men were boisterous now and there were shouts and laughter; they shook their rattles and looked around. From the darkness at the rear of the maloca where the women were sitting came shrill laughter. We could not see them, but once in a while, when the light flared up, one could perceive their huddled shapes in the darkness. All during this time some of the men had been playing their flutes, and the croaking, hackling noise of the turtle shell had not ceased for an instant. Again the men rose and danced, and this time the women came forward and joined them in a slow, solemn dance.

At nine o'clock Bëhpó blew again into his clay horn; Muhipu stirred the potion and began to chant "mamamamamá!" and we all had another draught. By now my pulse had dropped to 84. At 9:30 another round was presented, also preceded by the wailing sound of Bëhpó's horn. The dancers were now more animated, their voices more sonorous, their movements more precise. The man who had been playing the turtle shell was dancing alone, jumping back and forward very rapidly with closed bent legs while throwing his body backward and forward to counterbalance his violent jumps. With the right hand he stroked the turtle shell, while with the left he held a panpipe he was playing in shrill rapid notes. The other men were dancing in line with the women and were now singing more rapidly, but without raising their voices.

A quarter past ten o'clock Muhipu offered a new round of yajé, the fourth. He returned to his seat and began a monotonous recital. It was very dark inside the maloca. Some of the men were sitting slumped forward, as if asleep, their heads hanging low over their chests, but their arms were moving and their hands were gesticulating. "All painted red," said the man sitting next to me. His hand pointed to the housepost in front of us, but he spoke without looking up. "All painted red; the posts, the walls, the rafters! Hoooo— the flowers, the images, the sun!" he exclaimed and then, shaking his hand over his head, he bent sideways and vomited. The others were murmuring, a singsong, a few words. Someone started to play a flute. Suddenly I felt very nauseated; I went outside and vomited violently, but I soon felt better.

Muhipu was sitting to the far left, a little apart from the others and half-facing the first row of men. He had drawn up his legs so that his chin was almost resting on his knees. He was looking before him with half-closed eyes, his lips moving rapidly while he slowly stretched out his right arm, palm downward. The flutes stopped suddenly and the men were silent. Now Muhipu's voice could be heard chanting rapidly, and his hand rose and fell in an even rhythm. Biá was sitting in front of him, his arms embracing his up-drawn knees. Now both spoke rapidly, in singsong voices, without looking at each other, both motionless but for their lips and Muhipu's outstretched arm, which rose and fell with the tone of his voice. They were alternating in their recital, in different intonations, sometimes in a staccato followed by long-drawn sounds and a sharp catching of breath. The light from the torch had become dimmer and dimmer. Muhipu's voice became louder and rose sharply, again and again. Then it stopped. For a long while we sat in silence and almost complete darkness.

One of the men got up and went to light the torch again. Standing close to the smoke-blackened pole he carefully kindled the flames until its red light began to spread over the room. The men were coughing and spitting, and now they tightened the seed rattles on their ankles and rose to gather in front for the next dance. The deafening sound of the rattles filled the room as the men took up their positions once more, facing the interior of the house, stamping the floor—once, twice, three times—. "Hö!" they exclaimed; "Hö-hö!" Then they advanced and turned, singing and marking their steps with the hollow thud of the stamping tubes. The line advanced into the open space of the center. Turning around in a circle, each man with one hand on the shoulder of the one before him, they appeared again in the light, dancing slowly, round after round. The voices rose and fell, the thumping approached and receded, over and over, from light to darkness and back again into the red glow of the torch.

By now most of the men were having hallucinations. They talked about them in drowsy voices, describing what they were seeing and sometimes asking others to explain the significance of their visions. I myself had not felt the slightest effect so far; I was completely conscious of my surroundings and in control of all my actions. The general rhythm of the dance had become more and more coordinated as time went on. After the men had drunk three or four cups of yajé the steps, turns, and gestures had reached a precision that made the group appear to be one single organism moving in a highly controlled and precise way. The same was true for the songs; there was never a false note or an eccentric movement; song and dance had become completely fused. Moreover, the entire scene was far from being a frenetic orgy; it was extremely formalized and solemn. There was noise, but even the noise had a formal quality and was produced intentionally and at certain intervals. I noticed that during the whole night people hardly ever looked at each other; they seemed to avoid facing others and looking into their eyes. Each man talked and sang and danced, but he did not talk to a specific person, or dance with a specific partner or neighbor. Each man acted alone, but at the same time as a member of a highly organized team.

The men were resting again and there was music of flutes. One of the guests poured some *vihó* snuff mixed with tobacco on the palm of his hand, scooped it up with a straight bird-bone tube, and crouching before another man blew the powder into his nostrils. He then handed him the filled tube and the other man repeated the act. The exchange of snuff was very solemn, done with slow, deliberate movements. Not all of the men took snuff.

A few minutes after eleven o'clock we were served the fifth cup of yajé. There followed another dance with the women, more rapid than the preceding ones and this time not accompanied by songs but by panpipes. But soon the women retired into the darkness and the men continued to dance, now running rapidly in a zigzag, now in a figure eight, between the houseposts. When they sat down to rest there was jesting and laughing. "Hö-hö-höi!" the men called, and the women answered in a shrill falsetto. There was a short exchange of obscene remarks.

At midnight Muhipu served another round. By now I had developed a strong headache, and a few minutes after taking the potion I had a spell of diarrhea. Almost all the participants had suffered from the same effects and had also vomited violently. But soon after, I felt better; the headache was gone and I felt a peculiar lightness. About half an hour passed. The men were groaning and murmuring; there were sudden exclamations. Now all of them were in a trance once more.

It was very hot and still. Suddenly I saw a flash of light before me. I looked up and saw the men, the room, the red light of the torch. I let my head fall on my chest and stretched my crossed legs out before me, just like the others. There was another flash. I had the sensation that something opened before me like a huge door, and that I could see beyond it into a deep space. I saw something like red curtains catching the light somewhere. Then, suddenly colored patterns began to unfold before my eyes.

The following is a transcription of the tape-recording I made while having these visions.[3]

> I'm seeing something . . . well, like . . . it's dark, but I see
> something like the tail of a peacock . . . but at the same time
> it's like . . . everything in movement . . . like fireworks, no? Much
> like a . . . the background of, let's say . . . of certain Persian
> miniatures There's something Oriental about all this. Oh,
> tapestries, Tibetan tapestries. . . . Sometimes it makes me think
> of . . . that decorative Arabic script, some Sūra of the Qu'rān.
> Rather in dark colors; sometimes it appears white, but more
> often than not it is a dark red. It passes . . . it goes . . . it is oblique
> in my field of vision. It moves from top left to bottom right.
> There is a very gentle flow. Now it is changing . . . all the colors
> of the spectrum, as . . . yes, undulating . . . but in some way
> the arches of each undulation separate and form new motifs.
> At the bottom it is yellow; it changes continually and then passes

through all the colors of the spectrum. The motifs are . . . yes,
everything is curvilinear: semicircles, shapes like hearts that
are intertwined and then become flowers; suddenly, shapes like
a Medusa. Sometimes there are . . . yes . . . again these effects of
fireworks. But when . . . no, it isn't three-dimensional . . . it's flat
and fairly dark. Now it's gone. [*Some sounds of the flutes; the
dancers rest now.*] Something comes from above, from the right:
they are . . . it is like water from a fountain, but the light
passes through the jets of water, like a rainbow. These lines cross,
but they aren't lines, in fact they are interrupted by intervals.
Spots, with a . . . dark center, the exterior yellow . . . then, like a
flower, like ostrich feathers, curled. And again, feathers like a
peacock's. Sometimes like moss; like these mosses. Now very
much like fungi, like those fungi in the lens of a camera;
irridescent. A flower, but with three petals . . . three . . . yes. [*The
vision disappears for two minutes; the dancing starts over
again.*] I am very much awake again. When I open my eyes
wide open, I see the maloca, the darkness, the people; but this
way, when I half-close them, I again see these motifs. Sometimes
they are like microphotographs of butterfly wings, or of marine
corals. Sometimes the colors aren't . . . aren't pleasant. Now
there are more definite motifs: arabesques, horizontal bands. Yes,
just about everything comes in parallel bands, each a different
color. Yet always in motion. Often in these bands there appears
a kind of grid, a mesh. Centers form themselves. [*The music
becomes more intense.*] The grid is relatively static, only the
centers are in motion, they spin and change colors. Again . . .
now this whole scheme tilts, and moves about . . . almost 45
degrees . . . but, now almost vertical [*Strong rattling.*] Now the
pattern is becoming more horizontal. The bottom is almost
black. Sometimes there are concentric waves that move, like
very black waters in which a stone has fallen. Yes, yes, but all
very symmetrical. Hardly ever is there a motif which is not
symmetrical. Sometimes, like . . . ancient locks, these ancient
ornate plates on the lock of a door. It is all so baroque! [*Dance
with much percussion.*] A number of semicircles, like trees of
some sort, dark against a lighter, almost bluish background.
But it changed already! Like . . . like microphotographs of
plants; like those microscopic stained sections; sometimes like
from a pathology textbook. [*Some people are vomiting. All are
saying that they are having hallucinations; they claim that
they see the whole interior of the maloca painted in colors. But
they go on dancing.*] Now there is a change on the right side . . .

now . . . there is a Tibetan quality, blue Buddhas, and around them a yellow-red-blue halo or flames that end in little dots. [*The dancers rest; there is talking.*] It's like that sometimes. It isn't pleasant. Yes, it is spectacular as a color! And always this increase and decrease of shapes, of lights. They duplicate themselves . . . a circle appears, it doubles, it triples, it multiplies itself. Yes, they spin . . . everything moving very quickly. Like . . . like . . . that's it, like bubbles, transparent bubbles, those soap bubbles. And now darkness. No, I see no more. But I am feeling well. It's almost one o'clock. I have taken six cups of yajé: pulse 84, a light headache. After the fourth cup, I vomited violently, and after the fifth I started to get diarrhea. But otherwise I'm all right. A bitter taste in my mouth, nothing more. [*About two minutes go by.*] I continue to see things. Hexagons, all like a ceiling full of hexagons, some tilted 35 degrees, and at the center of every four of them, a blue dot. It's changed, now they are small stars . . . how many there are! They come and go, come and go; that is, they approach and recede. . . . Now they have almost disappeared. [*Monotonous ritual conversation beside me; virtually no music.*] Hmmm . . . like a basketry design. Ah yes, yes . . . Rouault's paintings, like stained-glass windows . . . colors . . . blots, surrounded by a thick black line. [*High-pitched sounds of flutes*]. Yes . . . or large, different-colored eyes. That symmetry doesn't exist any more! These things drawing near are like bodies . . . now they are like large caterpillars, with a lot of quills and fur . . . with a little bubble at the end of each hair. But again . . . like a microphotograph. It has changed now . . . like little red hairs, is it not? But now it is changing; those little bubbles are lengthening, and now they are gone. Again . . . well, it's so difficult! Now there appears a dark red color crossed by a series of yellow rays; the center is to the right, but I can't see it. These rays fall as if on a forest of little red hairs. Everything is tilted . . . again, above to the left and below to the right. It has now changed, now . . . they are thousands and thousands of stylized palms in perspective. They are like tapestries, aren't they? They change, they change, like stylized little trees. Yes, all of that is, for the most part, like certain ties in bad taste. Yes, now it is all disappearing. I see no more.

It was almost two o'clock in the morning. My vision had lasted for twenty minutes, interrupted twice by a few minutes during which I did not see anything. I had been speaking very slowly.

At 2:10 A.M. the men took another round of yajé, and at 3:20 the eighth and last one. They were dancing now in almost complete darkness. Then they rested, and occasionally there were long monotonous recitals. The music never stopped completely, and the croaking noise of the turtle shell continued hour after hour.

Dawn was coming. Bëhpó slowly took the feathercrown from his head and handed it to Muhipu, saying "má" take! in a loud voice. The other men followed his example. It was exactly 6:20 A.M.; the ceremony had lasted twelve hours to the minute. Muhipu handed the different ornaments to Biá, who carefully packed them away in their boxes. The men left the maloca and gathered in the chilly air in front of the house, yawning and stretching their limbs. There was but little conversation. The men looked tired but content. After a while some of them put up their hammocks and went to sleep. The women were starting to light their hearths, but there was little food that day and few people cared to eat. Nobody complained of any unpleasant aftereffects of the potion.

I was drawing in my notebook, trying to recapture some of the images I had seen. A man who was looking over my shoulder when I was making a series of dotted lines, vertical but slightly undulating, asked a question about it, and I answered that I had seen this design last night.

"Look!" he called to the others. Several people came and gathered around me, staring at my drawing.

"What does this image mean?" I asked.

The men laughed. "It's the Milky Way," they said; "You saw the Milky Way! You were flying up with us to the Milky Way!"

A long time before I myself had taken yajé my attention had been drawn to a certain relationship that seemed to exist between hallucinatory imagery and some decorative design elements I had observed among the Tukano. Before going further in the discussion of the yajé experience itself I must therefore refer back to these initial observations.

I had a box of colored pencils and some sheets of paper clipped to a drawing board, and I left these things lying about with the hope that someone would become interested in them. I myself never made a drawing in the presence of the Indians, so as not to provide them with a ready model. One day someone asked me what these pencils were for. "One can draw with them," I said. "I don't know how to draw," the man replied. "Draw anything you like," I told him. The man sat down and traced a red line. I left him to himself, but when I returned after some time he had drawn a fish, very carefully, and several people were standing around him making comments. Then someone else sat down and started to draw, and in this manner I soon had a small collection of pictures showing birds and tapirs, fish, a maloca. Some of them were painstakingly detailed, but they were stiff and lifeless, completely lacking in spontaneity. Anyhow, people did not like to draw these things; they soon became bored and often abandoned drawings they had begun to make.[4]

One day I said: "Why don't you make a drawing of what you see when you drink yajé?"

The man I had spoken to looked up in amazement. "*Gahpí ohori*"/yajé images, he exclaimed. He seemed pleased with the idea. He sat down and chose three pencils—red, yellow, and blue—and began to draw in bold, flowing lines. Others came and immediately recognized what he was doing. "*Gahpí ohori*," they said. They, too, wanted to draw some. An elderly man who had been watching left the maloca to bring some bits of wood and string. He began to fashion a set of drawing utensils: a straight ruler, a ruler with an undulating edge, a small circle, a semicircle fashioned like a bow. Each tool was a miniature replica of the ones used in painting the front walls of the malocas, an art which had almost disappeared in recent years and now was found only in some remote regions. The drawing of *gahpí ohori* soon became a favorite occupation of several men who would spend hours sitting over the drawing board tracing intricate designs in red, yellow, and blue. Sometimes they would trace with their fingers some outlines in the dust at their feet, copying them on paper afterward. There was disappointment that my box contained only one shade of yellow, and often the artists would ask me for other shades of this color, insisting that they were of importance to their work. They were pleased with these drawings and proudly showed them around. I tape-recorded their own explanations and the comments other people made.

I soon noticed that the drawings fell essentially into two categories: those composed only of geometrical design motifs, and others showing figurative motifs, although occasionally combined with abstract elements. I also noted that certain design motifs were

repeated in the drawings of different people, and that these motifs
were constantly interpreted by the men as having a quite precise
significance. "This is *vahsú*," they would say, or "This is the Anaconda-Canoe." The motifs were rarely exactly the same, but each
category had in common a certain basic shape, such as a zigzag line,
a triangle, a circle, or a U-shaped element. There were variations
in size, color, or elaboration, but the essential outline was the same
within each category and could easily be recognized. It could be
drawn in a single, a double, or a triple line; in one, two, or three
colors; with little appendages or other secondary additions; but the
basic shape was the same.

I now proceeded to isolate these design motifs by drawing each
of them on a numbered card and showing these around while so-
liciting an interpretation. The result was remarkable in that almost
all the Indians agreed upon the meaning of the individual designs,
and the few who did not were undecided as to any specific interpretation. From this experiment it seemed that the design motifs
taken from the larger drawings were somehow coded, and that this
code corresponded mainly to certain aspects of myth and social
organization. In making this suggestion—and I wish to point out
that it is no more than that—a note of caution is necessary. The
number of persons who thus identified the design motifs was limited and does not represent a reliable sample; there were about
forty men who agreed upon the interpretation of the designs, but
since most of them were inhabitants of neighboring malocas there
may have existed only a local consensus. Nevertheless, the general
agreement on the significance of the designs was so striking that it
seems to justify the presentation here of the results of this inquiry.
The following discussion, therefore, is based on incomplete data
and cannot be more than a suggestion for further research.

The design motifs that can be isolated as distinct units, together
with their interpretations, are approximately twenty (Fig. 39):

1. A triangle flanked by vertical lines ending in outward-turning
volutes or spirals. This is said to represent the male organ and is
designated as *vahsú*, the rubber tree.[5] The fruit is edible only
when boiled, and it has a seminal connotation because of its gelatinous flesh; the tree itself, because of its latex, is mentioned in
many myths and rituals as a "male" tree.

2. A rhomboid-shaped element said to represent the female or-

gan. By the addition of a dot in the center, the idea of fertilization is expressed.

3. An oval-shaped element which contains several circles or semicircles, said to represent a fertilized uterus.

4. A U-shaped element said to represent a "door," an "entrance" to the uterus, and, in a wider sense, "the heavens." It is said to mark the transition from one state of consciousness to another, as in a sequence of hallucinatory imagery. The design is seen as a frame surrounding a hollow space, and the protuberance at the top represents the clitoris.

5. Rows of dots or small circles said to represent drops of semen. In a wider sense they represent descent, or life itself.

6. Several parallel undulating lines drawn horizontally and in different colors, said to represent the Anaconda-Canoe of the Creation Myth.

7. A rhomboid-shaped element with a marked central dot, said to represent an exogamic group. According to the color—red or blue—of the dot, it is said to stand for "our people" or "other people."

8. A cluster of rhomboid elements in red and/or blue, with central dots of the complementary color (i.e., a red dot in a blue rhomb, etc.), said to represent the reciprocal relationship between two or more exogamic units.

9. A vertical line of connected rhombs, sometimes simplified as a zigzag line, interpreted as a line of descent, fertility, and social continuity.

10. A spiral element said to represent incest and to stand for women who are not eligible as marriage partners. It is said to be the sign for the *yuruparí* and to be derived from the imprint the twisted end of a flute would make if placed on the ground. By association, the spiral is said to represent a snail shell.

11. A design element similar to a fleur-de-lys, said to express exogamy. It is said to be derived from the image of two fish traps put back to back, and then seen from above. These traps of reeds are interpreted as "devouring" female organs and, in this case, the fish that enter them are male elements.

12. Two or more concentric rectangles, generally of an elongated shape, said to represent a box of feather ornaments. In many mythological and ritual contexts these boxes are said to be female or uterine elements.

13. A vertical pattern of little dots, sometimes arranged in undulating rows, said to represent the Milky Way.

14. A semicircle formed of several parallel lines, said to represent the rainbow. In some mythological contexts the rainbow is associated with the concept of a celestial vagina.

15. A circle with short lines radiating from it, said to represent the sun. If formed by several concentric circles it is said to be a female organ. Should the radii point inward toward the center of the circle, the design is also interpreted as a female organ.

16. A design shaped like a long-leaved plant (maize?) said to represent vegetable growth in general.

17. Several parallel undulating lines, drawn horizontally, said to represent the "thought of the Sun Father." It is said that it conveys the idea of procreation and is compared to the design of the Anaconda-Canoe (No. 6).

18. A rectangular design filled with parallel lines, said to represent the little wooden stools of the men. These are often painted with red stripes and, in some ritual contexts, are said to symbolize stability and good judgment.

19. Angular outlines, U-shaped or L-shaped, filled with short oblique parallel lines, said to represent different categories of gourd rattles.

20. A fork-shaped design said to represent the wooden cigar holder used in connection with rituals during which the alliance between exogamic units is reaffirmed.

It would perhaps be possible to enlarge this series, because there seem to be several other design motifs which appear to have a recognized ideographic value, but the list given above will suffice as a basis for discussion. Apart from the designs we have mentioned here there are also some more or less stylized representations of people, animals, flowers, and fruits, and the drawings also contain lines, colored areas, or ill-defined motifs which do not seem to have precise meanings; they are simply "things one sees."

One of the Indians said, when speaking of yajé trance: "When one takes yajé, first one hears something like a heavy shower. Then one feels the trembling of one's body. Then come the colored stars. Then everything turns dark. Then the houseposts seem to be covered with snakes." This idea of a sequence, of a slowly developing pattern of hallucinatory images, was expressed by everyone we

talked to. After the initial tremor and the sensation of rushing winds
—interpreted as the ascent to the Milky Way—the men recognized
essentially three stages of the trance: a first stage when colored
"stars" or "flowers" were appearing, a second stage when figurative elements were taking shape and whole mythological scenes
were visualized, and a third and final stage when there was only
a very slow movement of fleeting shapes and colors.

The images perceived during the first stage are often identified
by the generic term *noméri* (D), a word that could mean "to paint
with colored dots" but is also used to designate any patterned,
luminous sensation. Another term for the initial phase of *gahpí
ohori*/yajé-images, is *toondari*/sprigs, clusters; the term is derived
from *too* (D), a small herb or leaf, and the suffix *-da,* which expresses the concept of a string, a chain, a series. The images are visualized as small colored stars or flowers, clusters of fruits, or
feathery leaves. The term *toopuri*/too-leaves, is also used. More
specific images such as grid patterns, zigzag lines, or undulating
lines are called *tere* (D), a term which can also be applied to the
hot vibrating air on the horizon or over a fire (D: *gui-tere*). In any
case, it is said that, during the first stage, one experiences a pleasant
sensation while one watches the floating, ever changing kaleidos-
copic patterns of these little images. The second stage begins when
the former symmetry is disappearing and when larger shapes, looking like people, animals, or unknown creatures, begin to take form.
Those who have learned how to interpret these visions see in them
mythological scenes: the Sun Father and his daughter, the Anaconda-Canoe, the First Woman, the First Maloca, or the different
yurupari flutes; they also see the Master of Game Animals and his
abode in the hills or under the waters. One might see people dancing—the first dance executed by mankind—or fish running, or
plants growing and sprouting from the soil. There is music and
one hears the Sun Father's stick rattle. But others, less prepared
and unable to interpret readily what they see, might perceive monstrous jaguars, snakes, huge birds of prey, or other beasts approaching as if to devour the beholder, and then they become very
frightened. The second stage, then, is fraught with danger. In the
third stage all these images are disappearing. Now there is said to
prevail a yellow-greenish light of young coca leaves, the light of
ahpikondiá, the paradise. There are soft music and wandering
clouds, seemingly carried by a gentle breeze.

The idea of successive stages in the hallucinations produced by yajé was also expressed in the interpretation given to the drawings the Indians had made. "This is what one sees after two cups," they would say; or "This one can see after six cups." By simply glancing at a drawing a man would claim to know almost exactly how many cups of the potion had been consumed by the artist, so he could have seen what he had drawn. In many cases it was pointed out by the informants that the layout and certain details of the drawings varied with the specific kind of yajé consumed, and that certain design elements or combinations of them "pertained" to different exogamic groups. It appears, then, that the first stage of hallucinatory trance provides the models for the coded designs mentioned above, and, therefore, we must turn first of all to this aspect of the yajé trance.

The fleeting perception by the human eye of specks, stars, or irregular patterns, known as phosphenes, is a common phenomenon. Phosphenes are subjective images, independent of an external light source, and are the results of the self-illumination of the visual sense.[6] As they originate within the eye and the brain, they are common to all men. Occasionally, phosphenes can appear quite spontaneously, especially when the person has been deprived for a certain time of visual stimuli, as, for instance, during periods of prolonged darkness or of exposure to extremely unvaried sights such as a cloudless sky, the sea, or rain in open country. They can also be produced by external stimuli: pressure on the eyeballs, a sudden shock, or the act of looking into the darkness when one wakes up at night. In all these cases the eye may perceive luminous images varying from tiny dots to intricate moiré patterns, and from fan-shaped rays to glowing circles, all in different shades, generally blue, green, orange, and yellow.

Moreover, phosphenes can be induced by a number of chemical agents. Hallucinogenic drugs such as LSD, psilocybin, mescaline, bufotein, and harmaline are known to produce phosphenes of abstract design motifs, and frequently the afterimages can be observed for several months after the initial experience. Laboratory experiments carried out by Max Knoll,[7] who induced phosphenes with electrical impulses in more than 1,000 people, gave the following results: with the application of low-voltage square-wave pulses[8] to the temples, pulses in the same frequency range as brain waves produced luminous sensations in the visual field of the subjects, and about half of them perceived geometric design motifs. The patterns of these designs changed whenever the frequency of the pulses was varied, and it became possible to group these motifs into fifteen categories. The design pattern perceived by each subject was repeatable even after six months' time.

Now if we compare Knoll's categories (Fig. 40) with the designs we have isolated from the Indian drawings, we can observe a number of correspondences:

TUKANO NO.	KNOLL NO.
1	13
2	9
6	3
7	9
8–9	12
10	10
11	15
13	7
14	1
15	2
17	3
18	4

Moreover, Knoll's numbers 5, 8, 11, and 14 are found in numerous drawings. These correspondences are too close to be mere coincidences; they seem to demonstrate that the motifs seen by the Indians under the influence of yajé, especially those of the first stage of intoxication, are phosphenes which then are interpreted in cultural terms as having a specific significance.

It is important to remember here that the afterimages of phosphenes can repeat themselves for up to six months. Within this time span it is very probable in our case that the person will have taken part in one or more yajé sessions, or that he will have consumed another narcotic drug, and so the afterimages are likely to persist in a latent, chronical state, appearing in the visual field at any instant when they are triggered off by a change in body chemistry or by an external stimulus. As these afterimages might appear superimposed on the normal vision of the individual, and in plain daylight, the particular spectrum of phosphenes, together with their cultural interpretations, can be said to accompany the person in a permanent manner.

36. A Barasana artist
drawing hallucinatory
patterns in the sand;
Pira-paraná

37. A Barasana artist
drawing hallucinatory
patterns; Pira-paraná

36

37

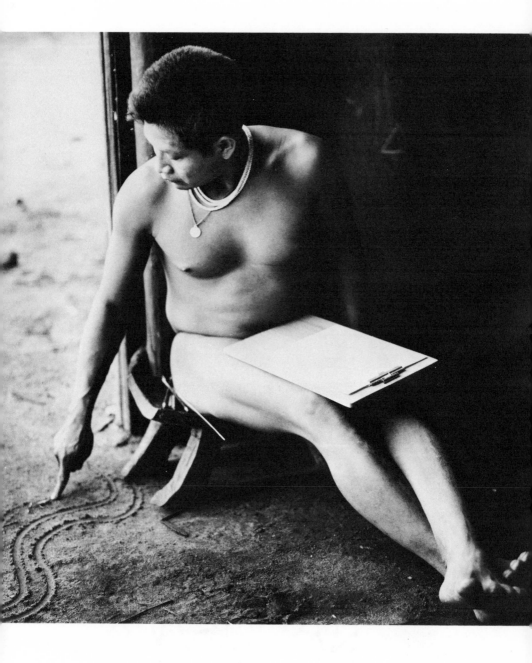

39. Hallucinatory design motifs of the Tukano Indians

40. Phosphene patterns (after Max Knoll)

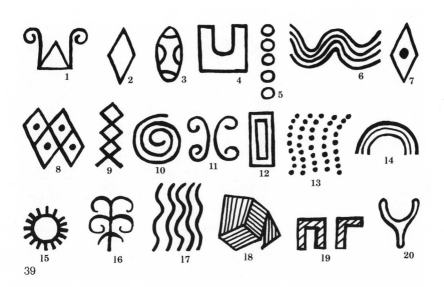

39

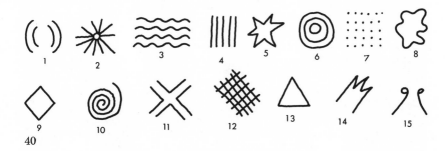

40

41. House decoration representing hallucinatory patterns; Pira-paraná

42. Wall painting on a Taibano maloca showing the Master of Game Animals and hallucinatory patterns; Pira-paraná

41

42

43. Wall painting on a Taibano maloca showing hallucinatory patterns; Pira-paraná

44. Painted snake on housepost; Tukano Indians, Vaupés River (after Koch-Grünberg 1909–10, 2:243)

45. Painted loincloth of tree bark (length, 43 cm.); Tatuyo Indians, Pira-paraná

46. Painted loincloth of tree bark; Tatuyo Indians, Pira-paraná

43

44

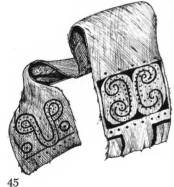

45

46

47. Stamping tubes with
painted designs; Tatuyo
Indians, Pira-paraná

48. Gourd rattle with incised designs (length, 42 cm.); Tatuyo Indians, Pira-paraná

49. Incised design motifs from a gourd rattle; Barasana Indians, Pira-paraná

50. Incised design motifs from a gourd rattle; Barasana Indians, Pira-paraná

49

48

50

51. Incised design motifs from a gourd rattle; Barasana Indians, Pira-paraná

52. Painted design from a drum; Tiquié River (after Koch-Grünberg 1909–10, 1:276)

53. Painted yajé vessel; Tiquié River (after Koch-Grünberg 1909–10, 1:298)

51

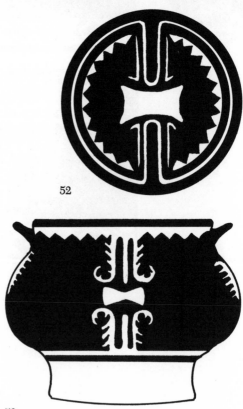

52

53

54. Drawing by a Barasana Indian representing the hallucinatory image of the first peopling of the world; Pira-paraná

55. Drawing by a Barasana Indian representing the hallucinatory image of the origin of yajé; Pira-paraná

56. Drawing by a Baransana Indian representing the hallucinatory image of mankind's first dance; Pira-paraná

54

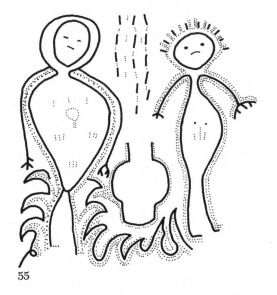

55

56

57. Drawing by a
Barasana Indian repre-
senting the hallucinatory
image of a jaguar, people
on the Milky Way, and
the U-shaped "entrance to
the other world"; Pira-
paraná

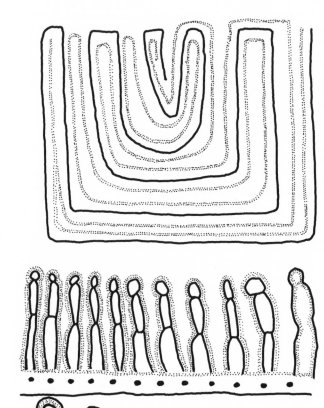

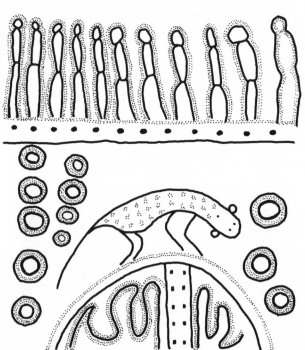

That phosphenes and their afterimages are occasionally rein-forced, brought into focus, or perhaps triggered off by normal visual perception is also quite probable. It has been observed experi-mentally[9] that, when flickering, shapeless phosphenes are com-bined with normal visual perception, the phosphenes begin to take a more definite form. This poses an interesting problem; such sud-den "color shocks" as, for example, the sight of a large spotted cat, a huge blue butterfly, or a brightly striped coral snake conceivably might combine with phosphenes and bring them into sharper focus, modifying the normal visual image and making it appear to be a "supernatural" apparition. The physical environment of the Indians provides several models; we mentioned earlier the fish traps and the spirally twisted flutes. Other models or stimuli almost permanently before the eyes of the individual, for instance, are the very symmetrically interwoven leaves of the thatched roof and of the walls of the maloca; when lying in a hammock one always has these patterns before one's eyes. Baskets and basketry trays are similarly patterned and there exist, of course, many patterns in nature, such as mosses, lichens, leaves, flowers, clusters of fruit, butterflies, and spiderwebs.

There are probably other stimuli present, many of which seem to be well recognized as such by the Indians. The intense red light of the torch seems to be an important factor in the production of phosphenes and, eventually, of true hallucinations. A Desana payé, when asked about the function of the red light, said, "The light of day is not the same as the light of the night," and he explained that the light from the resin-covered torch and that from a hearth fire were kinds of light that had to be specially prepared for certain purposes.[10] The red efflorescences of the Heliconia plant, which are a striking sight against the dark background of the jungle, are said by the Indians to produce jaguar visions and evil dreams if looked at for too long. The hypnotic, hackling noise of the turtle-shell in-strument, the heavy rhythmic thud of the stamping tubes, and the shrill sounds of the flutes are probably additional stimuli. I per-sonally recall that each time the dancers sounded their seed rattles the pattern of phosphenes changed immediately in shape and color. The general state of dehydration produced by vomiting, diarrhea, and copious perspiration may be another contributing factor, to-gether with the previous dietary restrictions and the abstinence from any food during the ceremony. It may also be pointed out that

while sitting on their stools the men often adopted a hunched position, embracing their updrawn knees tightly with their arms, a
posture which probably restricted their breathing capacity.

We must turn now to the cultural interpretation given by the
Indians to the phosphene-based designs. We have repeatedly mentioned the color symbolism of the Indians, and we have said that the
colors yellow and white tend to represent a seminal principle associated with the male sex or with solar fertilization. The different
shades of these colors indicate varying degrees of intensity of this
fertilizing energy. Now these colors are characteristic of many material objects or phenomena to which the Indians attribute a seminal character, perceived not only in the color but also in the particular shape or texture of the object. Saliva, dew, the exudation
from a damp rock, the gelatinous flesh of certain fruits, the sticky
sap of plants, manioc starch, honey, cotton, and feather down are
all examples of this seminal principal, as are a stalactite, a transparent piece of quartz, the sprouting yellowish shoot of a plant, and
a phallus-shaped mushroom. The red color represents the complementary opposite and stands for female sex and fecundity. It is the
color of fire, of heat, of the womb, of menstrual blood. Yellow and
white are designated as "cold" colors, while red is "hot," comple-
menting the male/female opposition; together they represent a
benefic principle. Another fundamental color is blue, and of it people say that it is sexually neutral and morally ambivalent. The blue
color represents above all a principle of communication. Tobacco
smoke blown ritually over a person or an object, or in a certain
direction, produces a contact in that it conveys a thought, a wish.
Songs and spells are imagined to be "blue." Now as the message
transmitted by that color may be benefic or malefic, the intrinsic
value of blue depends to a high degree upon its combination with
other colors, that is, with yellow or white or red. For example, a
combination of blue and yellow in approximately equal parts indicates a state of reciprocity and complementarity. A combination of
red and blue indicates an opposition of male and female principles,
say, of two exogamic groups or a single couple. But should the red
shade predominate, this balanced opposition becomes a struggle,
an evil influence of the female principle over the male; and should
blue predominate, it might also mean that an evil component is
present. The drawings and the individual design motifs must be
seen, therefore, partly from the point of view of their color sym-

bolism and its particular combination with specific "male" or "female" shapes.

In our case these "male" shapes are essentially two: the *vahsú* design (Fig. 39, No. 1); and the row of dots (i.e., "drops"), which are interpreted as semen (Fig. 39, No. 5). Shapes of a female connotation are far more frequent; the rhomboid design (Fig. 39, No. 2) is interpreted as a vagina, and a combination of them as a group of exogamic units (Fig. 39, No. 8), or a line of descent (Fig. 39, No. 9). The U-shaped design (Fig. 39, No. 4) is also a vagina, the same as the spiral (Fig. 39, No. 10), the double C (Fig. 39, No. 11), and, probably, the rainbow (Fig. 39, No. 14). The oval (Fig. 39, No. 3) is representative of the womb, and the box of ornaments (Fig. 39, No. 12) is interpreted in the same way. Combinations of male and female fertility can be seen in the Anaconda-Canoe (Fig. 39, No. 6), the fertilized womb (Fig. 39, No. 3), and the group of exogamic units (Fig. 39, No. 8). Other signs with fertility associations are the "drops" of the Milky Way (Fig. 39, No. 13), the sun (Fig. 39, No. 15), the sprouting plant (Fig. 39, No. 16), and the bifurcate motif, which is often interpreted as a crotch (Fig. 39, No. 20). Designs referring to the concept of communication are "thought" (Fig. 39, No. 17) and, probably, the wooden stools (Fig. 39, No. 18) which, according to the Indians, are above all instruments for meditation. The rectangular designs of the gourd rattle (Fig. 39, No. 19) may be connected with the idea of communication.

The most important designs are the pairs "male" and "female" (Fig. 39, Nos. 1, 2), and "incest" and "exogamy" (Fig. 39, Nos. 10, 11). They dominate and provide the emphasis to the entire hallucinatory imagery. In fact, the interpretation given to the signs revolves entirely around the problem of incest, a pervasive problem in the native culture, and the message transmitted by the code insists on the observance of the law of exogamy. The code is extended beyond the narrow confines of individual trance and is applied to the physical environment of everyday life. The designs and patterns seen during the yajé-induced hallucinations are transplanted to the concrete objects of material culture, where they constitute an art form. Practically all decorative elements that adorn the objects manufactured by the Tukano are said by them to be derived from hallucinatory imagery, that is, are based on phosphenes.

The most outstanding examples are the paintings executed on

the front walls of the malocas. These walls, made of large pieces of flattened bark, are covered wholly or in part with bold designs painted with mineral colors—occasionally with the admixture of vegetable dyes—and represent the same geometric design motifs we have discussed above (Fig. 39). Large eye-shaped designs, the wavy lines of the Anaconda-Canoe, the *vahsú* design, and the design for exogamy can be found painted on the house fronts, sometimes combined with figurative designs representing the Master of Game Animals (Fig. 42), or individual animals such as fish, frogs, or snakes. When asked about these paintings the Indians simply reply: "This is what we see when we drink yajé; they are *gahpí ohori.*"

In former times it was the custom to decorate the houseposts with colored designs, and occasionally one still can see some of these paintings (Fig. 44). Some show snakes—the snakes mentioned as twisting around the posts during the yajé trance—while others show figures and designs interpreted as *pamurí-mahsë*/the germinator, and the Snake-Canoe.

Further examples are numerous. The barkcloth aprons used during ritual occasions are painted with these designs (Figs. 45–46), and among the Cubeo and other groups that still manufacture barkcloth masks, these, too, exhibit the same patterns (Fig. 24). One apron (Fig. 45) shows the design of exogamy painted prominently over the genital region, while others are adorned with the sun, the rainbow, or other designs (Fig. 46). The large stamping tubes used by the Tukano to accompany their dances are covered with similar paintings showing zigzag lines, rhombs, and rows of dots. The gourd rattles are sometimes covered with phosphene patterns (Figs. 49–51). The large drums formerly used by the Tukano were generally painted with the ornaments of the Anaconda-Canoe, combined with the *vahsú* sign (Fig. 52), and occasionally a modern *cashirí* trough will be adorned with similar patterns. At present the Tukano have almost abandoned the manufacture of pottery, at least of small service vessels that are likely to be decorated. The older people assured us that formerly many pottery vessels were decorated with yajé-inspired ornaments, and even now one can occasionally find a small vessel adorned with these design motifs. The yajé vessels are always adorned with painted designs, often in red, yellow and white, showing wavy lines, rows of dots, or series of rainbow-shaped patterns. On many yajé vessels the U-shaped design of the "entrance" is painted on the foot of the vessel (Fig. 32).

In summarizing, with the exception of a few realistic designs of animals or houses, the entire art style of the Tukano can be said to be based on drug-induced phosphenes. Most of the elements that compose this art style carry the same message: exogamy. Everywhere, especially on ritual occasions, the individual is reminded of the law of exogamy, expressed by design motifs that adorn utensils or that are ever present in the spectrum of his phosphenes.

It may be of interest to reconsider for a moment my own interpretations of the phosphenes I had perceived. Formally, the most striking aspect was the marked bilateral symmetry displayed by the shapes. The underlying forms were those of a simple geometric kind: oblique stripes, undulating lines, circles, hearts, arches, grid designs, and aureolae. These shapes, together with their colors, provoked associations during the first ten minutes of the experience which referred mainly to Oriental art, while those provoked during the ensuing stage referred more to shapes found in nature. Both stages were interspersed with references to mechanistic elements. The first series of associations was: Persian miniatures, Tibetan tapestries, and Islamic calligraphy, combined with impressions of ancient locks and maps, a "baroque" air, fountains, fireworks, and basketry designs. There were references to World religions: the Qu'rān, Islamic calligraphy, Buddhas, Tibetan rugs, and stained-glass windows. The associations with nature were: medusae, butterflies, corals, caterpillars, eyes, trees, flowers, moss, fungi, feathers, water, fire, stars, and the rainbow. The interspersed physical allusions were: microphotographs, stained sections, and the color spectrum. All these phosphenes I readily interpreted in terms of my culture, comparing them to shapes and colors with which I was already acquainted, but this situation changed as soon as the second stage began and the abstract designs gave way to slowly moving masses of shapes and colors. Then I found myself at a loss because my culture did not provide me with the imagery the Indians could project upon these luminous sensations.

We must turn briefly to this second stage of the yajé trance, characterized, according to the Indians, by visions interpreted as mythological scenes. While the first stage is one of phosphenes, the second stage seems to be one of true hallucinations. The mass of details that marks the initial visions now dissolves into more coherent images, the smaller elements being now of a secondary nature. To the viewer the interpretation of these shapes and colors is far more difficult than that of the previous images. The floating shapes and colors cannot be easily identified in terms of preexisting models in nature, and the formation of a consensus of the cultural projections becomes, now, of major importance. This consensus is achieved, in part at least, by the viewer's communicating with others, especially with older and more experienced men. The individual hallucinations do not constitute a private world, an intimate or almost secret experience; they are freely discussed, and anyone will ask questions and solicit answers. People describe their visions and their neighbors will offer explanations. For example, a man might say: "A red shape is appearing on the left; it is approaching." The payé, or perhaps another man, will explain: "It is the Master of Game Animals; he is your friend." Or again, a man may see a swirling movement of many individual shapes and will be told that he is seeing a dance, a ritual scene enacted by mythological or otherworldly beings. In this manner a process of imprinting is brought into play, and any individual who is acquainted with the basic significance of color symbolism, of ritual paraphernalia, and of the corresponding music will soon be able to identify a number of images each time they appear in his visions. The interpretation, then, refers mainly to mythological motifs known by all—for example, *pamurí-mahsë* and the Anconda-Canoe, the creation of mankind, and the *yuruparí* flutes—which now the viewer can project upon his visions. There is, then, a process of feedback, of reinterpretation and elaboration; the viewer, it seems, will sometimes create his own translation, based upon previous cultural experiences, and will explain it to others who, eventually, will accept the explanation should it coincide with their own experiences and expectancies.

This second stage of the yajé experience was discussed in detail with many informants and from their comments it appears that this stage is interpreted, in all essence, as a return to the maternal womb. It is a visit to the place of Creation, the *fons et origo* of everything that exists, and the viewer thus becomes an eyewitness and a participant in the Creation story and the moral concepts it contains. The yajé vessel is said to be a female body, the maternal body, and by drinking its contents the individual is enabled to enter it through the "door," the vagina one often sees depicted at the base of the container. There is a kind of struggle, a contest, between the vessel and the consumer. We have mentioned that the men, addressing the vessel, exclaim: "I shall drink your contents and then I shall fill you with dirt!" or that they will threaten to kick the vessel or to defecate into it. The men "are afraid," it is said, and they bolster their courage by challenging the danger. They know they will soon be overwhelmed by its contents.

The "danger" is that of incest. From what we were told, the return to the maternal womb is imagined as consisting of two steps: first the individual enters the vessel's vagina as a phallus, and then he assumes an embryonic state which, eventually, leads to his rebirth. In other words, he commits incest and then, becoming his own progenitor, is reborn. There exists, then, a strong sexual component in the yajé experience. One of our informants, a man who had been educated by the Catholic missionaries, expressed it in these words: "To drink yajé is a spiritual coitus; it is, as the priests say, a spiritual communion." In the myth which speaks of the origin of yajé it is clear that a sexual element was involved, and we must remember that hallucinogenic substances, yajé or others, are said to be divine sperm. The narcotic intoxication is often compared to an orgastic rapture, a state of "drowning," of sinking into a trance, half-blissful and half-anguished. In fact, several Indians pointed out that during the sex act "one sees images similar to those produced by yajé." The return to the womb implies a direct and intentional modification of time. When the individual becomes an embryo, it is a reversal of time, but—it was said—"when one drinks yajé, one dies," and this means an acceleration of time. Return and rebirth take place outside the normal biological time scale, and this state of standing outside the empirical universe is produced by the drug.

Again, as in the first stage of the yajé trance, the central theme is the law of exogamy. The mythical scenes constantly emphasize the need for exogamic relationships and the importance of reciprocity patterns in these contacts. The collective ritual of yajé trance, then, is an experience from which the individual emerges with the firm conviction of the truthfulness of the traditional origins of his culture, and of the guiding moral principles of the Creation story.

9

SPIRITS
OF THE
FOREST

Bush spirits of one sort or another are said to be common in the rain forest, and most Tukano have more or less elaborate beliefs about them. To call these spirits mere superstitions and let it go at that is not sufficient; they are cultural projections and, as such, are patterned and express cultural problems. An encounter with a bush spirit is not a casual matter. It is triggered by certain circumstances, and the form the encounter takes is likely to reflect a person's fears or expectancies with regard to his social relationships. In this chapter, then, we shall refer to these ghostly apparitions because, in a sense, they are hallucinations and therefore are related to the central theme of our inquiry.

Among the many forest spirits of the Vaupés, one is feared above all others—the *boráro*. In Lengua Geral this creature is generally known under the name of *curupira*,[1] and all over the Amazon basin there are tales about this spirit-being. In most Tukano languages he is called *boráro*, a name that, according to the Indians, imitates his fierce cry, a long-drawn *o-á-o;* people say they can hear it sometimes, after sunset, coming from the depths of the forest.[2]

Although individual descriptions of the *boráro* may vary, they coincide in certain basic features. The *boráro* is imagined as a monstrous manlike being, covered with shaggy black hair, with huge pointed fangs protruding from his mouth. He has big, pointed ears and a large penis. His feet are twisted so that his toes face backward and the heels forward, and his knees have no joints so that when he falls he has great difficulty in rising again. Some people say that his feet have no toes at all, and others say that he has no umbilicus. At night, the bats are the *boráro*'s companions, but during the day he is often accompanied by huge blue Morpho butterflies and by that colorful bird typical of the Vaupés forests, the cock of the rock.

The *boráro* kills people by grasping them in a crushing embrace which turns the flesh into a pulpy mass but does not tear the skin or break the bones. He then pricks a small hole in the top of the head and sucks out the pulp until only the limp skin is left covering the skeleton.[3] He now blows up the skin, and the victim, although dazed and behaving as though in a dream, walks back to his maloca where he dies shortly afterward.[4]

There are many tales about the *boráro,* some of them hearsay, but many of them accounts of personal experiences. Lonely hunters or travelers, almost always men, claim to have seen the *boráro* or to have been attacked by him, or they tell of their headlong flight, with the monster persecuting them for hours. The twisted feet of the *boráro,* people say, often mislead the person who comes upon the tracks into believing that the monster went in one direction while, in fact, he was walking the opposite way. One should put one's closed fist into the track because this gesture will make the *boráro's* legs stiffen so that he can advance only slowly; others say that one should follow his example and run backward, facing him, in order to escape. In any case, a sudden encounter with the *boráro* almost always has dire consequences; the person will fall ill—develop a high fever and strong headache—and it then falls to the payé to recite the appropriate spells for curing this dangerous condition.

We mentioned earlier that the *boráro* is said to dwell in the cliffs and hills where *Vaí-mahsë,* the Master of Animals, has his abode. He is not a river spirit and is not associated in any way with water; his domain is the forest, where he wanders about armed with his hoe and often in the company of a herd of peccary. Birds and insects, the *boráro's* "servants," flutter around him, and a heavy, evil stench pervades the air whenever the *boráro* is near. His favorite food is small crabs he gathers in the creeks of the headwaters of the larger streams, and he also likes to eat the fruits of the *barbasco*[5] tree, which otherwise are used as a potent fish poison. According to some Indians, the *boráro* will sprinkle his human victims with his urine and, because this secretion is a strong poison, will cause them to become fatally ill.

At first, these stories appear to be faintly amusing; they seem to be anecdotes, tales to be told at night around the fire—to pass the time, one might think, or to entertain a visitor. But then one will note that at the back of all these fantastic stories there lurks an element of fear, of stark terror, and that people do not talk lightly of these matters. What is it, then, that people are afraid of? What is it that makes them see these apparitions, and how are these perceived and interpreted? Why should a man say, all of a sudden: "I have seen a spirit and I shall fall ill"?

A Desana text (Text No. 104) runs like this:

"A Makú and his wife were lost in the forest. They came upon the house of the *boráro.* It was in the middle of the forest. Nobody was there, but there were some cooking utensils. The two went to the creek to catch some fish. In the evening the Makú and his wife went back to the house; the *boráro* and his wife were there. The *boráro*'s woman had one single breast.[6] Together they ate the fish they had caught.

" 'These fish of the creek are rotten, cousin,' said the *boráro;* 'Tomorrow we shall catch some fish in the river,' he said. 'My wife will accompany you,' said the *boráro,* 'and I shall go with yours.' He said it as a joke: 'We shall swap our women.' 'All right,' said the Makú. But to his wife he said: 'He is going to devour you; this is the *boráro.*' He knew by now.

"The next morning they went to fish; the Makú went with the wife of the *boráro,* and the *boráro* went with the wife of the Makú. After having walked a short distance the *boráro* devoured the wife of the Makú. The Makú went with the wife of the *boráro* and he carried his blowgun. After having walked for a while she said to him: 'This is a good spot to have intercourse.' 'No,' said the Makú; 'Let's walk for another while.' In this manner the wife of the *boráro* was trying to seduce the Makú. As they were walking along they came upon a tree heavy with fruit. 'There is a lot of *caimo*[7] fruit,' she said. 'Go and get them!' she said, and he said yes. 'You go and fetch a forked stick,' he told her. Meanwhile he prepared himself to climb the tree. 'Yes,' she said and went and brought a forked stick. While preparing the forked stick he said quite casually: 'Find me another,' saying this so she would fetch a very hard stick that would take some time to get. Meanwhile he climbed the tree, and when the woman returned he was already up there. 'You climbed up after some hesitation,' she observed. Once he was up there he began to throw down some fruit. He put poison on the fruit and threw it down to her. When she was already under the influence of the poison, he hit her in the back with some darts from his blowgun. Up there in the tree he was protected by the leaves. When she died, she urinated and, although he had hurt her only a little bit she died vomiting. When she was dead he made a large basket, put her into it and carried her away. On his return he cooked her and then added some peppers; then he broke all the vessels. He also broke the gourd vessels. When he had done this he went to the landing place where there was a large tree and there he hid. When the *boráro* returned to his house he ate the cooked meat, and when he became thirsty he wanted to drink and so he went to the landing where the Makú was hiding. If the Makú had not broken all the vessels there would have been water and he would not have had to go to the landing. While eating the meat he had come upon the breast of the woman and said: 'For sure, this is my wife! Is not this the breast of my wife?' he said looking around. When the *boráro* returned he brought the Makú's wife with him. So when he went to the landing to drink water the Makú hit him in the back with several darts from his blowgun, but the *boráro* thought the mosquitoes were biting him. Then he felt the effect of the poison and he fell down and died, screaming loudly. In this way the Makú killed the *boráro* and his wife. And so he returned home."

Stories of this type are numerous. They speak of magic flights and ruses, of loyal dogs defending their masters, and of the supernatural strength of the monster. Often, the *boráro* appears as a sexual aggressor who "devours" women or, on other occasions, carries them off to his forest abode.

A tale told by a Tukano proper is this:

"My father once told me of a man who had killed a *boráro*. That was over at Pari-Cachoeira. My father knew the man, and the story is true. I shall tell you what my father told me.

"A Desana had gone hunting with his shotgun. He met the *boráro*. He shot and killed him. Three years later he was hunting near that spot and he went to look for the bones; he wanted some of the *boráro*'s teeth. He hit the jawbone with a stick to get the teeth loose, but the blow made the *boráro* wake up. The skeleton was almost covered with roots and leaves, but the blow revived him. The *boráro* rose and was pleased that the man had revived him. He gave him a stick rattle and told him to plant it firmly in the ground at a certain spot in the forest, whenever he wanted meat.

The man did as told and all the game animals fell dead when they came near the stick rattle. In this way he always had meat. The other Desana wondered how he got so much game, but he said he was a good hunter. One day another man followed him and observed what happened. After that the stick rattle lost its power. The Desana hid it under water, in a deep pool. There was a famine and the Desana dived into the pool to recover the stick rattle, but there was a huge electric eel that killed him."

Another Tukano told us the following story:

"We were living near a hill called Aruitera in Lengua Geral. That was over at the Rio Negro. I was a boy then. One day my father and I walked to our field, and we had two hunting dogs with us. It was an open trail and the dogs were running ahead of us. We had walked for some time, when suddenly the dogs came running back, very frightened. They passed us by and ran back over the trail. My father said: 'They must have seen some strange animal.' We went on and came to a small clearing. The *boráro* was standing there. He was huge and naked, and was wearing a red headdress. He was standing with outstretched arms and was looking at the sun. On his left arm two cocks of the rock were sitting, and on his right arm there were three. The birds were fluttering and crying: *pe-peó*. We became frightened and turned back. A storm was coming and suddenly it was very dark. We could hear the *boráro* scream behind us. We ran and ran, and then we found our canoe and crossed the river and arrived at our maloca. My father said: 'We have seen the *boráro*.' My mother gave him fish and cassava bread, but he did not want to eat. 'I am frightened,' he said. He went to sleep for a while and then he woke up and vomited. He had a headache. I, too, had a headache and some fever. Then my grandfather came and said some spells and we felt better."

The following is a Desana text (Text No. 155):

"A man went up a creek. There he found the *boráro* sitting on some leaves on the riverbank. The *boráro* rose, but the man had not seen him yet. The *boráro* approached the man, making a humming noise; he was looking quite friendly. He was wearing a red tassel on his head. The man tried to run away and jumped into the water; there he watched the *boráro* from behind the roots of a hollow tree. Crouching near the water the *boráro* stretched out his hand searching for the man and just missed him. Then he rose and began to talk in a mumble. Once more he searched for the man. This went on for quite a while. The man was watching him without moving; the *boráro* made a loud noise and his eyes were like lightning. Once again he reached for the man. When the *boráro* is angry he makes a noise like a *yurupari* flute. When he is furious it is as if the leaves were falling from a tree. The man had no spells against the *boráro*. Now he had been in the water for a long time. The *boráro* retreated to watch the river from a distance. The *boráro* was watching the water and did not move. Again he went to the water's edge and searched for the man. For a long time he watched the water. He looked and watched it from different spots. It was late when the *boráro* left. Sometimes the *boráro* makes a noise like monkeys, or he makes a noise like peccaries. This happened in Taracuá, in Brazil; he calls like a monkey. This happens quite often, over in Brazil."

We should note here that the man in our story did not have a spell against the *boráro*. There are a number of spells and incantations which, depending upon their elaborateness, can be pronounced by any person or only by a payé. They are very similar to the spells used against the Master of Game Animals, or against evil jaguars. The following description given by a Desana (Text No. 154) contains some interesting details:

"The *boráro* always carries a hoe that has a handle of *vahsú* wood.[8] He uses everything of the *vahsú* trees, not only their fruits. The *boráro* grabs his victim with the hooked *vahsú* hoe. He wears a crown of all sorts of feathers. They [the payés] give him the essence of milk and of *vahsú* fruit, and while he is eating they take away his headdress and his hoe, and so he is left powerless. They give him the designs and the colors of the sieves,[9] and the yellow and red colors of edible ants, and this makes him see the firmament.[10] They make him sit on a mat of the same design and coloring. All the colors of the reeds one uses to make basketry trays they put on the sieves. They put the color of the quartz crystals on the sieves. Also the shape of the quartz crystals. All this contains the essence of crabs.[11] The *boráro* is fierce when he wears the red headdress. They give him the essence of milk and of sweet berries. All these things of bright colors they put upon the sieves. Then come the colors of all kinds of monkey hair. Also those of *mararay;*[12] these, too, are put on the sieves. The *boráro* wears the red color of the feathercrowns; all this is taken away from him, and in its stead they give him milk and honey. They put the feathercrowns on the sieve which is full with the essence of milk and honey. The *boráro* wears a headdress on top of which there are tassels of yellow, red, reddish, green, and blue colors. They take off this headdress and give him instead the essence of milk and honey. He carries a stick-rattle; they take it away from him and leave him only with the sound of the rattle. Everything is put on the sieve which contains the essence of milk and honey. The *boráro* is fierce only when he wears these things. This spell is made with tobacco smoke."

It is important to observe the many sexual connotations of the objects associated with the *boráro* or given to him to appease him. The milky sap of *vahsú* and the mucilaginous consistency of its fruits have been mentioned already. The colors yellow and red stand for male fertility and female fecundity; the color of quartz crystals also has a seminal meaning, and edible ants are a "male" food to which occasionally aphrodisiac properties are attributed. Monkey hair, symbolizing pubic hair, figures prominently in the curing of diseases, and the stick rattle and hoe have been mentioned as phallic symbols. "Milk and honey" are both of a seminal character and are mentioned in many spells.

Some aspects of the spell against the *boráro* were elaborated by a Desana payé in the following text (Text No. 142):

"The *boráro* of the rocky hills carries a quartz crystal of the same color as the stones of the hills. When he carries this crystal he is fierce;[13] to stop his fierceness one must take the crystal away from him. Once this has been done, one has to confine him to his dwelling place inside his hill, with his face turned toward the wall. In this position he is given to eat the essence of *umarí*,[14] of *vahsú*,[15] of groundnuts, and of starch. The *boráro* of the green-, white-, and rose-colored hills carries crystals of the same colors and his earrings are also of these colors. They give him the same things to eat. With *Vaí-mahsë* it is the same. While he [the *boráro*] is eating all this, he can do no harm to people. There are also the hills of sand, and the spirit-beings there wear things of a sandy color. One must give them coca and milk. Then the *boráro* cannot do any harm to people."

It is interesting to compare these accounts given by Desana informants with that of a payé of the Tukano proper. According to him, the *boráro* lives underground, beneath the small clearings in the forest we have mentioned. There he shares his "house"—called *ditá vii*/earth-house (T)—with the *ditá mahsá*/earth-people, spirit-beings that are closely related to the *vaí-mahsá*. Also, *yaí-uá-*

mahsá/jaguar-people (T) live there. All these spirits become very annoyed should someone walk over these spots in the forest while eating "cold fish or cold meat" because "it is as if one was insulting them." Should a menstruating woman pass by, the house of the *ditá-mahsá* would become filled with blood. The *ditá-mahsá* have a mirror, and in it they see the people who are approaching the spot. Should these people be eating,[16] the image in the mirror will darken, and should a menstruating woman approach, the mirror image will turn blood-red. Then the *ditá-mahsá* will say, "Who is this?" and they will emerge from their abode. "You have no right to do this here!" they will say to the passerby, and then they will punish him by leading him astray. The *boráro*, too, becomes very annoyed and sallies forth to punish the offenders.

According to the Tukano payé, every time *cashirí* beer is being prepared from fermented fruits that grow below the ground— manioc, yams, taro, and the like—a special spell must be said "so that the *boráro* will not see it" (T: *nihí seári mahsë*). With this spell the *boráro* is deprived of his headdress and is made to return to his abode; once he has entered it, he is made to turn toward the wall and to sit down. Several kinds of coca are conjured in this spell—*karé patu*/caimo-coca,[17] *yuhkë patu*/tree-coca, and *vaí patu*/fish-coca—and the tobacco that is smoked during the spell must be of three kinds: *uári moënó*/mojarra-tobacco,[18] *seápihkana moënó*/sardine-tobacco,[19] and *dóe-piá moënó*/dormilón-tobacco.[20] This procedure is called *nihí sease moënó püi*/"not to be seen by the boráro" (T), and *kumuáse moënó püi*/"to make him think of something else." In this way, all his "weapons" (T: *uámo*) are taken away from him and are put on a special mat (T: *bahtípakaro*) woven of leaves of the *muhí* palm,[21] while the *boráro* is falling asleep.

We have checked a number of cases in which people claimed to have seen the *boráro*, and from their accounts we can reconstruct the following pattern: they were walking over a small clearing in the forest; there was a foul smell in the air, and the humming of insects; suddenly they perceived the *boráro* "sunning" himself and then rising at their approach. The consequences of the encounter were severe headaches, fever, and a general malaise, but more often than not these symptoms subsided after a few days and the cure was attributed to dietary restrictions and shamanistic spells.

The recurrent details of this experience are of interest because

of their specific associations. Small, isolated clearings in the forest
are often thought to be uncanny spots, and a man crossing such a
clearing will be apprehensive. And there are good reasons for this:
on a clearing one is exposed, one can be seen by others who may
be hiding in the forest. Moreover, there are likely to be snakes, and
one might come upon a jaguar. One is seen by birds, which are
likely to give their warning calls and thus betray the hunter's
presence. The sight of blue butterflies, fairly common at these spots,
will also alert the person, and a waft of foul-smelling air, perhaps
from some carrion, from rotten timber, or from certain mushrooms
growing upon it, will do the same. There are also likely to be some
strong-smelling flowers in such a clearing.

Now if there should be some shape, some shadow, some detail
that, together with others, seems to form a whole, an image might
arise quite suddenly under the preexisting tension and might
readily be perceived as a spirit-being, the associations of which are
falling into a pattern. It is at this point of "closure" that the person
suddenly sees the apparition, that is, that the internally latent image
finds a screen upon which it can be projected. And once a man
starts to run in headlong flight, some animals that have been hiding
silently will become scared and scamper or flutter noisily, with the
result that the frightened person believes he is being followed.

It is probable that sexual tensions lie at the back of these experiences. Clearings and fields are symbolically associated with a
female principle, with intercourse and fertilization; in fact, to clear
a field for planting is synonymous with intercourse. Moreover, odors
—especially body odors—are highly emotion-charged among the
Tukano and readily lend themselves to chains of associations. Humming sounds, like those of insects, are menacing in Tukano thought
and are associated with sexual restrictions.[22] Besides, the *boráro*
himself has many traits that make him appear to be a phallic being:
his jointlessness; his red headgear; his "fierceness"; his collapsing
and rising again; his association with odors, bats (i.e., vaginas),
stick rattles, hoes, devouring fangs, and uncouth hairiness. All these
make him appear to be an image of male sexual power, dangerous
because not subject to cultural norms. The *boráro*, then, seems to be
the projected image of the hunter's own repressed impulses, and
the punishment for having allowed himself this projection is the
characteristic precarious state of health of those who claim to have
seen this monster.

58. Wall painting in black and white from a Bará maloca, representing hallucinatory patterns; Pira-paraná

59. Zoomorphic design from a Bará maloca; Pira-paraná

60. Fish design from a painted stamping tube; Tatuyo Indians, Pira-paraná

61. Anthropomorphic design from a Bará maloca; Pira-paraná

62. A painted stool carved from a single piece of wood (length, 33 cm.); Tukano Indians, Vaupés River

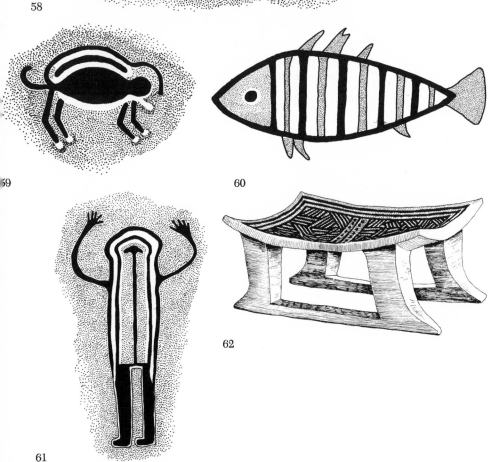

58

59

60

62

61

63. Design motif from a Bará maloca; Pira-paraná

64. Wall painting from a Bará maloca, representing hallucinatory patterns; Pira-paraná

65. Wall painting on a Taibano maloca, representing hallucinatory patterns; Pira-paraná

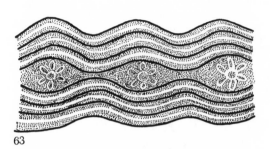

63

64

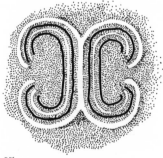

65

We have mentioned already the *vëari-mahsá,* another category of spirit-beings which is greatly feared. The imagery of the *vëari-mahsá* is considerably more complex than that of the *boráro* or other bush spirits. According to the Creation Myth, when the "germinator" (*pamurí-mahsë*) was ascending the rivers in his Anaconda-Canoe, his passengers consisted not only of a representative of each major group—Tukano, Arawak, Makú, and so on—and of each exogamic unit, but also of the exact double of each individual person. These doubles are called *vëari-mahsá* and, in some myths, are designated as the people whom *pamurí-mahsë* "had in excess." During the slow ascent and the peopling of the riverbanks these *vëari-mahsá* made themselves obnoxious by constantly opposing the germinator's orders; they always criticized and contradicted, causing confusion and discontent, until *pamurí-mahsë* decided to kill them all. But the Sun Father took pity on them and banished the doubles to the hills, where they continue to have their dwelling places together with the Master of Game Animals and the other spirits or spirit-animals that are said to exist inside these dark places.

The *vëari-mahsá* are, in every aspect, the exact doubles of every man or woman, and when occasionally they emerge from their hills and appear to people, they cause great confusion. They are likely to appear on lonely trails deep in the forest, or they might come at dusk to a landing place on the river, to a field, or even to a maloca. There they will behave just like human beings, imitating in detail the voices or gestures of close relatives, and will try to abduct people. A *vëari-mahsë* may appear to a woman as her brother or father and ask her to accompany him, perhaps to fetch a basket or to help in gathering some fruit. And then, when the woman accompanies him, he will rape her. A lone hunter may come upon a *vëari-mahsë,* see in him a close kinsman, and then be led astray by him. Children will be abducted by *vëari-mahsá* appearing as their parents, and it is said that a group of *vëari-mahsá* may appear at a dance and mingle with the crowd, trying to induce someone to follow them into the bush.

A person never meets his (or her) own Doppelgänger, but the double of a close relative—a sibling, parent, or uncle—who, then, will assault the victim sexually, or at least lead him astray and abandon him at some lonely spot. It is said that in times past the payés made use of the *vëari-mahsá* during intertribal wars to confound their enemies, and during the mythical time of chaos the *vëari-mahsá* abducted and seduced many people. The only recognizable trait of a *vëari-mahsë* is that he casts no shadow. But at dusk, or in the darkness of the forest, this is difficult to see and the doubles will rarely appear in full daylight.

The idea of the double, the mirror image, is fundamental to many Tukano concepts. Inside the hills, the Master of Game Animals is, in all essence, the double of the payé, and the animals themselves are the doubles of those found in the forest. Within the hills, these spirit-beings lead an existence identical with that of human society: they have their dances, their music, their food and drink, and they take narcotic drugs. The same happens in the underwater "houses" in the deep pools, where the Masters of Fish lead their existence. There is, then, "another world" matching in detail our world of empirical reality, and between these two "worlds" there is thought to exist a thin shell (D: *gahsíru*), an invisible wall which can be penetrated only in a hallucinatory trance. Under the influence of *vihó* or yajé people say they have visited this other dimension and have seen its inhabitants dancing, hunting, fishing, or otherwise behaving just like ordinary people in this world. The payés claim to know in detail the interior of the "houses" of the Master of Animals.

Apart from this collective sphere, of human and animallike spirit-beings in the "houses" of the hills and the waters, the idea of the double is found in other contexts. The shadow a person casts on the ground is a double, related to the mirror image one sees when standing at the water's edge and looking down upon one's reflection. In both cases, the person is connected with his double by the feet, a reversal which, according to the Indians proves the existence of this complementary world. The subterranean *ditá-mahsá* use mirrors to watch the approach of intruders into their territory; in one myth, the moon sees his spots in his reflection in the water, and in one of the tales about the *boráro* a man sees the reflection of a jaguar before him in the water. Large mirrors are the payment given to a payé by his apprentices, and we may recall the little mirrors set in pitch in the containers for narcotic powders. Of course, the entire complex of "turning into" or of "entering into" another dimension by the use of narcotic drugs is a process of *dédoublement*.

The concept of the double can be observed also in certain aspects of the social organization of the Tukano, especially in the opposition of two complementary exogamic groups. The members of one's complementary unit are called *verenígiri-mahsá/*"conversation-people" (D), that is, the people with whom one sustains a dialogue. They are called the "eco-people," because between two such units there is an "eco," an exchange.

This preoccupation with symmetry and reciprocity seems to pervade many aspects of Tukano culture, and, seen now within this context, the concept of the doubles—the *vëari-mahsá*—appears to represent something more than a mere alter ego, more than a simple projection of one's "other" personality into another sphere. On one level, one's *vëari-mahsë* is one's self, devoid of all cultural restrictions, incestuous and aggressive. A person is never confronted with himself, but with his close kin; and this is the fearful thing. But on another level, one's double is simply part of a great collectivity of doubles, of "the other half" as the Desana say, of Creation.

The forest and the rivers are believed to be peopled by a great number of minor spirits called *uahtí*. The term seems to be derived from *uahú/*hair, *uahuári/*to become covered with hair (D), and these spirits are imagined as small hairy beings that lurk in the dark and frighten lone hunters. More often than not they are quite harmless and do not attack people, but some are said to be rather similar to the *boráro*. Many strange noises that come from the forest or the river after dusk are attributed to *uahtí* spirits, and practically everyone can tell of some personal experience with one of these spirits.

A dangerous kind of *uahtí* called *pihsu-bári uahtí/*"to call–to devour–spirit" (T) is described as a manlike monster, but different from the *boráro*. He will cry "ë-ë-ë" in the forest, imitating the call of a person who has lost his way, and should a man answer this call, the monster will appear and kill him.

Other *uahtí* spirits are described as obscene, potbellied creatures, sometimes similar to monkeys, at other times to huge toads, which will suddenly emerge from a hollow tree, a cave, or a pool and frighten the passerby. It is said that occasionally *uahtí* spirits wear necklaces or carry blowguns, and then they tend to become confused with the *saaropë*, the "little people" said to live in the interfluvial regions.

We shall describe here a personal experience among the Tatuyo Indians which conveys some of the ambivalent attitudes toward these and other ghostly apparitions.

One moonlit night we were sitting at the door of a maloca, talking and looking out over the slope toward the river. There were eight men sitting in a semicircle, and the headman of the house was sitting in the middle, right in front of the door. He had been telling about the time when he was traveling on the Rio Negro, when, suddenly, he exclaimed: "People!" It was almost midnight, and all inhabitants of the maloca were accounted for; the next maloca was several hours' travel away, and so the approach of strangers was rather disquieting. The man explained that he had seen two men jump across the trail before us and disappear into the underbrush, at some hundred meters from where we were sitting. I myself had not seen anything, but all the others insisted now that they, too, had seen the shapes of two strangers rapidly cross the trail before us. While some of the men were posted as sentries at the two doors, the others retired to the center of the maloca where the matter was discussed until dawn, each man suggesting an explanation for this unusual event.

The first theory, which was advanced by most of the men, was that two *uahtí* spirits had been wandering by and that, when they saw us, they had become frightened and had gone into hiding. This idea was rejected when the headman explained that *uahtí* spirits did not travel in the rainy season on this part of the river, much less at moonlight, and that, anyway, spirits were not afraid of human beings and did not run away from them. By now the women had joined us and had begun to wail that surely the strangers were Indians from downriver who had come to abduct one of the nubile girls in our maloca. The girl in question seemed to be rather pleased with this prospect, but the men were very serious and disregarded what the women were saying. One of the men now explained at length that he was certain that they were going to be attacked by a raiding party of Kuripako Indians. He and the others talked in detail about the route by which these Indians might have come, and there was a long discussion about distances, place names, and portages. This explanation, too, was abandoned after a while, and now a very old man began to expound his theory. According to him the mysterious strangers were Indians who had fled from a rubber camp on the Apaporis River and were trying to find refuge here. When they approached the maloca they saw a white man sitting at the door, and, thinking he was a rubber collector, they had fled again. After some discussion this theory was rejected on the grounds that there were no rubber collectors on this part of the river and so the runaways would have had nothing to fear; besides, they would be foolish to travel at night.

All these different possibilities were argued at great length. People were extremely nervous, and on several occasions some men rushed to the door armed with clubs and bushknives, claiming to have heard some noise outside. The tension rose when a large cloud covered the moon and some birds that usually were silent at night began to croak loudly near the landing place.

At last, the headman who had initially given the warning of the strangers took the stage. He explained that the strangers had been Kuripako Indians, "but not real people"; they were the spirit-substance of Kuripako Indians who were wandering in a yajé trance. The real Kuripako were far away, and what they had seen were only their spirits; there was nothing to fear, therefore. "I travel a lot when I drink yajé," he said; "Surely people must have seen me wherever I went. But one cannot harm others when one travels that way." This explanation was accepted by all; an agreement had been reached and the incident was not mentioned again. When daylight came and I suggested looking for tracks, people shrugged their shoulders and the headman told me that "when one drinks yajé and travels, one does not leave any footprints."

For the Indians, the matter was settled. They had seen the spirit-substance of two hallucinating Kuripako Indians, potential enemies but, in this case, inoffensive. But, what was it they had "seen," after all?

In the foregoing pages, when speaking of the *boráro*, we have adduced some arguments that may point to sexual repression and to the phallic character of certain bush spirits. We have suggested that these tensions might lead to the projection of images of a frightening and, apparently, of a supernatural character. But this interpretation—if at all valid—should not be generalized. There are other reasons, other motivations which may produce similar effects, and one of them is fear. The nagging fear of known or unknown enemies, of ill-intentioned people, or, perhaps, of a hostile payé is an ever present factor in many malocas. Fear, indeed, is a great hallucinogen.

The fleeting shadows the headman had seen jumping across the trail had been interpreted as drug-possessed enemies.[23] The first consensus was established when all the others claimed to have seen the same apparition, thus identifying themselves with the headman, a highly respected person. The various interpretations given at first—*uahtí* spirits, a raiding party, or fugitives from a rubber camp—rather expressed a range of individual fears and expectancies. The *uahtí* were a commonplace explanation for all sorts of uncanny appearances; Kuripako raiders were feared above all by women; and the old man who suggested they were fugitives had had his own experiences with the rubber collectors. But all these interpretations were neutralized by the headman's authority, and again, there was agreement as to what had happened: there were enemies, but this time only their wandering spirits had appeared.

A further reconstruction of the particular circumstances of the event is revealing. At that time, the headman and others of his household were living an uneasy life. He himself was feared by many of his neighbors, who accused him of casting evil spells; several close relatives of his had died quite recently, and now another was seriously ill. A short time ago the headman had organized a gathering; he had prepared *cashirí* beer and had invited people from the neighboring malocas, but there had been tensions and doubts about this reunion. For days, during the preparation of the gathering, the headman had listened to the screeching and croaking of his two tame macaws. The birds flew back and forth over the forest, stopping at the other malocas, where they roosted, and then they went off again. It was thought that the birds might overhear some words, some remarks the neighbors might make concerning the invitation, and then repeat them on their return to the headman's maloca. But the screeching of the birds did not make sense. There were long nightly discussions: would the neighbors come and what would be their attitude? When finally the day came, only a few people arrived. The ritual greeting was brief; the *cashirí* beer was sour. There was no dancing and the conversation was dull. After two days the guests left, ill-humored and sullen. Moreover, there was little food at that time. The men went hunting and fishing, but often they returned empty-handed. Many people were suffering from severe colds and were lying listlessly in their hammocks.

It was in this atmosphere that we had been sitting at the door of the maloca when the spirits appeared. The headman had been talking about the hardships he had endured on the Rio Negro, traveling and working in a rubber camp, and these memories were not pleasant ones. He had been very ill and had almost died. He was in a somber mood when he talked of those times. It turned out that several other members of the maloca, all of them men, had recently had frightening experiences. At night they had heard strange, unexplained voices; near the landing they had seen shadowy beings, in the twilight after the sun had set, and one man told of a gigantic peccary he had seen in the forest, walking upright on its hindlegs. Deep in another section of the forest an old woman had been found who had gone astray from a neighboring maloca and was dying of exposure. People said that her face was deformed and looked like a tapir's trunk. She was not human any more; she was turning into a tapir.

It is perhaps small wonder, then, that in these circumstances people should believe in seeing spirits. Feeling surrounded by dangers, they are likely to interpret any unexplained noise or shape as a threat to their security. But there is another aspect that may explain some of these apparitions. In all the cases we were able to check in some detail, the beholder of the illusion was a frequent consumer of yajé and, less frequently perhaps, of narcotic snuff. Now it is possible that these drugs contain cumulative components, or that they produce irreversible effects, predisposing the person to experience sudden flashes of hallucinatory imagery every time a certain set of stimuli falls into a pattern. Changes in body chemistry may be responsible for these receptive states of mind, and they may trigger the frightening, threatening shapes of forest spirits, their voices, and their lurking movements in the shadows.

And then there seems to exist a paranoid streak in some aspects of Tukano personality. In speaking of shamanistic cures we have mentioned several syndromes that are recognized as such by the payés: the fear of being attacked by large, armed, anonymous crowds; the sensation of the sky's descending upon the earth and enfolding the person in darkness; and the feeling that the universe is steadily diminishing until the person is left perched upon a tiny remaining spot, in imminent danger of slipping off and falling into the void. Anxiety states like these are serious symptoms. But it would be an oversimplification to search exclusively for a social etiology; narcotic drugs may well be responsible for many of these states.

10

CONCLUSIONS

We have arrived at the end of our survey, and we must try to summarize some of our observations. Both the historical and the modern published sources, as well as our personal observations, have shown that drug-induced trances and hallucinatory states are at the core of many aboriginal beliefs and are of great consequence in myth and ritual, and in many practical affairs of everyday life. It seems, then, that any attempt at gaining an understanding of these cultures must take into account this hallucinatory sphere and must, therefore, pay close attention to ethnobotany and the Indians' knowledge of narcotic substances.

The hallucinogenic properties of these plants were discovered by the Amerinds in the remote past, probably before their arrival in the Western Hemisphere, and continuous experimentation has led to the accumulation of a large body of empirical observations on the effects of certain plants, certain preparations, and certain combinations. The Indians' categories, in this case, vary widely from ours in that they are based on the *effects* a certain plant produces, and not on the concept of species. Let us take the case of yajé. While we, in accordance with our Linnaean classification, would identify a certain vine as *Banisteriopsis caapi,* the Indians would recognize in one single vine a number of "kinds of yajé," according to the height at which the stems to be used are cut, and according to the age of the plant. In terms of the effects of the potion the Indians are certainly right because the concentration of the hallucinogenic components is likely to vary from one section of the vine to another. Besides, the Indians will distinguish between different yajé potions according to the specific habitat of the vine. A *Bani-*

steriopsis caapi preparation made from vines collected at one spot in the forest does not necessarily produce the same effects as a preparation made of the same species but gathered at another spot. The chemical composition of the local soils is likely to influence the potency of the drug, and when, occasionally, the men go to great pains to collect yajé vines at some remote spot in the jungle, they do so because they are fully aware of these differences.

The various admixtures used, combining different species of yajé or adding some other plants to the preparation, are another point of marked importance. Nothing is left to chance, and the precise quality and quantity of the admixture is a matter of serious concern to the Indians because they know that the effects of the drug will vary.

In addition, the individual and collective preparations of the consumers of the potion are likely to orient or even determine the character of the total experience. Dietary restrictions, sexual abstinence, and ritual vomiting prepare the organism, and the setting of the particular occasion itself is likely to produce a certain range of expectancies in the participants. The strict ritualization of the event is another factor which contributes to the production of a particular type of experience; the songs and dances, the different musical instruments, the red lights, the details of ritual conversation, and the cyclic interruptions of the procedure form, each time, a specific setting which tends to mould the experience into a pattern.

The same is true of the use of narcotic snuff. Although the group of participants is generally limited to a few, the taking of snuff for hallucinatory purposes is also highly formalized and implies a number of prerequisites that have to be met by the individual user.

All this points to the fact that the Indians have a truly extraordinary knowledge of narcotic plants and of the specific effects they produce if administered under controlled conditions. In the foregoing chapters we have spoken mainly of two different narcotic complexes—*Virola* snuff and *Banisteriopsis* potions—but from the data at our disposal it seems that there are several other groups of narcotic drugs. The snuff complex itself is insufficiently defined because, apart from *Virola* powder, certain other substances are in use which, as admixtures or taken alone, produce trancelike states. For example, a special snuff prepared from small lumps of a hard reddish resin is spoken of as a very potent hallucinogen, but nothing is known about its precise nature. The possibility that other narcotic snuffs are prepared from certain insects such as cicadas or lantern flies is of special interest, since some *Fulgoridae* of the Old World are known to contain narcotic substances,[1] and according to information we were able to obtain from the Indians, there are other, smaller insects containing psychoactive substances. The occasional combination of narcotic powders obtained from different natural sources is, of course, of major importance in producing hallucinatory effects of a certain range and intensity. The addition of powdered tobacco, coca, bark, or lime to a base of *Virola* powder is never a casual matter; it is carefully controlled in order that specific effects will be produced in the user.

Similar procedures are found in the *Banisteriopsis* complex. On the one hand, the preparation of the hallucinogenic potion is not simply a matter of using the stems of a certain botanical species, but a process of carefully combining plant materials which, although pertaining to the same species, are classified by the Indians according to the age of the vine or according to its specific habitat. On the other hand, the admixture of a small quantity of stems, leaves, or flowers from entirely different botanical species is, once more, a carefully controlled procedure. In these circumstances it would be a gross oversimplification to say that the Tukano use *Virola* snuff and *Banisteriopsis* potions; these are merely a basis, but the desired effects—the true cultural use of the plants—depend entirely upon the details of preparation.

According to the Indians many other plant sources also produce hallucinations, but we have little or no precise information on them. An interesting case in point is certain small herbs the fresh juice of which is squeezed into the eyes. Two different effects are attributed to this procedure: a marked increase in night vision, and true hallucinations. As to the first effect, the drops seem to produce a strong dilatation of the pupils; in fact, the person now has "jaguar eyes" and "sees in the dark." Hunters and travelers, when lost in the forest, are said to use this plant to orient themselves and to find their way back home. Regarding the second effect—produced by a different herb—the users claim to be able to see what is happening in distant places. For example, if far from his home, a man may "visit" his family and may find that someone is ill, or that his prompt return is required. These hallucinations, then, do not refer to any otherworldly sphere, but to the illusion of a momentary horizontal translocation within the world of empirical reality.

The direct ingestion of psychoactive substances—orally, as snuffs, or as eyedrops—is only part of the entire complex of the intentional control of body chemistry. A number of other practices are likely to produce endogenously certain substances of no less importance in leading to altered states of consciousness. Prolonged fasting, dietary restrictions, sexual abstinence, physical exertion, intentional deprivation of sleep, breath control, and concentrated thought are practiced by many people, apparently quite consciously, in order to produce certain desirable states of mind. Many of these procedures are prerequisites on ritual occasions, or precede certain activities such as hunting or fishing. In these cases nothing is ingested, nothing is added to the organism, but the latter is deprived of certain gratifications, and the ritualization of these deprivations is thought to produce the state of mind necessary to the successful achievement of a balance, whenever individual or social survival is threatened.

Among the Tukano, narcotic drugs are certainly not used for purely hedonistic reasons; their individual or collective use is always connected with the aim to transcend the bounds of empirical reality and to obtain a glimpse of that "other world" where the miseries and trials of daily existence may find their remedies. And, in most cases, these aims are quite realistically expressed. Narcotics are used in a very matter-of-fact way as a means of obtaining very practical, but very different, ends. It would be misleading to say that narcotic drugs form, in any way, a single coherent set of knowledge and practice. There is a great difference between the man who claims to turn into a jaguar and the man who wishes to diagnose an illness. They pursue entirely different ends, and the suggestion that there exists a link between the two because both use narcotic substances is quite meaningless within the context of their culture. The quest itself is highly ritualized, but with the exception of the collective consumption of yajé it can hardly be said to have religious ends. Even the collective yajé session is not a shamanistic ritual. More often, drugs are taken for very practical purposes, and even if so-called supernatural personifications (Vaí-mahsë, Vihó-mahsë) are thought to be instrumental in them these spirit-beings are used and handled in a very practical way. The concept of offerings, of a cult, or of an imploring attitude before "divine" forces is entirely lacking; the narcotic drug constitutes a practical mechanism for the curing of disease, the obtaining of food, the correct application of marriage rules, and the settlement of personal animosities. The shaman, as we have said before, is not a mystic, and the mechanisms he employs are not sacred.

If this evaluation of shamanistic practice and drug use is correct, we may go a step further and try to consider the total hallucinatory experience. We have said that narcotic drugs are used to establish contact with the "supernatural" sphere. This Otherworld is, of course, nothing but a projection of the individual mind, activated by the drug. Unconscious mental processes—fears and desires—are brought into focus and are projected upon the shapes and colors of the visions, and the interpretations given to this imagery by the viewer or by the payé refer in all essence to problems of food, sex, disease, and aggression, that is, to problems of physical survival. But the visions are not simply colorful images to be watched; they are imbued with meaning; they have a special significance to the beholder who believes that, in these visions, the Otherworld manifects itself to him in answer to his quest. Correct interpretation, therefore, is of great concern.

The initial sequence of physical reactions seems to be fairly standard, and the sensations of dizziness, tremor, flying, and rushing winds are commonly interpreted as the ascent to the Milky Way. The phosphene-based sensations of scintillating lights are explained as a penetration into the celestial sphere of stars and rainbows. But once a state of true hallucination has been reached, the images acquire a more personal character, and now the beholder, the payé, or the occasional consultant—whoever it may be—can no longer generalize but must probe and question in more detail; he can suggest certain explanations, judging from his personal experience, but it is probable that the beholder himself has precoded his interpretations and will see in them the threats he fears or the gratifications he desires.

The question arises: To what degree is the shaman aware of the nature of the projective process and of its psychodiagnostic value? In some cases the payé is convinced of the reality of his, or his companion's, ecstatic flight, as, for example, during jaguar transformation or during visits to the abodes of the Master of Animals. But on the far more frequent occasions concerned with curing rituals, or with attempts to establish the identity of an enemy or to harm a distant foe, there is no need for this kind of ecstatic dissociation, and the hallucinatory experience is reduced to the detailed scrutiny of images—his own or those described by his patient or client—for diagnostic clues and viable procedures. In these cases, it seems, the payé is fully aware of the projective nature of the visions. The same seems to be the case when a payé is being consulted by people who have taken part in a collective yajé session and are preoccupied with certain disturbing details of their particular hallucinations. Then the payé will explain and admonish, often by referring to dietary restrictions, the hunting ritual, or to interpersonal conflicts, and thus he will try to guide the person toward a more practical and realistic interpretation of his visions. While for the common drug consumer all hallucinations are phenomena which occur outside the person, outside ordinary reality, and, therefore, in the sphere of what he believes to be that of supernatural forces, for the shaman they constitute an all-important diagnostic tool, a mirror in which he observes the workings of the subconscious of his patients and clients, indeed of his entire social group. No matter whether or not he is fully aware of the projective processes involved, the interpretations he gives correspond to a social reality, and in this manner the payé acquires a powerful influence over his society and the cultural patterns guiding its behavior.

If we observe the close relationship between drug-induced hallucinations and such aspects as mythology, social organization, and artistic creation, we must conclude that the study of hallucinogenic plants and their use by native shamans provides the key to an understanding of many basic cultural processes. It is the hallucinatory experience which, at least among the Tukano, constitutes the common basis of most cultural activities, and the same is probably true for many other native cultures in which ecstatic states are known to be part of shamanistic practice.

But, as we said at the outset of this study, this is a border region of research, and the only safe pathways to an enlargement of our understanding of the relationships between drug use and cultural dynamics are the ones which botany, pharmacology, neurophysiology, and experimental psychology can reveal to us.

APPENDIX

Desana Texts

1. irá vai mahsa mahanëgaráa marire doremonyora. 2. iráa
iríríi iii mëë yeri peyarure iririkënyora. 3. dahá arikë yatutu
peyaru ii nyahiamara peyary iriré irá irinyora. 4. iriré amaruriráa
mahanyora viriporogere. 5. rogere mahanëgaráa mahsare dore
moanyora. 6. diroa mahsa irá vai poya surare ehobiranyora
mahsare. 7. dahiróo keri gorove-ororo mahsare. 8. iraré mari
kerogere ehobiranyora maripë iraré bayoro. 9. vai ariperekanyora
mari kerogere. 10. dahá arikë vaimëra dii ariperekanyoro.
11. dahá arikë vaimëra dii ariyoro kerogere. 12. iriré inyaráa
irá mahanëganyora vii tëërorigere irá vai mahsá. 13. dahiráa
marire doreyeebiranyora. 14. iri nyahá vari peyarure irinyora iri
ebobohó dehkore irinyora peyarure. 15. mari kerogere iriré marire
tiabiranyora. 16. dahigë peyaru irinigi kesuyoro goroveregë
kerogere. 17. marire dahá ohokariri miukarata yinyora. 18. marire
dore yeera arira. 19. igë turi bero mahka piru goa turibero
ariyoro. 20. umu poari vehko poari maha poari buyakëyoro.
21. mahaka piru bogë mahaka nyigë turikëri bero ariyoro. 22. igë
umu amigëga umu nyigë pore turiberokëribero ariyoro. 23. dahá
arikë irirú tereduu amiduga vëaduu ahpanyora. 24. dahá arikë
buhurú diaduu boreduu nyiiduu ahpanyora. 25. iriré irá puribiranyora irá vai mahsa. 26. mari kerogere peyaruu irii marire siu
puribiranyora. 27. dahiráa iraré ahpikó suu tooka ahpikó suu
tuunyeanugukama. 28. irá mahsa gumure ai tuunyeanugu ai varáa
ahpikó suu ookama. 29. irá peyaru saari sorori ariyoro irisare
ahpikoo suu ookama. 30. igë buyá puuveherinyee ahpikoo suu abe

205

keyage koamemuhkama. 31. irogé pasuamepeokama. 32. igë
mahka piru goa berosare ahpikoo suu koakama. 33. irisáa ëmaroge
vabë abeya keyage. 34. irirú buhurusaa ëmarogeta vabë abeya
keyage. 35. iriré ahpikoo suu abeya keyage simepeokama. 36. iriré
iraré mohotanyora irá yohoka dëhpërii ariyoro. 37. dia koragë
mahiri puuridohka yahsadigë puuridohka boredigë iri mahiri
ariyoro. 38. iri mera marire dohte dëa yuhpë igë vai mahsë.
39. dahiráa iri yohoka dëhpërire ahpikoo suu tooka ahpikoo suu igë
mohokëro mariboroga ai koameyuukama igë mahasa gume ai tuu
nyeanugukama. 40. iro abe keyageta ai pasuame peokama. 41. iri
mohokëgë gua yuhpë arima. 42. irigë oaa gahsirore gahsirukë
yuhpë. 43. iriru mera irá tuara panyora mahsa ya perare. 44. vii
bora mahagëgeta ira ya gahsirure díritura parakanyora. 45. irotá
igë bári parire buúma pare. 46. iripá soropa boreripa nyahsari
gorikëripa dia gorokëripa aiyoro. 47. irá bua barisaa dahta iri para
nëhkë ariyoro. 48. iri pari mera marire siu banyora. 49. iri
parire ahpikoo suu tooka ahpikoo suu ai vara viame buukanyora.
50. irá ya gahsiruge viamesaukanyora. 51. iri igë bari ariperero
mari barinëhkë soro pari parita ahpanyora. 52. píriri parisaa
iripeta ariyora. 53. iriré ahpikoo suu tooka ahpikoo suu ai viamé-
buukami. 54. iraré ahpikoo suu tooka ahpikoo suu iraré mahsa
gumu buukami. 55. tuu mahime buu iraré ai tuunërë mesaukami
gahsirugere. 56. irá gahsiru diripaora dare borerida iridá piasada
iri mera dirinyora. 57. iriré ahpikoo suu tooka ahpikoo suu ai
tëapamebuukami. 58. irirú gahsirure ahpikoo suu tooka ahpikoo
suu ai tuumeyuukami. 59. iri mahi ëhtabohoo bore mahi pea diari
mahi pea sahsari mahi ariyoro. 60. iri ëhtaboho mahisáa iripeta
ariyoro boreri mahi diari mahi ariyoro. 61. irirú gahsirure simeyuu-
gëta ëhtaboho mahire mesáa simé yuukayuhpë. 62. iri mahiri
mera me muhtume dihukami diagere. 63. iripeta aráa inye.

TEXT NO. 179

1. iriré inyagë vai gahpire iri yuhpë igë yeepëa paree. 2. iri
niarisibú baya yuhpë pare. 3. igë bayakë deyoro bëga muri
nëgaka yoro buime dohpa deyorinyee. 4. igë yee nyahsaruu umu
poari buyakëduu ahpamii. 5. iriru mera pagamerasama soa.
6. iri vahkari iri ëhtáa ari perero ai gamera yuhpë. 7. irirú mera iri
doreré nyadihuu yuhpë yee ëhtaye mera. 8. igë bayira murunyee
mera iriré puri yuhpë pare. 9. igë yeepëre deyokaka vahkari

ëhtayeeri varo. 10. gahsibure opata duakami iri vahkarire ai
koakami. 11. marisare deyokabë vahkari ëhtayari. 12. oore
moamure irá birasibure aridoo aribë 13. iipa vahkari aima nyu-
munyuu vahkari aribëro. 14. iri vahkari saa bore diari ebohó sura
aribë. 15. iritá nimakëri nyee ariyoro gahi nyee ehtokari nyee.
16. iro dohkaga nahsíi poaruga nigibë diriye marikerero vihiranyee.
17. iri nyee ariyoro marire mesiamerekë yiyirinyee. 18. iri vahkata simpora puri vahka aroyoro. 19. gahi vahakasáa iripa vahkata
aribë. 20. iri vahkare mahsë poada bero vihidoo aribë. 21. diriri
marikerekë obó vihiráa nyee ariyoro. 22. gahipëre boré aribë
doha gahipëre ebohó. 23. iri nyeesaa nimakëri ehtokari ahpayoro.
24. dii mera ehtomáa siririnyee aroyoro. 25. iriré ahpidigë dahá
yii ari verenigi yuhpë. 26. ëhtapëge taaborerogage yapikadigë
arimi. 27. iriré gahpí niarisibu buaa bayameguu yuhpë pare.
28. ëmaroge inyáa igë yaru shsaru mera game vagusamigë pare.
29. iri vahkarire murú purii ai mërimi gëyadëaraa iri noho. 30. igë
aibirikëre iri vahkarita bugakabuyuro. 31. iri vahkarita vihtú sare
bëgakë yiyoro pora. 32. buhpú pari mahsa iri porare inyamarii
buhpú panyora. 33. iri merata nimakërii ehtokarii misiamererii
ariyoro. 34. dahá vakëree vaisaa ehatuabirinyora vai mahsa
dahata. 35. irá vai peora geare ëhëtërikanyora vaibahara.
36. dahiráa iri yoo vahtearore mëë diapë dihukakoma dohkapë.
37. iri soró nimakërisoro sare dahata irogeta koakoma. 38. iri soro
vai mahsë gahpisoro ariyoro variavayoro irá koakë. 39. iri sorosáa
mari ya soro dohpata arika irisoro sáa. 40. bëariti saa arika mariya
soro dohpata deyoka. 41. irogeta nimakëri mëra sanyakoma oáa
mëréa. 42. iri bëariti parimakë mari mahsare nurikoma. 43. oáa
peasaa iriré bohkatiubeama iriré mahsibeama.

TEXT NO. 31

1. meresiamë poá suriro ariyoro. 2. iri surirore tooka suu ahpikó
suu ai tuuveame yuukakoma. 3. dia ahpikó dihtarugere óme
yuukakoma. 4. meresiamë borégë diagë ari yuhpë. 5. iri suriro
tooka mera suu ahpikó suu ai tuuveame yuukakoma. 6. dia ahpikó
dihtarugë óme yuukakoma. 7. ariperea vaimëra mera dahá
yikoma. 8. ukuámë sare dahata. 9. iropërëta arikumi mahsa véhe.
10. iri aripereri ahpikó dihtarugë vaka. 11. gahkía ariperera
vakoma pare. 12. iri surita mahsare surikë yiká. 13. iropërëta
arikoma oá vërá. 14. irisáa dia ahpikó dihtarugeta. 15. iro përëta

árika vehkë poa suriro. 16. dihpuru niarire bayira. 17. igë abé
buimébero diari bero. 18. peame diari bero bahá arika. 19. iri
sorori marire sorokë yika. 20. iri darire ahpikó suu tuuveyukakoma.
21. iriré ahpagëë marire dihpuru niabirika.

TEXT NO. 30

1. igë pamuri mahsëta iriru abé yerure ahpa yuhpë. 2. matá
pamuka yuhpë. 3. matá irá mari gubuta mahara yea arikanyora.
4. iri yee bari vahó arinyoro. 5. pirú bari vihó mahsa vihó ariyoro.
6. vëarí-mahsa viu nuguri vihó aroyoro. 7. abé yeru dahá vakë
yiyora. 8. iri vihiri dihpagugeta vayororo. 9. biarikuduu ariyoro.
10. matá dahá ariduu ariyoro. 11. iri vihóre vihí mora irigure
nuakanyora. 12. irá dehko piripi kanyora. 13. no gamegure
menyahaa mayoro. 14. asia maanyora. 15. iri porunyahaku dahá
vayoro iraré. 16. dahí turage irigure vihinyora. 17. iri abé yerure
vihí yi nihara siaka murinyora. 18. simpora diita nyome siaka-
murinyora. 19. dahí tuarata yee banyora. 20. dahira sipeama
diha vanyora. 21. irá simporare duura dahá onyora. 22. diapu
serore koapero arika yoro. 23. dahira irá peayéke siribirinyora.
24. irá virikësare oá yea nëgë viri mahara saa guaperekanyora.
25. óre dia dihpare yee vii arika. 26. dahá ari verenigi ma.
27. dahira irá oo dohkagere kurikomo yea bakurira. 28. yoabirika
iragere. 29. yuhúgo bëró iraré oma ehóko. 30. yuhuká iraré irá
nyehko bëró turi yohpo yësare mëa yea barire aigarike ari turi
yohpo. 31. aë arinyora. 32. dahá yii mahsë gohsore aí duharanyora
korá mera goha gohsore. 33. ai duharii soropage saakanyora igó
ehadego duharakëë verenyora meabëro mëë baduarore airabëgëa
arinyora. 34. iriré bisoro nihago bake arinyora. 35. igopë mahsa
gohsora inyamariago turi yohpo iraré. 36. mahá irá vihó vihí beré
ehodigë saa yeeta vaaka yuhpë. 37. mahsë dedirikë igë mahá
yee bamuri yuhpë. 38. igë vihó meré ehodigë yeegora vaka mëri
yuhpë. 39. igë igirure diiru diita ahpagë goaraka muri yuhpë.
40. dahiturata igë goare ai mërinyora. 41. oá yeeagorasaa bohé
arira yinyora irasáa. 42. bohema viri ahpakoma irasáa.

TEXT NO. 99

1. irá abé yeeru vihirá daháa yimërinyora ii në arikë vihinyoraa ii
në arikë iri yeea bari vihore vihiiráa. 2. irá yeea bari vihore vihiráa.

3. irá vihore irá dehko nuakanyoraa iri abé yerugëre aa irá dehko.
4. sëripuriye dohpa beharoge diikëyoro dahá me bohkatiurayé iriyere nuanyoráa iriyere nuayurii. 5. nuáa irá piri dobokanyoráa.
6. irá dehko piridobí yikë noo iri sëagëre me nyahamaayoro pare me nyahamáa aa më nyahaayoro. 7. iri me nyahaamákë asiamanyorá asiamáa. 8. iripeeta vakayoro iripeta vaka aa gahigësare dahta doha me nyahámayoro. 9. asiapereanyorá asiapera. 10. iriá asiapereromerá iraré vihó vihiro dohpa vasayasio aa dahta ariyáa.
11. irá dahí pare iri vihó beresiará pare irá yeea bamërinyorá.
12. iri surí iri yee suri me nyahará dahá vanyoraa. 13. nyomebirinyoráa nyomebiri pea vihtú behána siakanyora simpora diita nyomekayoro yoo daháa yee bakuriráa. 14. daháa yikurimërinyorá arimáa dahá ariri. 15. iri yee suri me nyaharagé sipë yuamahima vanyora. 16. iro paarupë ira sugëperogoa arikayoro ariká.
17. dahiráa sipë me nyahama nëganyorá dahatë. 18. noo irá vahagëra vererare yee bakurimërinyoráa. 19. iri nëre irá yeea barinëri irá yeea guapurikanyorá guapurikáa guapurikáa. 20. yeba mahara yeeasaa guarinyoráa guarii. 21. guatarinyorá guarinyoráa.
22. ari veregimáa ari veregiri. 23. oore igë dihpurure igë koa pero ariyoro koa pero koapero mera piribua peonyoráa. 24. yuhugëre yee banyora yee bayuríi. 25. igë inyá igëre veheanyomáa aríi igë buhii veheyuhpë igë buhii neheyuríi igë buhi veheyuríi. 26. yuhugë yee mahsa imugë ariyuhpë yee. 27. igë mahsëre nyebugë përëpërë ariyuhpë. 28. dahigë mari gahigëpëre inyarisibú përëpërë erá nyeayuhpë nyéa. 29. igëre nyea batua igë dihpurure gumu vehká piridobokamërinyora piridonokáa. 30. daháa yimërinyorá arimá ariri aa aa. 31. babirinyorá barapëa irá yeba viri maharapë banyoráa irá vaimërape vaimërapë. 32. irá mahsa yeeapë babirinyorá babiri aa yuhu diayeta vehekanyoráa irapë irare bakorenyoráa. 33. ari verenigimërimá ari verenigimëriri aa aa. 34. soo arú muurá vaaraa poeri vararé mëgarameremërinyorá mëgaramere. 35. deyoro oyamuhukanyorá deyoro irá inyakëre. 36. dahá yii igëre arubu iiyagë vagëre nyeanyorá nyeayuhpë igë yee nyeayuríi. 37. yikariyuhpë igë gamero turugë igëre nyeakanyorá. 38. irisibureta ehayuhpë igë buhíi eháa. 39. igë mëënyehkë poro igë mëënyehkë poro. 40. ehá igëre yee vehegëra ariyuhpë ariyuríi aa aa. 41. igë yë buhí eranyumí ari igëpë arúu poogë vaayuhpë aa yea bahara aranyorá yeea bara arira yianyorá irá arikë vabirimëriyuhpë vabirimëriyuríi. 42. koe yë buhí eramí pare ari viria yuhpë pare viriá pare. 43. arú poogë vagë pare

poogë vagë pare. 44. iro mëëpora arú igë muura oyamërisayasóo.
45. iraré guigë poogë vamahsibiri, ëriyuhpë. 46. igë pootua
maharigëre igë yee igëre nyeayuhpë nyeaka. 47. igë dahikë inyáa
nyamikage deyobiriyuhpë deyobiriyumí. 48. daháa yianyumí ari
gahinëinyaráa vanyoráa vayuríi. 49. irá inyagaaborore igë
dihpuru diita doakayoro. 50. dahá arikë goarii oyayoro oyáa.
51. iriré seasá oreduhariké ariyuhpë ariyuríi. 52. daháa yii irá
duharinyorá duharíi. 53. irá kore igëpëa ëmaroge keyá vabunihagë
inyapeyayuhpë inyapeyáa. 54. igësáa yeeta ariyuhpë yeeta.
55. igësáa marinohota arisanyumíi obó wiragëta ariyuhpë wiragëta.
56. igë peyaro dohkaga erá orenyorá taría orenyora doha. 57. irá
ore aharimari duharo arituanyorá arituayuríi. 58. ërera arinyorá
igë bueára ërera. 59. erarée vihó peogë yuhugëë ariyuhpë yuhugë
igëta ariyuhpë. 60. igë dihsipoábu diisihsipoabu diita arikayoro.
61. igëre nyeadigë arikebáa. 62. igë bueara ëmëtanyoráa igë
bueara. 63. ërera tarimanyora tarimáa. 64. arimari igë dohkare erá
pepiyuhpë pepinyumíi. 65. igë iro erá yuanyágëre yëre peayegëmë-
haba arigë árigë yiariyuhpë igë yee igëre peayebeo yuhpë vëgo-
begora. 66. irotá me mereháa yiriayuhpë pare siriavaa pare.
67. igë sirigëre igëre nedu viritabeokayuhpë viritabeoka. 68. dahá
yii igëre veheyuhpë dahá yii igëre veheyuríi. 69. gahinë ohokariro
mahagë sirimáa vayuhpë deyoropëre. 70. igë pësáa igë viragë
arigëka igëre daháa yiyuhpë arikebáa igë verenigiro mera daháa
yiyuhpë aa dahatë aa. 71. irá bahsíi game vehera yisanyosoa.
72. iri vihóreta ahpaa yësáa ari vehegamimëriyuhpë arimáa.
73. gahigëre megá siugëre bayuhpë megá siugëre. 74. irasáre
perageta nyeakayuhpë peragetaa. 75. nyeáa iraré banyoráa
báyurii. 76. irá yeba viri maharapëa yeba viri maharapëa.
77. batuanugúu ira dihpure gumu vehká dobo muhuunyora.
78. irá vehenara taragamerapu korebehanyorá koré pare. 79. vehenyorá irá buegëre yuhugë igë bëgëre yuhugë vehenyoráa
veheyurí. 80. ira perá vehenyorá perá. 81. igëgorapë deyobiriyuhpë gahirapë deyonyorá. 82. pesipurikayuhpë pesipurukáa, aa.
83. daháa yii pare irare vehetuamugu ari duháa soenyora pare
perageta. 84. irá mamayeare vehekanyorá mamayeare. 85. peamé
vëari peamé diú irare soenyorá varo uirá ëhëmorata irá oreporemaa
ványoraa po'tooo gahigësa dahta po'tooo. 86. dëhpë veremaa
várayinyorá dëëhpë veremáa. 87. dëhpë veremáa goekanyora
goekaanyomáa. 88. irá suriro vehekanyoráa irá surirose. 89. irá
yea bari mahsamerata irá vëari-mahsa virinyora vëari-mahsa.

90. daháa arikë irá piru bára irisibureta piru banyorá. 91. vaha-gëráa vereráa vereráa. 92. diapëre pirú ari baharopëre yee ari dahá arikë vëari-mahsa ari irá viriguanyoráa. 93. virimërinyora ari-mërimáa ariri aa aa. 94. irá abé yeruu vihiráa abé yeruu vihiráa. 95. daháa yii gamé vahagëra veremërinyorá veré. 96. iriboherigere gëhyapërikamëriyoro. 97. iripeta aráa iripeta aa aa.

TEXT NO. 140

1. mahsa iri vihore vihí mora nëhkë yuhu bero doanyora. 2. iri bahsíi opaa doarare menyahamáa vayoro. 3. abé yerure vihiráa irirure tëaduabeokanyora pare. 4. ira iriré vihiráa yohká sumuga diita irinyora. 5. vera poga irá popaoragare iriré iriré irinyora ira mahsa. 6. ëre aberi vaboro niagariyoro pare iri vihó. 7. niagarirota mërakëgarika yoro. 8. iro pare igë hímatua yuhpë pare.
9. hihihihihi vakayuhpë vaka. 10. dahigëta gahiropa aribirika ari igë marapore barigë suriyuhpë pare. 11. igë dahí makëta igë mahsëë himaaka yuhpë pare. 12. dahś arimá aa. 13. dahá varota varo parimáa vayoro varé vayoro. 14. iri yeba virimaha varo parikayoro varo deyoro tererigiri. 15. dahá varoreta iri suapurumuhuu yuhpë yeesuri. 16. iro diá gorosirigere vëhë ai yuhpë. 17. piru babugë uahtikenyarure sua yuhpë. 18. irotá inyakuu nugubeokayuhpë matá. 19. daha varota ii vëari-mahsa surii suanyora. 20. iri suri matá dahá arira arika iria. 21. iri saa yeea virigeta arika. 22. iri surire sanyaráa mehnyaháa ipë yua-peamahimenugakoma. 23. parupëre sugogoa arika. 24. dahirá oo diapu serore koaruperore piripeonyora. 25. yëre pavari agrigëë iinyere varo kamotagë yiyuhpë. 26. dahá yii igë siu vamavayuhpë te igë noo varo. 27. iritá irá vahagëra verero vayoro pare. 28. noo nëgëë vagëre yuu nyaka yuhpë igëre veheka yuhpë. 29. mahsare vehegëë yohoka mera tebe yuhpë. 30. dia gorosiri mahagë yee irare bueyuhpë. 31. yee mahsibigë noho mata veheka yuhpë mahsibigë noho vehebiriyuhpë. 32. neo gorare oáa boreka pora iriré ahpanyora. 33. irireta irá ëmëko vihó arima. 34. irá suriarin-yeesaa matá nëgaká yoro. 35. iri nohore vihiranoho varo tari-perebirinyora. 36. ipëpëre oá bëgëyeri pora turaro yeea bamërima arima. 37. irá turaro nyearasibure tari porare turaro nyeana arima. 38. oa nome nyeeriabëra igë marapopë yohá nyukú moabiri-yohpó. 39. igëpë nyamigakeya vaa vai vehegë vagë yiari yuhpë. 40. dahá guagë nyamigakeya veheri vahsú aigáa vayuhpë.

41. irisibureta irapë vihó vihiraa yinyora. 42. iró vamáa yoaya dia
vehkage omabuahayuhpë igë yee. 43. igëpë mahsëpë diagere
gumuge garisia yuria vehegë yiyuhpë. 44. veheyuhpë vareré iro
yuría gahí dihtaru doaha yuhpë doha. 45. igë diage inyame
paorore diagere gumuge taribuháa yuhpë. 46. igë mahëpë igëre
gui omagarigëta tarage mebiadoa vayuhpë. 47. igëre nyeagë
varigë yeero igë poro memerehayuhpë yee vëagë. 48. igë dahigëre
tabeyuhpë diapësero gora. 49. dii turaro viriyoro yeepëre igë
mahsëpë turaro piyu yuhpë mahsare. 50. yëre yee bagë aridëagë
obó ye ye ye ye ye ye vakayuhpë. 51. ira mahsapë turaro gagini-
gigari nyora mahsa bahara. 52. irá mahsa arikuú vaavayuhpë
yeero. 53. irá dahá yeea barasibure dahá vayoro arima. 54. gahi
në doha bëgëyerimagë doha peayevagagë vagë yiariyuhpë.
55. igë peaye kurigëre erá bakayuhpë yeeró vëagë. 56. igë
marapopë igëre yeea bara yianyomaa arii inyagáa yuhpo. 57. irotá
peagë oyanigiyoro irokoregaa igë mahsë dihpuru ayayoro.
58. dahaa vakë inyaa igë yeere salisáa vehenyora pare. 59. saliro
tamu yuhpë igë yee vëagë ari yuhpë igë yee. 60. pea baha aitía
soenyora igëre irotá orepore maavayuhpë. 61. dahá varore igë
siria vayuhpë igë mahsupë. 62. iri vihó niaripee mahsare bakurin-
yora. 63. iri niari perekë irá mahsa mahsáavanyora doha. 64. irotá
iraré irá goerodohpa vakayoro. 65. iripeta ohogororikëa.

TEXT NO. 96

1. ee iipë ariká arikuri aa vihó gahsiru vihó gahsirú aa aa. 2. iro
diaa gorosiripë aa. 3. ii dihpuru arikáa ii dihpuru arikurii. 4. ii
dihpuru diara dihpuru diara dihpuru aa. 5. iri dihpuru áriro
aráa arikebá iri gahsí mera ariro ii dihpuu ii dihpuu ariro mirunye
mera aráa. 6. soo vëri gahsí dohpá ariro yiia arikebáariro vëri
gahsí dohpá aa dahatëë. 7. irinyée miru bogá aráa iri mirunye.
8. dahina oáa iipëë mahrapë vihó vihimá arikebá vihii iriré
bohkatirira iri bohkatiriraa. 9. vihó vihimáa dohá vihó
vihi. 10. ii gurunyá veraré ii gurunyá veraré dihpaseri vihó
dihpaseri vehó. 11. ii dehko vihó dehko vihó. 12. dahirá irogere
doha irá doha vihó arinyora doha iri gahsigere iri gahsigere. 13. irá
mahsa porakëra marire keegoroveonyorá keegoroveo marire kerogere marire vehedëara yiaribëra. 14. dahá aribë dahá ariri gamúu
aa aa. 15. iri ariyoro iri aroyoro. 16. iroo oo inyée ii dihpuru
diara dihpuru ariaribëra diara dihpuru. 17. iro përë iri poraka

dihpuru poraka dihpuru. 18. iri poraka dihpuruta guayoro
guayuríi. 19. irá vihó mahsa iipë mahara doha irá bohkatirinyora
bohkatiriyuríi. 20. dahiro turaro buhpú paayuhpë paayuríi.
21. dahá aráa arimáa dahá ariyuríi. 22. iropërë ii poraka dihpuru
përëta nihtia dihpuru ariyoro doha ariyurí. 23. iri ii dihpuru
dihpururi gëhyaribërë gëhyaro iraya noho sibú diita gëhyaribëro
aa dahta aribë dohpagere ahari mára. 24. iri ariyoróo iri mirú bogá
iri gahsí mirú bogá ariyoróo ariyuríi dahara irá mirunye mera
arimáa arikebáa aríi gëhyama arikebáa. 25. dahá aráa arimáa
dahá aráa ariri. 26. vëri gahsíi yiro dohpáa ariyoro vëri gahsíi yiro
dohpá. 27. dahirá marire kerogere marire keeri goroveoaribëro.
28. mari bayaráa inyagamearibëro aa arikegë bayararee. 29. ii
mahapoári buyakënáa ariaribëráa aritarikama obóo. 30. ii dehkó
vihó mahsa ira surisá bayaráa mahsa gumú ahpanyora. 31. ii nyee
ii mahapoári maharáa ii dihpaseri vihó ariyoro dihpaseri vihó.
32. ii yuiturí maháa ariyoro ii nyee dehkó vihó dehkó vihó.
33. daháa yiira mahsa gumukëra mahsa gorovenyoráa dahatë
gamú. 34. iri marire dorenyora doreyeyurii nye oaa nomé arinyora
ii gahsii maharata ii gahsii maharata. 35. dahigë mari dorekëro
gameyoro dorekëro gamé. 36. dahá ari verenigimáa dahá ari
verenigiri. 37. ba iripeta araa iripeta aa.

TEXT NO. 207

1. igë kurikure buhpú guhya birika gahiropa arikumi. 2. dia
gorosiri mahagë ari yuhpë yee nyigë dia dihpamahagë nyi dorora
arinyora. 3. ohopu yeea irá nyamá yeea. 4. yuhuka mahsë iguré
nomé gamebirikë sua va yuhpë. 5. irisibureta bohkaha yuhpë
yuhëgu mahsëre yeerota ari yuhpëgë. 6. dia gorosiri mahage.
7. yuhuu saku oma yuhpë igëyá suriré irogé saa yuhpë.
8. igutá serepi yuhpë nooge vaari arigëë yëre nomé gamebirikë dahá vaa dedirikagë vagë yia ari yuhpë. 9. noo
arari igó nomea ari yuhpë? 10. iró aramo ari yuhpë aë yë
mure nyea bohsaëra ari yuhpë. 11. yohoka dëhpë peyádigë ari
yuhpë. 12. dahira oá yeea yohoka dëhpëre buyákënyora.
13. mahsa yeea diita ahpanyora iriré. 14. yee bara iri dëhpë
mera irá nyeanyora. 15. igorá koré igë surirogë menyahá yeegero
vahka yuhpë. 16. igopëa sorobure ai mabuari yohpo. 17. igo
buarikë yohoka dëhëe mera pasá beoka yuhpë. 18. igupë inyakëre
yeero ai burima suá vahuhpë. 19. mahsapë inyakuré dii maro

dita óyakáyoro. 20. mahsë gere ehá via yuhpë igoré. 21. igotá
gamebirarí mëre ari ehá via yuhpë. 22. iná yë mera vake yë dia
dihpa maha viige peyaru irigë vagë yia ari yuhpë. 23. irá saa
igëe merata vaanyora. 24. mahsapëa peamëe diuu yi yuhpë.
25. nyee nohore mëá bámëriri mëá ari yuhpë. 26. gëá vaimërare
bamuribë arinyora irapë. 27. mëá bake arika yuhpë babea yëá
arika yuhpë. 28. ira kari peredo suri nyahá yeegero oyaká muri
yuhpë. 29. ira kari vagá inyanyora igërë yee vëaridiagë oyamisii
arinyora igupë peká yuhpë. 30. igë gamiririre savé savé yibeo
yuhpë peea arigëë. 31. iripeta tuuveabeo ka yuhpë iri surirore.
32. mëá dohpá arira yirí mëá ari serepi yuhpë. 33. mëá yëre
guibiri kake ari yuhpë. 34. yaa suriré sanyagë opaa vaa
yëë. 35. viri nuhkë nyahá mërianyora. 36. viiri nuhkë dahá yi
mëriaka yuhpë. 37. iraré imugagu yi yuhpë. 38. vari gabore
ehanyora. 39. amerota duyaká pare ari yuhpë oota yëë surirore
dehkó bohorigëra yëë ari vere yuhpë. 40. igë dohpá yiburire varo
vere peoka yuhpë. 41. igë ya suri saare varo imupeo ka yuhpë
igë dihsipoari sare dahata yee vëari diagë ari yuhpë. 42. igë yee
buhurure koa yuhpë. 43. irá makera ohogoro ehá inyabeo
nyoraviigero arika yoro ohorikëri viiro ari yoro. 44. igë porerure
nyeaké ari yuhpë irogé nyeá nërësiake ari vere yuhpë. 45. irá
ariperera ohpota ari yuhpugë. 46. irogé bayagë vagë yi yuhpë.
47. iri në gora era yuhpë. 48. gahira saa bohká tiri gari tuanyora
bahari diara arinyora. 49. nyigurore pakoretu marinyora. 50. igëré
bohká tiri sererata yanorara. 51. ira saa igë poreruta nyeatuyaka-
nyora. 52. iri viigere nyahágëta suri vere ma va yuhpë. 53. iroré
bayanyora bayatuarata aririnyora pare. 54. yeasaa murita
hinyora. 55. mëá iriré vere mera ohokariraka ari yuhpë mëá verera
matá yu poroge vaaraka arika yuhpë. 56. mëá yoharo siribirikëre
oota ará mëare siugá gëra ari yuhpë. 57. yoari bohe vakayora irá
dédiriro yuhu bohori varo vaya. 58. dahigëe igë mahi yuriagë yi
yuhpë. 59. gahirapë sare piarinyora iraré verebiriyora. 60. peri
gari bore verenyora. 61. iri nyamireta kari nëgari siri kanyoara.

TEXT NO. 102

1. igë gamisiri gori ariyoro igë gamisiri gori aa aa. 2. nyee gaabëgë
vihtú arikáa aa aa. 3. iriré gami siagë guayuhpë guayuri aa aa.
4. dahá arikë turibero turibero aa aa. 5. buyakë yuhpë buyakë yurii

aa aa. 6. dahira igëre iribero tuuvea aikakoma aikáa aa aa. 7. dahá
arikë yohoka dëhpë yohoka dëhpë aa aa. 8. dëhpë mera tabeyuhpë
tabe yurii tabëgë yiyuhpë aa aa. 9. aa marire nyeagë nyeagë aa aa.
10. patamepiuka yuhpë patamepiukaa aa aa. 11. dahiráa igëre
buyá emara yikomá arikebá iri yohoka dëhpëre tuuvea aikakomáa
aikáa aa aa. 12. tuuvea ai abeya keyage peokakoma peokáa aa aa.
13. igë ëya gamiri siarisare dahta dahta aa aa. 14. dahá aribë
arimá ariri aa aa. 15. igëre nihisoráa iriré buyakëkë guayuhpë
guáa aa. 16. dahira igëre dohará dahá yikomá dahá ookuri aa
aa. 17. igëya viige igëre tuumahidoba gahkuukakomáa igëya viige
aa aa. 18. buya pabeo tuumahidobogahkuukoma aa aa. 19. iripeta
aráa iripeta aa aa.

TEXT NO. 100

1. yee dohári aráyoro iriré pedëayuhpë aa aa. 2. nee kurira
arisanyomaa aa iroreta pagara vaikëmará. 3. igë kariri gorore yeere
dohagë peame purisuhameregëta yipuru. 4. dahigë karirigorore
peame diugë ëmëgë diusakumisi ëmëgë diukuri. 5. igë iriré
diugëta iri imikeyaru mahsemékëduu dhtimékëduu seosirime
garisiukayuhpë. 6. dahá arikë nyahpukeri imikeyaru mohsá
mekëduu nihti mékëduu seosirime garisiukayuhpë. 7. nyee nyumu
yokeri imikeyaru dahta iri mera igë seosirime garisiukayuhpë.
8. iri daháa yii igë dahá maa moabeo yuhpë pare dia dihpamaha
viige. 9. irogé maa moabeoyuhpë iipëpëre maa moabeo yuhpë
ipë dia gorosirige maa moamenugu yuhpë. 10. irá bohsoa oáa
nyamáa irá buía iraré bari moabeoyuhpë dahigë ige maripëre inya-
peobiri yuhpë irinyee imikeyaru irogé mari arikasuyoro. 11. iri
pearé igë pea moa yihpë dohaa. 12. iri mihigë pea ariyoro dahá arikë
iri gohá nyuri peá iri baraská soo. 13. iri peá barari noho diitare
peá moakumí peamarámu nigikanyoro igë inyakë. 14. igë dahigëta
igë gamuyeri uahtíre mohomahime garisiu yuhpë iri imikeyaru
përëpërëre. 15. iri veheri vahsú nyiri vahsú tubia vahsú nyiri
vahsú dahá arikë iri vahsú moaburebu vahsú moho moayuhpë.
16. iri sirari vahsú iri vahsuri mera imikeyaru përëpërëre dahá
taramarikurika yuhpë pa pa pa pa pa. 17. dahá ariyuhpë arimí
ariri. 18. opáa yii dohakoma igë nohore dohara arimíi. 19. ipëpëpë
igë abé mëririropë igë maa moabeokomá arimí. 20. daháa arikë
igë abé nyaharopë dahigë igë imikeyaru arimi arinyumí. 21. dahigë

igë marire tuabiriyuhpë arimíi aridëagësaa soo nohoge pepi taria
vayuhpë arimíi. 22. dahá ari verenigimërimáa arimíi ariri.
23. iripeta aráa iripeta aa aa.

TEXT NO. 210

1. nyeé ka va'atí. 2. dia ka vaáa. 3. vai niri ya. 4. vai yo mairi
ya. 5. dia kase vaáa. 6. vai yo mairi ya. 7. vai niri ya. 8. vai
yo mairi. 9. nëëri ya kore. 10. vai niri ya. 11. vai yo mairi ya.
12. kaa vaaro vaáa. 13. yohaya nii kore niké. 14. kunyá kurinya
koyere. 15. ko yarore nërinya. 16. ko yarore. 17. tiya vai niri
ya. 18. vai niri vai yo. 19. dia kapi. 20. koo vaago varemo.
21. vai niri yare. 22. to ya vai niri ya. 23. vai nirore nii vai yo.
24. dia kapi. 25. koo vaago va'amó. 26. vai niri yare. 27. vai
yo mairi ya.

TEXT NO. 173

1. opa arikë verenigidoama gahpí purisaráa. 2. perá arima iriré
purisara noho. 3. marire dahá varoka ariaribëra nyaguí piromera
nugamá. 4. igëre ai mamari moama igë nyagí pirure. 5. gohori
vahsëagë gohori dërëgë gohori boregë omaa. 6. ii mahká piruu
boregë nyigë omaa. 7. igë ari yuhpë vii gumú kupë maha gumú
igë boregë ari yuhpë. 8. ii borari iritá ariyoro iri viire moara
yinyora. 9. igëtá iri borarire seamëri nëga yuhpë. 10. gohori
dërëgë gohori vahsëagë irá mëriarakoma ariaribëra. 11. ii yonero
gohori dërëgë gohori vahsëagë igë vagëkumi ariaribëra. 12. ai
nomeri tuugahkuariboora. 13. iropërë ii boreka piruu igá ya nomeri
ai tuu gahkuma. 14. iropërë ii mahka pirure oma pare. 15. igë
nomerire ai tuugahkumaa vii poekagere. 16. boregë ari yuhpë
gohori vahsëagë gohori dërëgë ari yuhpë. 17. igë ai tuu muhuu
borarigere viigere. 18. iri nomerire inyarakoma ariaribëra.
19. dahá ari iri murunye gere purituu mërima doha. 20. iri muru-
saa muru siuraa verenigirita aribë pagari. 21. iri buia bayara
airaa gurunya mera ai diabiri veagahkumaa viire. 22. daha arikë
bahsíi ii ebobohó nomeri moaa tuu gahkuuma. 23. iri buyá ai
dëhka torikë nëgahayoro poekagere. 24. boré iri dehkore vayoro
iri gurunya mera varo deyoro vayoro. 25. marire dahá varoka
mari iriré irikë ariabëra. 26. daha doakabirima viire iri nomerire
moadoaraa. 27. ii boresereri vahtopëkë nëgaharoka ariaribëra.

28. irirú nahsika tuu irirú nomeruu ahkarokë moanëgëmi. 29. iri vahsupë berori ai ahkaro moanugumi. 30. marire gahpi niakëgere marire iri pekë yiyoro viigere. 31. marire miriro dohpa vakayoro. 32. igë nyamá nyigë diagë irá ya goarire airáa arika. 33. iri goari mera ahkaro moanugu yuuma viigere. 34. oré-oré-oré-rooo-rooo-rooo-rooo-eruuu-eruuu-eruuu. 35. irireta pekasubë marire niarisibu. 36. irá pursiarata dahá vakabë. 37. dahá vakëta igë nyamá diagë goa doha bihsimáa. 38. pi-pari-pa-pira-puuu varibëra. 39. dahá vakëta mari aharimari doasuyoro pare. 40. iro arikumi ii sëii igë ya bihsiri mera. 41. mooo-mooo-vira-vira-vira—moo-mooo-vira-vira-vira-mo-mo-vira-vira-vira vabë. 42. iritá aribë irá verenigi mesara muru mere irá purisaráa. 43. irotá vabë doha irirú teredú irirúu bihsiri mera. 44. te-to-te-to-teto-te-roo-te-roo-teroo vabë marire. 45. irá vereri nyee mera ahkaro moama muru mera purisama. 46. marire iri marikaporo ai ariraa bahsimerata ai tuumuhu nugukama. 47. diari mera ai tuu nyeanugukami iri nyere. 48. irá dahá yikërée nomeri soroaro maribë mahsare. 49. varo baya poro ariráa maha poari mera si sinyeanugama. 50. dahá yibirikëree bayaro mahsiye maribë. 51. ii nyee iripeta aráa.

TEXT NO. 141

1. ii vai gahpida marire soyaro ahpayoro. 2. vai gahpida aa aa. 3. peame diaridáa peame boreridáa arikáa arikurii aa aa. 4. iridare ai ahpikó suu ai tuunyanugukakomáa aa. 5. ai tuunyeanugú ai nomeri tameyuukakomáa aa aa. 6. aa nomeri seapameyuukakomáa nomeri tuusirimeyuukakomáa aa. 7. irokáa ii daa dia dihpamaha dáa iri nimakëridáa arikáa aa. 8. poe gahpidáa yahsari dáa diari dáa boreridáa arikáa aa aa. 9. iridá tuusororo mariroboroga ai nomeri tayuukakomáa aa. 10. irá vai mahsa ira iriri aráa arikebáa aa aa. 11. irayá bayapia arikáa aa aa. 12. iri bayapia iri soyara ahpakë yikáa aa aa. 13. iri bayapia keeri diari keeri boreri iri yahsari arikáa aa. 14. mariya sáa iripeta arikáa aa aa. 15. keeri yahsari keeri diari keeri boreri arikáa aa aa. 16. iri soyaró ahpá aa aa. 17. iriré ahpikó suu tooka suu marire tuunëmëro mariroboroga ai tuunyeanugukamáa aa aa. 18. ai tuunyeanugú ai nomeri tayukamá ai dehkobogá takamá aa. 19. iri me siamereri bayiri aráa aa aa. 20. iroka abé yeeru vihó ariyoro doha aa aa. 21. iri daata paa siburi paa ariyoro aa aa. 22. iri puikarogë pea oyodiigë

pea peakëyoro aa aa. 23. iriré ai veasiripiukanyorá aa aa. 24. ai tuunyeanugu iri nomerire tayuukama. 25. ai nomeri seapameyuukama. 26. iró përëta ii gurunyaverá arika gahíi. 27. iri marire maha poari mahare goroveoka. 28. iriré oármahsa pora ii bayapia marire soyaro ahpakë yiia. 29. iriré ai mahsa pora ai tuunyeanugukama. 30. iro merata ai nomeri taamemuhukama dia gorosirige. 31. iri nomerire seapamemuhuukama. 32. iro ihogoro irá vai mahsaya bayapia arika doha. 33. keeri diari keeri boreri keeri yahsari arika. 34. iriré soyarire nomerire ai tamemuhuukama. 35. iro ohogo mariya gahpi arike pare. 36. mariya gahpida korepida merepida duhtu-puusereda. 37. iro përëta arika gahpi sorori. 38. iri soro gahpi soró mata soro ebobohó gohorikëri soro boré serikëri soro arika. 39. iri ahpikó mera iri gohorire iri serire ahpikó suu tooka ahpikó suu iri ahpikó mera ai tuunyeanugukakoma. 40. iri dëhpë gahpi gorari dëhëe arika. 41. gahpi soroakë yiro dohpata marire soroakë yiká. 42. iriré ahpikó suu tooka ahpikó suu tameyuukakoma. 43. dahá yii nomeri seapameyuukakoma.

TEXT NO. 174

1. iri gahpi moaraa dihsiporoge ariperero deama. 2. iri purire yuhuu tarapiaribëra. 3. iro përë deama turaro bihsikë yimá turaro viaribëra. 4. irá moreri purisaa aribë irisare mohe dearibëraa. 5. iro përë sirurigere iri gahpi soro. 6. irotá murugëre siá irá bayidigëre siá purisaribëra pare. 7. dahá yiirata irisoro poekagere piveadoboma pare. 8. irá sigiri pasaa bohema pa aribë. 9. viigere ainyaháa nyahariporoga doboma. 10. aridëariro arii perá irinyama. 11. mëhtariga aribë ii pa koaga. 12. pe koa irinyaa turáa arima varoka arima ira bansíi. 13. iripeta irigë yeegëre mohoyeama pare. 14. irigëre mohonyea veregë vaaribegë pare. 15. baya vihariro dohka ehanuga ehá verenigimi. 16. iro ehá nuga veremi irikoa aráa gahpirira mari arimi. 17. dahá aritua yuririmi doha. 18. irotá irá bayamora game vere muhuma irá perata. 19. ariperera gamé yahpirira mari arima. 20. iripeta kaavëri përë muhuuma. iiii aaaa ëë iiii aaa ëë arima. 21. dahá vado përëta dehkogere omaranugami. 22. igëta nyamiubeo pemohotori mera sinigimi. 23. kaari maharage viriríi erá irimá iratá iri nëgama. 24. pesibú iríi mahaavama doha irá doarogere. 25. irá dohka mahara piarima doha irá sáa irima doha. 26. irá mërageta turaro paakeo maha maha vamadoha irá doarogere. 27. ariperera mahsa irogeéta vihá

irimá. 28. irirá nëhkë dahá parikëkará timá irá mahsa. 29. irá
dahi perero irá bayamëra virima para. 30. irageta yee yuhkë
ahpáama vabero sare irageta sisuaribëra. 31. irá iri pesibu irimá
irasáa mahinëga paabeo pare yeegëre. 32. vapuriro sëabë ii paa-
dëarisaa dahata vahagëreta padëamara. 33. iro përëta buya
veama pare iraré siu bayagë vaiture nyeami. 34. ariperera mahsa
buyakëtua pera yeri viháa dehokogere.

TEXT NO. 78

1. igë iri soro gahpi soro ai mëririgë arigë oá mari mahsa tirare
iri dehko koa ehatuaro mosuarigë arigë yiia arimí arinyumíi aa aa.
2. oorike arimuhuma oorike oorike aimuhunyoma iraré gahpi
morero vake arimi gahpi morero vake arinyomáa ma-ma-ma-ma-ma
arimi arinyumí. 3. yuhupë mohotomahara arima mamára mamára
aa aa. 4. igë gahpi sorore goragë yuhugë arimi igë gahpi koare
ahpamí ahpari gorari dëhpë mera gorari dëhpë mera. 5. igë irí
tiabugë igë nyee yimi arikeba iri sorore ahpami ahpari aa. 6. igë
tiagë irigë vererimi arikeba vererinyumí. 7. mari igo yë nomekëri
mahsó yahpirira mari arimi yahpirira mari arinyumí. 8. doá yë
daha yirore yahpi tamurike arimí arinyumíi. 9. ari mahí yuria vami
mahí yuria ai mëriri puru muhumi ai mëriri puru muhunyumi.
10. igë ai mëririkëta iráa iipë maharopë vii maama viimaari.
11. ee-ee-ee-aë-aë-aë turamuhukare igë matá igë matá nye puriro
oá vai irá ariperero igë ehtokapi kurakë arima arinyoma igë matá
gaginigi oyakorekë arimá ariri. 12. ee ee ee dihpabú vakama
dihpabú vakanyomá igë vago mera aa daháa yikare irisoroborore
arimá ariri. 13. nye iripeobeo nihkumera diye dobokari arimáa
arinyomá. 14. tuanugú këraturamehe kari arimáa arinyomáa aa
aa. 15. noo irá ariro arikama arikanyomáa gahigëë irisoroboro
iripeobeo gëri dobo kari amimí ariri. 16. arí iripeta viriami viriari
irogé dehkoge oo bayá viharí tabú dohka nigimí nigiríi. 17. nyahpamihiri siadigë nyahpamihiri siadigë. 18. ópaa simí arikebá
irokoare opa siri iri koare. 19. daháa irá viriri ma! viririri viriri
chavé eranëgamá irá erá óma pee koa ori aa iri tua mahaama
maharí doha paarikë mahaama paarikë mahaari. 20. baa! gahira
viririma viririri doha irá dahata doha irasáa chavé eranëgama
eranëgari irare oomi doha pee koa aa ameroga yuhuka ahku
yuurika yuhuka ahkuyuriga. 21. irá mahaama doha gahira arima
doha arinyoma doha chavé eranëgama doha iraré oomi irasaa

iritua mahaama mahanyomáa. 22. irá maháa gahira arima arinyomá doha. 23. irasáa chavé ernëgama eranëganyomáa aa dahta
yinyomá. 24. irasá mahaama iritua mahanyomá gahira viririma
doha. 25. iipë mahaka peremá iipë mahaka arima ariri doha
eranëgama irá yiido dohpata doha chavé eranëgama aa daha
siita. 26. irasáa peremá irá bayama dëhyabë pare aa bayá baa.
27. irá vabera sisuaa irá yohoka dëhpëri peyana ariaribëa peyanaa.
28. gëyadë puribë aritia yë gëyadëapuriya chavé aränëga vamáa.
29. maa! arimí arinyumíi mari ohokariri vai goari arimi vai goari
arinyumíi. 30. iraré oomi pekoa pee koa irigëre yeegëre yurimere
paabeo ooge komeparoge patumi kiriri kiriri kiriri kiriri pëëë
vahagë bure arimi kiriri kiriri kiriri pëëë vahage bure vahagë bure
arinyumíi aa aa ariri. 31. yëë pagësëmara vahadigë bure arimí
arinyumíi aa. 32. pera ariaribëra yëë pagësëmara vahadigë bure
igë dihpuruborore igë yeegë mera nyohsepiupi beokari arimi
arinyumíi. 33. ari ma yuriami arima yurianyumi. 34. ehanëga
guburo moabeome kiriri kiriri kiriri pë pë pë pë vahagë bure arimi
arinyumíi piumepikare iribure arimi arinyumí aritua mahaa vami
mahaavanyumíi. 35. aritua mahá doaha vami doahaa vanyumíi.
36. iri sorore ai yoo nyea ai guburo moáa gubukë ehanëga vami
aí yoyuria vaami tee viigorogumuge vii gorogumuge doha irogë
ehanëga vami dihpabáa ehanëga vami ehanëga vanyumí. 37. ehá
nëgaháa ai maháa dobokamí dobokaa pare. 38. iripeta arituabë
arituaya marire goari naragaro ariro goari naragaro gahi nyee mari
nyee yibë igë obó tiapeobirikëta gohpetëa taribë gohpetëa tari.
39. tsaaaaaaa adé më! mërëga arikabë arikáa. 40. turake turake
turake pi-paripa pira-pë-pirapuuu tsaaaaa vakabë vakayaaa aa.
41. te-toreto-teto-te-toro-toro-te-toro-to-toro-to-toro vakabë vaya
aa. 42. soo irá gahpi irá purisara varoge iri varoo iri noho aráa
arikeba iri noho. 43. ii suiri dahá aribë mahsa ņëhkë iire vere-
nigikoma ooa dihpari mahara dipe mahsa ariperera verenigima
arikebá verenigi. 44. iriré verenigiraa nye iinye suirinye irá
verenigirá vároo gahinyee diabiririnyee aráa gahinyee diabiririnyee. 45. diabiriri iri nomeri sororikë arikeba sororikë. 46. marire
opaa tuumurinëgaa tuumërinëgá. 47. miridoahaka miridoahaka
aa aa. 48. dahigë soo bohe irigë nohore bibu doboka arikebá.
49. ne verenigiri viubeami arikebá viubiri. 50. igë obo inyagoriri
doakamí inyagorori doaka. 51. mari dëpë ahënyëagë arikasëa.
52. soo dihsiro mahagë obo arigë vakamí. 53. soo verenigibiri-
digëpë verenigikamí. 54. dahá aririsibutá irá mërá baya mërage

bayara yima arikebá aa dahá aririsibutá. 55. dahira doadore-
birabëra doadorebiri puribirarisáa ariaribëráa. 56. turiri dihparure
tarusure ahpara puriaribëra. 57. dahira irá ohkaro moamá arikebá
móa. 58. igoa eheri goa eheri goa rerererere ohkarokëbë. 59. dahá
vakë iigoa nyama goa aharikë maabë doha pi-paripá peropuuuuu
paririririri pirararara dahá vakaro yia. 60. irá verenigira varo dahá
vaa arikebá. 61. dahá vakë igë sëiga bihsimáami doha mooo-mooo-
vira-vira-virara vaa baa vaa. 62. dahá várota yaaaaa tsaaaaa
veoveoveoveoveo arikabë arikaya. 63. mari dëpëpë naragakabë
naragaka pare. 64. dahá vakëta oa nome marire arimá dee simërë-
gare noo imudëaritagë vakabë pare. 65. dahá vakaro yibë dahá
vákaro. 66. dahá ahkarobë baa. 67. iipë doaro vaa iipë vaa vakabë
pare vakaa. 68. dahá varotá teredú bihsimáa bë doha teredú igë
verenigi meredo përërë. 69. irá ahkaro moara nyee dahá vabë.
70. ii nyeeribë arikebá nyeeribë. 71. irá baya mërage gunya turara
verenigima. 72. igë vabere sisua igë doakaribegë aa doakáa.
73. iinye vabera kuu pagarinyee kuu mëhtarinyee ai koresirirokë
doakayuhpë igë bayaru. 74. igëya seebero gohorikë sebero vahsero
gohorikë seebero ai doakayuhpë doakáa. 75. igë yeegë kurukëdigë
kurumaridigë ai nyapuhtu doaha doaka doakayuhpë doakáa.
76. ii nehka mahsa igë ya kuiyahkëri mera ai kuinyahkurikë yuhpë.
77. kuiyahkurikë doaka yuhpë. 78. gahigë igë bahsireta nomeri
tuahaporo aríi ai nomeri igë nereri mahsëpëa. 79. igë ai nomeri
tuuyunuguka yuhpë. 80. dahira igëpëreta iri nomeri tuuyuri-
nëhayoro doha. 81. ari verenigima ari verenigiri.

TEXT NO. 104

1. vihsigë yiyuhpë igë marapo mera ariyuhpë. 2. irogé pihanyoráa
boraro viigé. 3. nëgë dehkoge ariyoro. 4. mahsa marinyorá ari-
yoró irá moabaríi bihiri parí ariyoro. 5. daháa yii maë vai piara
ehanyorá. 6. nyamika duhará igë puyësáa igë marapo mera igë
borarosáa arinyoráa. 7. igë marapo bëro yuhupë ahpiru ahpago
bëro arikayohpo. 8. duhará irá maë vaire aigoe sora siubanyorá
iraré. 9. maë vai baharidiara boara yiama pagomë ariyuhpë.
10. nyamiga boyoro seará vara arihuhpë. 11. yë marapo mëre
imugo vagokomo ariyuhpë yëpë mëmarapo mera seagë vagëra doha
ariyuhpë. 12. paputariro ariyuhpë opa game yirá ariyuhpë. 13. aë
ariyuhpë igë puyësáa. 14. arí mëre bákagëkumigë ariyuhpë
boraroata arimasoa mahsikayuhpë. 15. ari gahinë nyamiga vama-

vayuhpë igë puyëpë bora nome mera igë boraro poyo nomero mera vaanyora. 16. aí máa igo poyore amerota vaa bakanyumí bákaa. 17. igëpë suamáa yuhpë buhuru koa suayuhpë. 18. suáa amerota vamáa igë oota yëre biramërimí ariyohpo aribea soonyari váramari ariyuhpë mahsikayuhpë. 19. daháa arigáa yohpo igo igë puyëre. 20. iro vaa bohkahanyorá irigë nia dëhkagëre karebahaga aráa ariyohpo. 21. teagë vanyaké ariyohpo aë ariyuhpë. 22. irisibutere mëë vahserore peago vake ariyuhpë. 23. igë dahá arigëëta puikarore beroyibeo yuhpë. 24. igopë aë vaa peayohpo. 25. iri vahserori pego dabero peabeokayohpo gahigëre ariyuhpë igëpë daháa yii pare nyohkadigëre bohkahayohpo irigëre pearigo yeboyohpo pare. 26. iripeta igë puyëpë mëriatuayuhpë igë soonoho ariké omarayohpo. 27. gunya mahsigë mëria mëbuu ariyohpo. 28. mëria teayuhpëgë pare baháa. 29. iri nima vahakari mera puu medihuu mëriyuhpë. 30. dipée yoado përe nimamere yohpo pare igë pësáa purime dihumëriyuhpë igë përërëpere. 31. igëpë ëmarogere varo puupeasuabehakayuhpë igo sirimáa goreyohpo pare igëre daberoga peremayoro igopë ehtooka siria vayohpo. 32. igo dahá vakë inyaa igore baaro suabeo omayuhpëgë igë igore omaa duhaa vayuhpë. 33. duhahá igore tabesáa sorayuhpëgë nyaikë inyáa iri soroparire bohepeokayuhpë. 34. iri koare varo peokayuhpë. 35. daháa yitua bua iro peramare yuhkëgë vëadigëre ariyoro irigëre inyapeyuhpëgë. 36. igë boraro duharáa iriré bayuhpëgë baa dehko iridëayuhpëgë igë dehko iridëakëta soroburo buatuayoro iri soro bahsíi igëpë inyapeya yuhpëgë. 37. igë bohepeobirido arikëre iri vasookaburuyoro igëre igë bahsíi buaribiribudigë ariyuhpë. 38. iro baarige igo ahpiruro bohkayuhpë igo vii paago muhsimogo ariyuhpë. 39. aribea igota arikanyobá arigëta iri ahpirure inyayuhpë. 40. igë bara suriropëre ai duhari peokayuhpë. 41. iripeta buaríi dehkore iriyuhpë pareigë dahigëre igëpëpuribeoyuhpë igë goroperogere bahasibiru puriyuhpë igëpë yëra nurira yikoma arikayuhpë igë boraropë. 42. nimameregariyuhpë pare igë boraro pare tuuru siriyuhpë dahá siriyuhpë pare turaro gaginigi siriyuhpë pare. 43. daháa yii perageta vehekayuhpë igë puyë. 44. daháa yitua duhaa vayuhpë.

TEXT NO. 155

1. maëgére maha yuhpë. 2. igë boraró pëa miurure tará medihuu doanigika yuhpë igë mahsë mahaborore. 3. mahsëpëa inyuu biri yuhpë igë vagaa kuta voo vayoro. 4. iripeta arika yuhpë mahsëge-

rota arika yuhpë díaguro. 5. dipuru vehkata diari yëhsëro
tupeogure ari yuhpë. 6. igë mahsëpëa dihtaruge murinyahá nuguri
dohkage oho nyahaa paya yuhpë. 7. iroré buara nëgá iguré momá
yuhpë pare oo nohota aigë mohotoro buimáa muriyoro. 8. dahata
yii vaganugá urugá muri yuhpë doha. 9. dihpaturí momamuri
yuhpë doha. 10. dihtarure dahpa vaka yuhpë. 11. irotá pou pou
pou igë dahá yikë puri bururo dohpa vakayoro buhpusáa dahata
miaro dohpá vakayoro. 12. dahá yitua moma yuhpë doha.
13. igëta mahsamëra dohpa bihsika yuhpë. 14. iri purisaa bururo
dohpa vakayoro. 15. igë mahsëpëa butirire maë yuhpë. 16. yoari
bohe dahpa vayoro. 17. irotá maháa gumú ohogere gora ehá inya
nigikurika yuhpë. 18. ne nyomebiri yuhpë mahsëpëa inyaka yuhpë
iguré. 19. dihpaturi buara yuhpë doha. 20. irotá mahanuga
inyanigë kurika yuhpë. 21. bahasiriburi inya yuhpë yoanyariro-
keya. 22. yoado përë vaa yuhpë pare. 23. igëta ari yuhpë gahkía
dohpa veregë. 24. iró beregoara nyorore dahá yayayoro dahá
goara arinigi yuhpë iroré.

TEXT NO. 154

1. igë boraró yohoka duhpureta ahpa yuhpë. 2. tara vahsaru
duhpë ariyoro. 3. iri duhpumera marire nyea yuhpë. 4. rinyesare
mahapoari nyere buyakë yuhpë. 5. iri aripererire tooka sumohsa
ahpikó sumohsa ai tuuveabeokanyora. 6. siburú gohoriku duu
diáduu miapora dohpa gohorikuduu aime peokakoma. 7. irirú
sihburú vehkágere. 8. iropërëtamare viumá vaitu dari mera ariperero oma. 9. ohta bohorusaa dahata ariyoro. 10. iri piorisare
dahata ariperero óma. 11. nahsikamu gami keri kaarikë duu
arinyora. 12. iri diabiririre ahpagëë gua yuhpë. 13. iri ariperere
tooka ahpikó subeo tuuveabeokama. 14. iroge diita vakabuu iri
siburu vehkagere. 15. irirú kaaduhkaru. 16. mahsá bayari sanyarí
buyaku peoka yuhpë. 17. aripereri vabu irirú siburu vehkage.
18. iri vehkó pigë yëhsë diari boreri yahsari ariyoro. 19. iriríré
taraveabeokama. 20. irigú yeegëre mohoku yuhpë iri varo siya-
beokama. 21. iri aripereri vayoro siburu vehkage. 22. iriré moho-
kugu guayuhpë. 23. iguré purigúu murunye mera gameyoro.

TEXT NO. 142

1. ëhta buru mahagë arikumi ëhtabohoru buyadigë. 2. iri tabure
ahpagúu guapurika yuhpë iri tabure tuveabeokakoma. 3. dahá

yitua tuu mahidobo kakoma. 4. igú poga koa yatutú vahsú muu
pogá ariperero okomá. 5. iro puruta ëhtabohó vii yahsari vii bore
vii diari vii arika iri mahirire tuveakakoma. 6. aripereró iguré bari
okomá. 7. igusáa vai mahsusaa dahta arikumi. 8. irá ariperera
irireta bakoma iriré bara mari inyapeobirikoma. 9. iri imipa vii
mahagusaa dahta arikumi. 10. ahpire opeakakoma ihpikosare
dahata. 11. dahira marire inyapeobarikoma.

DESCRIPTION OF YAJE HALLUCINATIONS[*]

El delirio en sus principios es todo esplendores, sensaciones
gratísimas, goces del empíreo. Varios blancos que han tomado el
yagé, me han referido sus visiones, supremamente bellas, pero
diferentes de acuerdo con los diversos gustos, ambiciones y apetitos.
A su decir, la exaltada imaginación del más ardiente poeta no
podría idear, ni expresar la lengua más elocuente, lo que son en
toda su magnificencia esos ensueños en los dos ó tres primeros
cuartos de hora que se siguen á la libación del magnífico licor. La
vista se recrea entonces sobre verdes llanuras, bajo cielo azul con
nacaradas nubes; éntrase luégo á floridos verjeles, donde al alcance
de las manos cuelgan de las ramas los árboles frutas de áureas ó
rojos colores y de gusto exquisitamente delicado; el oído se goza
entre tanto en música inefable; y al salir de los verjeles, y al són
de ésta, en otros verdes cármenes, danzan y cantan deliciosamente
bayaderas celestes calzadas con el clásico coturno, elegantes cual
las palmeras del desierto; hembras de blancas y sonrosadas carnes;
vestidas de rasos, terciopelos y gasas; desnudos los brazos, la gar-
ganta y el mórbido seno, ceñidos aquéllos, esa y el donoso talle
con brazaletes, pulceras, collares y cinturones en que brillan
deslumbradores diamantes, esmeraldas, zafiros y rubíes; mujeres
de mirar que fascina, sonrisa encantadora, boca dulce como la
miel, hermosas, en fin, como la esposa del cantar de los cantares. Y
terminada la danza, brindan en copas de topacio al soñador,
postradas ante él, amorosas y sonrientes, olímpico néctar que
embarga suavemente el pensamiento. Eso ven unos; otros se
sueñan senores poderosos á cuyas plantas se humillan los emperadores y los reyes; aquéllos deliran dueños de todas las riquezas
del universo; quiénes son místicos y ven coros de ángeles y vírgenes
y al mismo Jehová sentado sobre encendidas nubes ú oculto en

[*] Reprinted from Rocha 1905, pp. 43–45.

la ardiente zarza; cuáles son epicureos y glotones, y se deleitan con gustosos manjares y sabrosas carnes de monte; cabritos asados de rica sazón y provocativo olor; y para terminar, los indios se ven en medio de bosques poblados de caza; dantas y venados que huyen veloces, pero que no se les escaparán, porque convertidos los indios mismos en tigres, corren tras la pieza con velocidad felina ó bien se sienten gustando de blando reposo á la sombra de frondosos árboles y rodeados al propio tiempo de cántaros rebosantes de inagotable y dorado licor de chontaduro. . . . pero á las visiones placenteras del *yagé* se sucede con sólo el paréntesis de una corta somnolencia, el delirio de lo horrible. Poseído de éste el yajófago, siente violentos dolores, y ebria la mente, trémulos los miembros y vacilante el cuerpo, para no caer, quiere agarrarse de las mismas ramas de los árboles de donde cogió las exquisitas frutas y las ramas se truecan entonces en serpientes que se envuelven en el cuerpo de él y rabiosas le muerden una y otra vez; las bayaderas celestes se convierten en hidras y furias infernales que le azotan; los reyes y emperadores que se humillaban delante de él en verdugos que le abofetean, la vapulan y le dan de puntapiés; los ángeles y vírgenes que veían los místicos, ceden su puesto á los demonios que los sumergen en calderas de plomo derretido é hirviente, y el Dios bondadoso en Dios justiciero, que airado los entrega á Satanás.

NOTES

1. Christopher Columbus's reports are known to us through the writings of his son Don Ferdinand Columbus and of Father Bartolomé de las Casas (1474–1566). The quotation is taken from Ferdinand Columbus's work and is preceded by these words: "I shall quote the very words of the Admiral, which he left in writing in this form" (see Colón 1944, p. 161). The first edition was published in Italian in 1571. Las Casas's *Historia* was begun in 1523. (See also Anghiera 1912; Bourne 1907; Navarrete 1825, Vol. 1.)

2. The original Spanish text says: "Tienen en esta casa una tabla bien labrada, redonda como un táller, en que hay unos polvos que ponen sobre la cabeza de los dichos *cemis*, haciendo cierta ceremonia; después se meten en las narices una caña de dos ramos, con la cual sorben el polvo. Las palabras que dicen no las entiende ninguno de los nuestros; con estos polvos salen de juicio, quedando como borrachos" (Colón 1944, pp. 161–62). Bourne's English translation of this text is frequently quoted, but it contains a few errors. Referring to the *tabla*, Bourne's translation says that it was "round like a wooden dish." This is not quite correct; the Spanish word *táller* (or *tálero*) does not mean dish but is derived from the German *Taler*, that is, a thaler coin, and the snuff tablet must have been much smaller than the word *dish* would imply (Bourne 1906, pp. 4–5). Further on, Bourne's translation says that "they lost consciousness." The Spanish expression *salir de juicio* means "to go out of one's mind" and does not imply a loss of consciousness.

3. "I have gone to great pains in trying to understand what they believe in" (Colón 1944, p. 163); in Spanish: "Me he fatigado mucho en entender lo que creen."

4. Colón 1944, p. 169, quoting Román Pane's report.

5. The spelling of this native term is not consistent throughout most of the literature; the older editions mention *cogioba* and *cohoba*, a fact that has led some authors to suggest that Pane was speaking of two different kinds of snuff (see Wassén 1964, pp. 101–2). The Buenos Aires edition of Ferdinand Columbus's history uses *cogioba* all through. See also n. 23, below.

6. Colón 1944, p. 172, quoting Román Pane's report.

7. Safford's (1917, p. 394) translation seems to be erroneous when he writes: "[He] gives it all its titles as if it were some great lord, and asks

it. . . ." The Spanish text reads: "Hecha la *cogioba* se levanta en pie y refiere todos sus títulos, como si fueran de un gran señor y le pregunta . . ." (Colón 1944, p. 176). It is rather to be thought that the shaman refers to himself in enumerating his own titles and dignities in a kind of presentation, before addressing his questions to the tree.

8. Colón 1944, pp. 176–77, quoting Román Pane's report.

9. The Spanish text (see n. 10 below) has the verb *toca*, which might stand for *touches*.

10. I have retranslated Bourne's English version of the text because it seems to contain a few minor errors (see Bourne 1907 or, for a recent quotation of this text, Wassén 1964, pp. 100–101). For the scene described here see also Las Casas 1909, pp. 445–46.

11. Las Casas 1909, p. 445. The original Spanish text reads: "tenian hechos ciertos polvos de ciertas yerbas muy secas y bien molidas, de color de canela o de alhena molida."

12. Las Casas, 1909, p. 445. The original text reads: "plato redondo, no llano sino uno poco combado ó hondo, hecho de madera, tan hermoso, liso y lindo que no fuera muy más hermoso de oro ó de plata; era cuasi negro y lucio como azabache."

13. Las Casas 1909, p. 445.

14. Oviedo 1851–55, 1: 130; illustration, ibid., Plate 1, Fig. 7. The original text reads: "los caciques e hombres principales tenian unos palillos huecos del tamaño de un xeme o ménos de la groseza del dedo menor de la mano, y estos cañutos tenian dos cañones correspondientes á uno como aquí está pintado, e todo de una pieza."

15. A *xeme* (from the Latin *semis*) is the maximum distance between the tips of the thumb and the forefinger.

16. Oviedo 1851–55, 1:130.

17. Ibid.

18. Ibid., p. 131. It is interesting to note that, according to Oviedo, the term *tabaco* was not used to designate the plant, but the snuffing tube. The chronicler writes that "the above-mentioned tubes the Indians call *tabaco*, and not the herb or the sleep that overtakes them (as some have been thinking)." The original text says: "á las cañuelas que es dicho llaman los indios *tabaco*, é no á la hierva ó sueño que les toma (como pensaban algunos)." On this point Ernst (1889, p. 134) suggests that the original word might have been *taboca*.

19. Las Casas 1909, p. 445: "hablaban como en algarabia, ó como alemanes, confusamente "Las Casas was an eyewitness to the snuffing ritual; he writes: "Several times I have seen them celebrate their cohoba, and it was a sight to watch how they took it and what they chattered." In the original: "yo los ví algunas veces celebrar su cohoba, y era cosa de ver cómo la tomaban y lo que parlaban" (ibid., p. 446).

20. Oviedo 1851–55, 1:131: "este tomar de aquella hierva é zahumerio no tan solamente les era cosa sana, pero muy sancta cosa."

21. Ibid., pp. 138–39.

22. Safford 1917, pp. 393–97.

23. The identity of the two words can be suggested from the fact that Friar Román Pane's term *cohoba* would be written *cogioba* when transliterated into Italian, the language in which Ferdinand Columbus wrote his original report. In the translations back and forth, through several editions, it seems that the two ways of writing became mixed, giving the impression that

two different plants were involved. Unfortunately, the original Italian manuscript is lost. See Wassén 1967, p. 237 n; Lovén 1935, pp. 386–98, 681–82, 697 (Addendum 1); Friederici 1947.

24. On the present taxonomic status of *Piptadenia peregrina* see Altschul 1972.

25. Oviedo 1851–55, 1:347. The text reads: "llevan unas arvejas ó havas negras é redondas é duríssimas é no para comerlas hombre ni algund animal. E aquesta cohoba lleva unas arvejas que las vaynas son de un palmo é más ó menos luengas, con unas lentejuelas por fructo que no son de comer" (A *palmo* is about 21 cm.)

26. Ibid., p. 130: "esta hierva es un tallo ó pimpollo como quatro ó cinco palmos ó menos de alto con unas hojas anchas é gruesas, é blandas é vellosas."

27. Ibid., p. 131: "Esta hierva tenian los indios por cosa muy presçiada, y la criaban en sus huertos y labranças."

28. Ibid., 2:403. Chibcha is a linguistic family, while Muisca is the name of a Chibcha-speaking tribe; the two should not be confused.

29. Ibid., 4:603.

30. The origin of the word is uncertain. Lovén (1935, p. 387) believes it to be taken from the Achagua language, an Arawakan dialect spoken widely on the Colombian Orinoco Plains during the eighteenth century. However, in a contemporary source the Achagua term is given as *nuba* (Neira and Ribero 1928, p. 116).

31. Vargas Machuca 1892, 2:81. The original text says: "Mascan hayo ó coca y jopa y tabaco, con que pierden el juicio, y entonces les habla el diablo."

32. The term *mohan* (or *moján*) is often used in the early literature to designate a shaman or priest.

33. Vargas Machuca, 2:82. The text reads: "el cacique de ellos, que era hechicero o mohan, habiendo tomado la jopa para hablar con el diablo." See also ibid., 2:97–98.

34. Ibid., 2:111: "Jopa es un palo que echa unas vainillas como arbejas y los granos dentro son á su modo, pero más chicos. Esta toman los indios molida en la boca para hablar con el diablo."

35. Friar Pedro de Aguado is one of the most important sources on Colombian Indian cultures in the second half of the sixteenth century. See Bibliography.

36. Aguado 1956, 1:599.

37. Friar Juan de Castellanos is another important source on aboriginal cultures in the sixteenth century. He arrived in the Indies in 1534 and died in Tunja, one of the main centers of Muisca culture. Castellanos wrote his major historical works in very bad verse. See Bibliography.

38. Castellanos 1847, p. 93. The original text reads: "Uno toma tabaco y otro yopa / Para poder saber lo venidero; / Estaban plazas, calles y caminos / Llenos de hechiceros y adivinos."

39. Simón 1882–92, 5:60. This author is a good source on the aboriginal cultures of the early seventeenth century. However, his and Oviedo's descriptions of the use of yopo among the Muisca leave one with the impression that the Indians were hiding the true reason for their use of the drug; there was more to it than simple divination by mucus flow.

40. Arce 1634.

41. Aguado 1956, 1:599.

42. Uricoechea 1871, p. 197. This is in all essence a reedition of the "*Gramática, Catecismo y Confesionario de la Lengua Chibcha*" by Friar Bernardo

de Lugo, published originally in Madrid in 1619. Another, more recent work on the Muisca language is by Acosta Ortegón (q.v.) and is also based on Lugo's grammar.

43. Pérez Arbeláez 1956, pp. 701–2; Safford 1922; Schultes 1963*b*, p. 153.

44. The principal species are *Datura candida, D. sanguinea, D. dolichocarpa, D. suaveolens, D. arborea, D. vulcanicola* (Schultes 1963, p. 153).

45. The alkaloids *hyoscyamine, scopolamine*, and *atropine* seem to be common to most species of *Datura* (Schultes 1963, p. 154).

46. The term *xeque* (or *jeque*) is a corruption of the Muisca word *ogque*/ shaman or priest (Simón 1882–92, 2:291).

47. Castellanos 1886, 1:65–66. The original text reads: "y para que no sientan las mujeres / ni los esclavos míseros su muerte, / antes de ver la cueva monstruosa / les dan los xeques ciertos bebedizos / de ebrio tabaco, y otras hojas / del árbol que llamamos borrachero."

48. Uricoechea 1871, p. 236.

49. Ibid., pp. 153, 197.

50. Ibid., p. 121.

51. Ibid., p. 204.

52. Oviedo 1851–55, 1:130.

53. Uricoechea 1871, p. 207.

54. Rivero 1883, p. 104.

55. Ibid., pp. 104–5.

56. Ibid., p. 210.

57. Ibid., p. 148.

58. Gumilla 1955, pp. 123–24.

59. Rivero 1883, p. 56.

60. Humboldt 1822, 8:312–13, 319. The original text reads: "ils se mettent aussi dans un état particulier d'ivresse, ou on pourroit dire de démence, par l'usage de la poudre de *niopo*. Ils cueillent les longues gousses d'une Mimosacée que nous avons fait connoitre sous le nom d'*Acacia Niopo;* ils les mettent en morceaux, les humectent et les font fermenter. Lorsque les graines amollies commencent à noircir, ils les pétrissent comme une pate; et, après y avoir melé de la farine de manioc et de la chaux tirée de la coquille d'un Ampullaire, ils exposent tout la masse à un feu tres-vif sur un gril de bois dur. La pate durcie prend la forme de petits gateaux. Lorsqu'on veut s'en servir, on la réduit en une poudre fine qu'on place sur un plat de 5 ou 6 pouces de largeur. L'Otomaque tient ce plat, qui a un manche, dans sa main droit, tandis qu'il aspire le *niopo* par le nez à travers un os fourchu d'oiseau dont les deux extrémités aboutissent aux narines. L'os sans lequel l'Otomaque ne croiroit pas pouvoir prendre cette espèce de tabac à poudre, a 7 pouces de longeur: il m'a paru être le tarse d'un grand Echassier. . . . Le *niopo* est si excitant que les plus petites portions font éternuer viollement ceux qui n'y sont pas accoutumés." From this description it would seem that the Otomac were using *Anadenanthera peregrina* seeds. Humboldt was mistaken in his identification of the plant. Codazzi, the Italian geographer (1841, pp. 111–12), repeats Humboldt's information and adds: "Not only the Otomac but also the Guahibo, Yaruro and other tribes of the Orinoco use *Niopo.*"

61. Humboldt 1822, 8:312.

62. Spruce 1908, 2:427–28.

63. Ibid., p. 430.

64. On the Guahibo see Bürger 1900, pp. 347–48; Chaffanjon 1889, p.

198; Crévaux 1883, p. 550; Reichel-Dolmatoff 1944, pp. 453–54. Of the Llanos (Orinoco Plains) tribes in general, Díaz Escobar (1879, p. 52) writes that the Indians also use yopo as a prophylactic against common colds. Speaking of the snuffing apparatus, this author describes it as "an instrument worthy to be imitated by civilised man."

65. Rivero 1883, p. 56. Rochereau, Monsalve, and Parra (1914, p. 164) write: "They snuff a very strong alkaline powder they call *yopo* and whose origin we ignore. This powder they keep in the beak of a toucan bird; they put a bit in a wooden platter and absorb it through the tubular bone of a pajuil bird." See also Rochereau 1919, p. 521.

66. Wilbert 1961, p. 41.

67. Cooper 1949, p. 546; Reichel-Dolmatoff, personal observation during field work in 1941.

68. Reichel-Dolmatoff, personal observation among Baniva Indians traveling on the Vichada River, that is, outside their tribal territory, which lies to the south.

69. Reichel-Dolmatoff, personal observation, 1941.

70. Crévaux 1883, p. 371. This information is somewhat doubtful; the Huitoto territory lies outside the range of *Anadenanthera peregrina*. Perhaps they were using powdered tobacco.

71. For distributional studies see, above all, Altschul 1972; Cooper 1949, pp. 536–37; Schultes 1967a, 1967b; Serrano 1941; Wassén 1964, 1965, 1967a, 1967b; Wassén and Holmstedt 1963.

72. Schultes 1954, pp. 248–50. See also Seitz's description of a Tukano shaman from the Papurí River (1967, pp. 335–36).

73. Schultes 1954, p. 248; Wassén 1965, pp. 99–100.

74. Schultes 1954, p. 242; Wassén 1965, p. 100.

75. Uscátegui 1959, p. 295.

76. Schultes 1954, p. 242; Goldman 1948, p. 796.

77. Reichel-Dolmatoff, personal observation; see also Schultes 1954; Seitz 1967, p. 336; Uscátegui 1959.

78. Holmstedt and Lindgren 1967, pp. 399 ff.; Stromberg 1954.

79. Agurell et al. 1969.

80. Becher, 1960, p. 89. On macropsia see Holmstedt (discussion) 1967, pp. 376, 378; Holmstedt and Lindgren 1967, p. 339; Seitz 1967, pp. 330, 369.

81. Quoted in Holmstedt and Lindgren 1967, p. 339.

82. Agurell et al. 1965, pp. 903–16; Schultes and Holmstedt 1968, p. 133.

83. Schultes 1954, pp. 248–50.

84. Ibid., p. 251.

85. Szara 1967, p. 374.

86. Wassén (1971, pp. 60–61) has recently pointed out the use of narcotic snuff in modern Thailand.

87. On the archaeological evidence for snuff use, see Wassén 1965, 1967a, 1967b, 1971; Wassén and Holmstedt 1963.

88. As a footnote to the history of snuff we should like to add the following observations: The Synod of Santa Fé de Bogotá in 1556 outlawed the use of tobacco and yopo by the Indians. The text says that "the priests in charge of Indian curacies shall not permit the sale of yopa . . . nor that they cultivate tobacco in their fields or houses, nor that they consume it" (Romero 1960, p. 368). However, tobacco—smoked or snuffed—had become a favorite with the Spanish soldiers (Simón 1882–92, 4:361) and soon became popular all over the Kingdom of New Granada. In all probability, the use of

tobacco snuff was introduced in Europe directly from Colombia. According to the chronicler Alonso de Zamora (1930; first edition, Madrid, 1701), the first tobacco mill for the manufacture of snuff was established at Tunja, followed soon by several mills in Bogotá. From here the snuff was taken to Cartagena of the Indies whence it was shipped to Spain, "where they call it tobacco of Tunja, because it was in that city where they began to grind it and to snuff it, a vice that, having been taught by the Indians, the Spaniards excel in, and almost all foreign nations" (Zamora 1930, p. 41). This snuff was "made from [tobacco] that is grown in an Indian village called Samacá, and from others, from what is called La Laguna, behind this city: it is a smallish and short tobacco plant, yellowish, but admirable when ground" (Simón 1882–92, 4:362). Rereading the Synodal Constitutions (Groot 1869, 1:503–4), we find that they also prohibited the ownership of books: "We order . . . that no one, no matter his station, possess books in his house." To prohibit books *and* tobacco strikes one as a rather cruel measure.

CHAPTER 2

1. On the Vaupés territory and its native inhabitants, see mainly Biocca 1965; Brüzzi 1962; Goldman 1948, 1963; Koch-Grünberg 1905, 1906a, 1906b, 1909–10, 1922; Reichel-Dolmatoff 1971. For additional references see Bernal, 1969, pp. 681–719; O'Leary, 1963.

2. Spruce 1874, 1908; Wallace 1889. For a recent biography of Wallace see Williams-Ellis 1966.

3. Bates, 1863 (several editions). Although this traveler did not visit the Vaupés proper, his book is excellent and one should read it along with those of Spruce and Wallace.

4. Wallace 1905, p. 150.

5. Wallace 1889, p. 194. Compressed into a short paragraph we are given here a most vivid and true picture of the Tukano Indians.

6. Spruce 1908, 2:419–20.

7. Ibid. The first references to Spruce's caapi samples were published under the title "Journal of a Voyage up the Amazon and Rio Negro by Richard Spruce, San Carlos del Rio Negro, June 27, 1853," in the *Hooker Journal of Botany and Kew Garden Miscellany,* Nos. 6 and 7, 1855.

8. Spruce 1874. At present the genus is named *Banisteriopsis,* and not *Banisteria;* see Cuatrecasas 1959, pp. 486–87.

9. Spruce 1908, 2:415–16.

10. Ibid., p. 419.

11. Villavicencio 1858.

12. Spruce 1908, 2:424.

13. Ibid., pp. 424–25.

14. Wallace 1889, p. 205.

15. Villavicencio 1858, p. 373.

16. Chantre y Herrera 1637–1767.

17. Martius, who did not visit the Vaupés, refers only indirectly to the use of caapi, probably basing his information on Spruce's collections (see Martius 1858, pp. 1–6; 1867, p. 388).

18. Humboldt 1822.

19. La Condamine 1745.

20. Coudreau 1887.

21. Stradelli 1890*a*. This author observed the use of yajé among the Pira-Tapuya, a Tukano group, during a ceremony of endocannibalism, when the ashes of a corpse were mixed with a fermented beverage.

22. Koch-Grünberg 1909–10, 1:299.

23. Ibid., p. 319.

24. Ibid., p. 300. According to one of our Tukano informants, *kuli gahpí* means "knotty yajé," that is, with a knotty stem. It is also called *gahpí dëhpëri/* 'arm yajé,' and is said to be very strong.

25. Rocha 1905, pp. 43–46. I find it most difficult to translate Rocha's glowing words into English, but for the benefit of Spanish readers I have reproduced the original text in the Appendix, both because it is an important document and because Rocha's book is very rare, even in Colombian libraries.

26. See, for example, Kok 1921–22, 1925–26.

27. Goldman 1940, 1948, 1963, 1964.

28. Goldman 1963, pp. 210–11.

29. Brüzzi 1962.

30. Ibid., pp. 230–31.

31. Calella 1935, pp. 51, 52; 1940–44.

32. Calella 1944*a*, 1944*b*.

33. Whiffen 1915, pp. 139–40.

34. Reichel-Dolmatoff 1944, p. 454.

35. Uscátegui 1959, 1961.

36. Reichel-Dolmatoff 1960, pp. 130–31.

37. Rocha 1905, pp. 43–46.

38. Villavicencio 1858.

39. Reinburg 1921.

40. Rouhier 1924, 1926.

41. Fischer Cárdenas 1923.

42. Schultes 1967*a*, p. 48.

43. The idea that yajé has telepathic properties has, of course, fascinated the credulous. Zerda Bayón, who traveled among the Indians of the upper Putumayo River in 1935, declares that yajé produces visions in which the person develops telepathic faculties. García Barriga (1958, pp. 66–68) mentions this traveler and writes: "Savage Indians who have never left their forests and who, of course, can have no idea of civilized life, describe, in their particular language, and with more or less precision, the details of houses, castles, and cities peopled by multitudes." The fact is that even fairly isolated Indians know a great deal about "civilized" life, having been told of its marvels by missionaries, soldiers, rubber collectors, traders and travelers, and having seen pictures in calendars and illustrated journals.

44. Basic botanical research was carried out by, among others, Morton (1931), Rusby (1923, 1924), and White (1922) (see Schultes 1957). On the pharmacological and chemical aspects, early research was carried out mainly by Barriga Villalba (1925*a*, 1925*b*), Fischer Cárdenas (1923), Michiels and Clinquart (1926), Perrot and Hamet (1927*a*, 1927*b*), Reutter (1927), Wolfe and Rumpf (1928). For more recent studies see Agurell, Holmstedt, and Lindgren 1968; Bristol 1966*a*, 1966*b*; Deulofeu 1967; Hochstein and Paradies 1957; der Marderosian, Pinkley, and Dobins 1968; Mors and Zaltzman 1954; Plutarco Naranjo 1969; O'Connell and Lynn 1953; Ríos 1962.

45. Perrot and Hamet 1927*a*, 1927*b*.

46. Fischer Cárdenas 1923.

47. Barriga Villalba 1925.

48. Keller and Gottauf 1929.
49. Chen and Chen 1939.
50. Williams 1931.
51. Quoted in Schultes 1957, p. 33.
52. *Peganum harmala* is a zygophyllaceous shrub widely distributed in southern Russia, Hungary, Egypt, Syria, and also Spain, where it seems to have been introduced by the Arabs. In the Middle East and India it is used as a narcotic and a spice. From the seeds of this plant, harmine, harmaline, and harmalole have been isolated. See Claudio Naranjo 1967.
53. Hochstein and Paradies 1957.
54. O'Connell and Lynn 1953.
55. Claudio Naranjo 1967.

CHAPTER 3

1. For an excellent introduction to the jaguar-shaman transformation complex see Furst 1968, esp. pp. 154–64. A useful summary is given in Walter 1956.
2. Coe 1970. This interesting paper by a specialist on Olmec civilization tries to relate the jaguar imagery to the concept of kingship.
3. Uricoechea 1871; Lehmann 1920, 1:50–52. The earliest Spanish sources on the Muisca language use the letter *y* to transcribe what was probably a short *ë*.
4. The title *zipa* was given to the lord of the Bogotá district, while that of the Tunja district to the north was *zaque*.
5. Simón 1882–92, 2:324.
6. Ibid., 2:139.
7. Ibid., p. 138.
8. Ibid., p. 316.
9. Piedrahita 1881, pp. 12–13.
10. Simón 1882–92, 2:210; Piedrahita 1881, p. 131.
11. Simón 1882–92, 2:285.
12. Ibid., p. 287. *Nen-* is probably an error in the transcription and should read *Nem-*.
13. On the Kogi (or Kágaba) see Preuss 1926; Reichel-Dolmatoff 1950–51. A fairly complete bibliography of the Sierra Nevada tribes is given in Reichel-Dolmatoff 1963.
14. The relationship between the jaguar and the moon is mentioned in chapter 6.
15. Reichel-Dolmatoff 1950–51, passim.
16. Reichel-Dolmatoff, personal observation. See also Reichel-Dolmatoff 1963.
17. The individual in question was also a shaman.
18. Reichel-Dolmatoff, personal observation during field work in 1941.
19. Piedrahita 1881, p. 36; Simón 1882–92, 2:320.
20. Zamora 1930, p. 127. The original reads: "disfrazes de varios animales ajustadas con tanta curiosidad las pieles, que representaban muy al vivo Ossos, Leones, Tigres."
21. Simón 1882–92, 5:191.
22. Reichel-Dolmatoff, personal observation during field work in 1941. See also Reichel-Dolmatoff 1944, pp. 454, 480, Fig. 4. Carrying-bag of jaguar

skin/*negüíti bókoto-doro;* headdress of jaguar claws/*kotíberi, kotibirebure;* necklace of jaguar teeth/*negüíti uónoto;* snuffing tube of bird bone/*siripu.*

23. Reichel-Dolmatoff 1950–51, passim; for illustrations see Preuss 1926, Figs. 30–34.

24. Castellanos 1886, 1:50; Simón 1882–92, 2:286.

25. Piedrahita 1881, p. 13.

26. Aguado 1956, 1:598.

27. Stoddart 1962, p. 148.

28. Simón 1882–92, 4:327.

29. Anonymous 1928, p. 356. The original text in Siona reads: "Ayroiay creesique aquero? Junica yay somiye, roctasique aquero?"

30. Rocha 1905, pp. 75–77; see also Calella 1935, pp. 51, 52; Castellví 1944, pp. 111, 112.

31. Several reports exist on shamans who were killed for sorcery.

32. Whiffen 1915, p. 182.

33. Calella, 1944a, p. 34.

34. On the Páez see Bernal 1953a, 1953b, 1954a, 1954b, 1956; Nachtigall 1955a, 1955b; Otero 1952.

35. Nachtigall 1955a, p. 308; 1955b, p. 223.

36. Ibid.

37. Reichel-Dolmatoff 1945, p. 5.

38. Reichel-Dolmatoff 1944, p. 478.

39. Romero (1960, p. 369) writes: "It is an ancient custom among them to fear and reverence the devil."

40. Oviedo 1851–55, 6:303.

41. Simón 1882–92, 2:293.

42. Ibid., p. 197.

43. Ibid.

44. As we shall see later on, intoxication with narcotic snuff is often accompanied by the sensation of strong winds and rushing noises. It is also possible that shamanistic séances took place during thunderstorms; many Indians have an extraordinary capacity for weather prediction and can often forecast a thunderstorm well in advance.

45. Mártir 1944, p. 617.

46. Anonymous 1866, p. 488.

47. Simón 1882–92, 2:286. Father Asensio, a Spanish priest of the sixteenth century, tells the following anecdote: A Muisca shaman from the village of Ubaque asked the devil where to hide his gold from the Spaniards. He was overheard by a mestizo who understood the language and answered in the devil's stead, directing the shaman to bury his treasure at a certain spot. The shaman did so and realized his mistake only when it was too late, and the mestizo had got away with the gold. See Romero 1960, pp. 369–70; Simón 1882–92, 3:150–54.

48. Simón 1882–92, 3:370. The original text reads: "sólo quería de la fiesta el tabaco en hoja y polvo, porque era manjar muy a su gusto."

49. Simón 1882–92, 3:150–51.

50. On macropsia under the influence of narcotic drug see, among others, Holmstedt (discussion) 1967, pp. 376, 378; Holmstedt and Lindgren 1967, p. 369; Seitz 1967, pp. 330, 334.

51. Markham 1864, p. 48.

52. Simón 1882–92, 4:172.

53. Anonymous 1865, p. 394. Italics mine.

54. Markham 1864, p. 59.
55. Simón 1882–92, 2:293.
56. Castellanos 1886, 1:51.
57. Vadillo 1884; on Dabeiba see Trimborn 1948, pp. 157–208.
58. Manuel Lucena Samoral, Instituto Colombiano de Antropología; personal communication.
59. This concept of ill omen is called *urúmo*, a native word of uncertain etymology used in expressions like *hacer urúmo*/to prognosticate evil, or *ser urúmo*/to be an evil omen. See Reichel-Dolmatoff 1961, p. 410.
60. Bernal 1953a, pp. 291, 292, 303; Rowe 1956, p. 154.
61. That the Pijao were cannibals is a historical fact, and the contemporary chroniclers speak of it in detail.
62. For another version see Nachtigall 1955a, p. 293.
63. One tale explains that, should a Páez Indian meet a Pijao or a jaguar, he must not tell anyone of his encounter before six to twelve months have passed, because otherwise he risks his life (Nachtigall 1955a, p. 305). These traditions are paralleled by the belief that in ancient times there were many jaguars in Páez territory (Bernal 1953a, p. 305). Nachtigall (1955a, p. 266) mentions that to dream of jaguars or cats means that one's house was built upon an ancient Pijao burial ground. This may cause sickness to the occupants. See also Bernal 1954a, p. 235.
64. It is interesting to compare the little Thunder-Jaguars of Páez mythology with the so-called baby-faced sculptures of the ancient Olmecs in Mexico. See Coe 1962, p. 85; also nn. 66 and 67, below.
65. The name is often mentioned as Juan Tama; other synonyms are Llibán or Juan Chiracol.
66. Ayerbe 1944, pp. 227–28; Bernal 1953a, p. 295; Nachtigall 1955a, pp. 270–71, 294, 297–98; id. 1955b, p. 223. In Páez mythology the story of the culture hero is often found encapsulated in a cycle of stories telling of the origin of the voracious little Thunder-Children. They are essentially one and the same.
67. Bernal 1954, pp. 221–22; Nachtigall 1955a, p. 269; id. 1955b, p. 222. In the State of Veracruz, Mexico, the center of the ancient Olmec area, many folk tales speak of the *chaneques*, small dwarfed beings said to live in cascades, who besides being rain-spirits are said to run after women (Covarrubias 1954, pp. 98–99).
68. Most Páez shamans are male (*tepits*), but occasionally there are female practitioners (*teui*); an evil shaman is called *nyij* (Nachtigall 1955a, p. 258).
69. There are many lakes in the surrounding mountains where these Thunder-spirits are said to dwell. Some of the best known are *Taibe* (Nachtigall 1955b, p. 212), *Hipndyk* (Nachtigall 1955b, p. 222), *Juan Tama* (Nachtigall 1955a, p. 293), *El Caspe* (Bernal Villa 1953a, p. 297; Nachtigall 1955a, p. 298), *Bugta* (Nachtigall 1955a, p. 302), *Vichaguau* (Bernal Villa 1953a, p. 292), and *Eshufi Ik* (Bernal Villa 1953a, p. 295).
70. Nachtigall 1955a, pp. 260, 262.
71. Bernal Villa 1954a, pp. 222–23.
72. Bernal 1954a, pp. 228, 233–34, 235; Nachtigall 1955a, p. 268; id. 1955b, p. 212.
73. Bernal 1954a, p. 224; Nachtigall 1955a. p. 297.
74. Ayerbe 1944, p. 228.
75. Sergio Elías Ortíz, Instituto Colombiano de Antropología; personal communication.

76. Bernal 1954a, p. 246.

77. Nachtigall 1955a, p. 311.

78. Bernal 1954a, p. 247.

79. Ibid., pp. 227, 237.

80. Hernández de Alba 1944, p. 222.

81. Nachtigall 1955a, p. 308.

82. Ibid., p. 264.

83. Ibid., 1955a, pp. 294–95; 1955b, 220–21. The Páez say that this plant no longer exists in their tribal territory, but that it can be found in the neighboring Cauca valley. The *yutse* plant is described by them, rather cryptically, as looking "like a caterpillar" (Nachtigall 1955a, p. 308). It is interesting to note that there exists a parallel for this tale among the Tukano Indians of the Vaupés. The forest monster *boráro*, who has many traits that make him appear to be a jaguar-spirit, grasps his human prey in a crushing embrace until the flesh turns into a pulpy mass he then sucks out through a small hole he pricks on top of the head. He then inflates the limp skin and sends the victim back to his family (Reichel-Dolmatoff 1971, p. 87; see also Chapter 9). The prohibition against telling of a hallucinatory experience connected with the encounter with a spirit-being, generally a jaguar, is mentioned in several Tukano myths. See also n. 63, above.

84. Bernal Villa 1954a, p. 259.

85. Otero 1952, pp. 89–91.

86. Bernal Villa (1953a, p. 291) summarizes thus his appraisal of Páez mythology: "The predominant, central motifs refer to sex and aggression."

87. On the Kogi see Preuss 1926; Reichel-Dolmatoff 1950–51.

88. Reichel-Dolmatoff 1950–51, 2:10.

89. Ibid., p. 19.

90. Ibid., p. 72.

91. Ibid., p. 39. The text says that "he devoured her . . . not with his mouth, but with his anus."

92. *Búnkuase* is the embodiment of the principle of good.

93. In Kogi thought, disease is, in all essence, the exterior manifestation of a state of sin.

94. Reichel-Dolmatoff 1950–51, 2:38–42.

95. The precise etymology of this name is not clear. It seems to be a jaguar-name.

96. Reichel-Dolmatoff 1950–51, 2:42–43.

97. *Námaku* means jaguar-lord; from *nam*/jaguar, and *makú*/lord, chief. His mother *Nabia* (also a jaguar-name) is occasionally designated as *hába Nabia*/mother-jaguar, which gives her the status of a divine personification.

98. The tale of *Námaku* contains the elements of great tragedy and is an example of the power and expressiveness of some aboriginal myths.

99. In this respect one might say that the Kogi practice a mystery religion, in contrast to the tribes of the Colombian Amazonian lowlands.

100. Among the Kogi, membership in one of these groups is exteriorized by colored stripes interwoven in the cotton cloth the men are wearing.

101. The associations of these different groups are many and include animals, plants, minerals, the ownership of songs and dances, and specific ritual functions. For details see Reichel-Dolmatoff 1950–51, 1:168–87.

102. Ibid., pp. 169–213.

103. In the archaeology of the Tairona area, peopled in the sixteenth century by the forebears of the Kogi, representations of jaguars in pottery, stone,

or gold are common. In many cases these objects show people wearing jaguar masks. For illustrations see Mason 1931, 1936, 1939.

104. This custom has been borne out by archaeology. During the excavation of a protohistoric ceremonial site of the Tairona culture, a jaguar skull was discovered near the main entrance of the construction.

105. Reichel-Dolmatoff 1950–51, 1:267–68.

CHAPTER 4

1. The total area of the administrative district called the "Comisaría Especial del Vaupés" is about 100,000 square kilometers. The neighboring "Comisaría del Guainía" covers some 78,000 square kilometers and formed part of the Vaupés territory until 1963.

2. The rapids and falls are commonly designated by the name *cachivera*, a local corruption of the Portuguese word *cachoeira*.

3. In the first years of the nineteenth century all communication with the capital of Colombia was practically cut. Humboldt (1882, 7:390) writes: "Lorsque j'étois à Santa-Fe de Bogotá, on connoissoit à peine chemin qui conduit, par les villages d'Usme, d'Ubaque ou de Caqueza, à Apiay et à l'embarcadère du Río Meta."

4. As far as I know, the first description by a scientific traveler who crossed from the Guaviare River to the headwaters of the Vaupés, is by Hamilton Rice (1910).

5. It seems that, originally, the term *Vaupés* (*Uaupé, Guapé,* etc.) did not refer to the river but to the local inhabitants know by that name among their Arawakan neighbors to the north and northeast. Even today it is considered to be a somewhat derogatory term because it seems to allude to an unpleasant body odor that, according to the neighboring groups, characterizes the local Indians. Humboldt (1822, 8:419) writes: "on retrouve dans les *Guaypes*, gouvernés par le cacique Macatoa, les habitants de la rivière d'Uaupés, qui porte aussi les noms de *guape* ou guapue." (See also Amorim 1926–28, pp. 186–87 n; Koch-Grünberg 1909, 1:208.) The Vaupés River is sometimes called *Cayarí*, an Arawakan word meaning "white water," or "white river."

6. On the expeditions in search of the "Dorado de los Omaguas" see Humboldt 1822, 7:383; ibid., 8:145 et passim; Langegg 1888; Simón 1882–92, 1:108 ff.

7. Much of the present toponymy of the Vaupés territory is Tupí; the Spanish-speaking population has adopted many words from this language, notably the names of animals and plants.

8. On the history of Catholic missions in the Vaupés territory see Aranha 1906–7; Builes 1957; Colini 1884; Coudreau 1887; 2:141; Goldman 1948, p. 768; Humboldt 1822, Vols. 7, 8, passim; Koch-Grünberg 1909, passim; Misiones del Vaupés 1966; Mochi 1902, p. 445; Stradelli 1890a, p. 433. Mitú, at present with a population of less than 1,000 inhabitants, is located on the right bank of the Vaupés, at lat. 1°05′30″N and long. 70°05′W.

9. For an excellent introduction see Ab'Sáber 1967.

10. This number is hardly more than a guess. Rodriguez Bermudez (1962, p. 77) mentions 8,300, but all census data published so far are doubtful.

11. This refers to the Colombian border post of Yavareté; across the river is the Brazilian mission station of Yavareté, of the Salesian Fathers, which

goes back to the nineteenth century. The name *yavareté* is Tupí and means "true jaguar."

12. Tipiaca has been renamed recently and is now called Fatima.

13. The Tukano of the Vaupés territory form the so-called Eastern Tukano group; the Western Tukano are formed by several tribes (Coreguaje, Macaguaje, Siona, Tama, etc.) which occupy the upper Caquetá River and maintain no contact with the eastern group.

14. On the Arawakan Indians of this general region see Civrieux and Lichy 1950; Koch-Grünberg 1906–11, 1911; Saake 1958a, 1958b, 1959, 1959–60, Wilbert 1960, 1961.

15. The Karihóna are remnants of the Umáua mentioned before. Some small groups live toward the southwest. Koch-Grünberg (1908b; 1909–10, 2:114) has suggested that the Carib-speaking Hianácoto-Umáua on the western fringe of the Vaupés territory are related to certain Carib groups of the Guianas, and that they represent a historically recent migration across the Orinoco.

16. On the Makú see, among others, Koch-Grünberg 1906b; Tastevin 1923; Terribilini and Terribilini 1961.

17. For general descriptions of Northwest Amazon cultures see Galvão 1955, 1959; Goldman 1948; Steward and Faron 1959. On the Vaupés area see Brüzzi 1962; Fulop 1954, 1955, 1956; Goldman 1948, 1964; Koch-Grünberg 1906–11, 1909–10, 1922; Kok, 1925–26; Moser and Tayler 1963; Reichel-Dolmatoff 1971.

18. This refers mainly to mother's brother's daughter (real or classificatory).

19. Goldman (1963) introduced the term *phratry* for Tukano exogamic groups and I have, somewhat uncritically, followed him in this (Reichel-Dolmatoff 1971). Until social anthropologists have decided on a better term, I shall use the expression *exogamic group* (or *unit*), or shall call them by their names, that is, Tukano proper. Desana, Pira-Tapuya, and so on. (For a detailed, but not always very precise, list see Brüzzi 1962, pp. 78–135; Sorensen (1967) is an excellent source. Some additional information can be found in Goldman 1948; Koch-Grünberg 1909–10, passim; Reichel-Dolmatoff 1971, pp. 4–6.) The names of these diverse exogamic units are causing a great deal of confusion; some names are derived from the Lengua Geral, while others are derived from Tukanoan or Arawakan languages. As each group speaks its own language, a variety of names exist by which, from a particular speaker's view, all other groups are designated, and the self-name each exogamic group uses also differs from the "common" name, that is, from Tukano, Desana, etc. For example, the name *tukano* is derived from the Tupí word for the toucan bird (*Rhamphastidae*); their self-name is *dáhsea*, the name of that bird in their language. The name *desana* seems to be taken from some of the neighboring Arawak languages; the Tariana call them *detsána* or *detsénei*, and the Ipeka, a group related to the Kuripako, say *desá*. Their self-name is *wirá*/wind, or *wirá-porá*/sons of the wind. According to some informants the term *wind* refers to an unpleasant body odor, flatulence, and so forth (see also n. 5 above). The Pira-Tapuya derive their name from the Tupí word for fish (*pira*) and the term *tapuya*, which, in the Vaupés, means "people." Their self-name is *vaí-kana*, from *vaí*/fish. (For a discussion of the term *tapuya* see Lowie 1946; and Schuller 1913.) The name *uanano* (or *guanano*) is also a Tupí word used to designate an aquatic bird (*Chenalopex jubatus*, according to Brüzzi 1962, p. 97); their self-name is *kótia* (*kótirya, kótidya, kótirwa*, after Brüzzi, ibid.), and the Tukano proper call them *ohkó-tikhara*/medicine-people, or,

perhaps, water-people. *Carapana,* the name of another group, is derived from the Tupí word *carapana,* a small mosquito of noctural habits; their self-name is *mëhtá/*mosquito. *Tatuyo* is derived from the Tupí word *tatú/*armadillo, and they call themselves *pamóa,* which is their name for this animal.

20. See Goldman 1940, 1963, 1964; Koch-Grünberg 1909–10.

21. Sorensen 1967. On the languages of the Eastern Tukano see, among others, Brüzzi 1962; Giacone 1939, 1965; Koch-Grünberg 1906a, 1913–16; Kok, 1921–22. On the nature of linguistic relationships Sorensen (1967, p. 675) says: "Structural interrelationships are generally close among the Eastern Tukano languages, but in the finer details of their similarities the languages do not coincide. In *broad* phonetic transcription, most of the Eastern Tukanoan languages share most of the same grid of phones, but the patterning of phonemes and the distribution of allophones vary from language to language."

22. I have dealt in another book (Reichel-Dolmatoff 1971) with some aspects of the general cosmogonic and cosmological ideas of the Desana. For the material culture of the Eastern Tukano, Koch-Grünberg's work (1909–10) is a basic source.

CHAPTER 5

1. The term *payé* is taken from the Tupi language and is widely used in the Amazon area (see Friederici 1947, pp. 468–69).

2. For a recent discussion of the seminal character of spiritual luminescence see Eliade 1971.

3. It is obvious that these sudden appearances of material objects out of nowhere must be attributed to sleight-of-hand of the master shaman.

4. There are many variations in the number and characteristics of these Thunder-stones; some payés use only a few, while others claim to possess many of them.

5. These yellow shiny cherts are fairly common on the Apaporis River, that is, outside the Tukano territory. Larger pebbles of the same material are used for burnishing pottery, especially the surface of the yajé vessel. Because of their color a seminal character is attributed to them.

6. Putting these splinters into the left arm is a precaution; during an insignificant quarrel or a drunken bout a man might strike out with his right arm and, should it contain these splinters, might unintentionally harm someone.

7. This might depend on local conditions and on individual preferences. Not all payés have the same spirit-helpers nor exactly the same physical equipment, and differences in technique, too, are frequently seen.

8. The fish a payé is allowed to eat in these circumstances were said to be: *yacundá* (LG), *uári* (T), a catfish, *yohua* (T) a small "sardine," and a fish called in Spanish *cabecita de almidón/*"little starch-head."

9. This ant is called *yamika* (T); it emerges about two hours before dawn.

10. For a discussion of the Master of Animals among South American Indians, see Zerries 1954; for the Vaupés area see Reichel-Dolmatoff 1971, pp. 80–86.

11. The reasons for these differences are not clear; perhaps they are due to local specialization. The Desana seem to emphasize *Vaí-mahsë's* weapons, while the Tukano proper consider thunder's weapon more important. It is not clear whether the neophyte actually dives into the pool or does so in his hallucinations.

12. These hills often form ecological niches where the fauna and flora differ somewhat from those of the surrounding forest. Being avoided by hunters, they are natural game reserves for many animal species.

13. The name *Curupira* seems to be derived from the Tupi language. For a discussion of this creature, see Zerries 1954, pp. 9–16, 337–39; Friederici 1947, p. 230. See also Chap. 9.

14. See Reichel-Dolmatoff 1971, pp. 89–91; see also Chap. 9.

15. Many tales about the *saaropë*, obtained from the Indians and rubber collectors, describe these creatures in very realistic terms, quite unlike those used in speaking of bush spirits. It is possible that these "little men" (or *bamberos*, as they are called in Spanish by the local rubber collectors) are in reality the remnants of an unknown archaic group of nomadic hunters and gatherers who continue to live in the interfluvial regions of the rain forest.

16. The etymology of this term is not clear. *Vëari*/large, spacious (D). See also Chap. 9.

17. The *vëarí-mahsá* are designated as *pamüíri-bëakana*/the "other half" (T), the people that *Pamurí-mahsë*, the Germinator, "had in excess." See also chap. 9.

18. *Uracentron werneri.*

19. *Plica plica* L.

20. *Bothrops* sp.

21. *Vaí-mahsë* is repaid in any case by the souls of people a payé kills and sends to the hills where they turn into servants, sometimes in the shapes of animals.

22. Characteristically, the same expression is used when yajé is being distributed.

23. One spell we collected makes reference to eighty-one different classes of fish.

24. The spell says, for example: "na vaí-mahsá naye dia poarire, pití tumahámínëko, pití tumahámisono, na vaí-mahsa vii seri, naye sinisé uamëperi diakó, duhtú patá diakó nyaino diakó, nayé pérutë pari . . ." (the *vaí-mahsa* face-grasp-turn, grasp-return to their houses, the *vaí-mahsa*'s houses, they drink . . . [three different kinds of beer]) (T).

25. *Yuruparí* flutes are used on certain major ritual occasions and are connected with the origins of exogamy. There are many different categories of flutes, and their respective mythical origins and specific ownership form a very complex body of beliefs and traditions. See Amorim 1926–28, passim; Bödiger 1965, pp. 127–43; Boje 1930*a;* Bolens 1967; Friederici 1947, pp. 336–37; Koch-Grünberg 1909–10, 1:314–20, 2:292–93; Reichel-Dolmatoff 1971, pp. 166–71.

26. Should the boys have had heterosexual contacts before their initiation, at their deaths their bones would turn into anacondas (T: *amoá piro boágë*/ "menstruation-snake–going into river").

27. The fences are described as very like those used in fishing.

28. Similar spells are used to distract the *boráro,* who, in these incantations, is made to "turn around," "sit quietly," "fall asleep," and so forth.

29. The symptoms described to us seem to be of a marked paranoid character. The patient develops delusions of persecution, not so much by individual enemies as by a large armed crowd. He will suddenly become panic-stricken and will incite others to flee with him and hide in the forest before an imaginary attack. Others suffer from the delusion that the sky is steadily descending in a threatening way and that "the world is coming to an end." A charac-

teristic symptom of another type is that the person, in full daylight, claims to be surrounded by darkness and walks hesitantly, with outstretched arms, as if in the dark. Cases of hysteroid behavior have been described elsewhere (see Reichel-Dolmatoff 1971, pp. 183–85).

30. The following leaves were mentioned: *káně, pehtásti pure, biël* (T) (similar to peppers), *barë* (with a strong aromatic smell), *piíkano* (a shrub), *bohta mihsida* (a vine), *mihsida* (a very small vine).

31. *Umarí,* Poraqueiba *paraensis; uamüë* (T), *mëë* (D). The term *umarí* is Tupi.

32. A kind of yam.

33. A divine personification; see Reichel-Dolmatoff 1971, pp. 76–77 et passim.

34. The *tooka plant* (unidentified) has small blackish berries that are of great magical importance and figure in many spells.

35. Unexplained.

36. Unexplained.

37. Unexplained.

38. A palm tree (*Leopoldina piassaba* Wallace); in the North (Orinoco Plains) the very strong fibers are commonly known as *chiquichique*.

39. See Reichel-Dolmatoff 1971, pp. 218–28.

40. A palm tree (*Jessenia bataua* Mart.).

41. *Fam. Fulgoridae.* Sometimes not a cicada but a large lantern fly is referred to.

42. The term *excrement* can also be understood as meaning any bodily secretion. The idea that hallucinogenic substances are a divine semen is common among the Desana and the Tukano proper.

43. This vine is described as having straight stems without nodules. The bark is said to be thin and smooth, and the flowers are said to be very similar to those of a coffee tree.

44. The distinction between relatives and allies is frequently made in myths that deal with animals.

45. The pattern of collecting herbs or approaching a hill from east to west via north, but avoiding the south, is unexplained.

46. Delusions of a diminishing universe under the influence of yajé are reported by Mallol de Recasens (1963).

47. Reichel-Dolmatoff 1971, passim.

48. Some of these fish may be eaten, but only after a spell has been pronounced over them.

49. Only on rare occasions may an old woman be allowed to take yajé.

CHAPTER 6

1. For a full version of the myth see Reichel-Dolmatoff 1971, pp. 28–29. The idea that a narcotic substance is jaguar's sperm is found in several Colombian Indian tribes. For example, among the Kogi of the Sierra Nevada of Santa Marta, the transforming substance is called "jaguar's seed" or "jaguar's testicle" (Reichel-Dolmatoff 1950–51, 2:39 n), while the Guahibo Indians associate the snuff tablet with jaguar's excrement (Bernard Arcand, Cambridge University, personal communication). Among the Sibundoy Indians of the upper Putumayo River, a narcotic plant (*Metistica emsianum* Schultes) is

called "jaguar's tongue" (Richard Evans Schultes, Harvard University, personal communication).

2. The concept of "doubles" (*vëarí-mahsá*) is discussed in more detail in Chapter 9.

3. *Umarí* is the Tupi term for *Poraqueiba paraensis*. The symbolic meaning attached to this tree and its fruits refers to a female principle of fecundity. Together with the "male" *vahsú* (*Hevea pauciflora* var. *coriacea*) it represents a pair of opposites among fruit trees. In many myths the tapir is the Master of *Umarí*.

4. To cut out the tongue of a game animal is common practice. This is done to prevent the animal's spirit from telling others of its fate.

5. The booming sound heard when a monster is burned is a common myth motif and means that only the material part has died, while the essence survives. It is, of course, a fact that a carcass when exposed to flame will develop gases and burst open with an audible sound.

6. The generic name for these caterpillars is *ii* (D), *iya* (T). The following specific names were given in Tukano: *batíya, iyá-nihtyá, viésa* (August), *uahsó-këya, nehtoá* (November), *sonasá, kaítoa* (other months).

7. The following are the Tukano proper names of some of the Masters of Caterpillars: *batíya vehkë* (of *batíya*), *yaí-ga* (of *viésa*), *kaí-vehkë* (of *kaítoa*), *nihtiá diáně* (of *iyá-nihtiá*).

8. Some of them seem, rather, to be lantern flies (*Fam. Fulgoridae*). The local Spanish-speaking population of the Vaupés call this large lantern fly *machaca*. It is greatly feared and is said to have a poisonous sting. The only antidote is said to be immediate sexual intercourse, and some extraordinary tales are told about certain emergencies.

9. It also announces the beginning of the season when new fields are cleared in the forest.

10. *Carayurú* is the Tupi term for *Bignonia chica,* a shrub from whose fruits a red facial paint is prepared.

11. November is the last month of the rainy season, and thunderstorms occur frequently then.

12. *Yuí;* unexplained.

13. Opinions differ as to the exact nature of dietary restrictions.

14. *Vëari-mahsë*/big-man. The name has two possible derivations; one is *vëari*/big, spacious; *vëaridiagë*/very big; *vëaro*/plenty, large; *vëagë*/large (of animals). The other is: *vëari*/rasp, scraper; *vëa*/name of a mythical being that "devours" people. In several myths the term *scraper* refers to an aggressive phallic being or to his "tool." Possibly the two words are related.

15. It is possible that the Tariano are meant, an Arawak-speaking group which, at present, is almost completely assimilated into the Tukano.

16. I wish to express my sincere gratitude to several distinguished zoologists who have most generously given of their time to discuss this matter with me. Information on feline behavior was kindly provided by Dr. George B. Schaller of the Bronx Zoo, New York; Dr. Frederick A. Ulmer, Jr., of the Philadelphia Zoological Garden; and Dr. J. Malcolm Hime of the Zoological Society of London.

17. In this story, the limit would have been at the Yuruparí Falls.

18. In another version, the girl's hand was stained with her menstrual blood.

19. The story pays tribute to the independent ways of domestic cats; each painted its fur in a different way, we are told.

20. A palm tree (*Mauritia flexuosa*).

21. *Bignonia chica;* see n. 10, above.

22. A palm tree (*Oenocarpus Batawa*).

23. *Moaburebu* is the name of the trumpeter bird (*Psophia crepitans*). According to our informants the word is derived from *moá,* a Cubeo word for meat, and the Desana verb *boréri/*to ripen, to shine.

24. *Gamuyéri* is derived from *gamé/*together, *yeéri/*to cohabit. It is often abbreviated as *gámura.*

25. The equivalence of food and sex, superposed upon the regional resources, implies many rules and restrictions, especially in the case of migrating animals which come from a "raw" region. The fish that run up to the Meyú Falls (Pira-paraná River) or the Jirijirimo Falls (Apaporis River), coming from the Caquetá, can be eaten only in special circumstances, when a person has received a "permit" to do so. One informant said: "The *balentón* and *bagre* [both catfish] which enter the Pira-paraná are people because they are in contact with *ahpikondía,* the paradise. Between the Meyú and Cuyucuyú Falls they are fertilized by fruits from trees, and so can be eaten. From Cuyucuyú to the headwaters they eat earthworms and are fertilized by the soil, and so can be eaten. But no one may eat fish from below the Meyú Falls, at least not large ones; not even piraña." Some of the migrating animals, or fruits from a "raw" area are said to be "poisonous," just as sexual relationships with "raw" people would be "poisonous." Bitter manioc or *vahsú* fruit are poisonous in a raw state and must be cooked to become edible. Exogamy, in Tukano thought, implies what we might call exophagy.

CHAPTER 7

1. The mythical canoe was shaped like an anaconda, and its outside was covered with zigzag designs in red, yellow, and black; the inside was red. The canoe is called *pamurí gahsíru* (D), from *pamuri/*to germinate, and *gahsíru/* a shell, a receptacle.

2. It is understood that this was the first maloca ever built on earth.

3. *Tooka,* also *too;* a small unidentified plant with round, blackish berries which is often mentioned in rituals.

4. *Bayapia* (D), an unidentified plant, probably a hallucinogen. The name seems to be related to *bayí/*spell, *bayári/*to dance.

5. The Tearing-in-Pieces (sparagmos) of the divine child is, of course, a well-known myth motif in the Old World. The pertinent part of our Desana text says: "gahira igë mohotóri igë dihpúru igë gubúri aí tuavea siria vanyora. Pamurí mahsá irá gahpí dáre aira" (Others seized its hands, its head, and its legs and dispersed them. Thus the Germination People got hold of their yajé vine).

6. Fertilization through the eye is mentioned in several Tukano myths.

7. *Sëmé* (D) is a leguminous tree with edible seeds.

8. *Boréka* is the name of the highest-ranking sib of the Desana. The name is that of the *aracú* (LG) fish (*Leporinus copelandi* Steind.). Another version states that the first group to obtain yajé was the Pira-Tapuya.

9. The proper name of the Creator is *go'á-mëe,* derived from *go'á/*a bone, a tube, and the suffix *-mëe* which indicates the power to produce something (D). An informant stated: "The bone-god is a penis . . . this tube, this bone

makes contact between man and *ahpikondiá* [the paradise]. . . . Between the visible world and the invisible there is a sexual contact." See also Reichel-Dolmatoff 1971, pp. 47–50.

10. For example, jaguars, squirrels, macaws, and almost any bird with yellow feathers.

11. For another version of this myth see Chap. 6.

12. Wainambí (also Uainambí, Guainambí) is a term token from Lengua Geral and is the name of a hummingbird (García 1929, p. 23). The Desana are traditionally descended from the hummingbird. For further symbolic associations see Reichel-Dolmatoff 1971, pp. 102, 192 ff.

13. The theme of the misleading *dédoublement* is treated in more detail in Chapter 8.

14. An interesting note on the relationship cohabitation/bedchamber/coemeterium/cemetery can be found in Jung 1947, p. 527, n. 21.

15. The hummingbird is a phallic animal; see n. 12, above.

16. The original text in Desana reads: "irigë yeegë ëmë dehko keoburigere nugunyari yuhpë (With his jaguar-rod he determined the center [middle] of the day); "irogeta yuhudiaye iri vahsero nugahayora pare irigë yeegë yuhudiaye" (On this spot the stick rattle stood erect).

17. In Tukano: Panoré.

18. Several Indians, when asked to draw the petroglyph of the Rock of Nyí from memory, drew a phallus and called it by that name.

19. The myth that tells of the First Couple has many local variants in the Vaupés. Among the Desana the theme seems to be little elaborated. According to one Tukano proper myth, the germinator descended to earth on a yajé vine (*pamuíri-mahsë duhítika-da*/to descend–vine), followed by the First Couple: *surí-pahkë* and *surí-pahkó*. In another Tukano proper version, *pamurí-mahsë's* daughter (*yepá-mahsó*/earth woman) became pregnant when she ate a *karé* fruit (*Chrysophyllum vulgare*) that was growing on a tree covered by yajé vines. The child was named *yepá-mahsë*/earth-man. According to one Barasana myth collected near the Rock of Nyí, the First Couple were *yepá*/earth-man, associated with the jaguar; and *yavíra*, a woman associated with the boa (?) snake.

20. The vine (in reality a palm: *Desmoncus horridus*) is called *vaítuda* (D, T), and the etymology, given by a Desana informant, is as follows: *vaí*/fish, *tuyári*/that which contains, that where are . . . , *da*/vine. According to some versions the Fish Girl was baited with a *poé* (D) fruit (*Pouteria Ucuquí* R. E. Schultes). In Tukano proper the fruit is called *puhpí*, and in Lengua Geral, *ukukí*. It is the size of a small mango and has a sweetish taste.

21. Honey is *momé* in Desana, a term equally used for sperm.

22. During the yearly run of fish, not all species travel together; certain species swim ahead, while others follow. There is an order, a sequence, and only the major rapids mark way stations on these migrations. The same phenomenon can be observed on the Magdalena River. Besides, some fish swim in a rapid zigzag, others proceed in tight shoals, and still others always keep to the riverbank. This yearly phenomenon seems to provide the model for dances, orders of precedence, indeed for the establishment of categories of women, that is, of rules of sexual and dietary permissibility or prohibition.

23. The term *maní fish* remains unexplained.

24. Our informants pointed out repeatedly that this is the "place of coca," where "no hunger is felt." As a matter of fact, the alkaloids of powdered coca

leaves mixed with lime anesthetize the stomach walls and deaden the sensation of hunger. Most Tukano Indians are avid consumers of coca (*Eritroxylon coca*). For details on *ahpikondiá* see Reichel-Dolmatoff 1971, pp. 46–47.

25. Reichel-Dolmatoff 1971, pp. 219–37.

26. *Yonéro* snake; not identified.

27. *Boréka*, a fish; see n. 8, above.

28. *Mahká*; boa constrictor.

29. *Buia*; not identified.

30. *Bignonia chica* and the red paint prepared from this plant.

31. Conical design; unexplained.

32. *Vahsú* or *vahsúpë*, the rubber tree (*Hevea pauciflora var. coriacea*). See also Chap. 9.

33. In this text three kinds of yajé were mentioned: *kuurikë-da*, a vine with knotty stems; *merepi-da* or *guamo* (*Inga* sp.) vine; and *too-da* (see n. 3 above).

34. *Puikarogë*, unexplained; *oyodiigë*, probably from *oyo*/bat, *dii*/blood, *-gë*/male suffix.

35. Cf. n. 33, above.

36. The vines are pounded in a wooden trough with a heavy club or stick. The pounding should be done with a certain rhythm, accompanied by singing and whistling.

37. This detail is important because it demonstrates that certain admixtures are used which are likely to modify the chemical properties of the potion.

38. It was mentioned by the informants that the admixture and the vessel in which it is prepared require a special song.

39. In this case, "to converse" refers to the ceremonial greeting addressed to the guests.

40. Circular shields of wickerwork (D: *vabéro*) used to be an important part of Desana ceremonial attire. Today they have practically disappeared.

41. Lengthy ceremonial conversations in which guests are greeted, mythical genealogies are recited, and the qualities of certain exogamic groups are extolled are the rule in most gatherings.

42. It is imagined that the back (or "female") part of a maloca occupies a slightly lower level than the front part where the men are. A person coming from the back part therefore "ascends" toward the front. See also Reichel-Dolmatoff 1971, pp. 106–8.

43. The expression was explained as referring to both saturation with yajé and saturation with the essence of the women of the complementary exogamic unit.

44. The vessel is addressed as if it were a woman, and the ritual insults refer to the danger this contact with a female principle involves. The idea that vomit, produced by poison, contains small fish is also found in other contexts.

45. The vessel is said to be "drunk," while the men who have consumed its contents defy the intoxication.

46. This is a ritual expression of exaltation and joy in which the upper arms are clapped sharply against the chest while the person exclaims *chavé!*

47. "Imposing"/*gëyadëári;* The word can also mean "serious," "solemn"; as it contains the idea of danger, it might also be translated as "awesome."

48. The term used is *gubúro moári*/to stamp ritually; literally, "to make foot." *Gubúro* also means "underground butt end of a tree stem," "origin of a family or an exogamic group." Occasionally the yajé vessel is placed upon a

decorated bench which is then carried at shoulder height by several dancers. It is interesting to observe that a similar dance was carried out by the sixteenth-century Guayupe Indians of the Guaviare River. The chronicler Pedro de Aguado describes a dance in which a vessel containing the ashes of a chieftain was carried by the men: "they put them on the bench on which the dead chief used to sit . . . and, carrying the bench with the vessels on their shoulders, they begin to dance with them" (Aguado 1956, 1:601–3). Afterward the ashes were mixed with "wine," and the men drank this potion. In the late nineteenth century, Stradelli (1890a) observed the Pira-Tapuya in a similar ritual, during which yajé was consumed.

49. The typical expression is *vahage bure*/"enemy-stupid" (D). The postposition of *bure* is an insult.

50. The gestures of defiance and the references to "enemies of our ancestors" appear to be survivals of a war dance and are, at present, quite out of place. From many myths and also from historical sources it seems that there existed a great deal of intertribal warfare in the Vaupés in former times.

51. This is the beginning of Text No. 111.

52. Here reference is made to the initial, nauseating phase, which is followed by red hallucinations. See also Chap. 9.

53. The difference remains unexplained.

54. Zigzag designs are, generally, associated with the Anaconda-Canoe.

55. Oropendola, in Desana: *umú, umusí*. This bird (*Icteridae*) is of symbolic importance (Reichel-Dolmatoff 1971, pp. 101–2, 179, 196–97).

56. *Caimo* (*Chrysophyllum vulgare*); a tree bearing edible fruits.

57. In several Desana myths a field or a garden plot symbolizes a female element. The "conversation-people" (*verenigiri mahsá*, in Desana) are the members of those groups with which marriage is allowed.

CHAPTER 8

1. *Inga* sp.
2. *Genipa americana*.
3. The original text was dictated in Spanish.
4. For a collection of drawings of Tukano Indians see Koch-Grünberg 1905.
5. *Hevea pauciflora* var. *coriacea*.
6. In these definitions I have freely used Oster's (1970) work on phosphenes, and my debt to this author is gratefully acknowledged.
7. Quoted in Oster 1970, pp. 85, 87.
8. About one volt, with only a milliampere of current (Oster 1970, p. 85).
9. Ibid.
10. A shaman of the Noanamá Indians of the Pacific coast of Colombia, while curing a patient of a disease caused by the influence of evil jaguars, used a large red-yellow macaw feather as a "lampshade" for a candle, so that the patient was under a reddish glow (I owe this information to Professor José de Recasens).

CHAPTER 9

1. On the *curupira* see Friederici 1947, p. 230; Reichel-Dolmatoff 1971, pp. 86–88; Zerries 1954, passim.

2. The name *boráro* is derived from *boréri/*to be white, to shine, to glow.

3. Compare with the Páez Indian tale, Chap. 3.

4. See Reichel-Dolmatoff 1971, pp. 86–88.

5. Probably *Piscida Erythrina* L. See Friederici 1947, pp. 80–81.

6. The same is said of several female forest spirits in other parts of Colombia.

7. *Caimo (Chrysophyllum vulgare).*

8. The rubber tree (*Hevea pauciflora* var. *coriacea).*

9. Unexplained; see the spell against the evil jaguar, Chap. 6.

10. Unexplained.

11. Crabs are the *boráro's* favorite food.

12. A Tupi term for a fruit tree.

13. The term *fierce* is sometimes used to describe sexual excitation.

14. *Umarí (Poraqueiba paraensis)*, a fruit tree; *uamüë* (T), *mëë* (D).

15. See n. 8, above.

16. The symbolic equivalence of eating and sexual intercourse was mentioned by the informant when commenting on this story.

17. See n. 7, above.

18. *Mojarra* is the Spanish (Arabic) name of a fish (*Cichlidae).* It is said to have very slow movements, and a yellowish part of its head contains a substance which is compared to sperm.

19. Many small river fish are designated by the Spanish term *sardina*. A seminal character is attributed to some of them.

20. *Dormilón* is the Spanish name of another slow-moving fish.

21. The *muhí* palm is said to be similar to *Mauritia flexuosa*. In LG it is called *caraná*.

22. Reichel-Dolmatoff 1971, p. 113.

23. Near the spot where the spirits had appeared several *Cecropia* trees were standing. Their large leaves are almost white on the underside, and as there was a slight breeze it seems that some of the leaves moved and caught the moonlight.

CHAPTER 10

1. In the district of Garhwal, Uttar Pradesh (India), the species *Phromnia marginella* Oliv. is reportedly consumed for its narcotic properties (Brehm 1915, 2:157).

GLOSSARY

Anadenanthera
peregrina

A leguminous plant the seeds of which contain potent hallucinogenic substances. Aboriginal names: *cohoba, yopo, vilca.*

Banisteriopsis

A malpighiaceous genus several species of which contain hallucinogenic substances. In the vernacular: *yajé, capi, ayahuasca.*

Barbasco

A leguminous plant used as a fish poison. Probably *Lonchocarpus.*

Boráro

A forest spirit (Tukano). Also known under the Tupí name *Curupira.*

Boréka

A fish (*Leporinus copelandi* steind. ?), in Tukano; also name of the highest-ranking sib of the Desana Indians. In Lengua Geral, the fish is called *aracú.*

Capi

Also *caapi;* see *Banisteriopsis.*

Cashirí

A slightly fermented beer made of water-soaked cassava bread, or of maize or palm fruits; a gathering during which this beer is consumed.

Cassava

Large breadlike cakes of coarse manioc flour.

Coca

Erythroxylon coca; a shrub the toasted leaves of which are powdered and mixed with the ash of *Cecropia* leaves.

Dabucurí

A ceremonial gathering during which gifts, usually in the form of food, are distributed.

Datura

A tree genus comprising several species which contain highly toxic alkaloids.

Maloca

Large communal house occupied by several nuclear families.

Manioc

Manihot esculenta Crantz, the staple food of the Tukano

Indians and their neighbors. The tubers contain hydro-cyanic acid and must be processed before consumption.

Pamurí-mahsë The "germinator"; a mythical being who established mankind on earth.

Payé Shaman or curer.

Uahtí A small, generally harmless, bush spirit (Tukano).

Umarí A wild-growing fruit tree *(Poraqueiba paraensis)*.

Vahsú The rubber tree *(Hevea pauciflora var. coriacea)*.

Vaí-mahsë The supernatural Master of Game Animals.

Vëarí-mahsá The supernatural doubles of mankind, who live in the abodes of the Master of Game Animals.

Vihó The Tukano name of a hallucinogenic snuff prepared from the bark resin of several species of *Virola*.

Vihó-mahsë The supernatural Master of *vihó* snuff.

Virola A *Myristicacea* from the bark resin of which a hallucinogenic snuff is prepared.

Yajé Hallucinogenic jungle vine of the genus *Banisteriopsis*.

Yopo Narcotic snuff prepared, in most cases, from the dried seeds of *Anadenanthera peregrina*. Also yop, yopa, niopo, etc.

Yurupari Large flutes of twisted bark, played during a ceremony known under the same name.

BIBLIOGRAPHY

Ab'Sáber, Aziz Nacib
1967. Problemas geomorfológicos da Amazonia brasileira. *In:* Atas do Simposio sobre biota amazonica (Herman Lent, editor), 1:35–67, Rio de Janeiro.

Acosta, Joaquin
1848. Compendio histórico del descubrimiento y colonización de la Nueva Granada en el siglo décimo sexto. Paris.

Acosta Ortegon, Joaquin
1938. El Idioma Chibcha o Aborígen de Cundinamarca. Imprenta del Departamento, Bogotá.

Aguado, Pedro de
1956. Recopilación Historial. 4 vols. Biblioteca de la Presidencia de Colombia, Bogotá.

Agurell, S., B. Holmstedt, and J.-E. Lindgren
1968. Alkaloid Content of *Banisteriopsis Rusbyana. American Journal of Pharmacy,* 140, No. 5, 148–51, Philadelphia.

Agurell, S., B. Holmstedt, J.-E. Lindgren, and R. E. Schultes
1968. Identification of Two New ß-Carboline Alkaloids in South American Hallucinogenic Plants. *Biochemical Pharmacology,* 17:2487–88, Pergamon Press, Long Island City, N.Y.
1969. Alkaloids in Certain Species of *Virola* and Other South American Plants of Ethnopharmacological Interest. *Acta Chemica Scandinavica,* 23:903–16.

Albarracin, Leopolodo
1925. Contribución al estudio de los alkaloides del yagé. Bogotá.

Allen, Paul H.
1947. Indians of Southeastern Colombia. *Geographical Review,* 37, No. 4, 567–82, New York.

Altschul, Siri von Reis
1964. A Taxonomic Study of the Genus *Anadenanthera. Contributions of the Gray Herbarium,* Harvard University, No. 193, pp. 3–65, Cambridge, Mass.
1967. Vilca and Its Use. *In:* Ethnopharmacologic Search for Psychoactive Drugs (Daniel H. Efron, editor), pp. 307–14, Public Health Service Publ. No. 1645, Washington, D.C.

251

1972. The Genus *Anadenanthera* in Amerindian Cultures. Botanical Museum, Harvard University, Cambridge, Mass.

Ambrosetti, Juan B.
1896. La leyenda del Yaguareté-Abá (El Indio Tigre) y sus proyecciones entre los Guaraníes, Quichuas, ... *An. Soc. Cient. Argentina*, 41: 321–34, Buenos Aires.

Amorim, A. Brandão de
1926–28. Lendas en Nheengatú e em Portuguez. *Revista do Instituto Historico e Georgraphico Brasileiro*, No. 100, 154:9–475, Rio de Janeiro.

Anghiera, Petro Martire d' (Angleria, Pedro Martir de; Peter Martyr)
1912. De orbe novo decadas: The Eight Decades of Peter Martyr d'Anhera. Translated from the Latin with notes and introduction by Francis Augustus MacNutt. 2 vols. New York (First Decade published in 1511).
1944. Décadas del Nuevo Mundo. Editorial Bajel, Buenos Aires.

Anonymous
1865. Descripción de los pueblos de la provincia de Ancerma. *In:* Colección de documentos inéditos relativos al descubrimiento, conquista y colonización de las posesiones españolas en América y Oceanía (Luis Torres de Mendoza, editor), 3:389–413, Madrid.

Anonymous
1866. Varias noticias curiosas sobre la Provincia de Popayán. Ibid., 5:487–93.

Anonymous
1928. Vocabulario de la lengua que usan los Yndios de estas Misiones, Ceona. *In:* Catálogo de la Real Biblioteca, Tomo VI, Manuscritos, Lenguas de América, 1:307–79, Madrid.

Anonymous
1933. Pelo Rio Mar: Missões Salesianas do Amazonas. Rio de Janeiro.

Anonymous
1934. Investigaciones lingüísticas y etnográficas en la Misión del Caquetá. *Senderos,* Biblioteca Nacional, 1, No. 6, 315–21, Bogotá.

Anonymous
1951. Vaupés. *Naturaleza y Técnica*, 1, No. 1, 18–20, Editorial Argra, Bogotá.

Anonymous
1964. Misiones del Vaupés: 1914–64. Bogotá.

Antze, Gustav
1922. Die Brasiliensammlung Vollmer aus der ersten Hälfte des 19. Jahrhunderts. *Mitteilungen aus dem Museum für Völkerkunde in Hamburg*, No. 7; *Beiheft zum Jahrbuch der Hamburgischen Wissenschaftlichen Anstalt,* No. 38, Hamburg.

Aranha, Bento de Figueiredo Tenreiro
1906–7. Archivo do Amazonas, Vols. 1 and 2, Nos. 2–6, Manáos.

Arce, Pedro Guillén de
1634. *In:* Visitas de Boyacá, 1:450r–660r, Archivo Histórico Nacional, Bogotá.

Ayerbe, Julio Manuel
1944. Tradiciones indígenas de Tierradentro. *Revista de la Universidad del Cauca*, No. 5, pp. 227–28, Popayán.

Barbosa Rodriguez, João
1890. Poranduba amazonense. *Anais da Biblioteca Nacional do Rio de Janeiro,* Tomo 14 (1886–87), Rio de Janeiro.

Barret, P.
1932. Le Yagé. *Journal de la Société des Américanistes*, N.S., 24, No. 2, 309–10, Paris.

Barriga Villalba, A. M.
1925a. Un nuevo alkaloide. *Boletín de la Sociedad Colombiana de Ciencias Naturales*, 14, No. 79, 31–36, Bogotá.
1925b. Yajeine: A New Alkaloid. *Journ. Soc. Chem. Ind.*, pp. 205–7.
1927. El yagé: Bebida especial de los indios ribereños del Putumayo y el Amazonas. *Boletín del Laboratorio Samper-Martínez*, Special Issue No. 9 Bogotá.

Bates, Henry Walter
1863. The Naturalist on the River Amazons. London.

Becher, Hans
1960. Die Surára und Pakidái: Zwei Yanonámi-Stämme in Nordwest Brasilien. *Mitteilungen aus dem Museum für Völkerkunde in Hamburg*, No. 26, Hamburg.

Bedall, Barbara G. (editor)
1969. Wallace and Bates in the Tropics: An Introduction to the Theory of Natural Selection. Macmillan & Co., London.

Beringer, Kurt
1928. Ueber ein neues, auf das extra-pyramidal-motorische System wirkendes Alkaloid (Banisterin). *Der Nervenarzt*, No. 5.

Bernal Villa, Segundo
1953a. Aspectos de la cultura Páez: Mitología y cuentos de la parcialidad de Calderas, Tierradentro. *Revista Colombiana de Antropología*, 1:279–309, Bogotá.
1953b. La fiesta de San Juan de Calderas, Tierradentro. Ibid., 2:177–221.
1954a. Medicina y magia entre los Páez. Ibid., 2:219–64.
1954b. Economía de los Páez. Ibid., 3:291–367.
1956. Religious Life of the Páez Indians of Colombia. Master's thesis, Faculty of Political Science, Columbia University, New York.
1969. Guía Bibliográfica de Colombia de interés para el antropólogo. Universidad de los Andes, Bogotá.

Betania, Hermana Maria de
1964. Mitos, leyendas y costumbres de las Tribus Suramericanas. Editorial Coculsa, Madrid.

Beuchat, Henri, and Paul Rivet
1911. La famille Betoya ou Toucano. *Mémoires de la Société de Linguistique de Paris*, 17:117–36, 162–90, Paris.

Biocca, Ettore
1963. Contributo alla conoscenza dei problemi etno-biologici dell'Amazzonia I. Gli Indi dell'Alto Rio Negro. *Rivista di Antropologia*, Vol. 50, Rome.
1965. Viaggi tra gli Indi: Alto Rio Negro-Alto Orinoco. Appunti di un Biologo. 4 vols. Consiglio Nazionale delle Richerche, Rome.

Bischler, Helena, and P. Pinto.
1959. Pinturas y grabados rupestres en la Serranía de la Macarena. Lámpara, International Petroleum Company, 6, No. 3, 14–16, Bogotá.

Blohm, Henrik
1962. Poisonous Plants of Venezuela. Wissenschaftliche Verlagsgesellschaft M.B.H., Stuttgart.

Bödiger, Ute
1965. Die Religion der Tukano im nordwestlichen Amazonas. *Kölner Ethnologische Mitteilungen,* No. 3, Cologne.

Boje, Walter
1930*a.* Das Yurupari-Fest der Tuyuka-Indianer. *Der Erdball,* 4:387–90, Berlin.
1930*b.* Am Rio Tiquié. *Welt und Wissen,* 17, No. 3, 57–65.

Bolens, J.
1967. Mythe de Jurupari: Introduction à une analyse. *L'Homme,* 3, No. 1, 50–66, Paris.

Bourne, Edward Gaylord
1906. Columbus, Ramon Pane, and the Beginnings of American Anthropology. *Proceedings of the American Antiquarian Society,* N.S., 17:310–48, Worcester, Mass.

Brehm, Alfred
1915. Tierleben. Fourth edition.

Brinton, Daniel G.
1892. Further Notes on the Betoya Dialects; from Unpublished Sources. *Proceedings of the American Philosophical Society,* 30:27–278, Philadelphia.

Bristol, Melvin L.
1965. Sibundoy Ethnobotany. Ph.D. dissertation, Harvard University, Cambridge, Mass.
1966*a.* The Psychotropic *Banisteriopsis* among the Sibundoy of Colombia. *Botanical Museum Leaflets,* Harvard University, 21, No. 5, 113–40, Cambridge, Mass.
1966*b.* Notes on Species of Tree Daturas. Ibid., pp. 229–48.
1969. Tree Datura Drugs of the Colombian Sibundoy. Ibid., 22:165–27.

Brooks, Jerome E.
1937. Tobacco; Its History Illustrated by the Books, Manuscripts, and Engravings in the Library of George Arents, Jr., 1:1507–1615, Rosenbach Co., New York.

Brüzzi, Alves da Silva, Alcionilio
1955. Os ritos funebres entre as tribos do Uaupés (Amazonas). *Anthropos,* 50:593–601.
1961. Discoteca Etno-linguístico-musical das tribos dos Rios Uaupés, Içana e Cauáburi. São Paulo.
1962. A civilização indigena do Uaupés. São Paulo.
1966. Estructura da tribo Tukano. *Anthropos,* 61, No. 2, 191–203.

Builes, Miguel Angel
1957. Cuarenta días en el Vaupés (Del 14 de Oct. al 25 de Novbre de 1950). Second edition. Yarumal, Colombia.

Bürger, Otto
1900. Reisen eines Naturforschers im tropischen Südamerika. Leipzig.

Calella, Placido de
1935. Los Indios Sionas del Putumayo. *Boletín de Estudios Históricos,* Nos. 73–74, pp. 49–52, Pasto.
1936–37. Apuntes etnográficos sobre el curaca y el yagé en los indios sionas del Putumayo. *Revista de Misiones,* 12–13, Nos. 131–43, 180–86, 161–69, Bogotá.
1940–44. Apuntes sobre los Indios Siona del Putumayo. *Anthropos,* 35/36, 737–50.

1944a. Datos mitológicos de los Huitotos de La Chorrera. *Amazonia Colombiana Americanista*, 2, Nos. 4–8, 33–37, Pasto.
1944b. Breves notas mitológicas de los Huitotos de Santa Clara (Amazonas-Colombia). Ibid., pp. 38–40.

Canyes, Manuel
1939. El yajé y sus relaciones con la americanistica. *Actas del VI. Congreso Interamericano de Bibliografías y Bibliotecas*, 2:301–17, Washington, D.C.

Carvajal, Jose
1962. L'art rupèstre en Colombie. *Style*, 2:58–67, Lausanne.

Carvalho, José Candido M.
1952. Notas de Viagem ao Rio Negro. *Publicações avulsas do Museu Nacional*, No. 9, Rio de Janeiro.

Casas, Bartolomé de las
1909. Apologética historia de las Indias. Historiadores de Indias, Vol. 1 (Serrano y Sanz, editor), Madrid.

Castellanos, Juan de
1847. Elegías de varones ilustres de Indias. Madrid.
1886. Historia del Nuevo Reino de Granada. 2 vol. (Antonio Paz y Mélida, editor), Madrid.

Castellví, Marcelino de (editor)
1944. Supersticiones de la mitad meridional de Colombia. *Amazonia Colombiana Americanista*, 2, Nos. 4–8, 94–119, Pasto.

Castillo, Gabriel del
1963. La ayahuasca, planta mágica de la Amazonia. *Perú Indígena*, 10:88–98, Lima.

Chaffanjon, J.
1889. L'Orénoque et le Caura: Relation de voyages exécutées en 1886 et 1887. Paris.

Chagnon, Napoleon A., Philip Le Quesne, and James M. Cook
1971. Yanomamö Hallucinogens: Anthropological, Botanical, and Chemical Findings. *Current Anthropology*, 12, No. 1, 72–73, Glasgow.

Chantre y Herrera, Jose
1637–1767 Historia de las Misiones de la Compañía de Jesús en el Marañón español. Madrid.

Chaves Mendoza, Alvaro
s.a. Reseña etnográfica de los Cobarías. Casa Colonial, Pub. No. 3, Pamplona.

Chen, A. L., and K. K. Chen
1939. Harmine: The Alkaloid of Caapi. *Quarterly Journal of Pharmacy and Pharmacology*, 12:30–38.

Civrieux, Marc de, and René Lichy
1950. Vocabularios de cuatro dialectos arawak del Río Guainía. *Boletín de la Sociedad Venezolana de Ciencias Naturales*, 8, No. 77, 121–59, Caracas.

Claes, F.
1931. Quelques renseignements sur les coutumes des Huitotos et des Coreguajes de Colombie. *Bulletin de la Société des Américanistes de Belgique*, 6:22–39, Brussels.

Clinquart, Edouard
1926. Contribution à l'étude de la liane Yagé et de son alcaloïde. *Journal de Pharmacie*, 36:671, Brussels.

Codazzi, Agustín
  1841. Resúmen de la geografía de Venezuela. Paris.
Coe, Michael D.
  1962. Mexico: Ancient Peoples and Places. Thames & Hudson, London.
  1970. Olmec Jaguars and Olmec Kings. Paper presented at the Dumbarton
     Oaks Conference on the Cult of the Feline, Washington, D.C.
Colini, G. A.
  1884. Cronica del Museo Preistorico-Etnografico. *Bollettino della Società
     geografica Italiana*, Ser. 2, Vol. 21, Rome.
Colon, Fernando (Columbus, Ferdinand)
  1811. History of the Discovery of America, by Christopher Columbus;
     Written by His Son Don Ferdinand Columbus. *In:* A General His-
     tory and Collection of Voyages and Travels, 3:242 (Robert Kerr,
     editor), Edinburgh.
  1944. Historia Del Almirante De Las Indias Don Cristóbal Colón. Co-
     lección de Fuentes para la Historia de América, Editorial Bajel,
     Buenos Aires.
Condamine, Charles Marie de la
  1745. Relation abrégée d'un voyage fait dans l'interieur de l'Amérique
     Méridionale. Paris (first English edition, London, 1747).
Cooper, John M.
  1949. Stimulants and Narcotics. *Handbook of South American Indians*,
     5:525–58, Washington, D.C.
Coppens, Walter, and Jorge Cato-David
  1971. El yopo entre los Cuiva-Guajibo: Aspectos etnográficos y farmaco-
     lógicos. *Antropologica*, 28:3–24, Fundación La Salle de Ciencias
     Naturales, Caracas.
Corothie, E., and T. Nakano
  1969. Constituents of the Bark of *Virola sebifera*. *Planta Medica*, 2:184–88.
Costa, Oswaldo de Al., and Luis Faria
  1936. La planta que faz sonhar. *Revista da flora medicinal*, Vol. 2, No. 10,
     Rio de Janeiro.
Coudreau, Henri A.
  1887. Voyage à travers les Guyanes et l'Amazonie. La France èquinoxiale.
     2 vols. Paris.
Covarrubias, Miguel
  1954. Mexico South. New York.
Crévaux, Jules
  1883. Voyages dans l'Amérique du Sud. Paris.
Cuatrecasas, Jose
  1957–58. Prima flora colombiana: 2. Malpighiaceae. *Webbia*, 13:343–64,
     Florence.
Der Marderosian, Ara H., Homer V. Pinkley, and Murrell F. Dobins IV
  1968. Native Use and Occurrence of N, N-Dimethyltryptamine in the
     leaves of *Banisteriopsis Rusbyana*. *American Journal of Pharmacy*,
     140, No. 5, 137–47, Philadelphia.
Deulofeu, Venancio
  1967. Chemical Compounds Isolated from Banisteriopsis and Related Spe-
     cies. *In:* Ethnopharmacologic Search for Psychoactive Drugs (Daniel
     H. Efron, editor), pp. 393–402, Public Health Service Publ. No.
     1645, Washington, D.C.
Díaz Escobar, Joaquin
  1879. Bosquejo estadístico de la Región Oriental de Colombia y medios

económicos para su conquista, sometimiento y desarrollo industrial y político. Second edition, Imprenta de Zalamea, Bogotá.

Dobkin de Rios, Marlene

1970a. Banisteriopsis Used in Witchcraft and Healing Activities in Iquitos, Peru. *Economic Botany*, 24, No. 35, 296:300, New York.

1970b. A Note on the Use of Ayahuasca among Urban Mestizo Populations in the Peruvian Amazon. *American Anthropologist*, 72, No. 6, 1419–21.

1971. Curanderismo con la soga alucinógena (ayahuasca) en la selva peruana. *América Indígena*, 31, No. 3, 575–91, Mexico.

Ducke, Adolpho

1957. Capí, caapi, cabí, cayahuasca e yagé. *Revista Brasileira da Farmacologia*, 38, No. 12, 283–84, Rio de Janeiro.

Elger, F.

1928. Ueber das Vorkommen von Harmin in einer südamerikanischen Liane (Yagé). *Helv. Chim. Acta*, 11:162–66.

Eliade, Mircea

1971. Spirit, Light, and Seed. *History of Religions*, 2, No. 1, 1–30, Chicago.

Ernst, A.

1889. On the Etymology of the Word Tobacco. *American Anthropologist*, 2:133–42, Washington, D.C.

Farnsworth, Norman R.

1968. Hallucinogenic Plants. *Science*, 162:1086–92, Washington, D.C.,

Fish, M. S., and E. C. Horning

1956. Studies on Hallucinogenic Snuffs. *Journal Nerv. and Ment. Dis.*, 124:33–37.

Fish, M. S., N. M. Johnson, and E. C. Horning

1955. Piptadenia Alkaloids. Indole bases of *P. peregrina* (L.) Benth. and Related Species. *Journ. Am. Chem. Soc.*, 77:5892–95.

Fischer Cárdenas, G.

1923. Estudio sobre el principio activo del yagé. Ph.D. dissertation, Universidad Nacional, Bogotá.

Flury, Lazaro

1958. El Caá-pi y el Hataj, dos poderosos ilusionógenos indígenas. *América Indígena*, Vol. 18, Mexico.

Freitas, Newton (editor)

1943. Amazonia: Leyendas Ñangatú. *Colección Mar Dulce*, Editorial Nova, Buenos Aires.

Friedberg, Claudine

1959. Rapport sommaire sur une mission au Pérou. *Journal d'Agriculture Tropicale et de Botanique Appliquée*, Vol. 6, Paris.

1965. Des Banisteriopsis utilisés comme drogue en Amérique du Sud. Essay d'étude critique. *Journal d'Agriculture Tropicale et de Botanique Appliquée*, Vol. 12, Nos. 9–12, Paris.

Friede, Juan

1948. Algunos apuntes sobre los Karijona-Huaque del Caquetá. *Actes du XXVIIIe Congrès International des Américanistes, Paris, 1947*, pp. 255–63, Paris.

Friederici, Georg

1925. (Review) Sven Lovén: Ueber die Wurzeln der Tainischen Kultur. *Göttingischer Gelehrte Anzeigen*, 187:32–43, Berlin.

1947. Amerikanistisches Wörterbuch. *Abhandlungen aus dem Gebiet der Auslandskunde*, Vol. 53, Universität Hamburg, Hamburg.

Fulop, Marcos
  1954. Aspectos de la Cultura Tukana: Cosmogonía. *Revista Colombiana de Antropología*, 3:99–137, Bogotá.
  1955. Notas sobre los términos y el sistema de parentesco de los Tukano. Ibid., 4:123–64.
  1956. Aspectos de la Cultura Tukana: Mitología. Ibid., 5:337–73.
Furst, Peter T.
  1968. The Olmec Were-Jaguar Motif in the Light of Ethnographic Reality. *In:* Dumbarton Oaks Conference on the Olmec (Elizabeth P. Benson, editor), pp. 143–78, Washington, D.C.
Furst, Peter T. (editor)
  1972. Flesh of the Gods: The Ritual Use of Hallucinogens. Praeger Publishers, New York and Washington, D.C.
Gallo M., Carlos I.
  1972. Diccionario Tucano-Castellano. Medellín.
Galvão, Eduardo
  1955. Mudança cultural na região do Rio Negro. *Anais do XXXI Congreso Internacional de Americanistas, Sao Paulo, 1954*, 1:313–19, São Paulo.
  1959. Aculturação Indigena no Rio Negro. *Boletim do Museu Emilio Goeldi de Historia Natural e Ethnographia*, No. 7, Belém do Pará.
Gansser, A.
  1954a. The Guiana Shield. *Ecl. geol. Helv.*, 47, No. 1, 77–112.
  1954b. Altindianische Felszeichnungen aus den kolumbianischen Llanos. *Geografica Helvetica*, No. 2.
Garcia, Rodolpho
  1929. Nomes de aves em lingua Tupi. *Boletim do Museu Nacional*, 5, No. 3, 1–54, Rio de Janeiro.
García Barriga, Hernando
  1958. El yajé, caapi o ayahuasca: Un alucinógeno amazónico. *Revista Universidad Nacional de Colombia*, No. 23, pp. 59–76, Bogotá.
Gheerbrandt, Alain
  1952. L'expedition Orénoque-Amazone 1948–1950. Gallimard, Paris.
Ghisletti, Louis V.
  1955. Existen cuatro cielos y un sólo Dios. *Semana*, No. 436, pp. 30–32, Bogotá.
Giacone, Antonio
  1939. Pequeña gramática e dicionário de lingua Tucana. Manáos.
  1949. Os Tucanos e outras tribos do Rio Uaupés, afluente do Negro-Amazonas. São Paulo.
  1955. Pequeña gramática e dicionário Portuguez Ubde-Nehern out Macu. Recife.
  1965. Gramática, dicionário e fraseologia da lingua Dahceie ou Tucano. Belém do Pará.
Goldman, Irving
  1940. Cosmological Beliefs of the Cubeo Indians. *Journal of American Folklore*, 53:242–47, New York.
  1948. Tribes of the Uaupés-Caquetá Region. *Handbook of South American Indians*, 3:763–98, Washington, D.C.
  1963. The Cubeo: Indians of the Northwest Amazon. *Illinois Studies in Anthropology*, No. 2, Urbana.
  1964. The Structure of Ritual in the Northwest Amazon. *In:* Process and

Pattern in Culture: Essays in Honor of Julian H. Steward (Robert A. Manners, editor), pp. 111–22, Chicago.

Granier-Doyeux, Marcel
1948a. Acerca de una toxicomanía indígena: El uso de la *Piptadenia peregrina. Gaceta Médica*, 56:13–18, Caracas.
1948b. El uso popular de la planta niopo o yopo. *Boletín de la Oficina Sanitaria Panamericana*, 27:156–58, Washington, D.C.
1956. Una toxicomanía indígena: El uso de la *Piptadenia peregrina* (ñopo y yopo). *Revista de Técnica Policial*, Vol. 2, No. 8, Caracas.
1965. Native hallucinogenic drugs: *Piptadenias. Bulletin of Narcotics*, 17:29–38.

Groot, Jose Manuel
1869. Historia Eclesiástica y Civil de Nueva Granada. 3 vols. Bogotá.

Gumilla, Joseph
1955. El Orinoco Ilustrado: Historia Natural, Civil y Geográfica de este Gran Río. Bogotá (first edition, Barcelona, 1791).

Gunn, J. A.
1937. The Harmine Group of Alkaloids. *In:* Handbuch der Experimentellen Pharmakologie (B. Hefter, editor), Berlin.

Hammerman, A. F.
1930. Le yagé en Amazonie. *Rev. Bot. Appl. Agric. Colon.*, 10:600.

Hanke, Wanda
1964. Völkerkundliche Forschungen in Südamerika. *Kulturgeschichtliche Forschungen*, Vol. 11, Braunschweig.

Harner, Michael
1968. The Sound of Rushing Water. *Natural History*, Vol. 72, No. 6, New York.

Hartmann, G.
1970. Masken östlicher Tukano-Stämme (NW-Amazonien) im Lindenmuseum. *Tribus*, No. 19, p. 119, Stuttgart.

Hernández de Alba, Gregorio
1944. Etnología de los Andes del Sur de Colombia. *Revista de la Universidad del Cauca*, No. 5, pp. 141–226, Popayán.
1946. The Highland Tribes of Southern Colombia. *Handbook of South American Indians*, 2:915–60, Washington, D.C.

Hochstein, F. A., and A. M. Paradies
1957. Alkaloids of *Banisteria caapi* and *Prestonia amazonicum. Journal of the American Chemical Society*, 79:5735–36.

Hoeffer, A., and H. Osmond.
1967. The Hallucinogens. Academic Press, New York.

Holmstedt, Bo
1965. Tryptamine Derivatives in Epena: An Intoxicating Snuff Used by Some South American Indian Tribes. *Archives Internationales de Pharmacodynamie et de Thérapie*, 156, No. 2, 285–305.

Holmstedt, Bo, and Jan-Erik Lindgren
1967. Chemical Constituents and Pharmacology of South American Snuffs. *In:* Ethnopharmacologic Search for Psychoactive Drugs (Daniel H. Efron, editor), pp. 339–73, Health Service Publ. No. 1645, Washington, D.C.

Holmstedt, Bo, et al.
1967. Discussion on the Psychoactive Action of Various Tryptamine Derivatives. Ibid., pp. 374–82.

Horning   *See* Holmstedt and Lindgren (1967), p. 369.
Humboldt, Alexandre von
   1822. Voyage aux régions équinoxiales du Nouveau Continent. Paris.
Igualada, F. de, and Marcelino de Castellví
   1940. Clasificación y estadística de las lenguas habladas en el Putumayo,
           Caquetá y Amazonas. *Amazonia Colombiana Americanista*, 1, Nos.
           2–3, 92–101, Sibundoy.
Ihering, Rodolpho von
   1968. Dicionário dos animais do Brasil. Editóra Universidade de Brasilia,
           Brasilia.
Ipiranga Monteiro, Mario
   1960. Pubertätsritus der Tucano-Indianer. *Zeitschrift für Ethnologie*,
           85:37–39, Braunschweig.
Jung, C. G.
   1947. Psychology of the Unconscious: A Study of the Transformations and
           Symbolisms of the Libido. Dodd, Mead & Co., New York.
Karsten, Rafael
   1920. Berauschende und narkotische Getränke unter den Indianern Süd-
           amerikas. Beitrag zur Sittengeschichte der südamerikanischen
           Indianer. *Acta Academiae Aboensis Humaniora*, 1, No. 4, 28–72.
Keller, O., and Franz Gottauf
   1929. Ueber einige im Heimatlande benutzte bolivianische Drogen. *Arch.
           Pharmaz.*, 267:373.
Kensinger, Kenneth M.
   1968. The Cashinahua and *Banisteriopsis*. Paper read at the 67th Annual
           Meeting of the American Anthropological Association, Seattle
           (mimeographed).
Keses, M., Pedro Alberto
   1956. El clima de la región del Río Negro venezolano (Territorio Federal
           Amazonas). *Memoria de la Sociedad de Ciencias Naturales La Salle*,
           16, No. 45, 268–312, Caracas.
Koch-Grünberg, Theodor
   1905. Anfänge der Kunst im Urwald. Berlin.
   1906a. Die Indianerstämme am oberen Rio Negro und Yapurá und ihre
           sprachliche Zugehörigkeit. *Zeitschrift für Ethnologie*, 1–2:167–205.
   1906b. Die Makú. *Anthropos*, 1:877–906.
   1906–11. Indianertypen aus dem Amazonasgebiet nach eigenen Aufnahmen
           während seiner Reise in Brasilien. Ernst Wasmuth, Berlin.
   1907. Südamerikanische Felszeichnungen. Ernst Wasmuth, Berlin.
   1908a. Einige Bemerkungen zu der Forschungsreise des Dr. H. Rice in den
           Gebieten zwischen Guaviare und Caquetá-Yapurá. *Globus*, 93, No.
           19, 302–5, Braunschweig.
   1908b. Die Hianákoto-Umáua. *Anthropos*, 3:83–124, 297–335, 952–82.
   1909. Das Haus bei den Indianern Nordwestbrasiliens. *Archiv für An-
           thropologie, Neue Folge*, 7:37–50, Braunschweig.
   1909–10 Zwei Jahre unter den Indianern. Reisen in Nordwest-Brasilien
           1903/1905. 2 vols. Ernst Wasmuth, Berlin.
   1911. Aruak-Sprachen Nordwestbrasiliens und der angrenzenden Gebiete.
           Mitteilungen der Anthropologischen Gesellschaft in Wien, 41:1–
           200, Vienna.
   1913. Ergebnisse meiner letzten Reise durch Nord-Brasilien zum Orinoko,
           1911–1913. *Korrespondenzblatt der Deutschen Gesellschaft für An-*

thropologie, Ethnologie und Urgeschichte, 64, Nos. 8–12, pp. 77–81, Braunschweig.

1913–16. Die Betoya-Sprachen Nordwest Brasiliens und der angrenzenden Gebiete. *Anthropos,* 8:151–95, 569–89, 812–32; 10–11:114–58, 421–49.

1917–28. Vom Roroima zum Orinoco: Ergebnisse einer Reise in Nordbrasilien und Venezuela in den Jahren 1911–1913. 5 vols. Berlin.

1922. Die Völkergruppierung zwischen Rio Branco, Orinoco, Rio Negro und Yapurá. *In:* Festschrift Eduard Seler (Walter Lehmann, editor), pp. 205–66, Stuttgart.

Kok, P.
1921–22 Ensayo de Gramática Dagseje o Tokano. *Anthropos,* 16–17:838–65.
1925–26 Quelques notices ethnographiques sur les indiens du Rio Papurí. *Anthropos,* 20:624–37; 21:921–37.

Kreitmair, H.
1928. Ueber Harmin (Banisterin). *Merck's Jahresbericht.*

Kuhne, Heinz
1955. Der Jaguar im Zwillingsmythus der Chiriguano und dessen Beziehung zu anderen Stämmen der Neuen Welt. *Archiv für Völkerkunde,* 10:16–135.

Kunike, H.
1915. Jaguar und Mond in der Mythologie des andinen Hochlandes. Leipzig.

Kusel, H.
1965. Ayahuasca Drinkers among the Chama Indians of Northeast Peru. *Psychedelic Review,* 6:58–66.

La Barre, Weston
1964. The Narcotic Complex of the New World. *Diogenes,* pp. 125–38.
1970. Old and New World Narcotics: A Statistical Question and an Ethnological Reply. *Economic Botany,* 20, No. 1, pp. 73–80, New York.
1972. Hallucinogens and the Shamanic Origins of Religions. *In:* The Flesh of the Gods: The Ritual Use of Hallucinogens (Peter T. Furst, editor), pp. 261–78, Praeger Publishers, New York and Washington, D.C.

Langegg, F. A. von
1888. El Dorado: Geschichte der Entdeckungsreisen nach dem Goldlande El Dorado. Leipzig.

Leete, E.
1959. The Alkaloids of *Datura. In:* The Genus Datura (A. G. Avery, S. Satina, and J. Rietsma, editors), pp. 48–56, Ronald Press, New York.

Lehmann, Walter
1920. Zentral-Amerika. 2 vols. Berlin.

Lent, Herman (editor)
1967. Atas do Simpósio sobre a Biota Amazonica, Belém do Pará, Junho 6–11, 1966. 5 vols. Conselho Nacional de Pesquisas, Rio de Janeiro.

Les Corts, Estanislao
1926. Un caso en que los tomadores jayrunas (Fam. lingüística huitoto) pretenden ver a distancia. *In:* Informes de las Misiones Católicas de Colombia relativos a los años 1925 y 1926, p. 105, Bogotá.

Lévi-Strauss, Claude
1964. Le cru et le cuit. Paris.
1966. Du miel aux cendres. Paris.

Lewin, Luis
  1928. Untersuchungen über Banisteria Caapi Spr. *Archiv für Experimentelle Pathologie und Pharmakologie.*
  1964. Phantastica: Narcotic and Stimulating Drugs. Routledge & Kegan Paul, London.
Lovén, Sven
  1935. The Origins of the Tainan Culture, West Indies. Göteborg.
Lowie, Robert H.
  1946. The "Tapuya." *Handbook of South American Indians,* 1:553–56, Washington, D.C.
  1948. The Tropical Forests: An Introduction. Ibid., 3:1–56.
Lucena Samoral, Manuel
  1971. Observación participante de una toma de yagé entre los Kofán. *Universitas Humanistica,* 1:11–21, Pontificia Universidad Javeriana, Bogotá.
Lunardi, Federico
  1933–34. Tradiciones Páez. *Boletín Histórico del Valle,* 1:241–84, 553–56; 2:49–191, Cali.
Maccreagh, Gordon
  1926. White Waters and Black. Century Co., New York and London.
Mallol de Recasens, María Rosa
  1963. Cuatro representaciones de las imágenes alucinatorias originadas por la toma de yajé. *Revista Colombiana de Folklore,* 8:61–81, Bogotá.
Mallol de Recasens, María Rosa, and José de Recasens T.
  1964–65 Contribución al conocimiento del Cacique-Curaca entre los Siona. *Revista Colombiana de Antropología,* 13:93–145, Bogotá.
Markham, Clements R. (editor)
  1864. The Travels of Pedro Cieza de León. *The Hakluyt Society,* First Ser., No. 33, Burt Franklin, New York.
Martius, Carl F. P. von
  1858. Nomina plantarum in lingua tupi. *Bulletin der Königlich Bayerischen Academie der Wissenschaften,* pp. 1–6, Munich.
  1863–67. Beiträge zur Ethnographie und Sprachenkunde Amerika's, zumal Brasiliens. 2 vols. 1: Zur Ethnographie, Leipzig, 1867; 2: Zur Sprachenkunde, Erlangen, 1863.
Mártir, *see* Anghiera.
Mason, J. Alden
  1931. Archaeology of Santa Marta, Colombia. The Tairona Culture. Pt. 1: Report on Field Work. Field Museum of Natural History, Publ. 304, *Anthropological Series,* Vol. 20, No. 1, Chicago.
  1936. Archaeology of Santa Marta, Colombia. The Tairona Culture. Pt. 2, Sec. 1: Objects of Stone, Bone, and Metal. Field Museum of Natural History, Publ. 358, *Anthropological Series,* Vol. 20, No. 2, Chicago.
  1939. Archaeology of Santa Marta, Colombia. The Tairona Culture. Pt. 2, Sec. 2: Objects of Pottery. Field Museum of Natural History, Publ. 446, *Anthropological Series,* Vol. 20, No. 3, Chicago.
Mead, C. W.
  1907. A Collection from the Tukáno Indians of South America. *American Museum Journal,* 7, No. 7, 108–9, New York.
Metraux, Alfred
  1949. Religion and Shamanism. *Handbook of South American Indians,* 5:559–99, Washington, D.C.

1967. Religions et magies indiennes d'Amérique du Sud. Gallimard, Paris.
Meyer de Schauensee, R.
1964. The Birds of Colombia and Adjacent Areas of South and Central America. Livingston Publishing Co., Narberth, Pa.
Michaux, Henri
1967. Connaissance par les gouffres. Gallimard, Paris.
Michiels, M., and E. Clinquart
1926. Sur les réactions chimiques d'identification de la yagéine. *Bull. Acad. Roy. Méd. Belg.*, N.S. pp. 5, 6, 19, Brussels.
Misiones del Vaupés
1966. 1914–1964: Los misioneros del Vaupés a sus amigos y colaboradores. Medellín.
Mochi, Aldobrandino
1902–03. I popoli dell'Uaupés e la famiglia etnica Miranha. *Archivo per l'Antropologia e la Etnologia*, Nos. 32/33, Florence.
Mors, Walter B., and Perola Zaltzman
1954. Sobre o alkaloide de *Banisteria Caapi* Spruce e do *Cabi paraensis* Ducke. *Bol. Inst. Quim. Agric.*, No. 34, p. 17.
Morton, C. V.
1931. Notes on *Yagé*, a Drug-Plant of Southeastern Colombia. *Journal of the Washington Academy of Sciences*, 21:485–88, Washington, D.C.
Moser, Brian, and Donald Tayler
1963. Tribes of the Pira-paraná. *Geographical Journal*, 129:437–49, London.
1965. The Cocaine Eaters. London.
Muñoz, G.
1925. Datos informativos sobre el vegetal llamado Yagé. *Boletín Estadístico del Valle de Cauca* (February), Cali.
Nachtigall, Horst
1955a. Tierradentro: Archäologie und Ethnographie einer kolumbianischen Landschaft. *Mainzer Studien zur Kultur-und Völkerkunde*, Vol. 2, Zürich.
1955b. Schamanismus bei den Páez Indianern. *Zeitschrift für Ethnologie*, 78, No. 2, 210–23, Braunschweig.
Naranjo, Claudio
1965. Psychological Aspects of the Yagé Experience in an Experimental Setting. Paper presented at the 64th Annual Meeting of the American Anthropological Association, Denver (mimeographed).
1967. Psychotropic Properties of the Harmala Alkaloids. *In:* Ethnopharmacologic Search for Psychoactive Drugs (Daniel H. Efron, editor), pp. 385–91, Public Health Service Publ. No. 1645, Washington, D.C.
Naranjo, Plutarco
1969. Etnofarmacología de las plantas psicotrópicas de América. *Terapia, Revista de Información Médica, Laboratorios "Life,"* 24, No. 1, 5–62, Quito.
1970a. Plantas psicotrópicas de América y bioquímica de la mente. *Anales del V. Congreso Latinoamericano de Psiquiatría—VIII. Congreso Colombiano de Psiquiatría*, pp. 162–74, Bogotá.
1970b. Ayahuasca: Religión y Medicina. Editorial Universitaria, Quito.
Navarrete, Martin Fernandez de (editor)
1825–37. Colección de los Viages de Descubrimientos, que hicieron por

mar los Españoles desde fines del siglo XV. 5 vols. Vol. 1: Viages de Colón: Almirantazgo de Castilla, Madrid.

Neira, Alonso de, and Juan Ribero
1928. Arte y vocabulario de la Lengua Achagua. *In:* Catálogo de la Real Biblioteca, Tomo VI, Manuscritos, Lenguas de América, 1:1–174, Madrid.

Niedenzu, F.
1928. Ueber die Stammpflanzen des Yageins. *Pharmaz. Zeit.,* 73:141.

Nimuendajú, Curt
1950. Reconhecimento dos Rios Içana, Ayari e Uaupés. *Journal de la Société des Américanistes,* N.S., 39:126–82, Paris.

Nuñez A., Lautaro
1963. Problemas en torno a la tableta rapé. *Anales de la Universidad del Norte,* 2:148–68, Antofagasta.

Nuñez Olarte, Enrique
1970. Aspectos farmacológicos del "Yagé," planta alucinógena colombiana. *Anales del V. Congreso Latinoamericano de Psiquiatría—VIII. Congreso Colombiano de Psiquiatría,* pp. 606–7, Bogotá.

O'Connell, F. D., and E. V. Lynn
1953. The alkaloid of *Banisteriopsis inebrians* Morton. *Journal of the American Pharmaceutical Association,* 42:753.

O'Leary, Timothy J. (editor)
1963. Ethnographic Bibliography of South America. *Behavioral Science Bibliographies,* Human Relations Area Files, New Haven, Conn.

Orton, James M. A.
1870. The Andes and the Amazon; or, Across the Continent of South America. New York.

Oster, Gerald
1970. Phosphenes. *Scientific American,* 222, No. 2, 83–87, New York.

Otero, Jesus M.
1952. Etnología Caucana. Editorial Universidad, Popayán.

Oviedo y Valdés, Gonzalo Fernandez de
1851–55. Historia general y natural de las Indias, islas y tierra firme de la mar océano . . . 4 vols. (José Amador de los Ríos, editor). Madrid.

Pane, Roman
1944. Escritura de fray Román del Orden de San Jerónimo. De la antigüedad de los indios, la cual, como sujeto que sabe su lengua, recogió con diligencia, de orden del Almirante. *In:* Fernando Colón, Historia del Almirante De Las Indias Don Cristóbal Colón. Colección de fuentes para la Historia de América, pp. 163–85, Editorial Bajel, Buenos Aires.

Pardal, Ramón
1937. Medicina aborígen americana. Humanior, Sec. C, Vol. 3, Buenos Aires.

Perez Arbeláez, Enrique
1956. Plantas útiles de Colombia. Third edition. Bogotá.

Pérez de Barradas, José
1950. Drogas ilusionogénicas de los indios americanos. *Antropología y Etnología,* 3:9–107, Madrid.
1957. Plantas mágicas americanas. Consejo Superior de Investigaciones Científicas, Instituto "Bernardino de Sahagún," Madrid.

Pérez, Felipe
  1862–63. Geografía física i política de los Estados Unidos de Colombia. 2 vols. Bogotá.
Perrot, E., and R. Hamet
  1927a. Le yagé, plante sensorielle des indiens de la région amazonienne de l'Equateur et de la Colombie. Compte Rendu de l'Académie des Sciences, 184:1266, Paris.
  1927b. Yagé, Ayahuasca, Caapi et leur alcaloïde, telepatheine ou yaqueine. Bulletin des Sciences Pharmacologiques, 34:337–47, 417–26, 500–14, Paris.
Pfaff, Franz
  1910. Die Tucanos am oberen Amazonas. Verhandlungen der Berliner Gesellschaft für Anthropologie, Ethnologie und Urgeschichte, Berlin, 1910, Jahrgang 1890. In: Zeitschrift für Ethnologie, 22:596–606.
Piedrahita, Lucas Fernandez
  1881. Historia general de las Conquistas del Nuevo Reino de Granada. Bogotá (first edition, Amberes, 1688).
Pinel, Gaspar de
  1925. Excursión apostólica por los ríos Putumayo, San Miguel de Sucumbios, Cuyabeno, Caquetá y Caguan. Bogotá.
Pinkley, H. V.
  1969. Plant Admixtures to Ayahuasca, the South American Hallucinogenic Drink. Lloydia, 32:305–14.
Prance, Ghillean
  1970. Notes on the Use of Plant Hallucinogens in Amazonian Brazil. Economic Botany, 24:62–68, New York.
Prance, Ghillean, and Anne E. Prance
  1970. Hallucinations in Amazonia. Garden Journal, 20:102–7.
Preuss, Konrad Theodor
  1921. Religion und Mythologie der Uitoto. Göttingen/Leipzig.
  1926. Forschungsreise zu den Kágaba. Beobachtungen, Textaufnahmen und sprachliche Studien bei einem Indianerstamm in Kolumbien, Südamerika. Anthropos Verlag, St. Gabriel-Mödling.
Rank, Otto
  1919. Der Doppelgänger. In: Psychoanalytische Beiträge zur Mythenforschung: Gesammelte Studien aus den Jahren 1912 bis 1914, pp. 267–354, Internationale Psychoanalytische Bibliothek, No. 4, Leipzig/Vienna.
Reichel-Dolmatoff, Gerardo
  1944. La cultura material de los Indios Guahibo. Revista del Instituto Etnológico Nacional, 1, No. 1, 437–506, Bogotá.
  1945. Mitos y cuentos de los Indios Chimila. Boletín de Arqueología, 1, No. 1, 4–30, Bogotá.
  1950–51. Los Kogi: Una tribu indígena de la Sierra Nevada de Santa Marta, Colombia. 2 vols. Bogotá.
  1960. Notas etnográficas sobre los Indios del Chocó. Revista Colombiana de Antropología, vol. XI, pp. 75–158, Bogotá.
  1963. Apuntes etnográficos sobre los indios del alto río Sinú. Revista de la Academia Colombiana de Ciencias Exactas, Físicas y Naturales, 12, No. 45, 29–40, Bogotá.
  1967a. A Brief Field Report on Urgent Ethnological Research in the Vaupés

Area, Colombia, South America. *Bulletin of the International Committee on Urgent Anthropological and Ethnological Research,* No. 9, pp. 53–61, Vienna.

1967b. Rock-Paintings of the Vaupés: An Essay of Interpretation. *Folklore Americas,* 26, No. 2, 107–13, Los Angeles.

1969. El contexto cultural de un alucinógeno aborígen. *Revista de la Academia Colombiana de Ciencias Exactas, Físicas y Naturales,* 13, No. 51, 327–45, Bogotá.

1971. Amazonian Cosmos: The Sexual and Religious Symbolism of the Tukano Indians. University of Chicago Press, Chicago.

1972a. San Agustín: A Culture of Colombia. Praeger Publishers, New York and Washington, D.C.

1972b. The Cultural Context of an Aboriginal Hallucinogen: *Banisteriopsis Caapi. In:* Flesh of the Gods: The Ritual Use of Hallucinogens (Peter T. Furst, editor), pp. 84–113, Praeger Publishers, New York and Washington, D.C.

Reichel-Dolmatoff, Gerardo and Alicia Reichel-Dolmatoff
1961. The People of Aritama: The Cultural Personality of a Colombian Mestizo Village. University of Chicago Press, Chicago.

Reinburg, P.
1921. Contribution à l'étude des boissons toxiques des indiens du Nord-ouest de l'Amazone: l'ayahuasca, le yajé, le huanto. *Journal de la Société des Américanistes,* N.S., 13:25–54, 197–216, Paris.

Reko, Viktor A.
1949. Magische Gifte: Rausch-und Betäubungsmittel der Neuen Welt. Third edition. Ferdinand Enke Verlag, Stuttgart.

Reutter, K.
1927. Du yagé ou aya-huasca. *Schweiz. Apotheker Zeit.* 25:289.

Rice, Alexander Hamilton
1910. The River Uaupés. *Geographical Journal,* 35:682–700, London.
1914. South America: The N.W. Amazon Basin from Surveys 1907–1908 and 1912–1913. Ibid., Vol. 44.

Ríos, O.
1962. Aspectos preliminares al estudio farmacopsiquiátrico del ayahuasca y su principio activo. *Anales de la Facultad de Medicina,* 45, Nos. 1–2, 22–66, Universidad Nacional Mayor de San Marcos, Lima.

Rivero, Juan de
1883. Historia de las Misiones de los Llanos de Casanare y los Ríos Orinoco y Meta. Bogotá.

Rocha, Joaquin
1905. Memorandum de Viaje: Regiones Amazónicas. Bogotá.

Rocherau, Henri
1919. Les Indiens Tunebos et Pedrazas. *Journal de la Société des Américanistes,* N.S., 11, No. 2, 513–24, Paris.

Rocherau, Henri, R. Monsalve, and Nestor Parra
1914. Los Indios Tunebos. *Boletín de la Sociedad de Ciencias Naturales,* 2, No. 6, 163–69, 195–97, 229–30, Bogotá.

Rodriguez Bermudez, José
1962. Población indígena de Colombia, segun los datos que existen en el archivo de la División de Asuntos Indígenas. *In:* Fernando Londoño y Londoño, Memoria del Ministro de Gobierno al Congreso de 1962, pp. 76–77, Bogotá.

Rodriguez Lamus, Luis Raúl
1958. La arquitectura de los Tukano. *Revista Colombiana de Antropología,* 7:251–70, Bogotá.
Roessner, Thomas
1946. El ayahuasca: Planta mágica del Amazonas. *Revista Geográfica Americana,* 26:14–16, Buenos Aires.
Romero, Mario German
1960. Fray Juan de los Barrios y la evangelización del Nuevo Reino de Granada. *Biblioteca de Historia Eclesiástica "Fernando Caycedo y Florez,"* Vol. 4, Bogotá.
Rondon, Frederico
1945. Uaupés: Hidrografía, demografía, geopolítica. Rio de Janeiro.
Roth, Walter E.
1915. An Inquiry into the Animism and Folk-Lore of the Guiana Indians. *Thirtieth Annual Report of the Bureau of American Ethnology, 1908–1909,* pp. 103–386, Washington, D.C.
1924. An Introductory Study of the Arts, Crafts, and Customs of the Guiana Indians. *Thirty-eighth Annual Report of the Bureau of American Ethnology, 1916–1917,* pp. 25–745, Washington, D.C.
Rouhier, Alexandre
1924. Le *yagé:* plante télépathique. *Paris médical,* partie paramédicale 52, p. 341, Paris.
1926. Les plantes divinatoires. *Revue Métapsychique,* pp. 325–31, Paris.
Rowe, John Howland
1956. An Ethnographic Sketch of Guambía, Colombia. *Tribus,* 4–5: 139–56, Stuttgart.
Rusby, H. H.
1923. The Aboriginal Uses of *Caapi. Journal of the American Pharmaceutical Association,* 12:1123.
1924. The Pharmacodynamics of Caapi. *Ibid.,* 13:98.
Saake, Wilhelm
1958a. Die Juruparilegende bei den Baniwa des Rio Issana. *Proceedings of the XXXII International Congress of Americanists, Copenhagen, 1956,* pp. 271–79, Copenhagen.
1958b. Aus den Ueberlieferungen der Baniwa. *Staden-Jahrbuch,* 6:83–91, São Paulo.
1959. Iniciaçao de um Pajé entre os Baniwa. *Sociologia,* 21:434–42, São Paulo.
1959–60. Kari, der Kulturheros, feiert mit den Baniwa-Indianern das erste Dabukurifest. *Staden-Jahrbuch,* 7–8:193–201, São Paulo.
Safford, William Edwin
1916. Identity of Cohoba, the Narcotic Snuff of Ancient Haiti. *Journal of the Washington Academy of Sciences,* 6:547–62, Baltimore.
1917. Narcotic Plants and Stimulants of the Ancient Americans. *Annual Report of the Board of Regents of the Smithsonian Institution,* pp. 387–424, Washington, D.C.
1922. Daturas of the Old World and New: An Account of their Narcotic Properties and Their Use in Oracular and Initiatory Ceremonies. *Smithsonian Institution Annual Report for 1920,* pp. 537–67, Washington, D.C.
Salas, Alberto Mario
1945. El antigal de Ciénega Grande (Quebrada de Purmamarca, Prov. de

Jujuy). *Publicaciones del Museo Etnográfico de la Facultad de Filosofía y Letras* (pp. 209–26, Area de dispersión de tubos y tabletas), Buenos Aires.

Schuller, Rudolf R.
1913. Zur Affinität der Tapúya-Indianer des "TEATRUM RERUM NATURALIUM BRASILIAE." *International Archive for Ethnology,* 21:78–98, Leiden.

Schultes, Richard Evans
1954. A New Narcotic Snuff from the Northwest Amazon. *Botanical Museum Leaflets,* Harvard University, 16, No. 9, 241–60.
1955. A New Narcotic Genus from the Amazon Slope of the Colombian Andes. Ibid., 17, No. 1, 1–11.
1957. The Identity of the Malpighiaceous Narcotics of South America. Ibid., 18, No. 1, 1–56.
1961. Native Narcotics of the New World. *Texas Journ. Pharm.,* 2:141.
1962. The Role of the Ethnobotanist in the Search of New Medical Plants. *Lloydia,* 25, No. 4, 257–66.
1963a. The Widening Panorama in Medical Botany. *Rhodora,* 65, No. 762, 97–120.
1963b. Hallucinogenic Plants of the New World. *Harvard Review,* Vol. 1, No. 18.
1963c. Botanical Sources of the New World Narcotics. *Psychedelic Review,* 1, No. 2, 145–66.
1965. Ein halbes Jahrhundert Ethnobotanik amerikanischer Hallucinogene. *Planta Medica,* 13:124.
1966. The Search for New Natural Hallucinogens. *Lloydia,* 29, No. 4, 293–308.
1967a. The Place of Ethnobotany in the Ethnopharmacologic Search for Psychotomimetic Drugs. *In:* Ethnopharmacologic Search for Psychoactive Drugs (Daniel H. Efron, editor), pp. 33–57, Public Health Service Publ. No. 1645, Washington, D.C.
1967b. The Botanical Origins of South American Snuffs. Ibid., pp. 291–306.
1968. Some Impacts of Spruce's Amazon Explorations on Modern Phytochemical research. *Rhodora,* 70, No. 783, 313–39.
1969a. The Unfolding Panorama of the New World Hallucinogens. *In:* Current Topics in Plant Science (J. E. Gunckel, editor), pp. 336–54, New York.
1969b. The Plant Kingdom and Hallucinogens. *Bulletin of Narcotics,* 21, No. 3, 3–16; No. 4, 15–27; 22 (1970): 25–53.
1969c. De plantis toxicariis e Mundo Novo tropicale commentationes V. *Virola* as an Orally Administered Hallucinogen. *Botanical Museum Leaflets,* Harvard University, 11:229–40.
1969d. Hallucinogens of Plant Origin. *Science,* 163:245–54.
1970. The New World Indians and Their Hallucinogens. *Bull. Morris Arb.,* pp. 3–14.
1972a. De plantis toxicariis e Mundo Novo tropicale commentationes X. New Data on the Malpighiaceous Narcotics of South America. *Botanical Museum Leaflets,* Harvard University, 23, No. 3, 137–47.
1972b. An Overview of Hallucinogens in the Western Hemisphere. *In:* Flesh of the Gods: The Ritual Use of Hallucinogens (Peter T. Furst, editor), pp. 3–54, New York and Washington, D.C.

Schultes, Richard Evans, and Bo Holmstedt
  1968. The Vegetal Ingredients of the Myristacaceous Snuffs of the North-west Amazon. *Rhodora,* 70:113–60.
Schultes, Richard Evans, Bo Holmstedt, and Jan-Erik Lindgren
  1969. De plantis toxicariis e Mundo Novo tropicale commentationes III. Phytochemical Examination of Spruce's Original Collection of *Banisteriopsis Caapi. Botanical Museum Leaflets,* Harvard University, 22:121–32.
Schultes, Richard Evans, and Albert Hofmann
  1972. The Botany and Chemistry of Hallucinogens. Charles C. Thomas, Springfield, Ill.
Schultes, Richard Evans, and Robert F. Raffauf
  1960. Prestonia: An Amazonian Narcotic or Not? *Botanical Museum Leaflets,* Harvard University, 12:109–22.
Seitz, Georg
  1965. Einige Bemerkungen zur Anwendung und Wirkungsweise des *Epena*-Schnupfpulvers der *Waika*-Indianer. *In:* The Use of Specific Kinds of South American Indian Snuff and Related Paraphernalia (Henry S. Wassén, editor), Etnologiska Studier, No. 28, pp. 117–32, Göteborg.
  1967. Epéna, the Intoxicating Snuff Powder of the Waika Indians and the Tucano Medicine Man, Agostino. *In:* Ethnopharmacologic Search for Psychoactive Drugs (Daniel H. Efron, editor), pp. 315–38, Public Health Service Publ. No. 1645, Washington, D.C.
Serrano, Antonio
  1941. Los recipientes para paricá y su dispersión en América del Sur. *Revista Geográfica Americana,* 15:251–57, Buenos Aires.
Simón, Pedro
  1882–92. Noticias historiales de las conquistas de Tierra Firme en las Indias Occidentales. 5 vols. Bogotá.
Sorensen, Arthur P.
  1967. Multilingualism in the Northwest Amazon. *American Anthropologist,* 69, No. 6, 670–84.
  1970. Multilingualism in the Northwest Amazon: Papurí and Pira-paraná Regions. Paper presented at the 39th International Congress of Americanists, Lima, 1970 (mimeographed).
Spruce, Richard
  1874. On Some Remarkable Narcotics of the Amazon Valley and Orinoco. *Geographical Magazine,* N.S., 1:184–93, London.
  1908. Notes of a Botanist on the Amazon and Andes. 2 vols. London.
Steward, Julian H., and Louis C. Faron
  1959. Native Peoples of South America. New York.
Stoddart, D. R.
  1962. Myth and Ceremonial among the Tunebo Indians of Eastern Colombia. *Journal of American Folklore,* 75:147–52.
Stradelli, Ermanno
  1890a. L'Uaupés e gli Uaupés. *Bollettino della Società Geografica Italiana,* Ser. 3, Vol. 3, anno 24, v. 27, pp. 425–53, Rome.
  1890b. Leggenda dell'Jurupary. *Ibid.,* v. 27.
Stromberg, V. L.
  1954. The Isolation of Bufotenine from *Piptadenia peregrina. Journal of the American Chemical Society,* 76:1707.

Szara, Stephen I.
　1967. Quoted in: Discussion on the Psychoactive Action of Various Trypta-
　　mine Derivatives. *In:* Ethnopharmacologic Search for Psychoactive
　　Drugs (Daniel H. Efron, editor), pp. 374–82, Public Health Service
　　Publ. No. 1645, Washington, D.C.
Tart, Charles T. (editor)
　1969. Altered States of Consciousness: A Book of Readings. Wiley, New
　　York.
Tastevin, C.
　1923. Les Makú du Japurá. *Journal de la Société des Américanistes,* N.S.,
　　15:99–108, Paris.
Terribilini, Mario, and Michel Terribilini
　1961. Enquête chez les Indiens Makú du Caiarí-Uaupés. Août 1960. *Bulle-
　　tin de la Société Suisse des Américanistes,* 21:2–10.
Torres Laborde, Alfonso
　1969. Mito y cultura entre los Barasana: Un grupo indígena tukano del
　　Vaupés. Universidad de los Andes, Bogotá.
Torres de Mendoza, Luis (editor)
　1864–84. Colección de documentos inéditos, relativos al descubrimiento,
　　conquista y organización de las antiguas posesiones españolas de
　　América y Oceanía. 42 vols. Madrid.
Trimborn, Hermann
　1948. Vergessene Königreiche. Studien zur Völkerkunde und Altertums-
　　kunde Nordwest-Kolumbiens. *Kulturgeschichtliche Forschungen,*
　　Vol. 2, Albert Limbach Verlag, Braunschweig.
Uricoechea, Ezequiel
　1871. Gramática, vocabulario, catecismo i confesionario de la Lengua
　　Chibcha segun antiguos manuscritos anónimos e inéditos, aumenta-
　　dos i correjidos. *Colección Lingüística Americana,* Vol. 1, Maison-
　　neuve, Paris.
Uscátegui, M. Nestor
　1959. The Present Distribution of Narcotics and Stimulants amongst the
　　Indian Tribes of Colombia. *Botanical Museum Leaflets,* Harvard
　　University, 18, No. 6, 273–304.
　1961. Distribución actual de las plantas narcóticas y estimulantes usadas
　　por las tribus indígenas de Colombia. *Revista de la Academia Colom-
　　biana de Ciencias Exactas, Físicas y Naturales,* 11, No. 43, 215–28,
　　Bogotá.
Vadillo, Juan de
　1884. Carta del Lycenciado Xoan de Vadillo a su Magestad, dándole
　　quenta de su vysita a la Gobernación de Cartagena, Cartagena,
　　Octubre 15 de 1537. *In:* Torres de Mendoza (editor), Vol. 41.
Vargas Machuca, Bernardo de
　1892. Milicia y descripción de las Indias. 2 vols. *Colección de libros raros
　　ó curiosos que tratan de América,* Vols. 8, 9, Madrid (first edition,
　　Madrid, 1599).
Villavicencio, M.
　1858. Geografía de la República del Ecuador. New York.
Wallace, Alfred Russell
　1889. Travels on the Amazon and Río Negro. Second edition. London.
　1908. My Life: A Record of Events and Opinions. 2 vols. New York.

Walter, Heinz
1956. Der Jaguar in der Vorstellungswelt der südamerikanischen Natur-völker. Ph.D. dissertation, University of Hamburg.

Wassén, S. Henry
1964. Some General Viewpoints in the Study of Native Drugs, Especially from the West Indies and South America. *Ethnos*, Nos. 1–2, pp. 97–120, Stockholm.
1965. The Use of Some Specific Kinds of South American Indian Snuff and Related Paraphernalia. *Etnologiska Studier*, No. 28, Göteborg.
1966. Sydamerikanska snusdroger. *Nytt och Nyttigt*, pp. 1–7.
1967a. Om några indianska droger och speciellt om snus samt tillbehör. Göteborgs Etnografiska Museum, *Arstryck 1963–1966*, pp. 97–140, Göteborg.
1967b. Anthropological Survey of the Use of South American Snuffs. *In:* Ethnopharmacologic Search for Psychoactive Drugs (Daniel H. Efron, editor), pp. 233–89, Public Health Service Publ. No. 1645, Washington, D.C.
1969. Om bruket av hallucinogena snuser av sydamerikanskt ursprung. *Sydsvenska Medicinhistoriska Sällskapets Arskrift*, pp. 70–98.
1970. A Naturalist's Lost Ethnographic Collection from Brazil; or, The Case from 1786: A contribution to the Study of South American Drugs. Göteborgs Etnografiska Museum, *Arstryck 1969*, pp. 32–47, Göteborg.
1971. Einige wichtige, hauptsächlich etnographische Daten zum Gebrauch indianischer Schnupfdrogen. *Ethnologische Zeitschrift*, No. 1, pp. 47–62, Universität Zürich, Zürich.

Wassén, S. Henry, and Bo Holmstedt
1963. The Use of Paricá: An Ethnological and Pharmacological Review. *Ethnos*, 1:5–45, Stockholm.

Wedel, R.
1934. Efectos del yajé sobre el paciente. *El País* (30 July), Medellín.

Whiffen, Thomas
1915. The North-West Amazons: Notes of Some Months Spent among Cannibal Tribes. London.

White, O. E.
1922. Botanical Exploration in Bolivia. *Brooklyn Bot. Gard. Rec.*, 11:102.

Wilbert, Johannes
1960. Nachrichten über die Curipaco. *Ethnologica*, N.S., 2:508–21, Sonderdruck aus Festband M. Heydrich, Cologne.
1961. Indios de la Región Orinoco-Ventuari. Instituto Caribe de Antropología y Sociología, Caracas.

Williams, Llewellyn
1931. The Death Vine: Ayahuasca. *Field Museum News*, No. 8, p. 3, Chicago.
1936. The Woods of Northeastern Peru. Field Museum Natural History Pub. No. 377, *Botany*, Ser. 15, p. 257, Chicago.
1945. Yopo: An Indian Narcotic of South America. *Bull. Chic. Mus. Nat. Hist.* Vol. 16, No. 4, Chicago.

Williams-Ellis, Amabel
1966. Darwin's Moon: A Biography of Alfred Russell Wallace. London and Glasgow.

Wolfe, O., and K. Rumpf
    1928. Ueber die Gewinnung von Harmin aus einer südamerikanischen
        Liane. *Arch. Pharmaz.*, 266:188.
Woodcock, George
    1969. Henry Walter Bates: Naturalist of the Amazons. Faber & Faber,
        London.
Wurdack, J. J.
    1958. Indian narcotics in Southern Venezuela. *Garden Journal*, 8:116–18.
Zamora, Alonso de
    1930. Historia de la Provincia de San Antonino del Nuevo Reino de Gra-
        nada. Caracas (first edition, Barcelona, 1701).
Zerda, Bayon, Rafael
    1915. Informe sobre mi excursión científica eń las regiones colombianas del
        Caquetá. Bogotá.
Zerries, Otto
    1954. Wild-und Buschgeister in Südamerika. *Studien zur Kulturkunde,*
        Vol. 11, Wiesbaden.
    1962. Die Vorstellung vom Zweiten Ich und die Rolle der Harpye in der
        Kultur der Naturvölker Südamerikas. *Anthropos*, 57:889–914.
    1967. Einführung zu dem Nachdruck von Th. Koch-Grünberg: Zwei Jahre
        bei den Indianern. Akademische Druck-und Verlagsanstalt, Graz.

INDEX

Ablutions, 90
Acacia Niopo, 230 n.60, 231 n.71. See also
 Anadenanthera peregrina
Achagua Indians, 16, 17, 229 n.30
Admixtures, narcotic, 9, 18, 21, 37, 39, 40,
 41, 116, 152, 200, 246 nn.37–38
Adultery, 57, 105, 118
Aggression (in interpersonal relations), 78,
 80, 81, 85, 86, 90, 96, 98, 99, 100, 103,
 104, 105, 108, 110 ff., 114, 118, 121,
 122, 128, 132, 193, 195
Agouti, 129
Agriculture, 67, 73
Aguado, Pedro de, 12, 14, 16
Ahpikondiá (Paradise, River of Milk), 95,
 145, 172, 245–46 n.24
Aldauhuíku, 55
Alkaloids, 39, 40 ff.
Alliances, 67, 74, 93, 94
Amazon River, 63, 239 n.7
Ambivalence, 59, 118, 130, 131
Ambu-ambu, 57, 58
Amorúa Indians, 19
Anaconda, 113, 114, 119, 138. *See also*
 Anaconda Canoe
Anaconda Canoe (mythical), 134, 143,
 146, 169, 170, 172, 178, 180, 191, 244
 n.1
Anadenanthera peregrina, 9, 12, 18, 19,
 20, 22, 24, 41, 43, 47, 230 n.60. See also
 Piptadenia peregrina
Andean Highlands, 14, 48
Anserma Indians, 49, 50
Antioquia, Indians of, 46
Ants, edible, 82, 88, 117, 130
Anxiety, level of, 74. *See also* Personality
Apaporis River, 16, 64, 65, 70, 126
Apocynaceae, 40
Aracú (fish), 143
Arawak (tribes and dialects), 16, 36, 65,
 66, 119, 191, 229 n.30, 239 n.14
Archaeology, 24, 44, 231 n.88, 237 n.103.
 See also Petroglyphs
Aristolochia, 37, 39
Arrows, 10, 47, 79; magical, 71, 73, 80,
 83, 84, 92
Art style, 179 ff.
Aruitera (place name), 186
Ayahuasca, 28, 29, 30, 31, 36, 37, 39. See
 also *Banisteriopsis;* Yajé

Axis mundi, concept of, 141

Bambero. See *Saaropë*
Banisterine, 39, 41
Banisteriopsis, 34, 35, 36, 37, 39, 41, 43,
 133 ff.; *caapi*, 28, 32, 36, 37, 38, 39, 40,
 41; *inebrians*, 39, 40, 41; *longlialata*,
 39; *lutea*, 39; *metallicolor*, 39; *quiten-
 sis*, 39, 40; *rusbyana*, 39, 40, 41
Baniva Indians, 19, 65
Barasana Indians, 16, 157 ff.
Barbasco (fish poison), 183
Barkcloth, 86, 100, 125, 178
Barriga Villalba, A. M., 39
Bates, Henry Walter, 26
Bathing, 73
Bayapia (plant), 134, 151, 152, 244 n.4
Becher, Hans, 21
Bench, 81. *See also* Stools, ritual
Bignonia chica. See Carayurú
Birds, 72, 85, 86, 98, 183; cock of the
 rock, 26, 84, 183, 186; duck, 96; harpy
 eagle, 78, 80, 128; humingbird, 73,
 140; macaw, 73, 110, 111, 116, 196;
 oropendola, 9, 94, 155; parrot, 73; sym-
 bolism of, 136; toucan, 94; trumpeter
 bird, 244 n.23; weaverbird, 73, 130;
 woodpecker, 96
Blood, 49, 82, 189
Blowgun, 83, 92, 123, 142
Blowing, magical, 80, 90, 94
"Blue ball," 55, 56, 57, 58
Boa, 92, 150
Bochica, 45
Bogotá, 10, 11, 44, 49
Bone, symbolism of, 244 n.9
Boráro (spirit), 72, 83, 84, 85, 99, 129,
 182 ff., 188 ff., 192, 193, 195, 237 n.83,
 241 n.28, 247 n.1, 248 nn.2 and 11
Boréka (aracú fish), 244 n.8; Desana sib,
 136, 244 n.8; snake, 150
Borrachero (Datura), 15, 16, 230 n.46
Botanical Museum at Harvard, 36
Botanical research, 9, 16, 18, 21, 26, 28,
 30, 36, 38, 233 n.44
Botanists, 9, 16, 18, 26, 28, 38
Bow, 79
Brazil, 25, 27, 34, 63, 66, 69, 141, 142,
 187

273

Brüzzi Alves da Silva, Alcionilio, 34
Bufotenine, 21
Búnkuase, 56, 237 n.92
Burial, 15, 67, 72, 74, 133, 137
Burial mounds, prehistoric, 10
Bush dog, 95, 96
Bush spirits. *See* Spirits
Butterfly, 71, 72, 175, 183, 190

Caapi, 27, 28, 29, 31, 32, 37, 38. See also
　Banisteriopsis; Yajé
Caapi pinima, 37
Caboclo, 27
Cachirí, 26, 67, 88, 89, 92, 93, 123, 135,
　140, 155, 159, 160, 161, 170, 189, 196
Cacique, 7, 14
Caimo fruit (*Chrysophyllum vulgare*), 156,
　248 n.7
Calella, Plácido de, 34, 47
Cannibalism, 3, 25, 51, 53
Canoes, 73
Caquetá River, 16, 19, 32, 34, 36, 38, 40,
　61, 62, 64
Caramanta, Indians of, 49–50
Carapana Indians, 66
Carayurú (*Bignonia chica*), 116, 150,
　243 n.10
Cardinal points and directions, 91, 122,
　124, 126
Caribbean Coast, 3, 10, 11, 20, 24, 48
Carib Indians, 10, 36, 65
Cartagena of the Indies, 10, 48
Carurú (place name), 94
Carurú Cachoeira, 34, 142
Casas, Bartolomé de las, 7, 8, 227 n.1
Casiquiare Channel, 25
Cassava, 63, 88, 117, 142
Castellanos, Juan de, 13, 15
Categories, native: of caterpillars, 243 n.6;
　of coca, 189; of foods, 88, 126; of
　jaguars, 122; of mats, 129; of patho-
　genic splinters, 94; of raw and cooked
　dishes, 126, 131, 148; of snakes, 138;
　of spotted things, 127–28, 130; of yajé,
　155, 198
Caterpillars, edible, 97, 115, 116, 243 n.6
Caterpillars, Master of, 97, 115–16, 243 n.7
Catholic missions, 238 n.8. *See also* Mis-
　sionaries
Cauca River, 51; Valley, 48
Caves, 3, 44, 56
Cemis, 5, 6, 7, 8, 227 n.2
Center, magical importance of, 111, 113,
　135, 140, 141, 148, 152
Central Andes, 44
Ceremonial centers, 54, 59
Ceremonies, 5, 27, 46, 54, 133, 157 ff.
Chagropanga, 40
Chaneques (Mexican rain-spirits),
　236 n.67
Chantre y Herrera, José, 30
Chen, A. L., 39
Chen, K. K., 39
Chía (village), 44
Chibcha Indians, 10, 44, 229 n.28; lan-
　guage of, 44, 45
Chieftains, 4, 6, 7, 8, 10, 11, 12, 14, 44,
　49, 57, 59, 67, 103
Childbirth, 67, 89, 138
Childlike spirits, 53
Chili peppers. *See* Peppers
Chimila Indians, 47
Chiripanga, 32

Chocó Indians, 45
Chroniclers, Spanish, 7, 10, 11, 12, 13, 44,
　45, 46, 48, 49, 62
Cicada, 97, 116. *See also* Lantern fly
Cigar, 74, 81, 88, 89, 94, 152; holder, 81,
　171. *See also* Tobacco
Coca, 12, 88, 145, 172, 189, 245–46 n.24
Cock of the rock, 26, 84, 183, 186
Cogioba. See *Cohoba*
Cohoba, 5, 6, 7, 9, 13, 19, 227 n.5,
　228 nn.7, 19, and 23
Color symbolism, 88, 90, 93, 94, 102, 111,
　124, 136, 156, 176, 180
Columbus, Christopher, 5, 8, 227 nn.1 and
　5
Columbus, Ferdinand, 5, 227 n.1
Condiments, 52, 88. *See also* Peppers; Salt,
　avoidance of
Confession, 46
Conflict solution, 103
Constellations and stars, 116, 137, 141
Conversation, ritual, 153, 246 n.41
"Conversation-people," 193
Correguaje Indians, 46
Cotton, symbolism of, 90, 102, 176
Coudreau, Henri A., 31
Couvade, 88, 102
Creation myth, 67, 70, 101, 111, 114, 133,
　136, 141, 142, 143, 145, 146, 147, 156,
　170, 180, 181, 191. *See also* Myths
Cuatrecasas, José, 39
Cubeo Indians, 21, 33, 34, 66, 154
Cucinemegua, 45
Cuduyarí River, 33
Cuiva Indians, 19, 47
Culture heroes, 3–4, 45, 51
Cumaná, Indians of, 48
Cumare Creek, 114
Cundinamarca Highlands, 10
Curing of disease. *See* Diseases, curing of
Curupa, 19
Curupira (*Kurupira*). See *Boráro*
Cuyucuyú Falls, 70

Dabeiba, 50
Dabocurí, 27, 67, 100, 101
Dance, 4, 26, 27, 46, 47, 54, 56, 67, 74, 78,
　79, 81, 85, 87, 100, 133, 154, 161 ff.,
　178, 192, 247 n.48; symbolism of, 124,
　143, 245 n.22
Dapa, 35
Datura, 15, 16, 40, 54, 230 nn.44–45. *See
　also* Borrachero
Daughter of Aracú, 143
Daughter of the Sun, 109, 127, 137, 172
Death, 50; origin of, 137
Decorative designs, 79, 86, 154, 169, 176,
　177, 178, 244 n.1. *See also* Drawings
Deer, 16, 58, 71, 122, 124, 129, 130
Deities, tribal, 4, 35, 44, 45, 54, 55
Desana Indians, 33, 66, 113, 114, 116,
　119, 121, 126, 129, 134, 139, 143, 155,
　156, 175, 185, 186, 188, 193, 245 nn.12
　and 15
Desana texts (original), 205–24; in English
　translation, 109, 111, 113, 115, 116,
　117, 119, 120, 121, 122, 124, 128,
　129, 131, 134, 150, 151, 152, 184, 186,
　187–88, 245 n.16
Devil: "talking with the," 3, 4, 5, 12, 14,
　16, 17, 47–48, 49; worship of, 3, 4, 5,
　8, 9, 46, 48, 50
Dew, 176

Dietary restrictions, 81, 82, 86, 87, 88, 105, 113, 117, 122, 175, 201. *See also* Fasting
Diroá-mahsë (Being of Blood), 92
Diseases, 84, 96, 102; categories of, 96; curing of, 6, 12, 19, 23, 35, 53, 55, 57, 67, 76, 79, 89, 90, 96, 97, 98, 102, 103, 108, 133; diagnosis of, 88, 89; etiology of, 71, 90, 93, 94, 102, 183
Divinatory practices, 4, 6, 11, 13, 14, 15, 16, 17, 18, 23, 29, 48, 52
Diving for power objects, 83
Disguise. *See* Garments, magical
Doppelgänger, concept of, 84, 191. *See also* Doubles
Dorado de los Omaguas, 62
Doubles, 84, 99, 110, 113, 114, 137, 191, 192, 193
Down feathers, symbolism of, 90, 102
Drawings, Indian, 167, 173 ff., 176
Dreams, 49, 59, 77, 92, 93, 102, 104, 128
"Drowning," concept of, 147, 150, 181
Drumming: on flat roots, 84; on water, 87
Duck, 96

Earpendants, 78, 79, 83, 135, 153
Eastern Cordillera, 68
Eastern Tukano, 66, 67
"Eco-People," 193
Ecstatis, 35, 49
Ecuador, 28, 29, 35, 36
El Dorado, quest for, 10, 62, 63
Eluitsáma, 55
Emberá Indians, 35
Emetics, 87
Endocannibalism, 12. *See also* Cannibalism
Enmity. *See* Aggression
Envy, 105
Equatorial line, 141, 142
Erytroxylon coca. See Coca
Exogamy, 58, 59, 66, 67, 93, 94, 105, 111, 119, 122, 126, 131, 133, 148, 149, 153, 170, 176, 177, 178, 192, 239 n.19, 245 n.23
Exophagy, concept of, 244 n.25

Falls, 68, 69, 70, 71, 73, 126, 137, 139, 140, 141, 143, 156. *See also* Rapids
Fasting, 52, 77, 91, 176, 201. *See also* Dietary restrictions
Fauna: general distribution, 70–71, 73; unexplained scarcity of, 72
Feathercrowns, 81, 88, 135, 148, 150, 159, 160, 187
Female symbolism, 93, 95, 106, 143, 149
Fence, symbolism of, 89, 100, 129, 130, 241 n.27
Fertility and fertilization, 3, 51, 53, 77, 90, 96, 100, 105, 111, 136, 141, 143, 170
Fire: preventive use of, 128, 129; symbolism of, 126, 131
First Couple (mythical), 143, 146, 245 n.19; woman, 172
First Dance (mythical), 172
First Maloca (mythical), 146, 172
Fischer Cárdenas, G., 37, 39
Fish, 76, 91; as food, 82, 85, 133; symbolism of, 106, 143, 149, 244 n.22
Fishing, 67, 78, 83, 87, 89, 108
Fish poison, 81, 133, 183
Fish songs, 144
Fish traps, 94, 170
"Fish yajé," 90, 94, 97, 151

Flagellation, ritual, 12, 87. *See also* Initiation
Fleur-de-lys, 170
Flutes. *See* Musical instruments
Food: categories of, 88; preparation of, 82, 88, 105, 131, 148; symbolism of, 105, 126, 142, 244 n.25
Food gatherers and gathering, 17, 18, 65, 67, 133
Franciscan friars, 46
Fruits, symbolism of, 102, 243 n.3

Gahpí (Banisteriopsis caapi). See Yajé
Gallery forest, 68
Game animals, 71, 72, 74, 76, 81, 84, 85, 100, 129, 144. *See also* Mammals
Garments, magical, 47, 112, 114, 120, 122, 124, 125
Gatherings, 74, 88, 133. See also *Dabocurí*
Genealogies, 77
Genipa americana, 159
Gift exchange, 27, 67, 93. *See also* Reciprocity
Gold, 10, 51, 52, 53, 63
Goldman, Irving, 33
Gottauf, Franz, 39
Groundnuts, 92, 93, 188
Guaca, Indians of, 49
Guahibo Indians, 17, 18, 19, 28, 35, 45, 46, 47, 230 n.64, 234 n.22
Guainía Territory, 31, 36, 64, 65, 119, 238 n.1
Guamo fruit (*Inga* sp.), 96
Guapé Indians, 63
Guaviare River, 12, 21, 36, 61, 62, 68
Guayabero Indians, 19, 20
Guayupe Indians, 12, 14, 16, 46, 247 n.48
Guiana-Shield, 64
Guillén de Arce, Pedro, 14
Gumilla, José, 17

Haemadictyon amazonicum, 37, 39
Hair, magical, 53, 80, 94, 95, 96, 188; symbolism of, 90
Haiti, 5, 7, 9
Hallucinations, 5, 9, 22, 29, 33, 34, 35, 41, 48, 49, 52, 77, 79, 80, 81, 82, 83, 85, 88, 100, 102, 103, 118, 133, 147, 163 ff., 174 ff., 179
Hallucinogens, 12, 15, 19, 21, 41, 43, 53, 54, 76, 78. See also *Anadenanthera peregrina; Banisteriopsis; Datura;* Snuff; *Virola* sp.; Yajé; Yopo
Hamet, R., 38
Harmala alkaloids, 40, 41, 42
Harpy eagle, 78, 80, 128
Hayo. See Coca
Hearth, symbolism of, 148
Heliconia bihai L., 81, 122, 124, 175
Herbs: aromatic, 71; magical, 81, 97; medicinal, 53, 81, 85, 90, 91, 97, 98, 121. See also *Bayapia; Tooka*
Hoe, 81, 92, 98, 101, 122, 187
Homosexuality, 105, 106
Honey, 67, 91, 143, 176, 245 n.21
Hosca. See Osca
House of Milk, 145
House of Thunder, 78, 100
Houses of the Hills and of the Waters (mythical), 70, 83, 84, 85, 98, 100, 134, 135, 139, 146, 147, 156, 172, 183, 188, 192, 241 n.12
Huitoto Indians, 19, 35, 46
Humboldt, Alexander von, 18, 30

Hummingbird, 73, 140
Hunting, 67, 71, 72, 73, 78, 82, 83, 84, 85, 89, 93; ritual, 44, 72, 81, 91

Igneri Indians, 13
Illness. *See* Diseases
Incest, 56, 60, 121, 127, 128, 130, 131, 137, 170, 177, 181, 193
Incubus, 102, 137
Infanticide, 12
Ingano Indians, 32, 34, 40, 46, 50
Inírida River, 64, 65
Initiation, ritual, 32, 35, 67, 74, 86–88, 91, 133
Insects, 67, 91, 136, 200; ant, 87, 88; butterfly, 71, 72, 175, 183, 190; caterpillar, 97, 115, 116, 243 n.6; cicada, 97, 116, 200; lantern fly, 200, 242 n.41, 243 n.8, 248 n.1; larvae, 82, 88; Morpho, 183; spider, 128; wasp, 87, 88, 128
Intermediaries, supernatural, 85, 86, 97, 108
Ipanoré (place name), 141; falls of, 27, 70, 156
Iquitos, 39
Isana River, 64, 65, 119

Jaguar: association with death, 50; association with fire, 44; association with mountains and caves, 44; association with sun and moon, 44; black, 124; general behavior of, 118 ff., 120 ff., 124, 243 n.17; Indian categories of, 120, 122, 124; man-eating, 46; mating behavior of, 120, 130; mythical creation of, 55, 56, 58; ritual burning of, 113, 115
Jaguar names, 44, 45
Jaguar People, 45, 55, 56, 57, 58, 59, 120
Jaguar skin, dresses of, 47, 120, 122, 123, 124, 125
Jaguar spirits, 43, 44, 46, 50, 51, 54, 78, 85
Jaguar transformation, 33, 43, 45, 46, 47, 50, 51, 53, 54, 55, 56, 108 ff., 234 n.1
Jeques (xeques), 15
Jesuit missions, 30
Jiménez de Quesada, 10
Jirijirimo Falls, 70, 126

Karihona Indians, 65, 239 n.15
Kashindúkua, 55, 56, 59
Keller, O., 39
Kew, Royal Botanic Gardens at, 28, 37, 38
Knoll, Max, 174
Koch-Grünberg, Theodor, 31, 32, 37
Kogi Indians, 45, 54, 55, 56, 58, 59; cosmogony of, 45, 55; myths of, 45, 55; priesthood among, 45, 46, 55; social organization of, 58, 59
Kumú, 67, 100
Kuripako Indians, 21, 65, 119, 194, 195, 196
Kurupira. See *Boráro*

La Condamine, Charles Marie de, 30
Lagoons, 70. *See also* Pools
Landing place, 73, 87, 92, 94, 99, 123
Languages, native, 5, 14, 15, 27, 44, 50, 51, 65, 66, 67, 229 n.30, 239 n.19, 240 n.21. *See also* Desana texts
Lantern fly (fam. *Fulgoridae*), 200, 242 n.41, 243 n.8, 248 n.1
Larvae, edible, 82, 88
Lengua Geral, 63, 67

Life cycle, rituals of, 67, 86–88, 133
Light, symbolism of, 93, 102, 136, 155
Lightning, 3, 53, 78, 99, 102
Lime (as admixture), 18, 21, 111
Litter, 11
Lizard, 84
Luminescence, shamanistic, 77, 109

Macaw, 73, 110, 111, 116, 196
Machaca. *See* Lantern fly
Macropsia, 22, 49, 231 n.80, 235 n.50
Macú-paraná, 137
Magdalena River, 10, 51; Valley, 12, 14
Makú Indians, 36, 65, 66, 185, 191, 239 n.16
Makuna Indians, 66
Mainas, district of, 30
Maipures, rapids of, 18, 28
Maize, 4; beer, 12
Maloca, 26, 65, 71, 73, 146; symbolism of, 148, 246 n.42
Malouetia Tamaquarina, 40
Mammals, 72, 136; agouti, 129; bush dog, 95, 96; deer, 16, 58, 71, 122, 124, 129, 130; monkey, 95, 96, 130, 134; ocelot, 44; paca, 129; peccary, 58, 71, 183; puma, 14, 16, 44, 45, 46, 53, 54, 55, 58; squirrel, 73, 134; tapir, 93, 95, 96, 130, 134
Manaos, 25, 63, 66
Manioc, 67, 73, 119
Mararay, 187
Marriage rules (Tukano), 88, 95, 156. *See also* Exogamy
Martius, Carl F. P. von, 30
Masks, 46, 53, 55, 56, 58, 86, 178
Master of Caterpillars, 97, 115–16, 243 n.7
Master of Fish, 76, 83, 94, 139, 192
Master of Game Animals, 3, 44, 67, 71, 76, 83, 85, 89, 91, 92, 93, 94, 102, 108, 129, 151, 172, 178, 180, 187, 191, 192, 240 n.10. See also *Vaí-mahsë*
Master of Umarí, 93, 96
Mats, symbolism of, 129, 130, 131, 189
Menstruation, 82, 137
"Menstruation People," 86, 189
Mesoamerica, 44
Meta River, 16, 18, 62
Meyú Falls, 70, 126, 141, 142, 143
Mice, 73
Migrations, 141, 146
Mihí, 33, 34
Milk, 94
Milk, River of, 95. See also *Alpikondiá*
Milky Way, 85, 98, 108, 115, 155, 171, 177; shamanistic ascent to, 98, 109, 172
Miraflores, 65
Mirití palm, 129
Mirror, 13, 14, 16, 189, 192
Mirror image, 84, 110, 189, 192. *See also* Doubles; *Vëari-mahsá*
Missionaries, 3, 4, 5, 15, 25, 30, 33, 34, 46, 62, 63, 65, 66, 74
Mitú, 26, 63, 65, 69
Mocoa, 40
Mohan, 12, 229 n.33
Mojas, 11
Monkey, 95, 96, 130, 134
Monsters, 53, 74, 118, 132, 139. See also *Boráro*
Moon, 3, 11, 49, 89, 127, 130, 192; spots, 127, 128, 192
Morpho, 71. *See also* Butterfly
Mosoco (village), 54

Mother Goddess, 45, 54, 55, 56, 57
Muisca Indians, 10, 11, 13, 14, 15, 16, 17, 44, 45, 46, 48, 49, 50, 229 nn.28 and 39
Mushroom, 176
Music, 26, 182
Musical instruments: flutes, 142, 151, 154, 160, 161, 175; gourd rattle, 79, 80, 90, 94, 160, 162, 163, 171, 177, 178; pan-pipes, 82, 87, 88, 161, 164; seed rattles, 81, 98, 153, 175; snail flute, 99, 154; stick rattle, 81, 85, 101, 111, 135, 140, 141, 145, 152, 153, 154, 155, 160, 172, 185, 186, 188; trumpet, 151, 160, 161; turtle shell, 160, 175
Mythical times, 4, 45, 51, 55, 66, 84, 134 ff., 142
Myths, 4, 45, 47, 51, 54, 55, 59, 66, 67, 70, 73, 77, 81, 88, 93, 101, 109, 111, 114, 119, 121, 126, 127, 131, 133, 136, 137, 139, 140, 141, 142, 143, 145, 146, 147, 156, 170, 172, 180, 181, 191, 192

Nabia, 57
Nabobá, 45, 55
Námaku, 45, 55, 57, 58, 237 nn.97–98
Names, personal, 44
Namsáui, 45
Namshaya, 45
Namsíku, 45
Napo River, 28
Naranjo, Claudio, 41
Narcotics, 5, 9, 11, 15, 16, 28, 30, 33, 43, 88, 89, 98; botanical sources of, 15, 36, 81; chemical composition of, 21, 31, 39; effects of, 27, 29, 32, 33, 39; use of, 5, 27. *See also* Hallucinogens; Snuff
Narcotic snuff. *See* Snuff; *Vihó*; *Virola*
Navigation, 25, 139
Nemequene, 44
Nemocón, 45
Nemqueteba, 45
Nemterequeteba, 45
Nencatacoa, 45
New Granada, Kingdom of, 10, 11, 13, 14
Niopo. *See* Yopo
Noanamá Indians, 35
Noánase, 55, 56, 57, 58
Noise, avoidance of, 82
Nompaném, 45
Nompasum, 44–45
Ñopo. *See* Yopo
Northwest Amazon (general), 239 n.17
Novices, shaman's, 52, 76, 77, 78, 80, 81, 122, 192
Nyí, Rock of, 141, 142, 156
Nyumú (palm), 129

Ocelot, 44, 59
Offerings, 52, 56
Omagua Indians, 63
Omens, 59, 90. *See also* Signs and portents
Orinoco Plains, 14, 16, 19, 29, 31, 35, 36, 45, 48, 61, 62, 68, 229 n.30
Orinoco River, 3, 18, 19, 25, 28, 61, 62, 64
Ornaments, ritual, 45, 78, 149, 150, 153, 170
Oropendola, 92, 94, 155
Osca, 11, 14, 16
Otomac Indians, 17, 18
Oviedo y Valdés, Gonzalo Fernández, 7, 8, 11, 14, 16, 48

Paca, 129

Pacific Coast, 3, 35, 50
Paddle, 79
Páez Indians, 47, 51, 53, 54, 59, 236 n.63
Paint, body and facial, 46, 49, 79, 97, 127, 148, 159
Palm trees, 93, 129, 189
Pamuri-mahsë (Germinator Person), 84, 110, 143, 146, 178, 180, 191
Panama, 35
Pane, Román, 5, 6, 227 n.4
Panpipe, 82, 87, 88, 161, 164
Papurí River, 25, 32, 33, 34, 64, 65, 69, 70, 137
Paradise, concept of. *See Ahpikondiá*
Paricá, 19
Pari Cachoeira, 142, 185
Parrot, 73
Payé (shaman), 19, 67, 76 ff., 100. *See also* Shamans
Peccary, 58, 71, 183
Peganum harmala, 39, 40, 234 n.51
Penis, 96, 101, 151. *See also* Phallic symbolism
Peppers, 52, 82, 87, 88
Perrot, E., 38
Personality (Tukano), 132, 197, 241–42 n.29
Peru, 31
Petroglyphs, 137, 141, 142, 143
Phallic symbolism, 81, 96, 101, 140, 141, 176, 188; attributes, 100, 135, 136, 141, 142, 190, 195
Pharmacology, 38, 39
Phosphenes, 173 ff., 178, 179, 202
Piapoco Indians, 19, 35
Piaroa Indians, 19
Piasaba (palm), 93
Pijao Indians, 12, 14, 16, 47, 51, 53
Pildé, 35
Pineapple, 56
Piptadenia peregrina, 229 n.24. See also *Anadenanthera peregrina*
Pira-paraná, 64, 65, 70, 126, 141, 157
Pira-Tapuya Indians, 33, 66, 121, 122, 124, 134
Poisonous plants, 98, 128
Political organization, 11
Pools, 70, 83, 84, 139, 140
Popayán, Indians of, 48
Portages, 68
Pottery, 178
Powder, narcotic. *See* Snuff
Power objects, 52, 76, 78, 79, 81, 83, 90
Prayers and invocations, 6, 8, 50
Pregnancy, 82, 91
Prestige, 105
Prestonia amazonica, 37, 39
Puberty, 88
Pubic hair, 95. *See also* Hair, magical
Puerto Nare, 65
Puffball, 58
Puinave Indians, 21
Puma, 14, 16, 44, 45, 46, 53, 54, 55, 57, 58
Purification, 87
Putumayo River, 34, 36, 40, 46

Quartz, quartzite, 79–80, 81, 93, 99, 101, 102, 176, 187, 188; cylinder, 80
Quechua (language), 50

Rain, 3, 50, 53, 54, 97
Rainbow, 53, 94, 95, 97, 171

Rapids, 66, 68, 69, 70, 71, 100, 126, 139, 140, 156. *See also* Falls
Raw and cooked, as categories, 126, 148
Reciprocity, 27, 67, 94, 153, 156, 170
Recitals, 77, 133
Red Dwarf, 83, 101. See also V*aí-mahsë*
Reinburg, P., 36
Religion, tribal, 4, 5, 8, 9, 35, 43, 54, 59, 133
Resin, narcotic, 81
Revenge, 104, 108, 113, 118. *See also* Aggression
Rio Negro, 18, 25, 26, 31, 37, 61, 62, 63, 64, 65, 66, 67, 186, 196
Ritual, 4, 5, 14, 44, 54, 59, 67, 72, 73, 76, 79, 86, 87, 88, 89, 90, 91, 133, 136, 140, 151 ff., 157 ff.; objects, 82, 180
Rivero, Juan, 17, 18
Rivers and river travel, symbolism of, 138 ff.
Rocha, Joaquín, 32, 33, 36, 46
Roller stamps, 159. *See also* Paint, body and facial
Rouhier, Alexandre, 37
Rubber, 25, 63, 169, 246 n.32, 248 n.8; collectors, 63, 65, 74, 194

Saaropë (forest creatures), 84, 85, 193, 241 n.15
Sacrifice, human, 15
Safford, William, 9
Salesian missions, 34
Saliva, 176
Sáliva Indians, 17
Salt, avoidance of, 52, 54
Santa Fé de Bogotá. *See* Bogotá
Santa Marta, 10, 49
São Gabriel, 70, 126
Schultes, Richard Evans, 22, 36, 37, 38, 40
Sebil, 19
Seclusion: during initiation rites, 88; during jaguar transformation, 111; during menstruation, 82; during power quest, 117; during shamanistic apprenticeship, 96, 117
Seminal symbolism and associations, 77, 90, 94, 96, 101, 102, 105, 136, 140, 145, 147, 149, 169, 176, 177, 188, 242 n.42
Sexual abstinence, 52, 77, 82, 85, 117, 201
Sexual aggression, 119, 121, 191, 192; in hallucinatory trance, 119, 127, 132; in myth, 51, 52, 53, 54, 56, 57, 58, 125, 131
Sexual intercourse, 73, 88, 94
Shamans: apprenticeship of, 52, 76, 77, 80, 122, 192; call to office of, 52, 76, 109; enmities between, 76, 79, 100; paraphernalia of, 13, 52, 94; social functions of, 4, 6, 76, 103
Shield, ritual, 153, 154
Shrines, 5, 8
Sibs, Tukano, 66, 119, 148
Sickness. *See* Diseases
Sicuani Indians, 19, 47
Sierra Nevada of Santa Marta, 12, 45, 50, 54
Signs and portents, 50, 59, 77, 90
Simón, Pedro, 13, 17
Sinú (valley), 10, 45
Siona Indians, 34, 46
Skins, 85, 98, 99, 112. *See also* Garments, magical
Slaves, 11
Sleep, deprivation of, 87, 201

Smoke-Person, 127
Smoking, 7, 78, 88, 89, 90, 97, 98, 150, 151, 152, 176, 188
Snail flute. *See* Musical instruments
Snail-shell container, 14, 16, 17
Snakes, 73, 121; anaconda, 113, 114, 119, 138; boa, 92, 139, 150; mythical origin of, 134; spirit snakes, 53, 55, 84, 85, 86, 98, 99, 100, 113, 114, 119, 139, 150; symbolism of, 138
Snuff: narcotic, 5, 6, 7, 8, 9, 11, 13, 16, 17, 18, 19, 20, 21, 22, 41, 46, 47, 48, 49, 78, 80, 81, 85, 97, 99, 102, 108, 109 ff., 116, 120, 163, 199; introduced in Europe, 232 n.88; reaction to, 5, 8, 11, 16, 17, 21, 22, 23, 110 ff.
Snuffing apparatus, 5, 6, 7, 8, 13, 14, 16, 18, 22, 24, 46, 81, 98, 192, 231 n.65
Sogamoso valley, 13, 44, 48
Songs and singing, 4, 46, 47, 74, 77, 78, 79, 80, 81, 85, 87, 90, 91, 93, 94, 97, 98, 133, 135, 136, 143, 152, 158, 159, 161 ff., 176
Sons of Aracu, 114, 119
Sons of Bëgëyeri, 114, 115, 119
Soul, 71, 77, 104, 113, 145
Soul birds, 86
Spanish Conquest, 3, 10, 45, 51, 62
Sparagmos (Tearing-into-Pieces), 135, 244 n.5
Spells, 72, 77, 78, 80, 86, 91, 100, 102, 104, 109, 113, 115, 124, 128, 131, 136, 151, 152, 176, 183, 187, 188, 189, 241 n.24; over cigars, 74; in curing, 88, 90, 183; over food, 88; against jaguars, 128, 129; against spirits, 89
Spider, 128
Spirit-animals, 84, 99, 191
Spirit-helpers, 76, 81, 97, 240 n.7. *See also* Intermediaries, supernatural
Spirits, 4, 35, 53, 72, 74, 86, 91, 108, 119, 130, 188; of the forest, 3, 71–72, 74, 83, 85, 181 ff., 241 n.15; of rivers, 3, 70
Splinters, pathogenic, 80, 92, 93, 94, 95, 240 n.6
Spoons, 14, 16
Spotted things (as a category), 127–28
Sprague, T. A., 38
Spruce, Richard, 18, 19, 26, 27, 28, 29, 30, 31, 36, 37, 38, 41
Squirrel, 73, 134
Stalactites, 111
Stamping tubes, 161 ff., 175, 178
Starch, 82, 87, 88, 113, 116, 176, 188
Star lore, 45
Star People, 155
Stars and constellations, 116, 137, 141
Status, 67
Stick rattle, 81, 85, 101, 111, 135, 140, 141, 145, 152, 153, 154, 155, 160, 172, 185, 186, 188
Stones, magical, 79, 80, 93, 94
Stools, ritual, 154, 171, 177
Stradelli, Ermanno, 31
Stress, 81, 118. *See also* Anxiety, level of; Personality
Sun, 3, 44, 77, 95, 127, 136, 137, 171
Sun Father, 84, 101, 103, 110, 111, 126, 135, 136, 137, 138, 139, 140, 141, 142, 143, 145, 146, 147, 149, 151, 155, 156, 171, 172, 191
Sun-god, 4, 11
Supai, 35
Synod of Santa Fé de Bogotá, 231–32 n.88

Taibano Indians, 66
Táife, 35
Tairona Indians, 45, 48
Tama (thunder deity), 51, 52, 236 n.65
Tama Indians, 46
Tapir, 95, 96, 130, 134; in myth, 93
Taracuá, 187
Tariana Indians, 65
Tari People, 114, 119
Tatuyo Indians, 66, 193
Telepathine, 39, 41
Temples, 11, 48, 50, 54, 59
Tetrapteris methystica, 37, 38
Texts, aboriginal, 111. *See also* Desana texts
Thorns, pathogenic, 80, 90. *See also* Splinters, pathogenic
Thunder, 3, 44, 50, 51, 53, 54, 78, 79, 80, 81, 83, 94, 97, 98, 99, 122
Thunderbolts, 99, 100
Thunder deity or spirit, 50, 51, 52, 53, 236 n.69
"Thunder excrement," 97
Thunder-stones, 79, 90, 97
Tierradentro, region of, 51
Tipiaca, 65
Tiquié River, 25, 32, 37, 64–65, 70, 142
Tobacco: chewing, 28, 48, 53; early description of, 7, 229 n.18; early use of, 7, 9, 12, 13, 15, 16, 17, 231 n.88; smoking, 7, 78, 88, 89, 90, 94, 97, 98, 150, 151, 152, 176, 188
Tongue, cutting off of, 243 n.4
Tooka (plant), 92, 93, 94, 95, 96, 134, 151, 242 n.34, 244 n.3
Torch, 160, 162, 175
Tota (village), 13
Toucan, 94
Trance and trancelike states, 5, 9, 29, 34, 35, 80, 85, 118. *See also* Hallucinations
Traps, 56, 139
Trinidad, 13
Trombetas River, 37
Trumpet. *See* Musical instruments
Trumpeter bird, 244 n.23
Tukano Indians, 49, 65; distribution of, 21, 34, 36, 65; economy of, 67; exogamic groups among, 66, 67; languages of, 46, 65, 66; missions among, 33; mythical migrations of, 66; mythical origins of, 66; social organization of, 66. *See also* Vaupés Territory, Indian population of
Tukano proper, 66, 121, 134
Tunebo Indians, 14, 16, 18, 19, 46, 50
Tunja (town), 11, 44, 45, 49, 50
Tupi language, 27, 63, 67
Turtle shell. *See* Musical instruments

Uahtí (spirits), 72, 85, 98, 129, 193, 194, 196
Uanano Indians, 66, 134
Uaupés. *See* Vaupés River; Vaupés Territory
Ubaque (village), 49
Umarí (*Poraqueiba paraensis*), 92, 93, 112, 188, 242 n.31, 243 n.3, 248 n.14
Umarí, Lake, 95
Umbilical cord, 134, 135, 136, 155
Umbrella bird, 26
Universe, structure of, 4
Urubú-coára (place name), 27
Uterine symbolism, 91, 101, 136, 137, 138, 139, 145, 148, 170

Vahsú (*Hevea pauciflora* var. *coriacea*), 150, 169, 177, 178, 187, 188, 243 n.3, 246 n.32
Vaí-mahsë (Master of Game Animals), 83, 84, 85, 86, 89, 91, 98, 100, 101, 102, 108, 183, 188, 201, 240 n.11
Vargas Machuca, Bernardo, 12
Vaupés River, 18, 25, 27, 64, 65, 67
Vaupés Territory, 232 n.1, 238 n.5; demographic succession in, 65; ecology of, 29, 64, 68, 71, 72; exploration of, 25, 26, 31, 33, 63; geological features of, 64, 71; Indian population of, 12, 18, 19, 21, 26, 36, 37, 64, 66, 239 nn.13 and 19; missions in, 33, 63; navigation in, 25, 62, 68, 69, 70; settlements in, 63, 65, 66
Vëarí-mahsá, 84, 85, 99, 110, 119, 191, 192, 193, 241 n.17, 243 n.14. *See also* Doubles
Venezuela, 21, 48
Vengeance, 85. *See also* Aggression
Venus (planet), 137
Vessels, symbolism of, 94, 140, 246 nn.44–45
Vichada River, 47, 62
Vihó (*Virola* sp.), 97, 98, 108, 109 ff., 114, 115, 116, 117, 122, 124, 163, 192. *See also* Snuff
Vihó-mahsë (Master of Snuff), 80, 81, 83, 85, 86, 89, 90, 98, 99, 100, 108, 201
Vilca, 19
Villavicencio, Manuel, 28, 30, 36
Villavicencio (town), 68
Virola sp., 20, 21, 23, 41, 108, 199, 200. *See also* *Vihó*; Snuff
Vomiting, ritual, 106

Waika Indians, 21
Wainambí Falls, 137, 245 n.12
Wallace, Alfred Russell, 26, 29, 31, 37
Warfare, 3, 4, 10, 11, 12, 51, 55
Wasps, edible, 87, 88
Water, symbolism of, 139
Weapons, 83, 189
Western Cordillera, 35, 48, 49
Western Tukano, 34
West Indies, 10, 13, 16
Whiffen, Thomas, 46
Williams, Llewellyn, 39
Women: avoidance or exclusion of, 87, 111; as symbolic equivalents to fish, 106, 143, 149, 244 n.22; as symbolic equivalents to vessels, 94
Woodpecker, 96
Worm Person, 97
Worms, noxious, 85
Wyndham, Percy E., 38

Xeques (jeques), 15

Yagé-úco, 40
Yajé: 27, 28, 30, 31, 32, 33, 34, 35, 36, 38, 39, 40, 78, 80, 90, 94, 97, 100, 121, 133 ff., 148, 198, 199; chemical composition of, 40; mythical origin of, 133 ff., 155; native categories of, 151, 157; vine, symbolism of, 135. *See also* *Banisteriopsis*
Yajeína, 39, 40
Yajenina, 39
"Yajé People," 35, 192
Yajé Person, 135. *See also* Yajé Woman

Yajé vessel, 95, 150, 151, 152, 153, 154, 158, 180
Yajé Woman, 134ff., 146, 147, 148, 149, 155
Yavareté: village, 34, 64, 65, 69; falls, 70
Yopo, yopa, 11, 12, 13, 14, 16, 17, 18, 19, 229n.34. See also *Anadenanthera peregrina;* Snuff; *Virola* sp.
Yupa. See *Yopo*

Yuruparí: flutes, 88, 170, 172, 187, 241 n.25; ritual, 88, 133
Yuruparí Falls, 25, 69, 93, 126
Yutse plant, 53

Zaparo Indians, 28, 36
Zerda Bayón, Rafael, 38
Zipa, 44